Advance Praise for *Sexual Obsessions in Obsessive-Compulsive Disorder*

"This is an exceptionally impressive and comprehensive book! Specific examples of hierarchies, step-by-step treatment descriptions for sexual obsessions are well written. Adding "third wave" treatments- ACT and Association Splitting provides richness to standard ERP/CBT approaches. Sexual obsessions are confusing for most clinicians. This book is among those considered a seminal resource for OCD practitioners and will receive high acclaim."

—**Barbara Van Noppen, PhD, LCSW**, Vice Chair for Faculty Development, Associate Professor, President, OCD Southern California, an affiliate of the International OCD Foundation

"Finally, a book dedicated to understanding sexual obsessions in OCD! Williams and Wetterneck, two leaders in the field of OCD assessment and treatment, have compiled an expert cast of authors who intimately examine how to conceptualize, assess, and treat sexual obsessive-compulsive symptoms. This valuable text belongs on the shelf of any clinician specializing in OCD and related disorders."

—**Eric Storch, PhD**, Professor and McIngvale Presidential Endowed Chair, Vice Chair & Head, Psychology, Menninger Department of Psychiatry and Behavioral Sciences, Baylor College of Medicine

Sexual Obsessions in Obsessive-Compulsive Disorder

A Step-by-Step, Definitive Guide to Understanding, Diagnosis, and Treatment

Edited by

MONNICA T. WILLIAMS
CHAD T. WETTERNECK

UNIVERSITY PRESS

UNIVERSITY PRESS

Oxford University Press is a department of the University of Oxford. It furthers
the University's objective of excellence in research, scholarship, and education
by publishing worldwide. Oxford is a registered trade mark of Oxford University
Press in the UK and certain other countries.

Published in the United States of America by Oxford University Press
198 Madison Avenue, New York, NY 10016, United States of America.

© Oxford University Press 2019

All rights reserved. No part of this publication may be reproduced, stored in
a retrieval system, or transmitted, in any form or by any means, without the
prior permission in writing of Oxford University Press, or as expressly permitted
by law, by license, or under terms agreed with the appropriate reproduction
rights organization. Inquiries concerning reproduction outside the scope of the
above should be sent to the Rights Department, Oxford University Press, at the
address above.

You must not circulate this work in any other form
and you must impose this same condition on any acquirer.

Library of Congress Cataloging-in-Publication Data
Names: Williams, Monnica T., editor. | Wetterneck, Chad T., editor.
Title: Sexual obsessions in obsessive-compulsive disorder : a step-by-step, definitive guide to
understanding, diagnosis, and treatment / edited by Monnica T. Williams & Chad T. Wetterneck.
Description: New York, NY : Oxford University Press, [2019] |
Includes bibliographical references and index.
Identifiers: LCCN 2019001026 (print) | LCCN 2019004618 (ebook) |
ISBN 9780190624804 (UPDF) | ISBN 9780190669539 (EPUB) |
ISBN 9780190624798 (pbk.)
Subjects: LCSH: Psychosexual disorders—Treatment. | Obsessive-compulsive disorder.
Classification: LCC RC556 (ebook) | LCC RC556 .S486 2019 (print) | DDC 616.85/227—dc23
LC record available at https://lccn.loc.gov/2019001026

1 3 5 7 9 8 6 4 2

Contents

Acknowledgments vii
Contributors ix

Introduction 1
Monnica T. Williams and Chad T. Wetterneck
1. Understanding Sexual Obsessions 7
Monnica T. Williams and Chad T. Wetterneck
2. Assessing Clients with Sexual Obsessions 39
Monnica T. Williams and Chad T. Wetterneck
3. Step-by-Step Treatment Manual 87
Monnica T. Williams, Chad T. Wetterneck, John Hart, Eric Lee, and Street Russell
4. Association Splitting: A Cognitive Technique for Reducing Obsessions 137
Terence H. W. Ching, Steffen Moritz, and Lena Jelinek
5. Treating Sexual Orientation Obsessions 163
Jenifer A. Viscusi and Monnica T. Williams
6. Treating Pedophile Obsessions 207
Chad T. Wetterneck and Erin C. Nghe
7. Relationship Issues 263
Monnica T. Williams, Jenifer A. Viscusi, and Chad T. Wetterneck
8. Troubleshooting Common Problems, Issues, and Resources 285
Monnica T. Williams, Erin C. Nghe, John Hart, and Chad T. Wetterneck

Appendices 313
   A. *Materials for Clients* 315
   B. *Measures* 353
   C. *Session Notes* 399
References 415
Index 435

Acknowledgments

- Simone Leavell Bruce, MA
- Ghazel Tellawi, PhD
- Emma Turner
- Sara Reed, MS
- Jasmine Fairfax, BA
- ABCT Listserv

Contributors

Terence H. W. Ching, MS
University of Connecticut
Storrs, CT, USA

John Hart, PhD
Behavior Therapy of Houston
Houston, TX, USA

Lena Jelinek, PhD
University Medical Center
Hamburg-Eppendorf
Hamburg, Germany

Eric Lee, PhD
Utah State University
Logan, UT, USA

Steffen Moritz, PhD
University Medical Center
Hamburg-Eppendorf
Hamburg, Germany

Erin C. Nghe, MSW, LCSW
OCD Set Free, LLC
Atlanta, GA, USA

Street Russell, PsyD
Louisville OCD Clinic
Louisville, KY, USA

Jenifer A. Viscusi, PsyD
Spalding University
Louisville, KY, USA

Chad T. Wetterneck, PhD
Rogers Memorial Hospital
Oconomowoc, WI, USA

Monnica T. Williams, PhD, ABPP
University of Connecticut
Storrs, CT, USA

Sexual Obsessions in Obsessive-Compulsive Disorder

Introduction

Monnica T. Williams and Chad T. Wetterneck

Sexual Obsessions in OCD: A Misunderstood Diagnosis

Obsessive-compulsive disorder (OCD) is a leading cause of mental health disability worldwide, with over 112 million individuals suffering from the disorder at some point in their lives (Ayuso-Mateos, 2006; Williams & Steever, 2015). Those afflicted with OCD may spend many hours per day tormented with unwanted thoughts and repetitive compulsions. As a result, people with OCD experience serious problems at work, at home, and in both casual and intimate relationships (Ruscio, Stein, Chiu, & Kessler 2010).

Worries caused by OCD may fall into a number of symptom-based categories, including contamination fears, symmetry concerns, doubts about causing accidental harm, and unacceptable/taboo thoughts (Abramowitz et al., 2010). Much research has been conducted to better understand the most well-known types of OCD, but less attention has been focused on understanding unacceptable/taboo thoughts, which include sexual obsessions (Williams, Mugno, Franklin, & Faber, 2013).

Sexual obsessions are perhaps the least understood manifestation of OCD. Common themes include doubts/obsessions about sexual orientation, infidelity, sexual deviations, incest, pregnancy, and blasphemous thoughts combining religion and sex (Gordon, 2002). Unfortunately, even mental health professionals have difficulty diagnosing sexually themed OCD (S-OCD). A recent study assessed clinicians' ability to correctly identify some common OCD presentations by devising vignettes, or short descriptions of a person with one of several types of OCD. Five OCD symptom vignettes were developed, and one was randomly assigned to each study participant, who was then asked to give a diagnostic impression. An astounding 77% misidentified the vignette on obsessions about sexual orientation and classified the problem as sexual identity confusion. Tragically, 43% misidentified sexual obsessions about children, with over a third classifying the problem as pedophilia. In a mental health setting, this could amount to innocent, treatment-seeking patients being reported to child protective services for trying to get help—which we have sadly witnessed on more than one occasion. In contrast, only 16% misidentified contamination obsessions as being indicative of OCD, and 29% misidentified religious obsessions as part of the disorder. You might wonder about the qualifications of the therapists who made so many serious diagnostic errors. In fact, all study participants were members of the American Psychological Association, randomly selected to participate from each state. Eighty-two percent were doctoral-level psychologists, 81% were licensed, and over half reported a cognitive-behavior therapy (CBT) orientation (Glazier, Calixte, Rothschild, & Pinto, 2013). If licensed psychologists can't identify common forms of OCD, there is little hope for laypeople with sexual obsessions to ever obtain a proper diagnosis. It's not uncommon for our clients to tell us horror stories of misdiagnoses from prior medical professionals who should have known better. These clients are the lucky few who figured out that their therapists were wrong and kept looking for answers.

Sexual Obsessions in OCD Are Common

As a result, it is difficult to know exactly how many people with OCD suffer from sexual obsessions. One of the largest studies of clinical OCD symptoms was the DSM-IV Field Trial, which included patients receiving treatment from top OCD specialty clinics at seven urban sites (Foa et al., 1995); 17% of patients reported current or past sexual obsessions as a primary or secondary concern (Williams & Farris, 2011). In a large nationwide study, 30% of those with OCD reported sexual and/or religious obsessions (Ruscio et al., 2010), but it is not known exactly how many of these experienced sexual obsessions since the two categories were combined. In another study, a quarter of treatment-seeking individuals were found to experience sexual obsessions at some point in their lives, and the authors of that study believed this was an underestimate (Grant et al., 2006). Between 20% and 50% of those with OCD report sexual obsessions in international samples (Rady, Salama, Wagdy, & Ketat, 2013; Tükel, Polat, Genç, Bozkurt, & Atli, 2004).

These sexual symptoms seem to complicate the treatment process, as such patients spend, on average, 3.4 years longer (over 30% longer) in treatment than people with other types of OCD (Grant et al., 2006). But because sexual obsessions in OCD are frequently misdiagnosed, many never make it into treatment at all. Thus, the number of those with sexual obsessions in OCD is probably much higher than what was found in the 20-year old DSM-IV Field Trial or even the more recent study by Grant and colleagues. Shame and embarrassment prevent many sufferers from telling anyone about their frightening sexual worries, even patients who may be in treatment for other forms of OCD (Newth & Rachman, 2001). Most people with OCD have worries in more than one area, and failure to address all symptom areas can facilitate treatment failure or relapse (Gillihan, Williams, Malcoun, Yadin, & Foa, 2012; Ruscio et al., 2010).

Why Another OCD Manual?

The current selection of available instructional materials does not provide much help for clinicians who want to better understand clients with sexual obsessions. Although we have written scholarly articles about this type of OCD, these are not accessible to the majority of mental health service providers, most of whom to not have access to academic databases. The selection of popular treatment manuals is not of much help either. Our own investigation into this matter found that none of the best-known OCD treatment manuals describe how to treat sexual obsessions, and only one had even a single page dedicated to this area. Likewise, we found that most self-help books for OCD omit the topic altogether.

Those of us with decades of experience treating OCD can easily use general CBT principles to develop an effective treatment plan for just about any symptom presentation, including S-OCD. But for the majority of clinicians who don't do this every day, it can be tough to turn abstract principles into action. With existing manuals, one is left trying to figure out how to take a sample exposure hierarchy written for a person who is deathly afraid of getting asbestos-related cancer and infer how to make it work for a patient afraid of molesting his four-year-old daughter. Even examples of how to treat violent or religious forms of OCD (which are likewise scarce) are likely to be of little help to the average therapist treating a client with sexual orientation fears. Therapists may struggle with not knowing what to do or how to do it. We are frequently contacted by clinicians encountering their first client with sexual obsessions. Inevitably, both the client and therapist are frightened and confused, and the sexual aspect of the problem makes therapists even more uncertain. Our practicum students routinely face skepticism and ridicule from their fellow student therapists when they describe treatment of their S-OCD cases in university supervision classes. Treating S-OCD requires courage and conviction by the therapist in the face of pervasive miseducation and lack of awareness.

Common questions asked by students, therapists, and others include:

- How do I know if this is OCD?
- What if a client really does have a paraphilia?
- Should clients be encouraged to explore alternative sexual experiences?
- Where is the line between reassurance and psychoeducation?
- How far is too far when it comes to sexually evocative exposures?
- How can one distinguish between anxiety and sexual arousal?
- What if the patient becomes sexually aroused during an exposure?
- How do you address mental compulsions?
- How explicit should imaginal exposures be?
- What does the client's partner need to know?
- How should the client and partner address stigma-related to sexual obsessions?

Special Features

There are no answers to these questions in any previous treatment manual, which is why we wrote this book. We take the best CBT strategies for the treatment of OCD and illustrate how to apply them to clients with S-OCD. This includes scientifically tested techniques from exposure and response prevention (Ex/RP), cognitive therapy (CT), and acceptance and commitment therapy (ACT) protocols (e.g., values-based exposure hierarchies and alternative defusion-inspired exposures), as well as useful mindfulness strategies. This manual contains direct, written step-by-step instructions for therapists as well as educational handouts and diagrams for clients to promote learning. We also include numerous exposure suggestions that we have used with real clients to provide a starting point for clinicians in addressing obsessional fears.

We understand that our clients live in a context that includes family members or important others who may be negatively impacted by symptoms. Sexual obsessions create a unique set of challenges for romantic partners who may be struggling to understand and cope with feelings of rejection, fear, and frustration. Partners may be unwitting participants in maintaining the client's symptoms by helping with rituals or providing excessive reassurance. We recently completed a study of married couples with OCD, and we bring these new insights to bear on how to help couples affected by the disorder (Tellawi et al., 2014; Tellawi, Viscusi, Miller, Williams, & Chasson, 2015). Sexual obsessions may also be stigmatizing to clients and their family members. Our work has shown that even well-educated psychology students and practicing therapists have stigmatizing attitudes toward sexual obsessions compared to other types of OCD content (Cathey & Wetterneck, 2013; Steinberg & Wetterneck, 2017). Thus, this form of OCD necessitates a higher level of instruction for therapists and special sensitivity when working with the afflicted families and significant others.

Summary

This book is designed to equip clinicians with the tools needed to successfully help clients suffering from unwanted, intrusive thoughts of a sexual nature. The first chapter provides an explanation of how sexual obsessions fit into our understanding of OCD, describes the most common types of sexual obsessions, and dispels myths about clients with sexual obsessions. The second chapter provides instructions on how to diagnose OCD in clients reporting sexual obsessions, guidance on measures to employ during assessment, and a discussion of differential diagnoses. Chapter 3 is a step-by-step manual describing how to provide treatment, using a combination of Ex/RP, CT, and newer CBT techniques. Chapter 4 describes new techniques for addressing S-OCD using the cognitive semantic association splitting technique. Chapters 5 and 6 present detailed case examples of pedophile OCD and sexual orientation OCD treatment approaches, along with a catalogue of specific ideas for in vivo exposures and detailed templates for imaginal exposures. Chapter 7 is focused on relationship issues that commonly emerge as a result of S-OCD and strategies therapists can use to tackle these problems. The last chapter is about troubleshooting common problems in S-OCD treatment. Also included are appendices of handouts for clients, validated tests and assessments, and other useful materials for therapists.

We use this manual to instruct our own trainees as well, including graduate students, and it makes a useful supplement in CBT courses. We sincerely hope you will find this material useful in your clinical practice when working with clients with S-OCD.

1

Understanding Sexual Obsessions

Monnica T. Williams and Chad T. Wetterneck

About Obsessive-Compulsive Disorder

When most people think of obsessive-compulsive disorder (OCD), they picture someone with a germ phobia, a person meticulously straightening a crooked picture frame, or someone arranging a collection of shoes by color in a painfully well-organized closet. We tend to laugh at these images in the media, but as clinicians we know that OCD is much more than a quirky character trait. In fact, OCD can be quite serious, and most people with the disorder aren't laughing about it. OCD is highly disabling, and nearly two thirds of those with the disorder suffer in nearly every major life domain, including family life, social life, work or school, and intimate relationships (Ruscio, Stein, Chiu, & Kessler 2010; Wetterneck, Knott, Kinnear, & Storch, 2017). People with OCD experience almost four times the unemployment rate of the general population due to the disabling nature of symptoms (Koran, Thienemann, & Davenport, 1996). In fact, OCD is considered one of the leading causes of disability worldwide, with a global impact comparable to that of schizophrenia (Ayuso-Mateos, 2006; Zohar, Fostick, Black, & Lopez-Ibor, 2007).

Almost all people with OCD have other diagnosable mental disorders as well, with 40% suffering from major depressive disorder, 76% suffering from an anxiety disorder or posttraumatic stress disorder (PTSD), 56% suffering from an impulse control disorder, and 39% suffering from a substance use disorder (Ruscio et al., 2010). These additional diagnoses can complicate treatment if not also managed. The average age of onset is 19.5 years and childhood onset is common, particularly in males (Fogel, 2003; Ruscio et al., 2010), but even among those who develop OCD in adulthood, most can remember having some symptoms as children.

OCD is defined by the presence of obsessions and compulsions. According to the fifth edition of the *Diagnostic and Statistical Manual of*

Mental Disorder (DSM-5; American Psychiatric Association [APA], 2013), obsessions are

> recurrent and persistent thoughts, urges, or images that are experienced, at some time during the disturbance, as intrusive and unwanted, and that in most individuals cause marked anxiety or distress; the individual attempts to ignore or suppress such thoughts, urges, or images, or to neutralize them with some other thought or action. (p. 237)

Compulsions are defined as

> repetitive behaviors or mental acts that the individual feels driven to perform in response to an obsession or according to rules that must be applied rigidly; the behaviors or mental acts are aimed at preventing or reducing anxiety or distress, or preventing some dreaded event or situation; however, these behaviors or mental acts are not connected in a realistic way with what they are designed to neutralize or prevent, or are clearly excessive. (p. 237)

Additionally, symptoms "are time-consuming (e.g., take more than 1 hour per day) or cause clinically significant distress or impairment" in an important area of functioning (p. 237).

For a diagnosis of OCD, symptoms must not be "attributable to the physiological effects of a substance or another medical condition" and are "not better explained by the symptoms of another mental disorder" (APA, 2013, p. 237). However, it is worth noting that some cases of OCD, particularly in children, are due to an autoimmune response typically trigged by a strep throat infection (pediatric acute-onset neuropsychiatric syndrome, aka PANS [Swedo, Leckman, & Rose, 2012] or pediatric autoimmune neuropsychiatric disorders associated with Streptococcal infections, aka PANDAS [Murphy, Storch, Lewin, Edge, & Goodman, 2012]).

The specific diagnostic criteria for OCD have changed in relatively minor ways from the fourth, revised edition of the *Diagnostic and Statistical Manual of Mental Disorder* (DSM-IV-TR) to DSM-5. The word *impulse*, which was previously used in the description of obsessions, has been replaced with *urge*. The word *inappropriate*, used to describe obsessional thoughts, has been replaced with the word *unwanted* (Abramowitz & Jacoby, 2014). The requirement that patients recognize their obsessions and compulsions as senseless and excessive has been removed. The insight specifier in DSM-5 now includes three options, which are "good or fair insight," "poor insight," and "absent insight/delusional beliefs." This was done to improve differential diagnosis as people with OCD have a range of insight into the senselessness of their symptoms (Foa et al., 1995). Thus, people with OCD may completely lack insight without being psychotic.

The most notable change is that OCD is no longer classified as an anxiety disorder. It is now included in a new category called "Obsessive-Compulsive and Related Disorders." This change was made primarily to group together disorders characterized by obsessive thoughts and/or repetitive behaviors, as there is increasing evidence that these disorders are somehow related (APA, 2013). However, this regrouping is not uncontroversial (Abramowitz & Jacoby, 2014), as several obsessive-compulsive–related disorders may be a better fit in other categories (such as impulse control disorders), and some disorders most similar to OCD were left out this new section entirely (i.e., illness/health anxiety).

Although people with and without OCD experience unwanted sexual thoughts (Smith, Wetterneck, & Harpster, 2011), people with OCD seem to get hung up on a subset of these unwanted thoughts and place too much importance on them (Rachman, 1997). These unwanted thoughts then become obsessions, which demand an action to produce relief. Any actions performed to alleviate an obsession are considered *rituals* or *compulsions*, although avoidance is also a common response. Thinking about the symptoms behaviorally, compulsions provide negative reinforcement by bringing about temporary relief through the performance of compulsions (Franklin & Foa, 2011; Mower, 1939, 1960). While compulsions may initially relieve anxiety caused by obsessions, they actually reinforce the behavior so that the likelihood of doing more compulsive behavior in response to obsessions increases. Continued use of compulsions to reduce OCD-related anxiety creates a reinforced behavioral response that becomes increasingly more entrenched and difficult to resist, leading to greater impairment. Thus, obsessions and compulsions are functionally related.

Like its predecessor, the DSM-5 permits a diagnosis if either obsessions and compulsions are present, but there is some scientific disagreement as to whether it is possible to have obsessions without compulsions (sometimes termed "pure obsessional" or "pure-o"; Williams, Crozier, & Powers, 2011). Research and clinical observations indicate that virtually all patients with OCD have both obsessions and compulsions (e.g., Leonard & Riemann,

2012), although compulsions without clear obsessions are sometimes seen in children and those who have a need for things to be "just right."

The Many Faces of OCD

OCD comes in many varieties; therefore, each person's symptom presentation may be different, and these presentations can change over time. Nonetheless, decades of research seem to point to four specific symptom dimensions that describe most OCD sufferers. These include (a) contamination obsessions with washing/cleaning compulsions, (b) symmetry obsessions with ordering compulsions, (c) doubting obsessions with repeated checking compulsions, and (d) unacceptable/taboo thoughts with mental/covert compulsions and reassurance-seeking (Williams, Mugno et al., 2013). People with OCD may have worries in one or all of these areas, although in our clinical experience most people have one major area of concern with smaller worries in one or two other areas. Because of the wide range of symptom presentations, OCD is misdiagnosed both in doctors' offices and among mental health professionals (Glazier, Calixte, Rothschild, & Pinto, 2013; Sussman, 2003); thus, a good understanding of the OCD presentations is vitally important for all clinicians to ensure a correct diagnosis. Here we briefly describe each major symptom dimension.

Contamination Fears and Cleaning Rituals

Although one of the most widely studied presentations (Ball, Baer, & Otto, 1996) and the one most often associated with OCD in the popular press, fear of contamination may account for only a quarter of obsessional fears among those with OCD in the general population (Ruscio et al., 2010). Nonetheless, such concerns are prominent in OCD sufferers worldwide (Williams & Steever, 2015). Fear of contamination typically involves excessive concern about the threat of illness or disease, difficulty tolerating the sensation of being physically unclean, or even a feeling of being mentally polluted in some way (Rachman, 2004). Feared contaminants are not limited to dirt and germs but may include such things as blood, household chemicals, and sticky substances or residues, as well as people who appear unclean or unkempt and various insects or animals. People may worry that if they become contaminated it will cause them harm in some way, or they will spread the contamination, leading to being responsible for harm to others, or a combination of the two.

To minimize exposure to contamination, individuals with this type of OCD may go to great lengths to avoid places and situations that might expose them to feared contaminants (e.g., public restrooms, crowded malls, etc.) and/or may involve themselves in a myriad of protective rituals. Such rituals may include disinfecting and sterilizing, throwing away "contaminated" objects, frequently changing clothes, and designating "clean" areas within the home that are off limits to others. If contaminants cannot be avoided, however, individuals often resort to excessive hand washing, showering, or housecleaning in an attempt to decontaminate themselves and their belongings. Among those with this form of OCD, contact with a feared contaminant often results in feelings of fear or disgust and, in some cases, may cause feelings of responsibility for spreading dreaded contamination to others, such as children or pets (Williams, Mugno et al., 2013).

Doubting and Compulsive Checking Rituals

The OCD symptom dimension we refer to as "doubt about harm/checking" has also been called "fear of harm" or "overresponsibility for harm." Individuals whose main obsessions fall into this category typically experience fears related to unintentionally harming themselves or somebody else due to carelessness or negligence. For example, two of the more common harming fears include the fear of hitting a pedestrian while driving and the fear of forgetting to turn off the stove before leaving the kitchen, thereby leading to the accidental death of a loved one in a house fire. Accompanying this fear of harm and heightened sense of responsibility are often extreme feelings of doubt, dread, or uncertainty. Repeated checking behaviors are used to neutralize these feelings by attempting to prevent the perceived dangerous consequence; thus, individuals engaging in these behaviors are often called "checkers" (although most people with OCD do some form of checking behaviors). In addition to checking, individuals with fears of harming often report other rituals that may have a "magical" quality, such as repeating "safety" words, phrases, or prayers; counting; or saying or withholding certain words or phrases.

People with this form of OCD tend to doubt their own recollections of past actions, and there has been some research into the idea that people who doubt and repeatedly check may have some actual memory deficits. Some studies have found that OCD patients who compulsively check are both less confident in their memories and have poorer performance on certain types of memory tasks (e.g., Woods, Vevea, Chambless, & Bayen, 2002). It is not completely clear if this is an actual neuropsychological deficit or simply a result of high anxiety. However, research suggests that in those with OCD repeated checking results in natural reductions in memory confidence, which is then worsened by an increased perception of responsibility for potential harm (Boschen & Vuksanovic, 2007).

Finally, research also suggests a relationship between the checking subtype of OCD and the experience of traumatic life events. For example, researchers found a significant, positive relationship between the experience of trauma and the magnitude of doubt about harm/checking symptoms and the symmetry/ordering symptom dimension, even after controlling for age, age of OCD onset, and mental health conditions (Cromer, Schmidt, & Murphy, 2007). It is not uncommon for people to have symptoms of OCD and PTSD intertwined. For example, someone who experienced a sexual assault might repeatedly check door locks for safety. In contrast, there was no association found linking the experience of traumatic life events to either the contamination/cleaning symptom dimension or hoarding.

Symmetry Obsessions and Ordering Rituals

Perfectionism is a common symptom of OCD patients whereby they are preoccupied with order, symmetry, and exactness. To reduce anxiety, these individuals tend to engage in compulsive behaviors that include repetitive arranging, organizing, or lining up of objects until certain subjective conditions are met. For example, they may experience intense discomfort if the objects on their desk are not symmetrically aligned or a certain distance apart from one another. It has been proposed that a common theme in the symmetry and ordering category is a feeling of "incompleteness," which has also been associated with compulsive slowness (Summerfeldt, 2004). People with this type of OCD may also engage in tapping and touching behaviors or fear not saying just the right thing. These behaviors are sometimes accompanied by magical thinking—that is, the belief that a thought can cause an event to occur or not occur (e.g., "If I don't align the silverware just right, my husband might have a car accident and die on his way home from work"), although there is also a large group of individuals who do not report unusual beliefs of this sort (Calamari et al., 2006; Taylor et al., 2006).

Compared to those with other OCD symptom dimensions, people with symmetry and ordering symptoms are much more likely to also experience dissociative symptoms (Grabe et al., 1999). Those with symmetry compulsions are also more likely to have comorbid tic disorders, be male, and have an earlier age of onset (Hasler et al., 2005; Leckman et al., 1995; Mataix-Cols et al., 1999). It is natural for most people to feel more comfortable and less anxious in an orderly environment. Thus, it may be that the compulsion to arrange things is based in an adaptive desire for orderliness; however, this need for order is taken to an extreme in patients with this particular form of OCD. It should also be noted that while people with OCD appear to be at higher risk for obsessive-compulsive personality disorder than those in the general population (with rates of 23% to 32% in OCD samples versus 1% to 3% in community samples; Albert, Maina, Forner, & Bogetto, 2004; Garyfallos et al., 2010; Samuels et al., 2002), there is some evidence that those with symmetry obsessions and ordering compulsions have the highest risk (Eisen et al., 2006).

Another finding that seems to be unique to the symmetry/ordering symptom dimension concerns suicide. One large study of clients being followed after having received cognitive-behavioral therapy (CBT) treatment found that those with symmetry/ordering symptoms were more likely to attempt or complete suicide in the six years after treatment than individuals with other symptom presentations. These patients were also more likely to have favorably responded to treatment initially only to have relapsed at a later point (Alonso et al., 2010). Other studies have found that ordering symptoms have the most consistent association with anger, including expression of anger toward others, holding in or suppressing anger, and difficulty controlling angry feelings (Tellawi et al., 2016; Whiteside & Abramowitz, 2005). It may be that anger is what drives the relationship between ordering symptoms and a higher risk of suicide. Alternatively, as noted previously, the experience of traumatic life events may also drive this relationship, given the connection between symmetry/ordering symptoms and trauma (Cromer, Schmidt, & Murphy, 2007). Taking all this into account, it is recommended that clinicians treating patients with symmetry and ordering assess for past trauma, monitor and address feelings of anger during treatment, and closely watch for suicidal ideation (Williams, Mugno et al., 2013).

Unacceptable/Taboo Thoughts and Mental Rituals

The unacceptable/taboo thoughts symptom dimension includes unwanted obsessions that are often of a religious, violent, or sexual nature. Traditionally, people in this group were referred to as "pure obsessionals" due to their lack of observable compulsive behaviors (i.e., Baer, 1994). It is now apparent, however, that these individuals do engage in ritualizing behaviors, but these rituals tend to be primarily mental in nature (e.g., praying, mental counting, etc.) or otherwise mostly covert (e.g., reassurance-seeking; Williams et al., 2011). This symptom dimension includes individuals whose obsessions often manifest as intrusive, unwanted thoughts, urges, or mental images of committing acts that severely violate their personal morals or values. Examples include thoughts of sexually molesting children, blasphemous thoughts about religious figures, and the experience of sudden urges or impulses to act out violently. People with excessive health concerns are also often represented in this category (Williams, Farris et al., 2014). Although violence is often a prominent theme in this particular category, those who have these thoughts usually have no history of violence, nor do they act on their obsessions; however, because such individuals think their OCD thoughts are dangerous and overly important (Obsessive Compulsive Cognitions Working Group, 2003), they put a lot of mental effort into trying to suppress the thoughts. Paradoxically, attempts at thought suppression have the unwanted effect of actually increasing anxiety and perpetuating symptoms. That is, purposefully trying not to think of a specific thing often has the opposite effect of making the thought more likely to return (Wegner, Schneider, Carter, & White, 1987).

Other ways people with this form of OCD usually try to control these thoughts include mental ritualization (e.g., arguing with oneself over the morality of one's character), neutralizing (e.g., mentally "canceling out" bad thoughts by replacing them with good thoughts or engaging in excessive prayer or confession), performing some form of mental checking (e.g., reviewing one's behaviors), and/or seeking reassurance from others. Avoiding known triggers is also especially common in this group. For example, sufferers may make excuses to avoid childcare responsibilities or religious ceremonies. Some research suggests that those with unacceptable thoughts may suffer with more severe obsessions than those with other forms of OCD (Alonso et al., 2001). For example, in one of our own studies, we found that patients with obsessions about their sexual orientation were much more distressed than those with different OCD worries, and they reported more interference in their lives as a result of their symptoms (Williams & Farris, 2011).

One of our clients wrote the following:

I am a 37-year-old woman who has had OCD about being gay since I was 11 years old. I have gotten CBT before, but the treatment only made me worse. I am currently on medication too. I've only ever dated men and only want to be straight. I have been doing well with the OCD until last November when I had a dream where I asked a dream figure "Am I a lesbian?" and he said "Yes, you've been in denial—but you've just been too scared to admit it!" This dream has terrified me so much that I attempted suicide a month ago. I am so scared that this is definitive proof that my subconscious is saying I'm gay and that it must be true. I realize that sexual content dreams are symbolic and don't mean what they appear; however, my dream was not symbolic with sexual content, but it straight out said I was a lesbian in denial. I am terribly concerned that this might not be OCD.

Sexual symptoms in OCD are the focus of this treatment manual, and most clients' with sexual OCD (S-OCD) will have primary symptoms that fall into the unacceptable/taboo thoughts category. However, sexual symptoms may be tied to other categories as well (e.g., contamination/cleaning dimension), and most clients will have some OCD symptoms in at least one other area. It will be important to understand and address all OCD symptoms in treatment to prevent symptoms from jumping to another area once the S-OCD is under control.

About Sexual OCD

Although many OCD patients report sexual obsessions as their primary symptom, sexually themed OCD remains understudied and misunderstood. Sexual obsessions may include fears about engaging in undesirable sexual acts, having unwanted sexual mental images, experiencing a change in sexual orientation, having sexual contact with a child, sexual thoughts about religious figures or incongruent with religious/moral values, sexual aggression, and becoming pregnant or impregnating others through unlikely means.

In one study of sexual symptoms in treatment-seeking OCD patients, out of a sample of 296 adults, researchers found current or past sexual obsessions among a quarter of patients (Grant et al., 2006). Patients with sexual obsessions were, on average, 38 years of age and included males and females fairly equally, which was not much different from those without sexual symptoms. Over 80% had an additional mental health diagnosis, and one in five were disabled due to their OCD symptoms. Both patients with and without sexual symptoms had a moderate level OCD severity; however, those with sexual symptoms had a slightly higher severity level. There were no differences between groups in amount of insight into OCD symptoms, indicating that those with S-OCD were just as aware of the senselessness of their symptoms as those with other forms of the disorder. In other words, sexual obsessions in OCD seem to be rather common, with more recent studies uncovering S-OCD in greater numbers than previously believed. Additionally, such symptoms appear to be uniquely distressing.

In one example of S-OCD, a 38-year-old woman came to one of the authors' outpatient clinics for help for upsetting thoughts about something that had happened a year ago. We'll call her Linda. She was born and raised in Indiana, and her husband was an East Asian immigrant. They were both devout Catholics and lived in an upscale neighborhood. She was a homemaker and homeschooled their five children, while he worked in advertising. One night while he was working late, she was in bed reading while her youngest child, aged three, had fallen asleep on the other end of the bed. Feeling a bit lonely missing her husband, she decided to masturbate before falling asleep herself. She had not thought much about that event for several months until one day she was reading a religious text that said that masturbation was a sin and a perversion. This made her reflect on this experience, and she immediately felt remorseful about it. She wondered if it meant she had perverted tendencies and if this was doubly so since her small child was in the bed with her. She reminded herself that her daughter was asleep and could not have known what was happening or been affected by it, but the nagging doubt would not go away. She decided never to masturbate again and spent much time praying about the incident and asking for God's forgiveness. She shared her fears with her husband who quickly dismissed her concerns and urged her to stop worrying. As time passed, the worries continued to grow, and she started to wonder if perhaps she had been sexually aroused by her child, which she surmised would make her a pervert. She then began to wonder if she had, in fact, done something illegal and should turn herself into the police. She imagined that she would be taken to jail and then face scorn and rejection from her family, church, and even God. These thoughts pushed her into a depressive spiral, and some days she was so sad that she could hardly speak to her husband or children at all.

Given the effects of these type of thoughts on the sufferer, it should be no surprise that rates of clinical depression are significantly higher among clients with sexual obsessions compared to other concerns in OCD (Dell'Osso et al., 2012; Grant et al., 2006). In fact, a preliminary analysis we conducted with data from a group of OCD patients in a residential facility showed a similar pattern of higher suicidal ideation (Osegueda, Wetterneck, Williams, Hart, & Bjorgvinsson, 2013), although there were no significant differences in OCD severity. Those with sexual obsessions scored significantly higher—almost twice as high on a measure of suicidality compared to those without sexual obsessions. We think this is due to the stigmatizing nature of such thoughts, leading to greater distress and despair and more depression.

S-OCD affects people of all ages and can even strike children. It used to be believed that S-OCD was rare in children, but it is more likely that S-OCD has been missed in children because sexual symptoms were being misdiagnosed as other problems. At an OCD treatment center in London, a quarter of their child patients were found to be experiencing unwanted sexual obsessions (de la Cruz et al., 2013). These children also suffered from more depression than the other children with OCD and were as young as eight years old.

In the case of Linda, one of her other daughters later began to show signs of S-OCD. This was triggered by having been accidentally exposed to a sexually provocative advertisement on the Internet, which had slipped past the stringent parental control safeguards that had been installed on her iPad. Linda was very upset when she learned about what happened. She blamed herself, became hypervigilant of her daughter's computer use and even wondered at times if her daughter could become a danger to the other children in the home. The good news is that such children have not been found to pose any risk to others (de la Cruz et al., 2013). Additionally, the results of the London study showed that treatment was equally effective for children with and without S-OCD.

When children present with S-OCD, it is common for adults to suspect that symptoms are an indication of sexual abuse. There are examples in the literature of S-OCD being linked to abuse in some cases but not others. Therefore, it is appropriate to consider sexual abuse when assessing S-OCD in a child, while keeping in mind that excessive questioning may be unnecessary or even harmful (de la Cruz et al., 2013). In the case of Linda's daughter, part of the intervention included resisting the urge to keep discussing what had happened, as Linda's repeated questioning of her daughter only served to perpetuate obsessional anxiety in both mother and daughter.

Sexual Obsessions across Ethnicity, Race, and Culture

S-OCD in Ethnic and Racial Minorities

Ethnoracial minorities in the United States tend to be wary of traditional Western mental healthcare, due in part to cultural mistrust, concerns about discrimination, and concerns that their groups' culture and values will not be appreciated. Widespread negative stereotypes contribute to a sense of stigma and shame among many people in minority groups. Among African Americans, for example, negative stereotypes include being lazy, poor, unintelligent, and, notably, sexually predatory or deviant (Williams, Gooden, & Davis, 2012). In one OCD study that we conducted, we found that at least 17% of African Americans experienced sexual obsessions either currently or in the past (Williams, Elstein et al., 2012), but African Americans with OCD may be hesitant to disclose sexual obsessions for fear of confirming stereotypes about being sexually deviant.

Safer, Bullock, and Safer (2016) reported on the interesting case of a 20-year-old African American college student with OCD and a sexual identity characterized by same-sex attraction. He presented for an evaluation for sexual reassignment surgery due to severe, anxiety-producing doubts about his gender identity. His worries started abruptly after the use of marijuana, at which point he began to question whether or not he was happy being a male. Specifically, he suffered from paralyzing obsessions of being transgender that caused him terrible distress, and as a result he engaged in mental and behavioral compulsions such as "testing" his reactions to certain thoughts or images and reassurance-seeking. He also experienced problems in school, depression, and fleeting suicidal thoughts. It may be interesting to consider possible reasons for why he experienced this previously undocumented form of OCD at that particular time. OCD symptoms often focus on what is most important to those afflicted, and sexual identity tends to be particularly salient to adolescents and young adults due to their developmental stage. Considering the greater awareness of transgender issues due to greater trans representation in the media (e.g., former Olympic athletic now known as Caitlyn Jenner), it is to be expected that we would see more questioning and worry about gender dysphoria among young people prone to OCD. In addition, the role of cultural issues in this case must also be considered. There is greater stigma of LGBTQ identity within the African American community, and transgender African Americans are disproportionately likely to experience discrimination and violence from hate crimes than their transgender White counterparts. This patient was already coping with the difficulties of his intersectionality—having an LGBTQ identity as a Black man—and becoming transgender would have been another massive stigmatizing hurdle to navigate. These social realities may have contributed to heightened anxiety and more obsessional worries in this particular patient (Williams & Ching, 2016).

Thus, treating ethnoracial minorities with S-OCD may involve more challenges and require a special patience and sensitivity. It is important for clinicians to take time to learn about the culture and values of their minority clients. Ignoring cultural values or differences using a colorblind approach may make minority clients more reluctant to open up about their concerns (Terwilliger et al., 2013). Making treatment a more collaborative process with minority clients may improve the process by giving the client more control over their recovery and establish more trust between the therapist and client (Williams, Sawyer, Ellsworth, Singh, & Tellawi, 2017). Furthermore, cultures differ in their attitudes about acceptable sexual behaviors. It will be important to understand and show respect for these practices and beliefs, even if they differ from mainstream Western practices and beliefs.

Treating OCD in ethnoracial minorities will usually require a considerable amount of rapport building, assessment, acknowledgement of cultural values, and psychoeducation. Traditional Western psychotherapy may not foster these ideologies, so it is essential for clinicians to be sensitive to a minority client's value system and potential negative cultural attitudes toward experiencing a mental disorder and mental healthcare overall. In a recent study of treatment outcomes at a major OCD residential/intensive treatment center, we found that ethnoracial minority patients were requiring longer stays, despite entering treatment with the same OCD severity as their White counterparts (Williams, Sawyer et al., 2015). It was thought that increased awareness of culturally appropriate approaches might improve future outcomes with patients from these groups. However, therapists should also remember that ethnoracial minorities are not a single homogeneous group; therefore, generalizing culturally relevant principles may not encompass the value systems of all minorities.

S-OCD Cross-Culturally

In Western cultures, it is widely believed that OCD is a mental condition caused by biological factors (Coles & Coleman, 2010), with washing, symmetry, and checking related dimensions more quickly recognized as OCD than sexual symptoms. Nonetheless, sexual symptoms in OCD have been reported around the world, including in India, Korea, South Africa, and Mexico (Williams & Steever, 2015). That being said, sometimes these sexual symptoms look very different than what we usually see in the United States.

In India, the culture-bound disorder termed *puppy pregnancy* is described as fear of being pregnant with a canine embryo (Chowdhury, Mukherjee, Ghosh, & Chowdhury, 2003). This condition is ironically more common among men than women and may emerge after having been bitten by a dog. Puppy pregnancy has been primarily reported in rural parts of West Bengal, India, and is thought to often be a variant of OCD. Puppy pregnancy includes a fear of internal contamination (from the puppy fetus), disability (impotence due to damage to internal sexual organs), and even death. For example, one case report involved a 27-year-old milkman who after having seen a dog licking milk cans was then bitten by the dog when trying to move it away. The subject became fearful of dogs, worried that he was being chased by a dog, and would check all milk cans, worried they had been licked by a dog. Gradually his obsessions about dogs increased, and he developed a severe doubt that all his household articles were contaminated by contact with a dog. He also experienced obsessive thoughts involving fear of dog bites and avoidance of places where dogs had been seen. He eventually became housebound and feared that he might die after painful delivery of puppies through his penis.

Another culture-bound disorder found mainly in Southeast Asian cultures is koro. This disorder is described as the phenomenon where sexual organs (penis in males and nipples/breasts in women) retract back into the body, disappearing and potentially causing death (APA, 2013). Although this condition has been noted as occurring within females, the majority of cases observed have been in males (Davis, Steever, Terwilliger, & Williams, 2012). Similar to obsessions seen often in OCD, koro can cause a lot of anxiety and disability in those suffering. Additionally, common reactions to symptoms that seem analogous to compulsions are tugging and pulling on genitals to stop the retraction process (Davis et al., 2012). More research is needed on the cause(s) of initial symptom manifestation, but in two cases studies the authors noted each koro sufferer began to experience symptoms after being warned about an outbreak via social networking (i.e., a phone call and local news reports). Each koro sufferer was checked by a physician for physical abnormalities, but none were found (Roy et al., 2011). Isolated cases have also been reported in the West, which indicates that koro may not be simply a culture bound syndrome but an OCD-related phenomenon with more universal constructs (Davis et al., 2012).

It has been suggested that sexual orientation obsessions in OCD (SO-OCD) are a Western cultural variation of OCD, as there have been no reports in the literature of this type of OCD outside the United States. This may be due to the societal tension around non-heterosexual orientations in the United States. In some Eastern cultures, homosexuality and transsexuality are embraced socially as a common form of lifestyle/expression. In some cultures, there is evidence of sexual practices between people of the same sex (which would be considered by Westerners as "homosexual") being seen as acceptable and separate from one's sexuality. That being said, we have been in touch with clients from around the world suffering from SO-OCD. This includes clients from cultures where same-sex behavior is frowned upon (i.e., India, Saudi Arabia, Philippines) and countries that tend to be very accepting of different orientations (i.e., Canada, England, Sweden). This leads us to believe that this form of OCD is universal and not simply a byproduct of cultural attitudes.

Types of Sexual Obsessions

Pedophile Obsessions

Pedophile obsessions (P-OCD) are perhaps the most troubling form of OCD, and this incarnation of the disorder can have specific or general obsessional targets. Some pedophilia obsessions involve specific family members or loved ones, while others may be about any random child, regardless of whether there is a pre-existing relationship. P-OCD can develop after a person has a baby (i.e., postpartum OCD) where they begin to fear it is inappropriate to touch a child's genitals while wiping, cleaning, or changing a diaper (Larsen et al., 2006). A parent may be concerned that they could become aroused by any of these acts, stimulate their baby, or even be aroused by stimulating their baby. As we will discuss in a later chapter, one woman we worked with felt as though her baby's penis moved too often or urinated while being wiped during a diaper change and feared she was a pedophile for continuing to stimulate him in this manner. Others fear that they must be doing something wrong during bathing, dressing, or changing a baby, and when someone else finds out, they will be accused of sexually harming the child.

As noted, P-OCD concerns are not limited to one's own children. A stray thought of being inappropriate around children during a routine "fun" activity (e.g., tickling or wrestling) or even when having a warm thought toward a child (e.g., "Oh, he's such a cute little boy" or "She looks so grown up in that dress") can balloon into much larger fears and unhelpful rituals or avoidance. Clients may wonder, "Did I enjoy being physically close to that child or become aroused at all? Did I accidentally touch them too close or directly on an inappropriate part of their body? Did I accidentally allow them to touch me somewhere? Maybe it wasn't an accident and I wanted to touch them or have them touch me? What is wrong with me?" Another line of obsessions may begin with the question, "Why did I have that thought about how they look? Was I seeing the child as an adult or someone that could be attractive? Would someone think I was a pervert for saying he was cute or commenting on her dress? I need to watch what I say or perhaps people will begin to question if I am a deviant of some sort."

The original obsessions themselves are met not only by more obsessional thinking but also behavioral changes or checking. The person may begin to have less physical contact with the child or any children and make excuses why they cannot wrestle, pick them up, hug them, or even give them a "high-five." They may avoid children altogether, making excuses to get out of their own childcare responsibilities or see other children or not allow themselves to be alone with a child. They might stop commenting on a child's appearance or refuse to look at a child below the neck so as to avoid sexualizing them. Others might engage or watch children from a safe distance, even occasionally to check their own reaction to make sure there is no arousal to seeing a child. Eventually they may try to avoid children altogether, despite not feeling aroused after numerous attempts to check because they could not bear if "the next time will be the time I am aroused."

We want to be clear that when a client has thoughts about children, their own or others, those with OCD are the least likely to do anything inappropriate. As a clinician, your primary question is to determine whether any of these thoughts are ever "wanted" or wanted to produce arousal. Those with OCD will deny wanting these thoughts (as they are ego-dystonic), and some will simultaneously cry or show great distress as they doubt why, then, they are having them. Having unwanted sexual thoughts about a much younger person is more common than most would know, as indicated by a traditional college-aged sample from Canada (endorsed by just over 50% for men and 25% for women; Renaud & Byers, 1999). Thus, asking these questions by normalizing the experience and finding out if the thoughts are wanted is crucial.

Sexual Orientation Obsessions

SO-OCDs were originally thought to be when a heterosexual person has an obsession about having a different sexual orientation (i.e., same-sex attraction or perhaps bisexual), and this was called homosexual OCD (H-OCD) in the first articles on this topic (Williams, 2008). This term evolved out of the OCD online self-help community in the early days of the Internet. We now know that people with sexual orientation concerns are not only present in those who are heterosexual but also that people who are gay or lesbian may have obsessions that they are straight/heterosexual, and so we revised the term to be inclusive and now call this presentation SO-OCD. Given the stigma that sexual minorities face in society, we do believe these obsessions are more likely to develop when stigma is greater, so those who are heterosexual are more likely to fear being LGBTQ than vice versa. This observation is mainly anecdotal at this point but is in line with our clinical observations.

There is research on the prevalence of SO-OCD overall from the large DSM-IV Field Trial ($n = 409$), which found 8% reported current SO-OCD and 11.9% with lifetime symptoms (Williams & Farris, 2011). More data, reported by Pinto et al. (2008) based on the OCD Collaborative Genetics Study reported approximately 10% of the sample ($n = 485$) acknowledged past or present obsessions related to same sex thoughts.

Similar to P-OCD, SO-OCD can develop in a variety of ways, with a number of accompanying compulsions. A heterosexual individual may initially have a thought when noticing a member of the same sex and finding that person attractive (e.g., a guy seeing a movie ad thinks, "That Brad Pitt is a sexy dude") and then questions the meaning of the thought. Other examples include a heterosexual male being complimented on his apparel by another male and then wondering if the person felt attracted to him and perhaps that is because him appears, acts, or actually is LGBTQ. Likewise, a very pro-LGBTQ–affirming lesbian may start to worry about being straight when noticing an attractive male and wonder if her orientation is changing.

As mentioned earlier, we believe these obsessions become much more challenging during periods where one has less experience and knowledge about sexuality, while also experiencing more physical reactions (or hearing about others experiencing reactions while they have yet to experience them); adolescence is a time where these concerns are heightened and where peers may be especially stigmatizing about differences, or when one feels as though these differences will be interpreted as negative.

One adolescent male client who came to our outpatient practice told us the following story:

> My mom was always talking about how cute Ryan Gosling was and told me I was just as cute as him. I told her that I did not think he was cute, but really had no idea who he was. My mom showed me a picture of him and said, "C'mon, you have to admit he's a hunk." He looked like a player, so I told my mom, "Ok, yes he's a hunk alright." We both laughed about it, but then I started considering that he was, you know, attractive, and then, did that mean, I was like, gay or bi- or something? It's so hard to even talk about this. I like to want girls and only girls, but the fact that I agreed must mean I could go the other way. I don't even want to watch any movies anymore because of it.

These obsessions could develop in other ways, including misinterpreting a bodily reaction. An episode of the television show *Seinfeld* illustrated such an example that we have heard referenced by a few clients. In the show, George, a fairly worrisome guy, is getting a massage and finds out what he thought would be a female masseuse is actually a male. During the massage, the masseuse applies slight pressure to George's lower back, and he immediately is distressed. Already heightened by the uncomfortableness of having a male touch him, he later tells his friends that he thinks "it [his penis] moved" and he worries that he might be gay. Although this example is from a sitcom, misinterpretations that are more easily explained by subtle movements, shifts in pressure around the genitals, or even a natural physiological arousal response to being touched may be the thought that begins SO-OCD. Conversely, absence of an arousal response (the failure to develop an erection or experience vaginal lubrication) when engaging in a physical, intimate behavior (e.g., kissing, hugging, caressing, or even groping or direct touching) with someone of the other sex that one is attracted to may also be interpreted as "Maybe I am really not straight."

These obsessions then lead to compulsions, which may present as the person checking for sexual arousal when around others or mental reminders about being heterosexual. Symptoms may also include avoidance, such as not watching television shows in which there is an LGBTQ character or keeping physical distance from others of the same sex (i.e., Williams et al., 2011). The individual may watch pornography with same-sex themes to determine whether it produces sexual arousal and compare that reaction to heterosexual pornography. Another compulsion is to increase sexual intercourse with an other-sex partner to demonstrate that the person's sexual preference has not changed.

We should note that SO-OCD is not caused by homophobia/heterosexism; the individual may or may not have negative feelings toward LGBTQ individuals (Williams, 2008). This is also different from internalized homophobia/heterosexism (IH), which occurs when an LGBTQ person has negative feelings about himself or herself due to sexual orientation or identity (Szymanski, Kashubeck-West, & Meyer, 2008), although LGBTQ people with OCD can also suffer from IH. Because it can be difficult for clinicians who do not have experience with OCD to distinguish between "sexual identity confusion" and SO-OCD, SO-OCD may be misdiagnosed (Glazier et al., 2013).

As you can see, there can be issues with identifying SO-OCD; however, we believe that through careful interviewing (e.g., establishing whether the thought is ego-syntonic or ego-dystonic and examining the function of the compulsions) and even some evidence-based measures (which we will share later in this book; see Chapter 3), clinicians will have more confidence in correctly identifying OCD concerns. We cannot overstate the importance of correct, thorough case conceptualization to allow clients to receive appropriate treatment and to reduce misdiagnosis, stigmatization, and other outcomes that prolong suffering and a less valued life.

Religious Sexual Obsessions (Scrupulosity)

Many types of obsessions fall under the category of religious sexual obsessions, either due to content or the client's beliefs about morality. An example of a content related religious obsession could have to do with having sexual images or thoughts about a religious figure. We have had clients report being distressed by images of acting sexually inappropriate with a religious role model in their life (i.e., anywhere from hugging or kissing to more sexual touching or intercourse with a pastor or church elder) or implausible sexual relationships with a religious figure, such as Jesus Christ. While these overt examples of religious sexual obsessions are distressing for some obvious reasons, the idea of scrupulosity is a complicating factor and is involved with other, more regular sexual thoughts and judgments about behaviors.

If one is scrupulous, it means they have identified scruples, which are moral or ethical standards and have to do with what one believes is right and wrong. It is important to note that people do not have to be religious or even knowledgeable about religion in any way to have scruples. In addition, not all OCD obsessions that involve scrupulosity are religious or sexually oriented. For example, clients may present with obsessions related to scruples about following rules correctly or conservation of resources and the environment. They may become distressed by thoughts that they have used too much water, which endangers our fresh-water resources, thrown away items in appropriate containers (i.e., not recycled items that are recyclable) making them responsible for pollution or inefficiency, or a number of other concerns.

Scrupulosity about sexual thoughts or behaviors does not have to be religiously influenced either. In the previous examples of those with P-OCD, knowing sexual activity with children is illegal maps onto the concept of scruples. For many with OCD, adding religious scruples to a sexual obsession adds additional consequences to illegal activities or creates immorality and consequences where it does not have to exist. Consider people with P-OCD, they may fear going to prison as a result of the ego-dystonic thoughts and now add the consequence of being judged by themselves and others and religious communities and a higher power, who may send the sinner to eternal hell after death.

Scrupulosity may also lead to obsessions about behaviors that may or may not be against one's religion. From most Christian perspectives, it is against God's law to "covet thy neighbor's wife" or enjoy "sins of the flesh." For those with OCD, an innocuous thought about a married person may lead to doubt about whether that reflects inappropriate interest in them. Other feelings or behaviors, such as having a physiological sign of sexual arousal, a thought of sex, or masturbating while thinking about the married person could be considered a sign of sinful thoughts or activities. When paired with the concept that one's higher power is everywhere and knows all, it leads to great distress and compulsive behaviors to alleviate associated anxiety and disgust (e.g., attending more religious services, frequent confessions, praying, etc.) and ultimately leaves less time for other meaningful life activities.

Religious obsessions present a unique challenge for the clinician as the evidence-based techniques will require actions that clients may feel challenge religious doctrine, even though many times the procedures are about areas open to interpretation. Clients often express early on that we are asking them to do things that feel wrong or are additional "sins." The idea is to create exposures that are anxiety-provoking but not sinful based on the accepted tenets of the client's religion. We will get as close to the line as possible without crossing it. We recommend communication with a religious/spiritual leader (more on this in Chapter 2) to assist and ease concerns for both the clinician and client.

Sexual Assault Obsessions

One of the most upsetting types of obsessions concern worries that a person may cause harm to others impulsively. Common OCD examples include the fear that the person will punch a friend when they are not angry but just because they can. People with aggressive obsessions may be concerned that they might push an elderly person into subway tracks or stab a loved one while using a kitchen knife. The focal point of these worries is usually loved ones but can be strangers or pets. Sometimes the person is not worried about harming others but worries about harming himself or herself, which is not to be confused with suicidal ideation, as people with these types of fears will do anything to avoid causing the harm they worry about.

Therefore, it should be no surprise that these sort of aggressive thoughts can involve sexual behaviors as well. People can have S-OCD focused on fears of seducing other people, sexual harassment, touching others inappropriately, or even violent rape. Here we recount the true story of a patient who struggled with sexual assault fears during his college years and later.

> Although I had always struggled with sexual fears and obsessions, through careful avoidance of potential "problem areas," I had been able to resist temptation. In high school I never dated, even turning down an offer to go to the prom for fear that I would rape the girl I was with. Sex was dirty. I vowed that I would either never marry, or I would marry my first girlfriend. This decision was fueled by the fear that I would lose control with a woman. I had no explanation for this as I had never been a violent person.
>
> In college, I avoided women my entire freshman year. I was afraid of being around the women at my dorm, and I had decided that I definitely would not date any of them because the situation was just too dangerous. If I dated it was inevitable that I would end up in a situation where it would be too easy to lose control. My worst fear was that I would lose my virginity in a sexual escapade. If that was gone, it would surely be a quick downhill slide from there. I knew only too well what it was like to lose control—I had struggled for many years with an eating disorder that almost killed me.
>
> My sophomore year I met someone I really enjoyed spending time with. I felt torn by the situation because she lived in my dorm. Part of me wanted to spend every moment with her but another part was terrified. I abruptly broke off the relationship, but somehow within a few weeks we were in bed together. Although we slept together for close to a year, I never lost my virginity. This should have proven to me that I indeed possessed a considerable amount of self-control. However, my feelings were just the opposite. I felt tremendous shame for being so close when we weren't married.

Even after I was married I continued to struggle with unfounded fears that I would cheat on my wife. As far as I was concerned, marriage was a lifetime commitment between two people that I had no desire to break. I blamed my weaknesses in this area on a variety of different factors: the fact that I had never dated in high school with no opportunity to sow any "wild oats"; my parents, for not communicating the facts of life to me at any point; sexual abuse perpetrated against me as a child by a close relative; an overly permissive society that allowed naked women to be brazenly displayed across the pages of a magazine available at any convenience store; but most of all myself. I blamed myself for having such a warped mind. I was convinced it was deadly character defect that would someday be my undoing.

I started a pattern of avoidance to keep my sexual obsessions at bay. I tried to never spend any time alone with another woman. I would even exhale when I passed a woman on the street so that I would not smell any perfume she might be wearing. I was convinced that any such stimulus could push me over the edge. When I walked down the street my eyes followed a tortuous path so that I would not look at a woman, even for an instant. If I looked at her, I was afraid I would begin to lust uncontrollably. There were times when I genuinely thought I was losing my mind, and I would call my therapist in a panic. He would talk me through it and I would feel okay for a while, but it was always only temporary.

When conceptualizing sexual assault obsessions, it is important to recognize that people with this sort of S-OCD find their thoughts immoral and do not wish to act them out. They are different from fantasies, as the obsessions are unpleasant and provoke guilt, rather than being enjoyable. As a result, the thoughts cause distress, which may be connected to unwanted emotions, such as lust, disgust, anger, and frequently guilt. This distress is directly related to the frequency of the sexual obsessions and may lead to depression, difficulties concentrating, anxiety, and avoidance of others.

Impregnating Obsessions

We once heard an interesting story about a German woman we'll call Gretchen, who got pregnant with a candle. She was a single woman with no current boyfriend, who lived with a female roommate in Berlin. When she felt so inclined, she would masturbate with a special candle in their apartment that she had determined was particularly well-suited to the task. Her roommate knew about the candle, and it had become a shared joke between the two of them. One day after her roommate had come home from a particularly unsatisfying sexual encounter with her boyfriend, she decided to finish the job with Gretchen's special candle, then she put it back in its holder on the mantle. When Gretchen came home later that evening, she used the candle for its usual purpose, and the residual semen on the candle, left there second-hand from the roommate's boyfriend managed to impregnate her. Gretchen was astonished to learn she was pregnant, and after the baby was born, she applied for public assistance. A paternity test confirmed the supposed route of impregnation, and her roommate's boyfriend was forced to pay child support. Could such a scenario actually lead to pregnancy? Or, was the candle a convenient excuse to hide an affair with a friend's boyfriend?

Getting pregnant from a candle seems far-fetched if not impossible. We may never know what actually happened, but for the person with impregnating obsessions in OCD, stories like this fuel terrifying worries of pregnancy occurring without even having sex. Women with this type of OCD may worry about getting pregnant from a toilet seat or in a swimming pool. Men with this form of OCD may fear impregnating others through sperm transferred by various means such as a handshake. The following is a typical account of a woman with frightening obsessions about pregnancy resulting from unlikely circumstances.

> I have been in a great relationship with a great guy for a while. But since we started having sex I totally freak myself out that I may become pregnant. I know there is no reason to be worried because I'm on "the pill," I insist we use a condom, and he pulls out every time. I ruin the experience for him afterwards because I am freaking out, and I didn't even enjoy the sex because of all the anxiety. And even now we hardly get intimate because of my fear that somehow I will get pregnant through just touching.
>
> When we're not having sex, I make myself sick with worry because it's all I think about. I start to feel pregnant with most of the symptoms, though in saner moments I know it's really all in my head. Last month I took at least 10 pregnancy tests, and all were negative. Then I went to see my gynecologist and got another pregnancy test, which was also negative. And even after I got my period I still think I'm pregnant. I read a story on

the Internet about a woman who kept having periods even though she was pregnant, and I worry that will happen to me too. I'll be the one in a million woman that gets pregnant but won't know it until the baby pops out.

I keep pressing my abdomen to see if I can figure out if my uterus is enlarging, and sometimes I actually feel like my tummy is getting bigger. The weird thing is that I lost four pounds, and you're supposed to gain weight when you're pregnant. Anyway, that doesn't stop me from freaking out. I'm crying all the time and thinking what I'm going to do if one day I wake up and my tummy is big as a watermelon. I keep searching the Internet for more and more information and waste so much time on it, sometimes hours at a time. I end up having panic attacks, worrying how I would hide it, what if it gets too late for an abortion, and then what would happen to me.

This example presents the obsessive-compulsive cycle in action. The obsessions are the ongoing, agonizing fears of pregnancy, and the compulsions are the repeated pregnancy tests and searching for answers on the Internet.

Are People with Sexual Obsessions Dangerous?

People with OCD are not dangerous. To clarify, they are not dangerous because they have OCD. In fact, they are less likely, in our opinion, as well as any OCD expert you ask, to engage in actions that they fear. Keep in mind, to have the disorder, the thoughts have to be unwanted—the thoughts are not in line with what a person values nor how they would like to be. But fear and doubt can be so overwhelming that, when combined with clinicians who have less experience with certain OCD presentations (or specialties in other areas that may also seem to explain the symptoms), there can be real concern. Your client is telling you they fear being sexually aggressive toward others, molesting a child (or in the case of aggressive violent obsessions, acting on those thoughts), or being "hypersexually aroused" and a danger. That's hard to hear and you want to do a great job ruling out the worst possible scenarios. It takes time to habituate to our own fears about doing therapy when the topics appear to be life-threatening, illegal, or include situations in which we are mandatory reporters. It gets easier over time, but if you have doubts early on in this book about your ability to diagnose or work with these presentations, we want you to know that is normal! All of our students and trainees express these concerns. And you will be able to help your client and get through it yourself as a clinician. You don't have to be 100% certain, and, ironically, this feels very much like what our clients have already been going through and will experience during treatment.

Back to the idea of danger. Understand that the function of all of client behavior is to keep the obsession from being a reality. Most avoid situations where harm or sexual behavior is even accidentally possible (e.g., the client with P-OCD avoids interacting with children, even their own; the person who fears touching a woman inappropriately does everything possible to maintain more space between them and females). Even situations where the client engages in something that could be a sign that the obsession is true (e.g., a client watches pornographic video that does not actually align with his or her orientation to check for signs of arousal) is done in the service of relieving anxiety and/or to disconfirm the belief. If the belief is not disconfirmed (e.g., a client has a physiological arousal response to the aforementioned video) it is met with fear, shame, or disgust and not acted upon in a manner that makes it a reality. There are no moments where a person with OCD is advertently testing to see if they will have a sexual reaction to something, experiences the sexual reaction (e.g., develops an erection or vaginal lubrication to the video), and then embraces the idea that they are a different sexual orientation, a pedophile, or a rapist and subsequently leads his or her life according to this belief. Our clients instead remain anxious, shameful, and disgusted; they increase self-loathing, restrict even more activities, and become depressed. They do not turn into what they fear.

What Is the Prognosis for People with Sexual Obsessions?

There are a lot of data indicating that those with OCD can get better with evidence-based treatment. However, there have been little data on treatment specifically for sexual obsessions as most studies using cognitive-behavioral interventions involving exposure and ritual (response) prevention (Ex/RP) have patient samples predominantly consisting of those with washing/cleaning and checking compulsions (Ball, Baer, & Otto, 1995; Williams, Mugno et al., 2013). There are less available findings for areas of unacceptable thoughts overall and few looking at only sexual and religious thoughts.

So far, a few case studies have been published on the successful treatment of SO-OCD (Williams, Slimowicz, et al., 2014) and fears related to P-OCD (O'Neil, Cather, Fishel, & Kafka, 2005; Reid et al., 2016). In addition, some studies have tried to compare those with sexual (Mataix-Cols et al., 2002; Starcevic & Brakoulias, 2008) or unacceptable thoughts in general in outpatient (e.g., Williams, Faris, et al., 2014) or residential treatment (Chase, Wetterneck, Bartsch, Leonard, & Riemann, 2015) to those with other primary obsessions. As previously mentioned, the studies that compared small numbers of those with sexual obsessions to those with other obsessions had a poorer prognosis. Nonetheless, those with S-OCD still were shown to make large and significant improvements. And the latter studies involving the unacceptable thoughts as a large group showed no differences in outcomes compared to those with other primary obsessions.

While more research is required before conclusions can be drawn, more successful outcomes are likely when treatment is tailored specifically to the symptom dimension—which is exactly our reason for writing this book! Sexual obsessions and other unacceptable thoughts may have features that are distinct from other symptom dimensions, including a more intense, repulsive, and morally reprehensible ego-dystonic nature; greater overall obsessional severity and distress; and greater time spent on obsessions, more covert mental compulsions and reassurance seeking than overt compulsions (Williams et al., 2011), and increased social stigma and shame (Cathey & Wetterneck, 2013; Grant et al., 2006). So, you made a wise choice to seek out the specialized knowledge and approach detailed in this book.

Treatment Options

Psychotherapies for OCD

OCD used to be considered extremely difficult, if not impossible, to treat. Psychoanalytic thought, based on Freud's theories of unconscious drives and wishes, produced many theories and interesting case studies that described sexual obsessions in a number of patients. However, his treatment of these obsessional states could not be reliably replicated. Nonetheless, due to lack of alternatives, Freudian approaches continued to be advanced as the treatment of choice for OCD, despite limited benefit (Williams, Powers, & Foa, 2012). This class of treatment includes psychoanalysis, psychodynamic therapy, and "insight-oriented therapy." Sometimes people call it "talk therapy." Sadly, people with OCD often ended up housebound or institutionalized.

It is now widely recognized that, for OCD, psychodynamic approaches have little evidence to justify their use. Concerning these therapies, the most current expert guidelines most tellingly note that "there is doubt as to whether it has a place in mental health services for OCD" at all (National Institute for Health and Clinical Excellence, 2006, p. 104). Nonetheless, such approaches for OCD continue to be widespread, despite their lack of efficacy. The good news is that today there are several effective treatments for OCD, including CBT, medication options, and their combination. Of the CBT approaches, Ex/RP (or ERP) has the most empirical support (Williams, Powers et al., 2012), although clinicians may use Ex/RP in combination with other therapies, such as cognitive therapy (CT), acceptance and commitment therapy (ACT), mindfulness, and functional analytic psychotherapy (FAP), which have shown some utility, particularly among those with unacceptable/taboo thoughts (Wetterneck, Williams, Tellawi, & Bruce, 2016).

There are other therapeutic techniques that may also help. Motivational interviewing may be useful to increase motivation at the onset of treatment to reduce ambivalence; motivational interviewing has been shown to improve treatment initiation and adherence when used before or with other treatments (Simpson & Zuckoff, 2011). Exercise has also been shown beneficial for mood and anxiety disorders, with studies suggesting some benefits in OCD (Rector, Richter, Lerman, & Regev, 2015). We believe these strategies should not be used instead of the evidence-based approaches but as additional ways to increase success in treatment. Finally, stress management CBT, consisting of relaxation and deep-breathing exercises, positive imagery, and problem-solving skills, has not been shown to be effective for OCD.

Alternative Treatments for OCD

We do not yet know whether other complementary and alternative therapies are useful for OCD. One study suggested that OCD patients can benefit from mindfulness meditation, and a Chinese study suggested that three weeks of electro-acupuncture was helpful, but these trials were small and not randomized; thus, more research is needed (Sarris, Camfield, & Berk, 2012). After some brief initial excitement, the over-the-counter supplement St. John's Wort was shown to be ineffective. Some people have also used 5-hydroxytryptophan (5-HTP) to combat symptoms.

Marijuana has not been demonstrated to be helpful in OCD, and, in fact, OCD symptoms have been linked to cannabis use in both case reports and epidemiological studies (Williams & Ching, 2016). Cannabis is known to predispose youth to motivational, affective, and psychotic disorders; there is strong evidence of the psychopathogenic effects of cannabis on the developing brain, and studies indicate that early cannabis use is associated with major depressive disorder and substance use disorders (Chadwick, Miller, & Hurd, 2013; Moore et al., 2007). Thus we strongly discourage its use by people with OCD, especially during adolescence and early adulthood. For several clients we have assessed, marijuana was actually the catalyst that triggered OCD symptoms, sometimes after just a single use. Furthermore, marijuana can impair verbal learning, which can interfere with the CBT treatment process (Bhattacharyya et al., 2009). However, there have been isolated reports of some people improving with cannabis use; thus, further study of the relationship between cannabis and OCD is needed. It could be that some components of marijuana are helpful and some harmful, and it could be that hazardous effects only occur in young people.

Medications for OCD

Although Ex/RP has been shown to be the most effective approach so far, it is rarely the first treatment received by those with the disorder. Many people simply do not have access to CBT for OCD because of a lack of therapists who use empirically supported treatments, particularly in rural areas (Taylor et al., 2003). Additionally, most clinicians do not receive training in Ex/RP or empirically supported treatments in general (Barlow, Levitt, & Bufka, 1999), resulting in a lack of therapists who can effectively treat OCD. As a result, would-be patients may have difficulty locating qualified providers in their communities. In fact, over half of those with OCD admit to uncertainty about where to go for help or who to see (Williams, Domanico et al., 2012). Less than a third with OCD obtain OCD-specific treatment, but just over half are seen by a general medical practitioner (Ruscio et al., 2010). Thus, the first-line treatment for OCD is typically a medication option, specifically selective serotonin reuptake inhibitors (SSRIs), due to their widespread availability and manageable side effects (Koran & Simpson, 2013). However, in most cases these medications only result in a modest decrease in OCD symptoms, leaving most people unsatisfied with the result.

When this happens, prescribers may augment the SSRI with other medications. Commonly prescribed medications for augmenting include benzodiazepines (e.g., muscle relaxants such as Clonazepam), mood stabilizers (e.g. lithium), and neuroleptics (e.g., Risperdal, Zyprexa, Seroquel). However, the efficacy of these add-on regimens is questionable, and, in some cases, they are unsafe. But we will discuss OCD medication issues more in depth in the next chapter.

Options for Treatment Refractory OCD

Although CBT for OCD can be extremely effective, this is probably a good place to mention that not everyone with OCD will be helped by even the best CBT therapy. Often clients are anxious about diving into CBT because they fear that nothing will help them and they don't want to be disappointed. We always encourage them by saying how effective the treatment is and also note that there are other approaches we can try if they happen to be in the minority that does not benefit from CBT. The sad truth is that all of us who work with OCD have had our share of treatment failures that were not due to lack of effort or expertise. When treatment-as-usual is not working, consider increasing the intensity of Ex/RP (e.g., intensive/daily outpatient care) or increasing the level of care, (e.g., a residential OCD program). If these are not effective, it is important for clients to know that additional options are available, although they are more invasive than therapy or medication.

Psychosurgery is an option for treatment-refractory OCD that essentially involves destruction of a small part of the brain. Psychosurgery can be controversial due to the now-discredited prefrontal lobotomy procedure and other surgical procedures that took place from the mid-1930s to the 1950s. These procedures were overzealously performed on people with issues such as schizophrenia, same-sex attraction, depression, autism, criminality, etc. A prefrontal lobotomy is a surgical procedure in which the frontal lobes of the brain are irreversibly severed. This procedure was abandoned in part because of common and severe side effects such as death, personality change, intellectual impairment, loss of emotional responsiveness, and paralysis. António Egas Moniz, who invented prefrontal lobotomies, sadly received a Nobel Prize—making it a good case study for anyone who believes that medicine has all the answers. In 1949, Moniz was shot by one of his own patients and was subsequently bound to a wheelchair. He continued his work until 1955, when he died just as lobotomies were falling into disrepute.

Modern medicine and psychiatry are different than in years past, with safeguards in place to prevent such travesties. Psychosurgery is much safer today than in previous years and much more judiciously performed. One must also take into account the reason it is even considered: for extreme, treatment refractory disorders. People with treatment refractory OCD often have some of the most debilitating symptoms, leading to a very poor quality of life.

The neuroanatomy of OCD is becoming increasingly better understood, although there is always much more to learn. Through imaging studies, doctors can see brain activity, lending evidence as to which parts of the brain are affected in patients with OCD. The evidence seems to point to the limbic system and its connection with the basal ganglia. The most commonly used psychosurgical treatments for OCD in the United States involve the use of radio-frequency waves (called a gamma knife) to destroy a small amount of brain tissue, which disrupts the specific circuit in the brain that has been implicated in OCD. This area is the corticostriatal circuit, and it is comprised of the orbitofrontal cortex, the caudate nucleus, the pallidum, the thalamus, and the anterior cingulate cortex. Surgical techniques for this purpose include anterior cingulotomy, capsulotomy, subcaudate tractotomy, and limbic leucotomy.

These are generally safe procedures that do not usually affect a patient's memory or intellect. The various methods all appear to be equally effective, with cingulotomies believed to be the safest. Long-term outcomes of these procedures appear to be about 70% effective in alleviating symptoms of treatment-refractory OCD (Martinez-Alvarez, 2015). Side effects include confusion, cognitive impairment, urinary incontinence, fever, nausea/vomiting, hallucinations, and depression, lasting between two and six months. Improvements appear gradually over the course of the two years after surgery.

Remember, psychosurgery is brain surgery. Because of the many ethical, legal, and social implications of psychosurgery, a relatively small number of these procedures are done at just a handful of medical centers around the world. It should not be considered unless the patient has failed several lengthy attempts at medication at the full dosage with augmentation and many months of focused and intensive CBT. Although psychosurgery should be a last resort, it should be considered as an option if nothing else is working.

Other brain-based techniques that do not involve the destruction of brain tissue involve neuromodulation, which means altering nerve activity through the delivery of electrical stimulation or chemicals to specific sites of the body. It directly treats the nervous system itself to rebalance the activity of neural circuits and manage symptoms. One neuromodulation technique for OCD is deep brain stimulation (DBS). DBS involves surgery whereby electrodes are implanted into the brain to target multiple neural circuits to reduce symptoms in patients with refractory OCD. The electrodes stimulate the brain by way of an implanted pulse generator (IPG), which is calibrated for best effects. To date, over 100 patients have undergone DBS implantation surgery for OCD. However, outcomes need to be cautiously interpreted due to the relatively small numbers of people using the technique (Sharma, Saleh, Deogaonkar, & Rezai, 2015). However, unlike psychosurgery, the effects are reversible and the electrodes can be removed.

Another less invasive technique is transcranial magnetic stimulation (TMS), although it is still considered experimental. TMS involves placing a magnetic coil near an individual's head to deliver small electrical currents directly through the skull into the brain, stimulating brain cells to relieve OCD symptoms. Research has demonstrated TMS can be effective in treating depression, and researchers are in the process of expanding this treatment to OCD.

Summary

OCD is a chronic, debilitating, and often perplexing disorder, with many symptom presentations, including those with sexual themes. These worries are the opposite of what clients want and are in no way predictive of future sexual behaviors. Ex/RP is the most well-supported approach to the treatment of all kinds of OCD, including S-OCD, although other psychotherapeutic approaches may be helpful as well. Not everyone will be successful in using CBT, and so it is important that clients understand there are other options for them, including medication and even more invasive approaches, such as brain surgery.

2

Assessing Clients with Sexual Obsessions

Monnica T. Williams and Chad T. Wetterneck

Consultation

Sexual fears in obsessive-compulsive disorder (S-OCD) can be difficult to talk about, and so a good therapeutic relationship with your client is essential. Clients need to be able to trust you enough to share their worst fears and then plunge into those fears head on. From the perspective of the client, it can seem like a reckless leap into shark-infested waters! Clients need to trust you to make that leap. Additionally, S-OCD clients often have concerns about the therapist having all the information necessary to make an accurate diagnosis and treatment plan. Thus, the consultation session is often a place to provide space for clients to discuss their history, pain, and fears. Although reassurance is a common compulsion that we need to address once treatment starts, it is important to provide some reassurance and hope to the client during the consultation session. It is critical that clients understand what is to come in treatment, so we like to provide a road map for what the treatment will entail. Here we discuss the details of that first critical visit.

Disarming Shame

Shame is an emotion involving self-evaluation in which the entire self, not just the behavior, is evaluated negatively. Shame has several dimensions, including components related to character, behaviors, and one's own body. Character shame includes feelings related to personal habits, manner with others, self-characterization, and personal ability; behavioral shame includes shame regarding doing something wrong, saying something stupid, and failing in competitive situations; and bodily shame relates to feelings about one's body characteristics, such as appearance or functioning. Shame negatively affects mood, sense of personal identity, and quality of life.

Although people with many types of mental health issues may experience shame, it appears to be especially prominent in obsessive-compulsive disorder (OCD), with approximately half reporting shame of their problem itself and even more reporting shame related to the need for outside help (Williams, Domanico, Marques, LeBlanc, & Turkheimer, 2012). As a result, many with OCD hide their symptoms from others. Given the role of thought–action fusion in OCD (i.e., people treating bad thoughts as real as doing the actions in the thoughts), it's easy to imagine that fears surrounding unacceptable thoughts can lead to character shame. Our own research found that unacceptable thoughts in OCD were significantly correlated to feelings of character shame, and shame was more negatively correlated to quality of life for unacceptable thoughts than other symptom dimensions (Singh, Wetterneck, Williams, & Knott, 2016). Shame may be greater in ethnic minority clients, as both mental illness and mental health help-seeking carry greater social stigma in those communities (Williams, Sawyer, Ellsworth, Singh, & Tellawi, 2017).

As a type of unacceptable thought, S-OCD thoughts seem to carry with them tremendous shame, more so than most other manifestations of this disorder. In one study, over half of those with S-OCD reported that feeling ashamed was a significant barrier to seeking treatment (Glazier, Wetterneck, Singh, & Williams, 2015). This can make it difficult for clients to disclose the extent of their symptoms right away. In fact, it is not uncommon for prospective clients to call for an appointment but refuse to give details of their symptoms to our administrative staff. In these cases, it is usually the case that the client is struggling with embarrassing S-OCD symptoms that are difficult to discuss.

As a result, people with S-OCD may initially tell their clinician a long narrative about many other life events and even other OCD symptoms before revealing their sexual worries (as in the case example of Reid et al., 2016). Additionally, we find that it is typical for clients to continually ask for reassurance before, during, and after a clinical interview. In some cases, the client may have sought multiple opinions, as a form of compulsive reassurance-seeking. In other cases, the person may not have shared their concerns with anyone due to shame (e.g., they may think, "I'm hopelessly deviant and damaged for having thoughts like this"), catastrophic fears that may be out of proportion with reality (e.g., "If anyone knew I had these thoughts, my life would be over and I would lose my job and family"), or a belief that treatment will be ineffective (e.g., Glazier, Wetterneck, et al.,

2015). Because these symptoms are often hard for clients to disclose and describe, it is critical to acknowledge the clients' courage in revealing their concerns and seeking help. Clients may experience self-loathing surrounding their thoughts, and this may be further compounded by a history of shaming from others, including therapists who may have previously expressed rejecting attitudes toward clients. It is important to always ask about past experiences with other therapists, because if prior work has been unhelpful or even hurtful, clients may have well-founded misgivings about moving forward. In such cases, it would be important to explain how working together will be different this time.

Make a point to normalize S-OCD symptoms and not express surprise or disapproval of the client's thoughts. Thoughts are not the same as actions, and we as therapists need to transmit our steadfast belief in this right from the start. Many uninitiated therapists express undue alarm at their client's disclosures, particularly if fears include anxieties surrounding sexually harming children. Even if therapists do not telegraph alarm on their faces, they can still communicate alarm by asking excessive probing questions about the client's fears. Therapists should show appropriate concern for the client's suffering at all times and at no point indicate that they think the client is bad or deviant. The main purpose of the consultation session is to build rapport and provide hope to clients that they can be helped. There will be ample opportunity to probe for details in the assessment phase of the treatment, which we will discuss further in the next section.

Most people have OCD symptoms in more than one category. We show clients a diagram of different categories of symptoms and explain how some of these categories are better known (like contamination or symmetry) while other categories are less recognized (like unacceptable/taboo thoughts; see Appendix A, Handout 1). We ask clients to point to the bubbles that represent their symptom categories. When they choose the unacceptable/taboo thoughts bubble, we then show them a second diagram with this category exploded further and again ask clients to point to the categories that represent their symptoms, where they can choose from sexual, violent, religious, and/or health concerns. Clients are often relieved to see their specific concerns listed as part of a pre-existing diagram. It shows that their fears are not unusual or unheard of, and they feel less alone. It also builds confidence that they are in the right place to get the help they need for their S-OCD.

Finally, rather than refer to OCD as a "mental illness," it is better to call it a "disorder" or "condition." The term *mental illness* often evokes images of someone who is psychotic, out of control, or prone to harm others if not restrained. In fact, over one in six people with S-OCD concerns feared coming to treatment because they thought they might be hospitalized against their will (Glazier, Wetterneck, et al., 2015). People sometimes ask if they are "crazy." You can say that they are not crazy because they have an awareness of the problem and want help—which is a very sane response to a medical problem. It can be useful to emphasize the biological and genetic aspects of the condition to help reduce feeling blamed or shamed for simply having the disorder. OCD is not something that can be fixed by will power alone. We emphasize that it's not the client's fault for having the OCD, but it is their responsibility to do what they can about it. And they have taken the right steps by coming for professional help.

For some of our clients, simply hearing the clinician try to normalize the thoughts or state that it is part of an anxiety disorder rather than a paraphilia is not enough. We often share findings from an article by Renaud and Byers (1999) that shows how common acceptable and "deviant" sexual thoughts are in a nonclinical sample (see Appendix A, Handout 7). Seeing that both men and women endorse a variety of unwanted and less acceptable sexual thoughts in a peer-reviewed journal provides a visual depiction and carries more weight with some of our clients.

Explaining the OCD Cycle

In the typical cycle of OCD, obsessions cause anxiety, leading to the sufferer engaging in compulsions in an attempt to alleviate the distress caused by the obsessions. Carrying out these compulsions, or rituals, does not result in any permanent change and, in fact, the OCD symptoms worsen. The OCD cycle has been conceptualized as consisting of four parts: obsession, anxiety, compulsion, and relief (see Appendix A, Handout 2).

We explain to clients the following:

OCD includes both obsessions and compulsions. Obsessions are unwelcome and distressing ideas, thoughts, images, or impulses that repeatedly enter your mind. They come into your mind against your will. They may be repugnant to you, you may recognize them as senseless or excessive, and they may not fit your personality. I know you hate these obsessions and just want them to go away.

The obsessions cause fear and distress that we call anxiety. You may or may not think of it as anxiety, as it could be a combination of negative emotions, including disgust, but it is truly *alarming* for you. In fact, it feels like an alarm urging you to do something about it. Anything you do to make that anxiety go away is called a compulsion. Compulsions are behaviors or mental acts that you feel driven to perform although you may recognize them as senseless or excessive. At times you may try to resist doing them, but this may prove difficult. After doing a compulsion, you may feel better for a little while (relief), but the worries always come back. In fact, the more your do compulsions, the stronger and faster the obsessions return. This is why OCD tends to get worse over time. The compulsions are the fuel that powers the OCD engine, and the more you feed it, the stronger it gets.

So, can you see where this is going? Can you guess what we need to do to bring your OCD under control? I know you want to make the obsessions just go away. I wish we could instantly do that for you; unfortunately, it is not that simple. We can't just take these thoughts out of your brain. The mind is additive, not subtractive. We cannot remove our experiences including thoughts or emotions. You can't stop obsessions directly. If you try, they only come back sooner. But you can stop compulsions. That will make your anxiety worse in the short run, but then eventually it will reduce and may go away altogether. The more you resist compulsions, the weaker your OCD will become, until it hardly bothers you at all. There is no 100% cure for OCD, but if we work together on it, I believe we can make your life manageable again, where the OCD is no longer in control and you're not worried all the time.

"Where Did My Symptoms Come From?"

Like anyone suffering from a mysterious illness, people with OCD often struggle to understand the cause of their disorder. Already prone to overthinking, many believe that if they can determine what caused their brain to go awry, they can figure out a way to fix it. People with OCD have been known to spend hours ruminating and searching the Internet to find "the root of the problem."

Many will report their OCD was triggered by a particular life event. Common triggers we have heard from clients include traumatic events, drug use, and random interactions that planted a seed of doubt in the mind that would not go away. For example, some clients may worry that their S-OCD was caused by a racy music video they saw as a child or being called "gay" while in middle school. Others remember worries starting after watching a movie or hearing a disturbing news story of a child sexual assault.

It is true that the specific content of obsessions can be influenced by events that occur in a person's life, and this can even be seen in cross-cultural studies of OCD. For example, OCD sufferers in Islamic cultures are more likely to have religious compulsions. However, in such cases, Islam is not the reason the person contracted OCD, it is only the mask worn by a disorder that, like a chameleon, tries to blend into its surroundings.

Interestingly, people who have had more stressful life events before the onset of OCD are more likely to engage in checking and symmetry compulsions (Cromer, Schmidt, & Murphy, 2007)—perhaps as an attempt to impose some order in a world filled with frightening unpredictability. Additionally, people with OCD and posttraumatic stress disorder (PTSD) together are much more likely to have sexual and/or religious obsessions (Fontenelle et al., 2012). However, despite the temptation to figure it all out, it is not possible to identify the exact cause of OCD in any particular person. OCD is not caused by religion, culture, or late toilet training. It is caused by a complex interaction of genetics, environment, personality, and stressors (Grisham, Anderson, & Sachdev, 2008). There is no one psychological factor that causes OCD in a particular person, and, likewise, no single gene that can be identified and excised. Some people are born with a predisposition to OCD, and then a combination of life events light the fuse. In other cases, the onset was like a ticking time bomb, destined to go off at the specified hour, regardless of the circumstances. Although most people can remember having some symptoms as a child, the average age of onset for OCD is around the age of 20—potential evidence for a sinister genetic plan unfolding at an appointed time.

Why Talk Therapy Won't Work

Although negative life events, such as a psychological trauma, can be the catalyst for the start of the disorder (Real et al., 2011), psychological exploration of these events will not cure OCD. These types of explorations are typical of treatment approaches like psychodynamic psychotherapy that are focused on understanding a person's past and unconscious as a route to resolving emotional problems. The goals of these forms of therapy include uncovering hidden motivations and gaining insight, leading to their designation as "insight-oriented therapies." Unfortunately, insight alone is not enough. People with OCD tend to be introspective and typically have already spent a great deal of time and effort ruminating about the origins of their disorder. In fact, this sort of rumination can be a mental compulsion, which will actually worsen the symptoms.

One problem is that too many therapists unwittingly participate in this counterproductive process. We have seen clients who previously spent years in therapy, as time and money were wasted trying to find the elusive root of the problem. And the irony is that even if a root were found, there is no evidence that an "ah ha!" moment would be curative. Over a hundred years of research has shown us that psychodynamic approaches are just not enough for OCD. Unfortunately, even cognitive-behavioral therapists are sometimes sucked into the temptation to dig for the roots. A little digging might help the client feel better understood, but it won't be enough to make the symptoms go away.

We are not suggesting that you quickly dismiss a client's inquiry into figuring it out how S-OCD started. That would be invalidating and interfere with rapport. We do suggest acknowledging the client's desire to know, be willing to discuss it to some extent, but planting the seed early on that we may not be able to figure it out and luckily we are able to treat it without having all of the origins identified.

People with OCD should be encouraged to refocus their energies on combating the symptoms through cognitive-behavioral therapy (CBT) for their OCD. Digging for the "root" of the problem should not be confused with identifying the client's core fear, which, in fact, is essential in guiding the development of appropriate exposure exercises. There's no cure for OCD, but clients can be assured that focused exposure and response prevention (Ex/RP)—not searching for the "cause"—is the best treatment science has to offer those plagued with these distressing obsessions and repetitive compulsions.

Doubting the Diagnosis

People with S-OCD often feel tremendous relief when they receive their initial OCD diagnosis. They are often afraid they have something much worse or much scarier than OCD, and so getting "labeled" with a mental health condition is not usually bad news for them. Therefore, therapists should not be anxious about being direct and honest about the diagnosis. However, it is to be expected that S-OCD clients will continually doubt their diagnosis and wonder whether, in fact, the problem is not their OCD, but some personal moral failing or stigmatizing defect. Clinicians should not be worried about it and often warn clients that they will come to doubt their diagnosis so that it does not come as a surprise to them. You might explain that OCD is the "disease of doubt," which in this case extends even to their diagnosis.

Sometimes we meet with clients who just want an expert to confirm their diagnosis. It is important to provide this service, but therapists should keep in mind that getting experts to repeatedly diagnose them can be a compulsion. Some professionals take advantage of people with OCD by offering expensive medical tests, such as functional magnetic resonance imaging (fMRIs), and these add nothing to the diagnostic accuracy or treatment plan. When asked by clients about these modalities, we discourage it. We have even had clients come to us from other OCD experts to confirm a diagnosis: In some cases, they admitted to being in treatment, and, in others, it was kept secret (perhaps to be a better test to dispel anxiety) and only found out later in the consultation. Sometimes clients think if they just knew *for sure* what it was and could confirm that it's not really the awful thing they're afraid it, they would feel better and have peace. So it is also important to emphasize that simply knowing the correct diagnosis is not sufficient in and of itself for getting better.

OCD Treatment: What to Expect

As mentioned previously, it's important for clients to understand what their treatment plan for OCD will look like. Foa, Yadin, and Lichner (2012) have published a 17-session protocol that is a gold-standard model for OCD behavioral treatment. This therapy includes 90-minute sessions twice a week. We find that most clients who are motivated and have no other conditions are typically able to complete treatment in about 20 sessions. However, as noted earlier, many clients have comorbid conditions that may also need to be addressed, and some have extremely severe OCD, low insight, and/ or extreme family accommodations that maintain the disorder. In our experience, about a third of clients do very well and no longer need treatment after the 20 sessions, about a third need periodic check-in visits, and a third require ongoing therapy for their OCD and/or related issues. People with comorbid personality disorders seem to have the most difficulty with the treatment program and should be advised that ongoing treatment will probably be needed to maintain gains once the 20 OCD-focused sessions are complete.

Here is an example of how you might describe treatment to new clients:

> *Exposure and ritual prevention* (Ex/RP) is a very effective treatment for OCD. It is also sometimes called *exposure and response prevention* (ERP). Ex/RP is a type of cognitive-behavioral therapy (CBT) designed specifically for OCD. Ex/RP includes both behavioral and cognitive techniques to help you get better. The main behavioral techniques we will use to help you include exposures where you confront things you would be inclined to avoid due to your OCD. This technique involves systematic, repeated, and prolonged confrontation with situations that cause you some anxiety, typically for 45 minutes or so at a time. You will feel anxious at first, but then you will learn that the anxiety will go away all by itself without doing any compulsions. We'll do this over and over until your brain catches on that it doesn't need to worry so much.

Once clients understand the essentials of what is to come they may seem more frightened or uncertain about beginning therapy. In response, we might say the following:

> I know the idea of confronting things you'd normally avoid can sound scary. Don't worry. The goal is not to expose you to your greatest fear all at once. We'll make a list of things you avoid and rank order them from easiest to hardest (your hierarchy). We'll start with some easier things first and slowly work our way up. The goal is for exposures to be challenging but manageable (and not impossible). We don't want you to freak out, because if you're freaking out, you're not learning that the exposure is actually safe. We want you to be challenged so that you can start to build a tolerance to the fears and get stronger over time. As we move up the list or hierarchy, you'll soon find that the items near the top that seemed so scary are not so scary anymore. You will learn (a) that your greatest fears won't come true, (b) to better manage anxiety, and (c) that anxiety goes away all

by itself without performing rituals. And *ritual prevention* is just a fancy way of saying that you're going to stop doing compulsions.

Another way to conceptualize it that is the hierarchy is like a pyramid with the greatest fears represented by the highest blocks and the more manageable fears at the bottom. We begin at the bottom and chip away at those blocks—as we do so, the pyramid itself starts to become less imposing and actually shorter as the bottom levels are removed. Unfortunately, it's not as easy as a game of Jenga for most, where removing a few blocks topple the whole thing! This decreases the distance and fear you will have as we are undermining parts of the pyramid that support the highest fear. By the time we reach the top levels, they are only half as high (and often half as scary) as they were at the beginning.

Make sure the client has the time and space to do the work involved in this treatment program. We state upfront that clients will need to come to session at least twice a week for 90-minute sessions and that there will be at least an hour of homework daily. We tell them to think of it like they would if they were taking a college course. If clients do not have the time for this work, you might help them problem-solve surrounding scheduling or advise them to come back when they can make proper time for treatment. In milder cases, we might accommodate two 60-minute session per week or one 90-minute session per week with phone check-ins between sessions. But because we offer specialized OCD treatment, most of our clients are severe and require the two 90-minute sessions per week.

Assessment

Intake Questionnaire

We have developed a short intake interview that we use to collect basic background information on our new clients with OCD. This interview is meant to be administered by a therapist in a conversational style and does not need to be administered in any particular order. The form helps to ensure that most of the important background information is collected early in the therapeutic process. The interview is intended to capture the following information:

- *Measurements summary*: A listing of the scores from any self-report measures provided at intake, along with an indication if any that are in the clinical range (see the table later in this chapter for recommended measures).
- *Background information*: Here the therapist will note the client's age, sex, marital status, race/ethnicity, and number of children, if any.
- *Presenting problem*: This is a place to describe current symptoms. You want to determine why the client is coming for help. Is this a new or recurring problem? When did it start (onset)? What are the triggers for symptoms? What is the client's explanatory model for their difficulties?
- *Current vocational and/or academic functioning*: Note what kind of work the client does. Determine whether there is any indication they are working below ability/education due to symptoms. Find out whether there have here been periods when the client was unable to work due to OCD or other emotional difficulties.
- *Other current problems*: Review any other recent symptoms that have been present in the past month, including depression, anxiety, drug/alcohol use, etc. Describe the problems and find out if it is a new or recurrent problem, the onset, and triggers.
- *Current treatment status*: Ask what sort of help the client has been getting in the past month and for what symptoms specifically. Describe the treatment setting, nature of treatment, duration, and outcome. List all current medications being taken and who is prescribing them.
- *Treatment history*: Find out when the client first attempted treatment and what symptoms were the main target of treatment. Describe the treatment setting, nature of treatment, duration, and outcome of treatment. It is important to know whether the client has been misdiagnosed by any mental or health professional and whether they have worked with others claiming to be knowledgeable about OCD treatment. We have encountered patients who have already been to someone who claimed to do Ex/RP and CBT for OCD and were less hopeful when we explained that was our approach. In most of these cases, we asked for a copy of the exposure hierarchy and were met with a response that indicated they did not have a hierarchy and, in some cases, did not know what an exposure was. Others had done Ex/RP but did not benefit, and we believed it was due to too few exposures/low dosing of therapy (e.g., sessions twice a month or only working on one exposure/exposures for 10 minutes a day), a lack of clinician-assisted

exposure to begin with or when needed (which sometimes increases the effectiveness of Ex/RP; cf. Franklin & Foa, 2014), and/or an inadequate understanding of the exposure process. All of these are key to assess to "undo" previous stigmatization or create more hope in conducting the treatment in the proper format when previously it was not done correctly or at too low of a "dose."

- *Family psychiatric history:* Many disorders run in families. Find out what diagnoses and/or symptoms are experienced by blood relatives. It is common to find OCD, OCD-related disorders, anxiety disorders, and mood disorders throughout the family tree. In fact, it is rare that the client is the only person in the family with a diagnosable disorder.
- *Previous and current relationship with parents:* Ask about the relationship with parents. Find out about the role of family accommodations, if any, growing up or currently.
- *Previous and current relationship with siblings (if applicable):* Find out how the client gets along with brothers and sisters, in childhood and currently.
- *Previous and current relationships with friends, co-workers, etc.:* Find out about the client's social life, friendships, how often they spend time with friends, quality of friendships, and what work relationships are like.
- *Dating/sexual history/current sexual functioning:* Gather information about the client's sexual history, including early sexual experiences, adolescence and puberty, messages about sex learned from parents, current sexual attitudes, religious beliefs about sex, past and current sexual functioning, and if OCD is impacting the client's sex life.
- *Previous and current relationship with spouse/partner (if applicable):* For clients with partners, understanding this relationship and how the OCD has impacted it is critical for treatment. Find out whether the significant other knows about OCD concerns and whether they will be involved in treatment (i.e., to discuss exposure work, reducing accommodations to symptoms, reducing giving reassurance, providing encouragement, etc.).
- *Diagnosis:* List the most likely *Diagnostic and Statistical Manual of Mental Disorder* (fifth edition; DSM-5; American Psychiatric Association, 2013) diagnoses. Also list diagnoses to be ruled out and a short note about why.

- *Plan/recommendation*: Typically, this would be Ex/RP, but if additional or other treatments are warranted, this can be noted.
- *Review*: If needed, review the rationale for treatment and the planned treatment for the client.
- *Homework*: Have the client review the handouts about the obsessive-compulsive symptom dimensions and the OCD cycle. The client should also be given the handout *Understanding S-OCD* to read for homework. Since there will be homework throughout treatment, it's best to start this right away so the client comes to expect it. It is also a good idea to start collecting data on the client's rituals. You can provide the *Compulsion & Avoidance Monitoring Log* and *Instructions* to the client to work on at home.

Comorbidity in OCD

Before we go any further with assessment, this is probably a good place to mention that OCD is highly comorbid with other mental health conditions, which is why a thorough assessment is so vitally important. In terms of lifetime prevalence rates, one major nationwide study (Ruscio, Stein, Chiu, & Kessler, 2010) found that over half of those with OCD had a comorbid unipolar depressive disorder (53.8%) and almost a quarter had a comorbid bipolar disorder (23.4%). That study also found that 75.8% also had an anxiety disorder (including PTSD), 55.9% had an impulse control disorder, and 38.6% had a substance use disorder. In total, 90% had some comorbid condition in one or more of those categories. OCD is also highly comorbid in women with eating disorders, and some have noted the similarities between obsessions about food versus typical OCD concerns.

Assessment Instruments: General Psychopathology Interviews

Given that comorbidity in OCD is the rule rather than the exception, in addition to collecting general demographic information and background information, we generally administer several clinical measures, including both clinical interviews and validated self-report measures. These are useful for determining diagnoses, developing a case conceptualization, and tracking progress over the course of therapy. Because OCD and comorbid conditions impact other important life domains, we utilize both OCD specific and nonspecific measures. We review these measures here, and they are also summarized in Table 2.1.

To assess for the most common psychopathologies, we use the Mini International Neuropsychiatric Inventory (MINI; Sheehan et al., 1998) to give us a comprehensive picture of all the common comorbidities a client may be experiencing. However, because OCD has such a wide range of symptoms, we do not ever use the MINI alone to diagnose OCD. The MINI module for OCD is more likely to capture more typical or well-known presentations, like contamination symptoms. For example, it directly queries whether the client repeatedly washes their hands or cleans excessively. The section on obsessions does include some wording that may signal intrusive sexual thoughts, but the section of the module devoted to compulsions does not adequately capture the mental compulsions, which are common with S-OCD. The MINI discusses physical compulsions, which are seen in more widely known forms of OCD.

Another structured interview often used to assess for OCD is the Assessment for Anxiety Disorders Clinical Interview Schedule (ADIS; Silverman & Albano, 1996). While the ADIS provides a more comprehensive view of obsessions that a client may endorse by listing symptom subtypes, its format is cumbersome for the interviewer, and there is no easy scoring system. It does not specifically mention pedophilic obsessions, but a client with pedophilic obsessions may relate to the section "Unwanted Sexual Thoughts/Images" and/or "Aggressive Urges" in the ADIS. The section that is structured to capture compulsions mentions "internal repetition," which may account for covert rituals like mental compulsions. While the ADIS does a better job of assessing for different manifestations of OCD, its adequacy in detecting S-OCD is unclear. Inexperienced clinicians would be susceptible to missing many important symptom manifestations in a client with S-OCD.

One other assessment that can be used to assess for OCD is the Structured Clinical Interview for DSM-IV Disorders (SCID; First, Spitzer, Gibbon, & Williams, 2002), which is widely used in research. Similar to the other structured assessments, the SCID does not ask specific questions about sexual obsessions or other taboo subtype OCD manifestations. After assessing for the presence of obsessions and/or compulsions, the

Table 2.1 Recommended Measures for Clients with Sexually Themed OCD

Clinician Administered	Measure Description
Yale–Brown Obsessive Compulsive Scale II—Severity Scale & Checklist (Y-BOCS-II; Storch et al., 2010)	The YBOCS-II is a 10-item semi-structured clinician-rated measure of OCD severity. Scores are computed for obsessions and compulsions, and a total severity score is the sum of all items. The checklist contains 60 items to assess specific OC symptoms.
Mini International Neuropsychiatric Interview (MINI; Sheehan et al., 1998)	The MINI is a semi-structured clinical interview that provides information about the participant's psychiatric diagnoses, age of onset and comorbid conditions.

Self-Report for OCD	Measure Description
Dimensional OCD Scale (DOCS; Abramowitz et al., 2010)	The DOCS measures the main symptom groups in OCD. The DOCS Sexually Intrusive Thoughts Scale (DOCS-SIT) is a variation of the DOCS focused on sexual obsessions (Wetterneck, Siev, Smith, Adams, & Slimowicz, 2015).
Sexual orientation Obsessions and Reactions Test (SORT; Williams et al., 2018)	The SORT is designed to help clinicians discriminate between people with sexual orientation worries in OCD and LGBTQ individuals without OCD.
Obsessive Compulsive Inventory-Revised (OCI-R; Foa et al., 2002)	The OCI-R is an 18-item self-report measure that yields distress ratings over the past month for six symptom areas: washing, checking, ordering, obsessing, hoarding, and neutralizing.
Adult OCD Impact Scale (AOIS; Wetterneck, Knott, Kinnear, & Storch, 2017)	This is a 58-item measure that assesses OCD-related dysfunction in multiple areas. It assesses work/school problems, intimate relationships, social problems, and home/family problems.
Barriers to Treatment Questionnaire (BTQ; Goodwin, 2002; Marques et al., 2010)	The BTQ is a 19-item self-report measure used in research studies and clinical practice to assess barriers to treatment of OCD in diverse samples (Marques et al., 2010; Williams, Domanico, et al., 2012). The BTQ has three subscales, including questions about shame/stigma and knowledge about where to find help.
Family Accommodation Scale (FAS-SR; Pinto et al., 2013)	The FAS-SR is a self-report measure given to significant family members to assess the degree to which family members assist the person with OCD in their rituals or avoidance behaviors. There are 15 items that query types of symptoms and 19 items that ask directly about family involvement in symptoms.

(*continued*)

Table 2.1 Continued

Other Useful Measures	Measure Description
Beck Depression Inventory (BDI-II; Beck, Steer, & Brown, 1996)	The BDI-II is a widely used 21-item self-report measure of depressive symptoms. It has been shown to have good psychometric properties.
Behavioral Activation for Depression Scale (BADS; Kanter et al., 2012)	The BADS is a 9-item scale used to monitor behavioral activation activities to reduce depression. It assesses engagement in pleasurable and productive activities and avoidance of stressful activities. It has good reliability and validity.
Beck Anxiety Inventory (BAI; Beck, 1990)	BAI is a 21-item instrument, consisting of common symptoms of anxiety. The BAI has good internal consistency and factor structure.
Penn State Worry Questionnaire (PSWQ; Meyer et al., 1990)	The PSWQ is a 16-item self-report measure that has been shown to provide a reliable and valid assessment of pathological worry, with good psychometric properties.
Sell Assessment of Sexual Orientation (SASO; Sell, 1996)	This updated version of the SASO is a self-report measure for assessing sexual orientation and may be useful for clients with sexual orientation concerns. It has high test–retest reliability and high construct validity with similar instruments.

SCID's module for OCD approaches the diagnosis in very general terms. The module assesses whether the client thinks about obsessive thoughts more than normal and/or whether they participate in compulsions more than they should. These questions seek to assess the client's level of insight into whether the time spent in obsessions and compulsions is excessive. The module asks the client to quantify the level of impairment they experience by asking how often other life tasks are interrupted by the condition and how much anxiety is experienced during an episode. However, very few specific examples of OCD behaviors are provided, and none include examples with sexual content. Thus, a client must already have a clear idea of their own obsessions and compulsions to answer these items correctly. Our own research into the utility of the SCID in identifying OCD found an unacceptably high miss rate among African Americans (33.8%), and more research needs to be done to determine whether this is a problem in other groups as well.

The newest version of the SCID, the SCID-5, does provide more concrete examples of OCD symptoms, but is only a minor improvement for those with S-OCD. The only question about sexual obsessions that is asked is, "How about having images popping into your head that you didn't want, like violent or horrible scenes or something of a sexual nature? (What were they?)" However, sexual obsessions may or may not include images. Additionally, no questions are asked about covert compulsions or compulsions clearly linked to sexual obsessions. Thus, the SCID-5 may also be of limited value for screening people for S-OCD if they don't already have a clear OCD diagnosis.

Assessment Instruments: OCD Interviews

The Yale–Brown Obsessive Compulsive Disorder Checklist and Severity Scale (Y-BOCS or Y-BOCS-II; Goodman et al., 1989; Storch et al., 2010) is the gold standard measure used for assessing the severity of OCD symptoms. The YBOCS checklist has over 60 items, with a four-item section devoted to sexual obsessions, bringing needed attention to this important symptom. We prefer the YBOCS-II (available online from the authors) as it has three detailed items about sexual obsessions, with a fourth item about doing something embarrassing or inappropriate that includes sexual contact and pregnancy as examples. There is also an additional specific item about excessive concern with becoming pregnant or of making someone pregnant. Thus, this measure captures a wide range of sexual obsessional symptoms.

The YBOCS severity scale rates the time occupied by obsessions and compulsions, how much they interfere with functioning, how much distress they cause, attempts to resist, and level of control, with the first five items addressing obsessions and the remainder focused on compulsions. Items are rated on a 5-point scale ranging from zero (no symptoms) to 4 (severe symptoms) and from zero (no symptoms) to 5 (severe symptoms) on the YBOCS-II. Both the YBOCS and YBOCS-II severity scales have shown good reliability and validity. YBOCS scores above 16 may be considered in the clinical range, and the mean for OCD patients is 21.9 (SD = 8). For the YBOCS-II, the mean for OCD patients in the original validation sample was 30.6 (SD = 7.4), which was similar to their scores on the original YBOCS (Storch et al., 2010). We like to see scores in the single-digit range before discharging them from treatment. Although we recommend administering the YBOCS or YBOCS-II via the clinician, a self-report version has also been validated (Steketee et al., 1996) and may be adequate if you are pressed for time. If you are considering this option, we recommend you give the severity scale via both self-report *and* interview format the first time you administer it to ensure there are no large discrepancies between total scores and items.

Assessment Instruments: Self-Report Instruments

The Dimensional Obsessive-Compulsive Scale (DOCS; Abramowitz et al., 2010) assesses OCD on the basis of four dimensions pertaining to contamination, responsibility for harm and mistakes, unacceptable thoughts, and symmetry/completeness. For each symptom dimension, individuals rate the amount of time spent on obsessions and compulsions, extent of avoidance and functional interference, degree of distress, and difficulty disregarding obsessions and refraining from compulsions. We like this measure because it helps to determine severity for each specific symptom area in OCD. However, the current DOCS may not do the best job capturing S-OCD symptoms because there is a single broad "Unacceptable Thoughts" category that includes anxiety about morality, violence, repeating, mental actions, mental prayers, and avoidance, as well as sexual concerns. Moreover, no specific mention is made of issues like sexual orientation or pedophilia. For that reason, as an even more specific option, we've developed a fifth DOCS scale to assess sexually intrusive thoughts (DOCS-SIT) by adapting content from the existing DOCS unacceptable thoughts scale and specifying a wider range of sexual obsessional content (Wetterneck, Siev, Smith, Adams, & Slimowicz, 2015). This new scale has good psychometric properties and appears to be distinct from the DOCS Unacceptable Thoughts scale. Both measures are included in Appendix B.

The Sexual Orientation Obsessions and Reactions Test (SORT; Williams et al., 2018) is a measure of sexual orientation concerns in OCD we recently developed, based on research we previously published in the *Archives of Sexual Behavior* (Williams, Wetterneck, Tellawi, & Duque, 2015). The purpose of the scale is to help clinicians discriminate between people with sexual orientation worries in OCD (SO-OCD) and LGBTQ individuals without OCD who may be experiencing a sexual identity crisis. We took 49 items from the larger pool of 70 items and gave them to a large sample of undergraduates, people in the community, and OCD patients. We examined each item and compared scores based on OCD status, type of OCD (sexual orientation concerns), and LGBTQ status. We identified 12 items that reliably discriminated between groups, with mean SO-OCD scale scores of 5.9 (SD = 5.8) for heterosexual undergraduates, 8.8 (SD = 7.5) for LGBTQ undergraduates, 6.3 (SD = 5.1) for LGBTQ people in the community, 21.6 (SD = 11.7) for heterosexual SO-OCD patients, and 12.4 (SD = 12.6) heterosexual patients with other forms of OCD. LGTBQ individuals with SO-OCD scored similarly to heterosexual individuals with SO-OCD. Those LGBTQ individuals who scored high in internalized homophobia/heterosexism did score a few points higher on the SO-OCD scale, but it was not in the OCD range. A score of 10 was found to be the optimal cut-off score for identifying SO-OCD. The scale demonstrated good reliability in the various samples. The measure is included in Appendix B.

The Obsessive-Compulsive Inventory–Revised (OCI-R) is an 18-item self-report measure of distress due to obsessions and compulsions (Foa et al., 2002). The total score ranges between zero and 72. The questionnaire also includes six subscales, including washing, checking, ordering, obsessing, hoarding, and neutralizing, but the OCI-R has no questions that address any specific sexual obsession. Subscale scores range between zero and 12. The OCI-R has shown good internal consistency, test–retest reliability, and discriminant validity (Foa et al., 2002). Although a clinical cutoff score of 21 differentiates OCD patients from nonpatients, African Americans tend to score higher and thus may need a higher clinical cut-off (Williams, Wetterneck, Thibodeau, & Duque, 2013). The OCI-R has been translated into multiple languages.

OCD can cause impairments in many varied life domains. The Adult OCD Impact Scale (AOIS) is designed to capture dysfunction in several important areas of life (Wetterneck, Knott, Kinnear, & Storch, 2017). The AOIS targets specific areas of psychosocial functioning impacted by OCD across a broad range of domains (work/school, significant relationships, social problems, and home/family problems), including intimate behaviors (especially relevant to many with S-OCD), which are excluded by almost all other OCD functioning measures. The measure includes a linear, widespread scoring system to encapsulate all measures of severity (time, difficulty, distress, and avoidance), while most other functioning measures only include one or two, often nonlinear, areas of severity. It may be useful in exposure hierarchy development to target areas most affected by OCD, and it is concise enough to be used regularly to show treatment progression. The items and factors also relate to valued living, which we consider to be as important as symptom reduction. It has demonstrated good psychometric properties as well. See Appendix B for this measure.

Barriers to Treatment Questionnaire (BTQ; Goodwin et al., 2002; Marques et al., 2010) measures clients' perceived barriers to seeking OCD treatment, based on similar questionnaires from the broader literature. The BTQ assesses barriers to treatment in the following domains: logistic and financial, stigma, shame and discrimination barriers, and treatment perception and satisfaction barriers. Clients are asked whether any of these possible barriers influenced them to not seek treatment. Given the hurdles that so many with OCD face in terms of finding treatment, this provides helpful background information on prior difficulties in finding help or adjusting expectations if they previously were misdiagnosed and/or went through a previous treatment that was not helpful.

Depression is a common problem among those with OCD. It can indeed be very depressing when one's thoughts continually veer off into frightening and seemingly dangerous territory. Additionally, severe depression can interfere with the efficacy of Ex/RP in outpatients (although we should note that those with severe depression have been shown to respond just as well as those with no to moderate levels of depression when provided with very high [residential] levels of care; Wetterneck et al., 2017). For this reason, it is critical to assess depression in all OCD patients. There are many good measures of depression, but one of the most popular is the Beck Depression Inventory (BDI-II;), a 21-item self-report scale that assesses the severity of affective, cognitive, and physiological components of depression. Total scores of 10 or less are considered normal, while scores of 20 or greater suggest clinical depression. The BDI-II has excellent reliability and validity and is used frequently in both clinical practice and treatment outcome research. However, the BDI-II is not freely available, so the original BDI is a good alternative. For clients who are depressed and concurrently receiving behavioral activation for their depression, the Behavioral Activation for Depression Scale (BADS; Kanter, Mulick, Busch, Berlin, & Martell, 2012) is an excellent way to track progress to help ensure clients are making time for activities that will improve their mood. The BADS is also related to valued living; as mentioned earlier, we consider this to be an important construct for life satisfaction. Interestingly, we often find it easier to get clients to do difficult exposure exercises for homework than enjoyable behavioral activation activities!

Other useful measures include the Beck Anxiety Inventory (BAI; Beck, 1990), a self-report measure that queries about the presence and severity of physical anxiety symptoms; each of the 21 items are rated on a scale of zero to 3, and it has good psychometric properties. The Penn State Worry Questionnaire (PSWQ; Meyer et al., 1990) may also be useful; it is a 16-item measure designed to assess the trait of worry. It is able to separate out worry from other types of anxiety and depression, and responses to the questionnaire are not influenced by social desirability. Finally, we also like to administer the Sell Assessment of Sexual Orientation (SASO; Sell, 1996), which is particularly useful for understanding the sexuality of our clients with sexual-orientation fears. We use a modified version with updated language surrounding the description of LGBTQ individuals, available in Appendix B.

Relationship Scales

Family accommodation in OCD refers to family members' participation in or facilitation of clients' rituals or avoidance. With research showing that accommodating is a predictor of poorer treatment outcome, the Family Accommodation Scale for OCD is an excellent way to determine the types of accommodating taking place in OCD families, and the severity. We use the relative self-report version (FAS-SR; Pinto et al., 2013), which you can simply give to a family member to complete, although there is also a patient self-report version (FAS-PV) and clinician interview version (FAS-IR) available as well. See Appendix B for these measures.

Differential Diagnosis

OCD versus Pedophilic Disorder

The assessment process can be challenging for clients with pedophilic obsessions due to the disturbing nature of these obsessions. For those who have not seen this type of OCD before, it can be difficult to assess for pedophilic OCD as there are few measures that adequately screen for these types of symptoms. Many clients come into treatment presenting with other types of well-known symptoms so it is likely that most OCD measures will adequately catch those symptoms, but pedophilic OCD may require greater probing. Thus, when assessing for OCD with structured interview assessments, like the MINI, clinical judgment must be used. In terms of OCD-specific measures, the Y-BOCS-II includes items on the obsessions checklist portion of the assessment that attempt to capture pedophilic concerns. The OCI-R has no items that point specifically to pedophilia obsessions; there are only two items that may indirectly refer to these areas OCD sufferers are likely to endorse, but these items may refer to other types of symptoms besides pedophilia obsessions.

An unstructured clinical interview is often the best source of information for clinicians when a client is presenting with pedophilic OCD. Many clients who seek treatment are reticent to disclose the types of thoughts they have been having out of shame or fear of legal or social punishment. Many clients may have already had negative experiences after disclosing their symptoms to other professionals, so this may contribute to reluctance to give details. In most cases, they have already done online research in an attempt to determine the root cause for the manifestation of intrusive pedophilic thoughts. Despite having recognized their symptoms as OCD, many still resist the idea that they are suffering from a mental disorder. Instead, they may feel they should be punished for having such thoughts.

Once clients open up about their obsessions involving pedophilia, they may begin a narrative detailing what events triggered these thoughts, along with evidence that they are not attracted to children. Throughout this story, therapists may repeatedly hear the client adamantly state that they never had these issues in the past. Clients may also ask repeatedly for reassurance from the therapist (e.g., "Do you think I am a pedophile?"). No matter how many times clients are reassured that they are not a pedophile, they will eventually come to doubt this information. They may express feeling as though they did not give enough information to help the therapist really determine whether they are actually a pedophile. As mentioned previously, getting a detailed history of the treatment they may have received in the past is important, as many clients have sought treatment from several other therapists as a means of compulsive reassurance-seeking.

It is important to note that people with pedophile-themed OCD feel distress because of the fear that they are horrible people who are sexually attracted to children. They have not actually committed crimes involving harm to children, and they are highly disturbed by the intrusive thoughts and images. They do not experience any pleasure when these thoughts and images persist. Instead of approaching children, they may go to great lengths to avoid contact with children. Some fears go much further than simply being attracted to children. Many worry that they will be deserted by their partner and/or loved ones and put in jail for the rest of their lives. Some decide that they will never have children and should never be around children because they worry about their capacity to do harm. Unfortunately, many clients make very definite decisions about their lives because of these fears, such as deciding to forego marriage or starting a family.

As mentioned previously, this type of S-OCD is frequently misdiagnosed, and due to the lack of knowledge about sexual forms of OCD, clients may face undeserved scrutiny when trying to find professional help. For example, one client experiencing severe pedophilic obsessions became so overwhelmed with obsessive thoughts and images that his wife took him to the emergency room, where he described obsessive sexual thoughts about his daughter. The medical staff there, being unaware of the difference between pedophilic OCD and pedophilic disorder, reported him to child protective services, which resulted in restrictions on contact with his young daughter. These actions and consequences were traumatic for the client and his family. Had the psychiatric staff at the hospital been knowledgeable about OCD, the family could have avoided these consequences.

There are very distinct differences between a true pedophile and one who suffers from pedophilic OCD (Bruce, Ching, & Williams, 2018). The term *pedophile* refers to an individual who is sexually attracted to children, who may or may not have acted on this attraction. Pedophilic disorder requires an attraction to children for a diagnosis, along with having acted on these urges with children, experiencing severe distress, and/or related interpersonal problems. For a diagnosis, the individual must be at least 16 years of age and at least five years older than the child(ren) of interest. It is not strictly the age of the child that defines whether or not the attraction is pathological, however, but the sexual development of the child. If the child is past puberty and has adult sexual characteristics, attraction would not be considered pathological, although sexual contact may be illegal depending on the age of both parties and local laws. Further, there are cultural differences surrounding what level of sexual maturity is considered acceptable or ideal in a given society.

Those with pedophilic disorder may experience pleasurable sexual arousal when coming in contact with children. Any fear or anxiety about this sexual attraction is more likely to be aimed toward society's hatred for people who sexually prey on children instead of toward their desire to become intimately close to children. These individuals prefer the company of children instead of romantic contact with age-appropriate companions. Pedophiles are likely to engage in grooming behaviors toward a child by finding opportunities to gain their trust Lang and Frenzel (1988). They may feign interest in activities that the child enjoys and may slowly get the child more comfortable with touching behaviors by creating opportunities to play fight or wrestle with the child. They seek opportunities to be alone with their victims to facilitate more intimate and inappropriate touching. When grooming children, true pedophiles experience sexual gratification from these interactions. Many pedophiles also meet criteria for antisocial personality disorder. It should be noted, however, that some people who are sexually attracted to children resist these urges due to fear of punishment or moral considerations and do not aggress against children. Although they are attracted to children and have sexual fantasies about children (perhaps getting pleasure via masturbation), they would typically not be called pedophiles, although they might be diagnosed with pedophilic disorder if they experienced distress or if their desires were causing interpersonal problems.

In contrast, people who are experiencing pedophilic OCD symptoms are generally avoidant of children. They may take extreme measures to avoid contact with even their own children to prevent themselves from the remote possibility of acting on their fears. Those experiencing obsessions that include thoughts and graphic images of sexual contact between themselves and children are repulsed by and highly disturbed by this, which may be accompanied by feelings of disgust. They may lock themselves away from others to decrease the chance that they may act out sexually toward a child or to prevent having their obsessional fears triggered. They do not find their symptoms sexually arousing or pleasant (and would not engage in fantasizing for pleasure or masturbation). Instead, many state that they would rather commit suicide than hurt a child.

Nonetheless, the compulsions conducted by someone with pedophilic OCD can make it appear as if the person wants to molest children. One known case study of pedophile-themed OCD published in the *Harvard Review of Psychiatry* (O'Neil, Cather, Fishel, & Kafka, 2005) describes a patient who was horribly afraid of molesting his two-year-old son. Despite his fear, he would intentionally replay an imagined molesting of his son in his head over and over to ensure he was not sexually aroused by the imagery. One could misinterpret this to mean that he enjoyed the thoughts and wanted this scenario to become real. However, he hated the thoughts, and they made him suicidal, even though he intentionally, compulsively replayed them in his mind. This case illustrates the importance of function of a behavior. The patient was playing out the images to make sure he was not aroused rather than to get aroused and engage in behavioral acts of pleasure. See Bruce, Ching, and Williams (2018) for more on differential diagnosis between pedophilic-themed OCD and pedophilic disorder.

Issues in Diagnosing Pedophilic OCD

People with pedophilic OCD are typically the least likely to harm a child. That being said, we wish we could say definitively that no person with pedophilic OCD would ever do anything inappropriate involving children. Although we have never ever seen harm come to a child due to pedophilic OCD, it is possible that someone with this form of OCD could do something inappropriate as a form of checking behavior. For example, we have heard of cases where someone with a worry about being sexually aroused by children touched a child—in an innocuous, nonsexual manner—to see whether this would produce sexual feelings to confirm or rule out his fears. We interviewed one middle-aged client who had been primarily asexual until one day at a social event she bumped into a teenager and felt a spark of sexual energy. Perplexed and fascinated by this, she bumped into the young person again. Suddenly, she realized this was inappropriate behavior and felt profoundly guilty and culpable. She was tormented by this experience for years and, at times, worried that she was a pedophile because of it. She wondered if she should turn herself into the police but also feared that doing so would cause distress to her unsuspecting "victim" and the family. The fears only grew over time, and after 10 years of carrying this obsessional burden, she attempted suicide.

Another more extreme example of inappropriate checking involves a legal case where we were consulted to determine the reasons behind a client's disturbing, compulsive use of child pornography. The client had OCD, which was complicated by comorbid PTSD from childhood sexual abuse. Beginning at the age of six, he was sexually molested by an older female cousin. The abuse included being coerced into kissing and fondling the cousin, which occurred off and on for six years. The cousin was eventually diagnosed with bipolar disorder and the abuse ended, but the client continued to be tormented by distressing memories and flashbacks of it into adulthood. He felt constant shame and mixed emotions, because although he was traumatized, an intense connection with her had also formed, which led to years of confusion and guilt. The client later came to believe that his cousin had also been sexually abused and that abuse had caused her victimizing behaviors toward him, which, in turn, led to a bond around their shared trauma.

At about the age of 14, the client began experiencing strong OCD symptoms. His obsessions first involved sexual orientation-themed intrusive thoughts, where he wondered whether or not he was gay. Over time, these intrusive thoughts evolved into worries about sexual activities with children. He became afraid that he might want to engage in sexual activities with a child since he was coerced into these acts in the past and was having upsetting flashbacks about them. He worried that he had been damaged as a result of his abuse and that this would lead him to becoming a pedophile. He turned to compulsive eating and marijuana to cope with the distress. He continued to experience these intrusive and distressing thoughts into college, as well as symptoms of depression. In his early 20s, he began looking at sexualized pictures of children on the Internet as a means to reassure himself that he was not actually attracted them. Over time, the material became more and more graphic. He would often seek out content that was the "most terrifying" to see whether he could stand it. He would attempt to masturbate to these pictures and videos to test himself and felt relieved if he could not do it. He also began to experience severe suicidal ideation and bought a gun to kill himself. In moments of intense despair, he loaded this gun and held it to his head, thinking this could be one way out of the daily agony he felt and the horrifying fear that he might be a pedophile. Finally, he began looking for a therapist. However, he worried that if he shared his illicit compulsive behaviors with a clinician, he would be told he was a pedophile. If that happened, he had decided he would definitely kill himself. So even though he started working with a therapist on his childhood trauma, he kept the child pornography use a secret.

By that time, the client had amassed a large collection of child pornography, and shortly after starting therapy he was discovered by authorities, arrested, and charged. He knew it was wrong and illegal to download child pornography and felt a great deal of shame and remorse for his actions. In terms of the charges, he said, "It makes me sad for these kids. I have the capacity to empathize with their situation, since it happened to me, and I should have made that connection. I wish I had disclosed my own molestation when I was younger." Although prosecutors in the case insisted the client was a danger to children and in the process of evolving into a bona fide sex offender, a comprehensive psychological evaluation and polygraph test confirmed that the client had no actual sexual attraction to children. Again, in this case, the function of the behavior was important to separate a potential pedophile from someone with P-OCD.

This might be a good opportunity to point out that there is a potential connection between OCD and PTSD, as PTSD can be a trigger for OCD. Almost one in five people with OCD have comorbid PTSD, with 60% getting OCD at the same time or before their traumas (Ruscio et al., 2010). As noted before, people with both OCD and PTSD are much more likely to have sexual and/or religious obsessions and increased suicidality, as well as increased depression and anxiety (Fontenelle et al., 2012), as was true in the case of the previously described client who was arrested for child pornography. The untreated trauma combined with the OCD symptoms had an intensifying effect for him, leading to criminal behaviors that would likely not have occurred if the client had suffered from either of these two disorders alone.

OCD versus Sexual Identity Confusion

Assessing SO-OCD using clinical measures can be difficult, as few screening instruments for OCD specifically address sexual orientation obsessions. However, these measures are still of value because it is very likely the patient will have obsessive-compulsive symptoms in other areas as well. Measures such as the OCI-R, YBOCS, and DOCS can be important tools to assist in gaining a comprehensive picture of OCD symptoms, although the original YBOCS checklist only has one question about sexual orientation fears, and the OCI-R has no questions about S-OCD at all. However, people with sexual orientation concerns tend to score high on the OCI-R Obsessing subscale. The YBOCS-II has three questions that ask about sexual obsessions, and one is specific to sexual orientation concerns (i.e., "Excessive concerns about sexual orientation or gender identity") with a prompt that reads: "Examples: person repeatedly wonders if s/he is gay even though there is every reason to believes s/he is heterosexual. *Distinguish from realistic issues around sexual or gender identity." Although the YBOCS-II says to make this important distinction, there are not instructions on exactly how to do this, which could be challenging for therapists without experience working with S-OCD. The DOCS Sexually Intrusive Thoughts Scale (DOCS-SI; Wetterneck et al., 2015), described previously, may better help to capture those with SO-OCD. We also recommend using the SORT, the SO-OCD scale we have developed for this exact sort of client.

Assessing SO-OCD in a clinical interview is how the disorder will first come to the attention of most clinicians. Many who seek treatment for this type of OCD are unaware that they are actually suffering from a form of OCD. They generally fear becoming LGBTQ and may want confirmation from a clinician that they are heterosexual. They may initially explain that they are not LGBTQ and have always been attracted to the opposite sex before revealing their sexual orientation worries. They may continually ask the clinician for reassurance and feel the need to provide excessive information.

As with other forms of S-OCD, the client may have sought other opinions, so it is important to inquire about who else may have been consulted about this problem. In some cases, the patient may not have shared their concerns with anyone due to shame or catastrophic fears that may be out of proportion with reality (e.g., "If anyone knew I had these thoughts, my life would be over and I would lose my job, friends, and family"). In other cases, the patient may have sought out opinions from numerous clinicians as a reassurance compulsion.

Typically, the distress experienced by the individual is not related to any actual same-sex experiences that have occurred but rather is attached to the worry that the patient will lose access to the opposite sex, something that they highly value. The person fears that the sex life they enjoyed (or may someday enjoy) will be suddenly taken and replaced with something unappealing and foreign (Williams, 2008). However, the person may have had some same-sex experiences as a child (either normal sex play or sexual abuse) but then placed too much importance on those experiences as possible evidence for their current confusion and worries.

Differential diagnosis is important, as mental health professionals who do not treat many people with OCD may fail to properly diagnose a patient complaining of unwanted sexual obsessions. Therapists may attribute the symptoms to an unconscious wish, emerging LGBTQ identity, or difficulties with sexual identity formation. This conceptualization of the problem may cause panic in an already distressed individual, resulting in the client becoming even more upset and confused. The key issue to understand is that the thoughts are ego-dystonic or ego-alien, meaning that the obsessions are mostly or completely inconsistent with the individual's fundamental desires, fantasies, and sexual history.

Sexual orientation-themed OCD is not the same as ambivalence about one's sexual orientation. LBGTQ individuals who have negative feelings about their own sexuality may be diagnosed with internalized homophobia/heterosexism, and these worries may overlap with SO-OCD. People in both groups may fear that same-sex attraction represents an end to lifelong dreams of a more socially desirable lifestyle, a traditional wedding, or raising a family; and in fact, these are concerns that many LGBTQ individuals work to process as they accept their orientation. People in both groups may suffer from anxiety, depression, and low self-esteem, and both may share concerns about being accepted by others. Nevertheless, a person with internalized homophobia usually has some positive feelings about their orientation and will enjoy same-sex fantasies, whereas the person with SO-OCD dreads the thoughts and finds them intrusive. People with SO-OCD generally see no consistency with same-sex romance and their actual sexual desires, though they may have no problems with others who are LGBTQ. It should not be assumed that people with SO-OCD are homophobic, as these individuals have a wide range of feelings about homosexuality.

To complicate matters, it is possible for LGBTQ individuals to have unwanted OCD-related sexual orientation obsessions as well. For example, a gay male may obsess about how a heterosexual relationship may affect his gay identity, and he might worry about being rejected by his peers if he was attracted to a woman. Another example is a married woman with bisexual tendencies who may fear that she will lose interest in her husband in favor of another woman, because she finds women attractive as well as men. These types of worries may occur for reasons unrelated to OCD, but what will distinguish these from reasonable concerns is an unwarranted focus on the *possibility* of these events happening, when the person's actual circumstances do not make them particularly likely to occur.

Issues Diagnosing S-OCD: Transgender Example

We have been approached by many people who would like an expert to determine whether they have OCD or are actually LGBTQ. In almost all cases, the person has been found to have OCD. Conversely, we have also been approached by a number of parents who have brought their child (teen or adult) into the clinic to make the same determination, and, in nearly all cases, the child has been LGBTQ. It seems the parents in these situations were struggling with the idea of their child being something other than straight and hoped that it was OCD instead.

One example of this involved a Palestinian American man in his mid-20s, who we'll call Adeeb, who was treated by one of our student therapists. His parents believed he was suffering from S-OCD and encouraged him to see us for an evaluation and treatment. After his first appointment, the parents made a separate appointment with the therapist where they asked her whether she had any "good news" to share with them, hoping for an OCD diagnosis. In interview, the client expressed a great deal of distress associated with presenting as a male. He even shared with the therapist a period of relief from these symptoms when he presented as female for a year, several years ago. Adeeb periodically experienced suicidal ideation, with a previous attempt after admitting his transgender feelings to his Muslim parents. His immediate suicidal ideation surrounded the fear of not being able to transition and subsequently losing the support of his family, with whom he was very close. This constellation of symptoms is contrary to what would be expected if this was a manifestation of OCD, as Adeeb's distress was a result of being closeted and not due to unwanted, intrusive thoughts. Thus, the client was diagnosed with gender dysphoria and not OCD.

Due to the complexity of this client's case, an integrative approach to therapy was used to target various areas of difficulty. Treatment began by establishing rapport and a safe space for discussing these sensitive topics. While the client expressed shame about being "too afraid to transition" due to family pressure, this was reframed as the client caring very much for the family and putting his life on hold for their sake. A need to create a balance as far as meeting the family's needs, while also meeting the client's needs to reduce distress was also discussed.

Upon establishing a trusting, warm therapeutic relationship, treatment moved into clarification of values and other acceptance and commitment therapy (ACT) principles. Through this, two of the client's identities were most prominent: "I am a woman, and I am a healer." Value-driven behaviors were chosen for each of these, including attending nursing school and beginning the process of transitioning by taking hormones. Suicidal ideation was managed and reduced through the use of a safety plan and attendance of a transgender support group to aid in feelings of common humanity.

CBT was then used to further reduce distress and suicidal ideation associated with thoughts that his parents hate him and will never accept him. Treatment also included normalizing the desire to hasten the transition process, while encouraging patience, and processing mood fluctuations associated with taking hormones.

Adeeb now prefers to be called Aziza. She is currently out to her family, professors, and several friends. She is one semester into nursing school and plans to hold off on larger, medically based procedures until she leaves her parents' home to reduce conflict and to respect their level of comfort, while balancing this with her own needs. Providing support, a knowledgeable therapist, and a safe space to discuss these issues was very important to her treatment.

Issues Diagnosing in S-OCD: Woman Claims to be a Pedophile

One particularly challenging conundrum involved a 20-something female client from rural Kentucky—we'll call her Claire—plagued by fears about sexual abusing children (Williams, 2016). The client was Amish, and so even coming all the way to our clinic in Louisville was a major hurdle because the family had to hire a driver to take them two hours each way. Claire would arrive at each session with her older sister, who had helped look after her over the years. The two were close, and the client wanted her sister to be involved as much as possible. Her sister was very kind and sincere and was only too willing to do whatever she could help Claire get better. She gave us a small book about Amish culture to help us better understand their ways.

Claire was suffering from a severe form of OCD that involved worries about causing harm to children. It is fairly well known that people with OCD often fear harming others accidently—for example, by leaving a stove turned on, thereby causing the home to catch fire. To prevent this feared outcome, a person with OCD would then engage in repeated checking of the stove. It is less well known that people with OCD also worry about causing harm on purpose, for example, by impulsively pushing someone onto subway tracks or stabbing them with a steak knife at dinner. OCD sufferers with these sorts of worries are generally very gentle people, mortified at the idea of violence against anyone, which is one reason these unwanted thoughts are so upsetting to them. In this case, the client worried excessively about harming children by touching them inappropriately, and thus she had become convinced that she was a danger to her community.

We spent some time getting a complete mental health history, and after only a few sessions, the client disclosed to me (MTW) that she had, in fact, sexually abused an identifiable small boy in the family general store. She gave a graphic description of event and seemed dead serious about her story. Of course, this was rather alarming. People with OCD generally have some insight into their worries and are able to admit their fears are exaggerated or even ridiculous. It is, however, possible for people with OCD to completely believe their fears will come true. But this was different. I had not encountered someone with OCD who believed that their feared outcome had already come true—especially something this horrible and with such certainty.

Claire's sister relayed to me that she had made many such statements in the past, and each time the situations were investigated and found to be untrue. She believed that Claire made these stories up to get attention. Correspondingly, there was no evidence that Claire had done any such thing this time either, yet she maintained her insistence that she had. Although I was fairly sure she had not abused any children, our field's ethical principles require disclosure of information learned in therapeutic sessions to protect others from harm, and state law requires a report if there is even a suspicion that a child has been abused. I did not yet know what was causing Claire to say these things and could not be 100% certain it was simply her OCD. On the other hand, I worried that if I made a report, it would harm our therapeutic relationship, and she would not continue treatment. Amish are a very communal and tight-knit group, and so it was quite likely that the client could only work with me with the permission of the community leadership. So, I further worried that a bogus Child Protective Services (CPS) investigation would erode whatever trust the community had placed in me as a psychologist to help this client, which might also have negative implications for future Amish from that community in need of outside mental health services.

I agonized over what to do about this. After careful consideration and consultation, I sat down with Claire and her sister together and explained the laws concerning my requirement to make a report. I asked her again if she was sure she had sexually abused a child, because, if so, I would have to call CPS and give them her name, address, and other pertinent details. I hoped and believed that she would tell me she was not completely sure about all this, which would be indicative of OCD and not something I would feel the need to report. Her sister was hoping she would just admit to having made it all up. Claire seemed confused that we didn't believe her and said, of course, she had done this act. I then left the client alone with her sister to discuss the matter between them, and I heard them having a loud argument in their native Amish language. Sadly, Claire would not relent, so I made the call to CPS. I explained to the social worker that my client was mentally ill, had made statements like this before, and that we did not think her admission was true. I said that Claire was likely suffering from psychosis in addition to OCD. I also informed Claire's psychiatrist of this, who subsequently added an atypical antipsychotic to her drug regimen.

However, as predicted, the trust was eroded, and the client did not return for treatment. I did hear later that she saw another therapist and that the medication change helped her a great deal. Yet I am still not sure if I made the right decision. In situations like this it's too easy to worry about professional liability and possible consequences of not making a report. At the time, it seemed like that was the legal obligation, but, in hindsight, I wish I had put more trust in my clinical judgment to effectively have helped Claire. I sometimes think about her and wonder if she ever got the help she so desperately needed. I also wonder about others suffering from psychotic OCD and imagine the hurdles they must face in getting the right kind of care.

Issues Diagnosing in S-OCD: Fears about Bestiality

One interesting variation of S-OCD surrounds fears of being sexually attracted to animals, which may be misdiagnosed as a paraphilia. One of our clinical students treated a 36-year-old Hispanic woman we'll call Malita. She had obtained her bachelor's degree in biology from a local state university and previously worked for the environmental services department of a local municipal agency. Malita was fired about six months prior to starting treatment, which was a result of being unable to perform her professional duties, primarily due to her inability to concentrate and anxiety about her performance. Malita lived at home with her parents and obtained a part-time job at a department store shortly after staring treatment but was let go from that job as well due to constant demands for reassurance about her work performance.

Malita grew up in a Catholic family but now simply describes herself as "spiritual." Her OCD symptoms started in her early 20s, and she believed that the OCD symptoms were a result of having watched pornography. She had suffered from obsessions in the past surrounding religion and scrupulosity (e.g., pleasing God, being moral/right), as well as occasional worries about contamination (e.g., fears of touching raw meat or eggs). Malita was now having even more worrisome thoughts that included molesting animals and children. This included upsetting sexual images about animals, children, and loved ones. She was concerned that she had engaged in sexual activity with her dog, who passed away about two years ago, and was now concerned that she would become aroused by her current dog and act on this by engaging in sexual activity with it. As a result of her obsessions, Malita mentally reviewed past interactions with her dogs in efforts to assure herself that she did not commit any acts of bestiality. When around her dog, she was also hyperaware of sensations in her vaginal area, such as muscle movement or possible arousal, to make sure she was not likely to molest the dog. Because the client was disgusted by the notion of bestiality and did not enjoy these thoughts, she was diagnosed with OCD rather than a paraphilia.

Prior to seeking treatment, Malita was in long-distance therapy for OCD treatment for approximately six years. She described therapy as "somewhat helpful" for understanding her personal views on religion, but she did not engage in Ex/RP or receive homework, rather her sessions were primarily discussing her worries with her therapist. This therapy felt supportive but was ineffective. Malita did not experience relief from obsessions and compulsions, which lead to seeking alternative OCD treatment. She subsequently engaged in Ex/RP treatment with our clinician and also joined our support group for S-OCD, which she found very helpful.

What Therapists Need to Know about Medications for OCD

Drugs, Therapy, or Both?

Conventional wisdom and older best practice guidelines advanced a combination of medication and CBT as the best approach for OCD. Since both have been shown to have some efficacy in reducing symptoms, it was assumed that combining them would result in an additive effect. However, Foa and colleagues (2005) executed a carefully designed set of studies to determine whether this was, in fact, the case. In the first study, researchers compared three groups—one receiving Ex/RP only, one receiving the serotonin reuptake inhibitor (SRI) medication clomipramine only, and one receiving both. The results showed that all active treatments were superior to a placebo, but the effect of Ex/RP plus clomipramine was no better than Ex/RP alone, and both were superior to clomipramine alone. In other words, medication was helpful, but Ex/RP was better, and including medication along with Ex/RP didn't improve the outcome.

Because most clients coming for treatment are already on an SRI medication, a follow-up study by the same group was conducted to determine whether there was anything about the Ex/RP that was unique to helping people with OCD, or if any type of CBT would be effective when combined with medication. So researchers compared the effects of augmenting an SRI with Ex/RP or stress management training, another form of CBT (Simpson et al., 2008). All subjects were already on an SRI but had received only partial benefit from it and were then randomized to either Ex/RP or stress management training. People in the stress management group learned deep breathing, progressive muscle relaxation, positive imagery, assertiveness training, and problem-solving to combat their OCD. After 17 sessions of treatment, those receiving the stress management training did not improve by much. People getting Ex/RP, however, improved by quite a lot, and their gains were maintained six months posttreatment.

An additional placebo-controlled study was conducted by Simpson and colleagues (2013), where either Ex/RP or risperidone (Risperdal) was added on for patients already using an SRI, but who had experienced only partial benefit from their medication. In this study, participants getting Ex/RP showed major improvements, but the addition of risperidone was no better than placebo.

For children with OCD, there do seem to be some additive benefits of selective serotonin reuptake inhibitors (SSRIs) plus Ex/RP. However, it is not clear what the long-term consequences of medication will be on these children. It might make sense to give a child an SSRI if therapy is not effective or not effective enough. However, we see a number of children with OCD put on an atypical antipsychotic for their OCD, and they are usually overweight and experiencing no obvious benefit from the medication.

We take the sum of these and other studies to indicate that Ex/RP should be tried first, and medication added if clients are having difficulty progressing in their Ex/RP. It used to be thought that very severe OCD required a combination of medication and therapy for best results, but this is not borne out by research. It is routine practice for many OCD specialty centers to attempt to put all patients on medications, whether they want them or not. We never suggest that clients try an SRI first, regardless of the initial severity of the OCD; many with the most severe OCD do just fine with Ex/RP alone.

That being said, there are some cases where we might consider medication at the onset, including for clients with complete lack of insight, psychotic symptoms, and with severe depression that is not responding to behavioral interventions.

"Why Did My Medication Stop Working?"

Many of the clients we see will tell us that they tried medication for their OCD, which helped a great deal for a period of time, but slowly the OCD somehow crept back in and the medication is no longer working. At this point, they may have tried several different medications, all with disappointing results. We explain to clients that OCD is progressive disorder that tends to get worse over time unless treated with an effective CBT approach. We refer back to the OCD cycle diagram and note that even though the medication helped, it did not help so much that the client stopped all compulsions. The compulsions are what feed and worsen the disorder, and so the medicine didn't actually stop working, rather the OCD just got worse. Hence, the need to now learn a new approach to the disorder (i.e., Ex/RP).

Serotonin Reuptake Inhibitors for OCD

First-line drug treatments for OCD include four SSRIs and the tricyclic antidepressant clomipramine, which, as noted previously, is an SRI (SSRIs are subsumed under the category of SRIs). The SSRIs that are US Food and Drug Administration (FDA) approved for OCD are fluvoxamine (Luvox), fluoxetine (Prozac), sertraline (Zoloft), and paroxetine (Paxil). Other drugs often used for the treatment of OCD include citalopram (Celexa), escitalopram (Lexapro), and vilazodone (Viibryd). Choice of SSRI for any given patient may be guided by patient or provider preference. Although not all SSRIs have been approved by the FDA, they all appear to be more or less equally effective in treating OCD (Koran & Simpson, 2013). However, these medications are not always prescribed properly. In a review of physician-reported data from 1997 to 1999, there were departures from empirically based practices for OCD, which included widespread underdosing, lack of adequate dose titration, and poor management of side effects (Blanco et al., 2006).

OCD is actually somewhat resistant to first-line SSRI interventions, with estimates of approximately 25% to 60% who were initially treated with an SSRI having an inadequate response (Van Ameringen et al., 2014). Relapse is likely within the first year of treatment; therefore, it is generally recommended that patients continue with medication for at least 12 months (Kellner, 2010). A trial of at least two, or occasionally three, SSRIs before changing to a different class of medication should be considered. Medication treatment is usually recommended permanently since relapse eventually occurs in 80% to 90% of patients when they stop medications (Bystritsky, 2004). Some patients are fine taking medication indefinitely, but most of the ones we see hope that they can be free of medications at some point in the future, so many resist the idea of being medicated.

It is also important to know that SSRIs include a "black box" warning for children and young adults up to age 25. A black box warning is the strictest warning put on the labeling of a prescription drugs by the FDA when there is reasonable evidence of a connection between a serious hazard and the drug in question. The reason for this warning is because a pooled analysis of many antidepressant studies found an increased risk of suicide in young people starting SSRI treatment, and so extra monitoring of symptoms is recommended in the first few months. Currently, there is no evidence for an increased risk of suicide in adult patients being treated with SSRIs over the age of 25. However, the FDA suggests that all patients treated with antidepressants for any reason should be carefully monitored and observed closely for worsening of symptoms, suicidality, and unusual changes in behavior, especially during the initial months of a course of drug therapy or when the dose changes.

As OCD clients tend to be risk-aversive, the black box warning may be rather terrifying. So it's worth taking some time to discuss the risk versus benefits of SSRIs with clients. Additionally, parents of young people with

OCD may be particularly alarmed at the thought of a drug causing their child to commit suicide. Although there is this small risk of suicide, we think that for patients who are severely depressed or those for whom CBT is not working well enough or quickly enough, medication should be considered. The risk of suicide from depression is much higher than the risk of suicide from an SSRI.

Though most people who try SRIs for OCD will be "treatment responders," research has shown that actual symptom reduction tends to be modest at best. Having a response to medication is not a complete cure, merely an indication that the treatment has reduced OCD symptoms by some measurable degree. Although there are reports of dramatic improvements from SRIs alone, on average, people with OCD will experience only about a 30% reduction in symptoms when on the maximally tolerated dose. Thus, many patients will be unsatisfied with the result. At this point, the psychiatrist will typically suggest trying a different SRI. Considering the long period SRIs may take to be effective, often four to eight weeks, the waiting and switching process can be frustrating to patients, and partial responders to one SRI are vulnerable to similar problems with other SRIs. For this reason, it is increasingly common to augment SRI medication with either CBT for OCD or another type of medication rather than continuing to switch from one SRI to another.

Sexual Side Effects in Sexual OCD

Other problems with SRIs include sexual side effects, which are a common reason for noncompliance or early discontinuation. SSRIs prevent or delay orgasm in 35% of patients, decrease libido in 20%, and cause problems with erectile function in 10% of men; the SRI clomipramine causes anorgasmia in 90% of patients (Segraves, 2007). Such difficulties may be more common in patients with OCD as they require larger doses of SSRIs than the depressed patients on which these problems have been generally studied. Sometimes sexual dysfunction will diminish on its own, but other direct means of addressing these side effects are often necessary.

People with S-OCD may become particularly alarmed by sexual performance difficulties and take these problems as evidence of their obsessional fears coming true (e.g., changing sexual orientation). Early psychoeducation about this specific side effect is especially important for this population. To combat sexual side effects, the addition of a drug that specifically targets sexual dysfunction—such as sildenafil (Viagra), vardenafil (Levitra), and tadalafil (Cialis)—can counter some of the sexual side effects of antidepressants in men and are generally considered safe (Schweitzer, Maguire, Ng, & 2009). To facilitate compliance with medications, clinicians should discuss of the possibility of sexual dysfunction with patients in advance. Since many physicians are not very good at these type of discussions, you may need to take the initiative to educate your clients about this yourself.

Other Medications Issues

As mentioned previously, people with OCD may also have been prescribed medications other than SRIs for OCD or other conditions. We are going to briefly review a few things therapists should know with respect to their clients for several classes of medications. We also want to underscore that clients should be warned not to stop any medications "cold turkey," as most of these medications should be gradually tapered down, and to consult with their prescriber before making any of the following recommended changes.

Benzodiazepines
Benzodiazepines are popular because of their speedy effectiveness in reducing immediate sensations of anxiety. These include drugs like alprazolam (Xanax), diazepam (Valium), clonazepam (Klonopin), and lorazepam (Ativan). However, these drugs can quickly become addicting and may require increasing doses over time. Although limited research on benzodiazepines suggests they can help to reduce anxiety from OCD symptoms, our assessment of the literature finds there is little evidence to support a recommendation for regular use of any benzodiazepine for OCD.

Furthermore, benzodiazepines have been shown to interfere with the effectiveness of CBT, which is why we require our clients to discontinue these drugs before starting CBT for OCD, whenever possible (Ahmed, Westra, & Stewart, 2008). Benzodiazepines are thought to interfere with CBT for two reasons: (a) When clients pop a pill every time they feel anxious, they don't learn that the anxiety will go away on its own, so the drug itself functions like a compulsion, and (b) benzodiazepines result in short-term memory loss for about four hours after taking them, which interferes with the learning process required for successful CBT. So, if clients are carrying around benzodiazepines and taking them "as needed" (i.e., p.r.n.), this is can result in CBT treatment failure. When clients absolutely must take these drugs, we require they be taken at the same time each day to break the reinforcement cycle and before bed so that the memory problems will have mostly worn off by the next morning.

Mood Stabilizers

People with OCD are more likely than the general public to have mood disorders, including bipolar disorder. If the client has a comorbid bipolar disorder, SSRIs may result in activation of manic symptoms (Greenberg et al., 2014). Therefore, in such cases, a mood stabilizer may be a better choice than an SSRI. Lithium was one thought to be helpful when used to augment SRIs, but the research on this is equivocal.

Antipsychotics

Adding atypical neuroleptics, or antipsychotics, was once considered the better method of approaching a poor response to SRI treatment. One of the first neuroleptics studied as an augmenter was haloperidol, but it was effective only for people with both OCD and a tic disorder. Small doses of newer, safer medications have since been added, namely second-generation "atypical" neuroleptics. These include risperidone (Risperdal), olanzapine (Zyprexa), and quetiapine (Seroquel). These medications are FDA approved for use in treating other disorders but are currently used off-label in the treatment of OCD. Research of olanzapine and quetiapine showed some positive results when compared to placebo, but risperidone had at one point demonstrated the most consistent performance based on three studies. Despite initial enthusiasm, recent research suggests poorer treatment response than previously reported. As mentioned previously, a very well-conducted randomized controlled trial found risperidone no better than placebo as an augmentation strategy (Simpson et al., 2013). Furthermore, these drugs lead to weight gain, excessive sedation, and some potentially serious problems such as cardiovascular issues. Therefore, we do not recommend any neuroleptic for OCD at this time (Williams, Davis, Powers, & Weissflog, 2014), although such drugs may be useful for comorbid depression or delusional thinking.

Hormonal Contraceptives

The effects of hormones in the body are complex and can vary among women, resulting in changes in both mood and sex drive. Hormonal contraceptives are made of synthetic female hormones and include oral contraceptives, as well as the patch, ring, and injectables. Male sex hormones, called androgens, affect both libido and feelings of well-being. Although women have less testosterone than men, the hormone is still important to normal sexual functioning, contributing to sex drive and sexual pleasure. Hormonal contraceptives lower free testosterone in the body, decreasing the frequency of sexual thoughts and sexual arousal (Graham et al., 2007). Additionally, it is not clear how long it takes for the hormone balance to return to normal after stopping hormonal contraceptive as many women continue to have lowered testosterone months or years after discontinuation (Panzer et al., 2006). Thus, such clients may find themselves no longer interested in sex and unable to become aroused by sexual thoughts or images. This could be a source of obsessional distress among women with OCD, especially since most doctors prescribing hormonal contraceptives don't think to warn women about this side effect; therefore, couples may not connect sexual problems to the drugs. These type of difficulties can exacerbate S-OCD concerns.

Communicating with Other Mental Healthcare Providers

Physicians and Other Prescribers

It is very important to collect a full medication history on your OCD clients, including exactly what they are currently taking and who is prescribing it. It is not uncommon for people with OCD to be getting their medications from a general practitioner or gynecologist, but the best resource for their medication management is a psychiatrist. Thus, we usually insist that clients who are on medication utilize a psychiatrist or doctoral-level nurse practitioner instead, especially if they require more than one psychiatric medication or if it appears that any change to their medication is warranted. Additionally, we find that many general practitioners are unaware that OCD often requires a higher dose of most SSRIs, and it can make for an awkward professional relationship when therapists have to tell physicians how to do their job. Therefore, it is best that clients see a doctor who is specially trained to prescribe for mental health issues, which is generally a psychiatrist or a qualified psychiatric nurse practitioner.

Because of limited accessibility to psychiatrists in many areas, clients may have no choice but to utilize a general practitioner. In such cases, it may be incumbent on you to advise the doctor of your client's medication needs. Don't be intimidated or afraid. In many cases, doctors recognize their limitations and appreciate the input. One resource that may be helpful includes an instructional article about medications for OCD that we wrote with some colleagues that you or your client can share with the doctor that covers many of the issues discussed here (see Williams, Davis, et al., 2014).

Open communication with the client's prescriber is particularly important when there are problems with medication (e.g., dosing, compliance, side effects) and when clients may pose a danger to themselves or others (e.g., suicidality, aggression). Fortunately, OCD clients are generally risk-aversive and therefore unlikely to harm themselves or others. Nonetheless, we will generally notify a client's psychiatrist if there is a worsening of depression or any suicidal ideation.

In our experience, most psychiatrists seem to be aware of S-OCD but not all are by any means. When mental health professionals do not understand S-OCD symptoms, they may give bad advice to their patients. One example is a male client who had been seeing a psychiatrist for sexual orientation worries in OCD. The doctor kept telling the client that he needed to explore his sexuality and should start going to gay bars to meet other guys. The client nervously took his doctor's advice and started to frequent a local gay bar once a week. He would look for other guys that he could possibly be attracted to but was continually perplexed by the fact that he found none of the male patrons appealing—despite the fact than many of the guys in the bar were interested in him. One day, he decided to get drunk to see whether that would enable him to be attracted to a man. One of the bar's patrons took advantage of the client's intoxicated state and lured him to his car, where he sexually victimized him. The client subsequently became even more distressed. He was not only traumatized from the sexual encounter but also confused about the meaning of the event for his sexuality. He remained unattracted to men—arguably less so since the traumatic encounter—but still struggled with sexual orientation worries. He soon spiraled into a deep depression.

In addition to our anecdotal experiences, at least one research study attempted to quantify how often certain symptoms dimensions of OCD would be misdiagnosed by primary care physicians. Overall, OCD was misidentified by doctors over half of the time (50.5%), with misdiagnosing occurring more frequently in the only two types of sexual obsessions examined in the study, sexual orientation obsessions (84.6%) and pedophile obsessions (P-OCD; 70.8%; Glazier, Swing, & McGinn, 2015).

Therapists

As previously noted, most therapists are not trained to treat OCD with empirically supported methods, and this is even more true for S-OCD. Therefore, when therapists realize that they are confronted with a client who needs help for S-OCD, the best response is to treat the client under the supervision of someone who is qualified or to refer the client to someone with the proper expertise to help that person. When the latter happens, it is important to take proactive steps to manage that professional relationship.

If the client has a good relationship with their therapist and is benefiting from therapy, treatment for OCD can occur simultaneously with other therapy or the client can take a temporary break from that therapy to fully engage in the OCD treatment. Generally, if the main problem is OCD and there are no other comorbid conditions that require immediate attention, we will encourage the client to take a break from their other therapist. There are several reasons for this. The OCD treatment is demanding and time-consuming, generally requiring a minimum of two visits per week, at least in the initial stages. It can be hard for busy clients to have enough time to make three therapy appointments in a single week, on top of the daily homework that will be required of the Ex/RP. Additionally, we find when therapists are referring clients to us it is often because their efforts at addressing the OCD were unsuccessful and, in fact, may even be counterproductive. For example, we have seen many clients whose therapists were making the OCD worse by reassuring clients that they are not pedophiles or who were utilizing outdated methods such as thought-stopping with a wrist rubber band. We don't want the client to be confused about what they should actually be doing to get well.

If the client has other conditions that merit ongoing work with the other therapist, such as a serious eating disorder, suicidality, or borderline personality, we will encourage the client to continue with the other therapist during the OCD treatment. In such cases, it is imperative to have an open line of communication with the other therapist. It can be tricky to tell other mental health professionals that they are doing the wrong thing with their client, so we generally advise them to continue working with the client on the other issues but to leave all OCD work to us. As treatment comes to an end, we might reach out to the therapist again to let him or her know what techniques were helpful for the client and encourage the therapist to remind the client to use the techniques they learned from us if they are struggling, or to come back for a few booster sessions if needed. We also make sure to inform the other therapist right away if we note a worsening of the client's clinical condition in any area.

Even though therapists are trained to be aware of biases and are expected to be skilled in the nuances of diagnosing, there is some research to indicate that stigma and misdiagnosis does occur. While stigma among the general population can discourage help-seeking, stigma among clinicians has the potential to be even more damaging. Despite the expectation that clinicians are trained to be free of bias, studies show they may hold a negative view of individuals suffering from mental illness mirroring that of the general public (Lauber et al., 2006; Kassam et al., 2010). For OCD specifically, we conducted a study primarily of therapists with less experience or those in training and found that there was a significant stigma by these treatment professionals when presented with a vignette about someone with sexual obsessions compared to other types of obsessions (Steinberg & Wetterneck, 2016).

There can be similar issues with misdiagnosing S-OCD in therapists. Glazier, Calixte, Rothschild, and Pinto (2013) conducted a vignette study and found that 38.9% of psychologists misdiagnosed the disorder; the failure rate increased dramatically when presented with more highly stigmatized obsessional content such as obsessions about homosexuality (77%) and sexual obsessions about children (43%). In contrast to this, it was reported that only 16% of the clinicians sampled ($n = 360$) misdiagnosed contamination obsessions.

Social Workers/CPS

Many social workers are proficient therapists that help people work through emotional difficulties, develop coping strategies, and adapt to challenging environments. Social workers also utilize their skills to help adapt the environment to the client. They may, for example, call employers of people who have special needs, act as case workers or case managers, or make community reentry plans for patients who have been hospitalized. Many social workers intervene in cases of family dysfunction, when there is evidence of harm occurring to children or other vulnerable persons. Social workers are typically prominent in agencies such as hospitals and CPS. As a result, social workers may be especially attuned to the possibility that a client's symptoms may pose a threat to others.

This emphasis on protecting others can create real problems for people with OCD that includes themes of sexual harm. Parents with P-OCD may fear that their children will be taken from them by CPS if they disclose their anxieties. In fact, we have seen this occur simply because a hospital social worker did not understand the difference between pedophilic fears in OCD and pedophilic disorder. One of our clients who ended up in the emergency room due to suicidal distress over his pedophilic fears reported that the hospital social worker said to him, "If you feel so worried and guilty about this, then you must have done *something*," implying that the client actually had harmed a child. Another parent in the same situation was barred from being around his three-year-old daughter unless supervised because a hospital social worker determined he was a danger due to his OCD.

Such statements and actions are truly harmful to clients and their families, as they introduce doubt about the intentions of the client and add stress to an already stressed family system. Furthermore, prolonged contact with the client's children is critical to facilitate recovery from the OCD. So, in such situations, we have not hesitated to intervene to provide corrective information surrounding the "danger" posed by such clients. A sample letter to children's aid services appears in Box 2.1.

Traditional Healers

Many people may turn to traditional healers to help address their S-OCD, and usually this includes a spiritual or religious component to helpgiving. Religion does not cause OCD, and so therapists should be particularly careful not to project a demeanor that blames a client's religion for symptoms. If the therapist believes that religion is somehow causing OCD, the therapist may try to control or suppress the person's beliefs to facilitate treatment. This is sure to undermine trust and empathy, leading to conflict

Box 2.1 Sample Letter to Children's Aid Services

To Whom It May Concern,

This letter is in reference to a request made by Children's Aid due to claims made by John Smith on September 4, 2014. We are aware that on September 4, 2014, Mr. Smith presented at Royal Victoria Hospital with details concerning inappropriate sexual thoughts involving his daughter. Due to the gravity of his statements, he was ordered to maintain a certain distance from his daughter. As you may be aware, Mr. Smith entered an intensive treatment program for those suffering from obsessive compulsive disorder (OCD). He received services at The Louisville OCD Clinic from October 20, 2014 through October 31, 2014. While in our care, Mr. Smith received the Mini International Neuropsychiatric Inventory (MINI) as well as the Yale–Brown Obsessive Compulsive Scale (Y-BOCS-II). This comprehensive psychological assessment revealed that he suffers from a severe case of OCD. While most treatment providers are unaware of the taboo/unacceptable symptom dimensions specific to this disorder, it is our finding that Mr. Smith was experiencing sexual obsessions, which is a symptom of OCD, afflicting 25% of sufferers.

While prudence in these matters is highly necessary given the risks, Mr. Smith's OCD diagnosis will not cause him to act out inappropriately toward his daughter. While we certainty cannot deem any person as completely safe, we can say with much certainty that his OCD diagnosis does not make him more dangerous than anyone else or pose any additional danger. It is my opinion that any type of supervision or restriction on his role as a parent is not necessary as he is just as capable of caring for his daughter as his wife Mrs. Smith. In fact, spending time alone with his daughter is an important part of his treatment and essential for his recovery. Impairment from OCD still remains, but this impairment does not make him incapable or unfit to fulfill his role as a parent. He will continue contact with providers at the Louisville OCD Clinic to manage and overcome his obsessive-compulsive symptoms.

It is my hope that this letter will serve as evidence of Mr. Smith's parental capabilities. Please feel free to contact The Louisville OCD Clinic directly with questions and concerns.

Sincerely,
Monnica T. Williams, Ph.D.
Clinical Director

and drop out. Therefore, we recommend working respectfully within the confines of the client's religious laws and traditions, which will ultimately facilitate treatment compliance. In fact, it's much more effective to recruit the client's religious values into service of treatment than to try to suppress it (Huppert, Siev, & Kushner, 2007). In most cases, the OCD has gotten in the way of carrying out proper religious duties (i.e., prayer, attendance at services, fellowship) rather than improving religious life (i.e., Himle, Taylor, & Chatters, 2012). For example, one client we treated had stopped going to mass due to OCD worries that she had committed a mortal sin by desecrating the host during communion. To motivate her to beat the OCD, it was necessary to help her understand that her OCD avoidances were not making her a better Christian but rather interfering with her spiritual life.

Other than mainstream religions, there are many other traditional healing practices that are connected to spiritual, medicinal, and psychic ways. Ethnic minority groups have introduced their approaches to health and well-being into the Western culture through immigration and globalization, and so your clients may also be making use of such practices. Often referred to as of complementary and alternative medicine, this may include Ayurveda, yoga, herbal medicine, acupuncture, Voodoo, astrology, Santeria, and new-age therapies (Moodley & Sutherland, 2010). Clinicians should be prepared to discuss the role of traditional medicine and healers in the client's treatment. It is important to show respect for these systems and acknowledge that indigenous, cultural, and traditional healing practices are time-honored methods that many people have historically used to alleviate both physical and psychological problems for hundreds or even thousands of years.

It is not uncommon for patients with OCD to enlist priests, rabbis, and other healers for reassurance-seeking when facing obsessive doubt. In the face of sexual worries, a religious leader may seem like the most appropriate person to provide guidance. However, sometimes well-meaning traditional healers provide help that is not actually helpful and may even make symptoms worse. Given a conflict between a therapist and a traditional healer, the client will usually side with the traditional healer and drop the therapist. Thus, it is better to collaborate with the healer rather than force the client to make a choice (Pouchly, 2012). With the permission of the client, the therapist can reach out to the traditional healer to describe the client's problem and the model for our CBT treatment approach. If the traditional healer is supportive, then that will go a long way toward helping the client feel motivated to fully participate in therapy. It can also be helpful for the traditional healer to know what practices are counterproductive for the client's progress, such as excessive reassurance.

Conclusion

The initial meeting with the client is an important opportunity to instill hope and disarm feelings of shame surrounding S-OCD. It is also a place to start the conversation about how S-OCD is maintained and defeated using CBT. A good assessment is essential to best understand the details of a client's OCD symptoms as well as other comorbidities.

Most people with OCD have suffered a long time before finding the right help, and, as such, it is not uncommon for many types of specialists to be involved in some facet of a client's S-OCD issues. These may include family physicians, psychiatrists, psychotherapists, social workers, clergy, and even traditional healers. It is important to be aware of all the services clients bring to bear for help in these situations to ensure harmonious and effective treatment for every client.

3

Step-by-Step Treatment Manual

Monnica T. Williams, Chad T. Wetterneck, John Hart, Eric Lee, and Street Russell

Introduction

Unwanted sexual thoughts have traditionally been considered difficult to treat because of their taboo and stigmatizing nature. Those suffering with such thoughts often experience intense shame and guilt, and so they are less likely to talk to others about their obsessive-compulsive disorder (OCD) due to fears of social rejection (Glazier, Wetterneck, Singh, & Williams, 2015; Grant et al., 2006). These fears are not completely unfounded, as unwanted sexual thoughts are shown to be less acceptable to others and more stigmatizing than other OCD themes, such as contamination or checking (Cathey & Wetterneck, 2013). People with unwanted sexual thoughts tend to attach more personal significance to their thoughts than other sufferers of OCD; they often have a self-punishing thinking style and experience difficulty having compassion for themselves (Jacoby, Leonard, Riemann, & Abramowitz, 2016; Wetterneck, Lee, Hart, & Smith, 2013). Reducing punitive thinking, decreasing self-criticism, and improving self-compassion will lead to greater success in cognitive-behavioral therapy (CBT), making this an important treatment priority, as an addition to those techniques focused directly on OCD symptoms.

Intrusive thoughts, and even sexual obsessions, are found among most people and occur across cultures and geographical locations (Williams, Chapman, Simms, & Tellawi, 2017). However, people with OCD are more distressed and attribute more responsibility to their thoughts than those without OCD. Because of the intensity of the distress, the OCD sufferer wants to suppress these troubling thoughts. Suppression, however, only leads to increased intensity, duration, and frequency of these disturbing mental intrusions.

As discussed previously, CBT is the most effective treatment for OCD (McKay et al., 2015; Öst, Havnen, Hansen, & Kvale, 2015). Meyer (1966) first developed the treatment by activating obsessions and encouraging patients to refrain from performing the corresponding a ritual or compulsion. Exposure and response prevention (Ex/RP), as it became known, has since been established as a gold-standard treatment for OCD (Abramowitz, 1996; Olatunji, 2013). In recent years, other CBT approaches that use exposure therapy in an indirect way or as an adjunct to exposure have also been developed.

Clients who are accustomed to nondirective therapies may find Ex/RP jarringly different as the therapist takes a more active role. Additionally, the format of sessions in Ex/RP differs from that of the traditional 50-minute session typical of other disorders. Ex/RP sessions are ideally 90 minutes long and occur twice weekly. The extended length of the session allows the clinician time at the beginning to review the client's daily homework that was completed between sessions and discuss areas of ongoing difficulty. The remaining hour of the session is spent doing therapist-guided exposure. The session length can be reduced to 60 minutes after clients have reached the top of their situation hierarchy, which will be discussed further in this chapter. Reducing the session length to 30 to 45 minutes may be appropriate once clients learn to develop and complete exposures on their own. For clients who express concern regarding the length and frequency of sessions (or insurance difficulties related to session length), reference the Troubleshooting chapter (see Chapter 8).

Psychoeducation

Unwanted Sexual Thoughts: Everyone Has Them

As previously noted, a large majority of people who don't have OCD will experience sexually intrusive thoughts during their lifetime (Wetterneck et al., 2011). For people with OCD, about a quarter of them will have experienced obsessional unwanted sexual thoughts (Grant et al., 2006). Common themes include sexually aggressive acts toward others, sexual acts toward family members or children, religious worries, and worries related to sexual orientation. Such thoughts can be images, perceptions, or intense subjective states that are not stimulating, gratifying, or enjoyable. Typically, people find these thoughts morally repugnant and contrary to their world view and personal value system. To illustrate just how common these fears are, we show clients Handout 7 (see Appendix A), a partial list of sexual thoughts experienced as unwanted by 292 undergraduate students. This helps to normalize and destigmatize their experience.

In the context of OCD, the unwanted sexual thought is the primary source of danger and distress. Repeated occurrences of the thoughts begins to take on a special meaning for the experiencer. For instance, if the thought is not sufficiently suppressed, then the probability that the feared action may occur is erroneously believed to increase. Alternatively, a person may be less concerned that he or she will commit the act but attribute the appearance of the unwanted sexual thought as evidence of a moral failing or a perverse aspect of their character. Moreover, the thought may be experienced as uncontrollable and the inability to suppress it may lead to hours of being consumed with related fears, worries, and ruminations.

In addition to attempts at thought suppression, people with unwanted sexual thoughts may use various other strategies to "neutralize" their experience. Examples may include various mental rituals that include thinking opposite thoughts, counting to good numbers, prayers, mantras, mental review of past events, analysis of emotions, etc. Unwanted sexual thoughts then become connected to behavioral rituals such as checking oneself, compulsive Internet searches, and seeking reassurance from others. Another dysfunctional response is excessive rumination as an attempt to seek an explanation, self-reassurance, or even self-condemnation for having the thoughts. Ruminations frequently lead to harsh self-judgment meant to discourage the reappearance of the unwanted thoughts and reduce fears of impulsive acting out. Individuals will avoid situations in which such thoughts may be triggered. This can lead to disruption in daily functioning, as valued, worthwhile, and necessary activities are avoided and one's life is arranged to reduce the possibility that the thoughts might occur.

Unwanted sexual thoughts can overlap with other themes of OCD, including contamination and scrupulosity. A person may feel contaminated by unwanted sexual thoughts and not want to spread the contamination to others or recontaminate themselves. This can lead to isolation from others and the development of related compulsions. A person may have a sexual OCD (S-OCD) thought in a particular place and will subsequently avoid it or ritualize until the place feels neutralized. Unwanted sexual thoughts are often experienced as a sin, making religious places, objects, or situations a potential trigger for obsessions.

OCD has commonly been associated with anxiety, but other distressing emotions are relevant as well. An inflated sense of responsibility for reducing risk and promoting safety often produces feelings of guilt when suffers feel that they are failing at controlling dangerous thoughts. The embarrassing nature of unwanted sexual thoughts increases shame, and the moral nature of these thoughts generates feelings of disgust.

Face Your Fears: How CBT Will Help

The distress caused by obsessional fears strengthens the pattern of avoidance and compulsions over time. This pattern is at the center of the growth and maintenance of the condition. Simply put, treatment of OCD, including S-OCD, is a reversal of this process. "Facing your fears" is primarily a task whereby the person with S-OCD is asked to face their own troubling thoughts and emotional responses, without ritualizing. S-OCD sufferers will often contend that they face their fears every day. However, an important goal of CBT is to encourage people to *intentionally* have their unwanted sexual thoughts rather than trying to avoid them (e.g., "Have your unwanted thought instead of it having you"). Additionally, individuals with OCD are encouraged to face their fears differently than they ever have before. For example, an S-OCD sufferer may face their fear of walking by a playground by intentionally doing it without performing a checking compulsion. This principle of intentionality is important since it helps S-OCD sufferers to change their behavior and relationship to their thoughts.

People with S-OCD have strong beliefs about the need to control their thoughts. Facing these thoughts through CBT helps the sufferer relinquish control and therefore increases the person's ability to have greater influence in decision-making in response to the thoughts in the long run. Instead of merely waiting around for an ambush of obsessions, individuals are taught to bring the fight to their OCD—like poking a sleeping monster with a stick. Clients are asked to stop being on the defensive against their OCD, and instead go on the offense and attack. Bringing on the OCD by making themselves have the unwanted sexual thoughts is a more adaptive form of empowerment. Likewise, encouraging S-OCD sufferers to face activating situations will better help them stay in control of their actions and increase their behavioral flexibility.

All of us have learned since childhood that facing our fears will help us to overcome them. When parents teach a child how to swim, they may start by helping them dip their toes into the water. This is followed by sitting in shallow water, splashing and playing in the water, and even experiencing what it is like to get water in their eyes. They may slip and fall, learning that getting water in your nose burns, or that having water in your lungs makes it impossible to breathe. Most parents instruct their child to get back up, wipe their eyes, and plug their nose next time they dunk their head under the water. It is a critical moment in overcoming their fear. The child who ventures out into deeper waters can ditch the life jacket or floaties as they become a more proficient swimmer and even learn how to dive head first into the water.

The process of successful exposure in OCD treatment uses a similar approach to help individuals face their fears. Fears are faced gradually at a rate that will help the individual gain experience and confidence in their ability to venture out into deeper waters. Many people are skeptical of exposure as a strategy to overcome their fears because the experience seems so daunting. The clinician must to tap into their client's innate understanding that facing fear is necessary for mastery of one's behavior when one is afraid and learning to conquer a fear. The swimming analogy is one that can be transposed to facing fears in other contexts, such as learning to roller skate, ride a bike, or play an instrument. The analogy should portray the learner taking small, attainable steps to becoming more proficient at their skill. Additionally, the learner in the analogy should experience adversity (e.g., falling down, scraping a knee, getting water in their nose) and then choose to overcome it by getting back up and facing the fear and, ultimately, overcoming it.

In this analogy, the learner is accompanied by a coach, parent, or mentor who will teach the skills needed to overcome the fear. A compassionate parent teaching their child to swim would never throw them into the deep end of the pool on their first lesson. Clients with OCD may have the mistaken impression that exposure entails facing the full extent of their fears, session after session. It is important for the clinician to emphasize that the treatment aims to expose them to feared situations in a controlled gradual manner, beginning with simpler tasks and ending with more difficult ones. Exercises are intended to be challenging but not overwhelming or impossible. Additionally, you will help clients to understand that their continued input throughout the entire process is taken into consideration, including in the creation of their treatment plan (e.g., the exposure hierarchy). Collaboration will increase their understanding in the process and willingness to adhere to the plan.

Commitment to Treatment: Building Mental Fitness

CBT for OCD is taxing, hard work. One useful metaphor for people initiating CBT for OCD is that of physical fitness. A successful exercise program starts slowly and must be consistently maintained. For example, an amateur runner who signs up to participate in a charity mini marathon in a few months will need to establish workable, short-term goals to build stamina and strength. They may start with running short distances in the first phase of their training program and making necessary changes to their diet in preparation for running longer distances. The joints, muscles, heart, lungs, and all other vital organs begin strengthening with further adherence to the program. Ultimately, the person sticks to the program and prepares their mind and body for the final task. This same success would not be possible for the amateur runner who decides to do the full length of the race without any training. Their body and mind would likely become overwhelmed by the physical and mental stress of such a difficult feat.

Exposure and response prevention for OCD prepares individuals to meet their wellness goals by gradually exposing them to fears that might otherwise be too great to face all at once. Changes will need to be made to their daily activities to make room for such a program. It will involve daily practice to strengthen mental fortitude and stamina as they face situations of slowly increasing intensity. Mental fitness is critical in the race with OCD. Success in treatment would be difficult for the individual who opted out of a gradual approach to exposure and wanted to jump to the hardest activity right away. The intensity of the resulting anxiety would likely become too overwhelming to sustain for the full extent of an exposure, decreasing the likelihood of staying in treatment.

Consider that people are willing to exercise because they believe it will increase their well-being. For various reasons, if people are going to put themselves in their most distressing situations, then they are best served if they can understand the reasons why they would willingly face such distress (e.g., "What am I doing this for?"). This can be facilitated by doing a brief activity aimed at identifying a person's values, such as a values card sort, or developing an inventory of everything they will gain when their OCD is under control. The limitations placed on a person by their obsessions prevents them from their pursuit of a valued path. A person may be more willing to commit to difficult treatment activities if they are clear how doing so will help them follow their values in the long run.

Exposure and Response Prevention

As noted previously, Ex/RP is an effective type of CBT treatment for all forms of OCD. The word *response* in Ex/RP is often replaced by *ritual* as the word *response* is too broad and not all responses are compulsions. However, it should be noted that avoidance may be the most common maladaptive response to unwanted obsessions.

Although behaviorally based, Ex/RP includes both behavioral and cognitive techniques. A more cognitive approach, called simply "cognitive therapy" (CT), is advocated by some clinicians and may be useful for clients who are resistant to engaging in exposures. However, Ex/RP and CT both typically include behavioral and cognitive elements. Ex/RP has been used in a variety of formats, including individual and group treatment, family-based treatment, computer-based treatment, self-help techniques, intensive programs, and residential care. This chapter will describe the primary components of Ex/RP and CT for OCD, along with acceptance and commitment therapy (ACT), mindfulness, and other techniques that can be incorporated into treatment.

Assessment

Chapter 2 addressed doing a full assessment of people with S-OCD. Don't make assumptions as to the function of a person's symptoms. When addressing the meaning of an obsession and the function of a ritual, try to avoid using the word *why*. Asking someone why they do something often puts them on the defensive and can make the person feel accused. People with S-OCD already believe they are in the wrong for having their thoughts in the first place, and they may believe that their compulsions are protecting themselves or others.

When probing the meaning of having an unwanted sexual thought, it is important to determine whether simply having the thought makes committing that act seem more likely to the client. Alternatively, the presence of the thought may not make the client feel there is an increase in the probability of it occurring, but rather the thought is simply disturbing, or even magical or impossible. In this case, the meaning may be that the thought is immoral, and, therefore, the client is immoral. This process is referred to as thought–action fusion, a type of cognitive bias that overvalues the significance and consequences of intrusive thoughts (Rassin et al., 2001). Thought–action fusion can cause a sense of increased probability or a violation of a moral standard in regards to the obsessional thoughts (Shafran, Thordason, & Rachman, 1996).

When doing an assessment of S-OCD, the therapist obtains an inventory of rituals that are used to neutralize or suppress obsessions. Rituals may be mental or covert (e.g., saying silent prayers, thinking the opposite thought) or overt behavioral action (e.g., checking a high school yearbook, making the sign of the cross, retracing steps). Also included in the assessment should be a list of the worthwhile or necessary activities that are avoided or interrupted because of the potentials for activating obsessions. For instance, a person who has intrusive thoughts about being a pedophile may avoid restaurants where there may be children or even family events where children's relatives may be present.

Another part of the assessment process is to determine what reassurance a person with S-OCD gets from other people. Reassurance-seeking is a common maintenance process for all forms of OCD. In its ritualized form, reassurance-seeking increases distress in the long term and is a source of interpersonal conflict, especially among partners and caregivers. Part of the Ex/RP plan would be to reduce the amount of reassurance a person seeks from others. This may require the assistance of family, friends, and others to help with the Ex/RP process, when appropriate (see Chapter 7 for how the family can be involved).

The assessment process itself can be a source of reassurance, and so keep in mind that not all reassurance can (or should) be avoided. The important thing to address is maladaptive ritualized reassurance. In some respects, a person may need to learn how to accept reasonable and effective reassurance by trusting their objective experience rather than others or the outcome of compulsive behavior. Ultimately, the best reassurance is when a person learns that they can function in a valued way without rituals, thought suppression, or behavioral avoidance.

Subjective Units of Distress/Discomfort

Before discussing exposures, the first thing clients need to learn is the Subjective Units of Distress/Discomfort Scale (SUDS; Wolpe, 1969). The SUDS is an important part of behavior therapy as it permits clinicians to quickly assess the level of OCD-related distress experienced by clients. It is a simple method that allows clinicians to anchor clients' self-rated discomfort in various provoking situations at baseline, monitor changes, and to evaluate the progress of therapy. The SUDS has been incorporated into many different treatment protocols for anxiety-related disorders.

Situations can be ranked from least to greatest amount of anxiety as measured by the client's reported SUDS, from zero (*no anxiety, calm*) to 100 (*very severe anxiety, worst ever experienced*). Sometimes the SUDS scale may range from zero to 10 instead of zero to 100, especially when used with children, and, in such cases, a SUDS pictorial thermometer may also be used. Although anxiety is the most common description of an OCD sufferers state, as discussed previously, other subjective states are often present (e.g., guilt, shame, disgust, not just right experiences, etc.), and we let clients know that any or all of these negative feelings can be part of the SUDS.

The therapist will teach the client how to create and use the SUDS (see Appendix A). You can explain to clients that this will be important for creating the hierarchy, giving ratings of distress during exposures, and recording discomfort caused by homework. Give the client the SUDS handout (Appendix A, Handout 8A second page) and explain it as follows:

> As you know, the treatment program consists of exposing you gradually to situations that make you anxious or uncomfortable. To put together your treatment program, I need to get from you a list of the specific situations that make you uncomfortable and how much discomfort each item generates in you. So that I know we're both on the same page in terms of your anxiety, let's put the degree of discomfort into numbers. Look at this scale, which we call the Subjective Units of Discomfort/Distress Scale or SUDS (see Handout 8), that ranges from zero to 100, where zero means that you feel no discomfort at all (perfectly at peace) and 100 indicates that you are very upset from anxiety; in fact, 100 should represent the most anxiety you've ever felt. Most people when experiencing this level of distress would be shaking, crying, or screaming.

Let's try it. We'll start with zero. Can you think of a time when you've felt no anxiety at all and experienced perfect peace? That would be zero on our scale. For many people it could being on vacation at the beach, watching the ocean. But some people don't like vacations, in which case that wouldn't be a good zero for them. What about you?

You can review the example SUDS scales in Handout 8b. Don't use examples from the patient's OCD. The distress caused by OCD is expected to change over the course of treatment, and we want to pick anchors that will stay the same. Assist the client in choosing anchor points for zero, 25, 50, 75, and 100 SUDS. It's ideal to choose real situations that the client has experienced, but sometimes the client will not have had any experiences that rise to the 90 to 100 level, and, in such cases, a hypothetical example will have to do. For example, a 100 might be, "You get a call from the hospital that your whole family has been in a tragic accident, and the doctors don't know if they will live or die."

The sample SUDS anchors will be used to rate the intensity of distress experienced during an exposure assignment. Make a copy of the SUDS anchors created during the session so that the client can use it as a reference for building their hierarchy, completing homework assignments, and filling out self-monitoring forms. Or two blank SUDS forms can be used and the therapist can make a parallel SUDS scale along with the client. A copy of the SUDS anchors should also be kept in the client chart to be used by the clinician as a point of reference in subsequent sessions. The more a person practices assigning ratings to their distress, the greater awareness they gain moving forward.

If accurate anchors are not established, clients may to overestimate the intensity of their anxiety by rating several activities in the 90 to100 range. For example, a person with a contamination obsession assigns a SUDS rating of 100 to the following two exposures: touching a doorknob and touching the rim of a toilet. Without an anchor as a point of reference, it is difficult for the client to discern a more accurate SUDS rating, and it is difficult to know which task would be more difficult for the client. If SUDS anchors were already established, the therapist might use the following amplified reflection: "So, touching a doorknob and getting a call from the hospital that your family was in a tragic accident are equally upsetting?" In another example of this false equivalency, a client with P-OCD may rate looking at a toy catalogue with child models as the same as touching a child in public. For this reason, establishing SUDS anchors prior to building a hierarchy is a critical step in developing a person's skill to accurately appraise their distress.

Building a Hierarchy

Beginning the Hierarchy

Constructed in collaboration with the client, distress-evoking situations are listed in a hierarchical manner, beginning with the least distressing and gradually proceeding to more distressing ones (see Appendix C, Session 4 note). The SUDS rating is used to determine the expected amount of distress associated with each exposure if the client was to imagine encountering the item without ritualizing or avoiding.

We find it best for the therapist to create the initial hierarchy because some people with OCD struggle with categorization and may have exhaustive lists of items for their hierarchies. Clients typically need help narrowing down their situations to be more specific and useful, particularly in a therapy setting. Therapists can choose items using information collected during the assessment or clinical interview. For example, Annette's fear of being a pedophile was endorsed on the YBOCS. The therapist then offers up situations that may trigger this obsession (e.g., driving past an elementary school, seeing pictures of children in a magazine, or watching shows of children on television), and asks the client to rate the situation using their SUDS anchors.

Ideas for exposure may also be derived from a consideration of external and internal factors—or bodily sensations—which have historically resulted in an increase of obsessions or distress for the client. For example, a client may report that pedophilia obsessions increase when his sister changes his niece's diaper or whenever he smells an odor of baby lotion. This information may lead to the creation of several exposures that could be included on the client's hierarchy incorporating these elements, such as smelling baby lotion or changing a diaper.

An important part of this process is to train the client how to do exposures at home and on their own. Therefore, it's best to select as many items as possible for the hierarchy (at least 15) that can initially be practiced in session with the therapist present. As shown in Table 3.1, In Annette's case, we have chosen situations that can be easily practiced not only in session or on a

Table 3.1 Example of a Partial Hierarchy for Annette's Fear of Being a Pedophile

Situation	SUDS
Driving past an elementary school	25
Looking at pictures of children in a magazine	35
Watching shows of children on television	45
Going to a public swimming pool where children are playing in the water	55
Being in the same room with a friend or relative's child (with other adults present)	65
Using the Internet alone (for fear of viewing child pornography)	75
Going to a fast food restaurant where children may be present	80
Being at a playground	95
Being in the presence of children without other adults around	100

daily basis between sessions at home. Other viable options might include reading children's books, driving around neighborhoods where children might be playing, or examining articles of children's clothing.

Although some situations may cause the client to experience heightened anxiety, not all options will be practical. For example, a client may report that seeing a specific child at the zoo carrying a red balloon made them very anxious. It would not be practical to spend time for a session searching for this specific child at the zoo. It would be more productive to help the client habituate to anxiety in locations where there is predictable child traffic, but not in search of a specific child carrying one specific item. As stated before, choosing practical exposures gives clients an opportunity to practice between sessions the very activity demonstrated to them by their therapist.

The importance of having a hierarchy is to determine a starting point and to organize a strategy. Depending on the client, the Ex/RP exercise should start just below the mid-point in their hierarchy. Any situations below this the typical client should be able to stop avoiding without help. For some more tentative or younger clients, the starting point may be at the lowest SUDS. A hierarchy is a working document that should be revised throughout treatment as situations are mastered and new distressing situations arise through expanded experience.

Table 3.2 Session-by-Session Treatment Schedule for Assessment and Treatment

Session Note	Session Description	Measures	Client Handouts	Client Activities	Homework Forms
C0	Consultation	A4: DOCS Other Applicable Self-Report Scales	A1: OCD Cycle A2: Symptom Dimensions		B1: FAS
C1	Assessment 1, Assessment & Diagnosis	MINI	A3a: Instructions for Monitoring A4a: Understanding S-OCD		A3b: Monitoring
C2	Assessment 2, Case Formulation Part 1	YBOCS-II			A3b: Monitoring
C3	Session 1		A5a: Unacceptable Thoughts A7: Unwanted Sexual Thoughts	A4b: Quiz: Understanding S-OCD	A3b: Monitoring
C4	Session 2 (also see A8a: SUDS Instructions)		A6a: Understanding CBT for OCD A8b: SUDS Examples	A5b: Quiz: Unacceptable Thoughts A8a: SUDS Forms	A3b: Monitoring
C5	Session 3			A6b: Quiz: Understanding CBT for OCD In-Session Exposures	A3b: Monitoring A9: Exposures
C5	Session 4–8			In-Session Exposures	A3b: Monitoring A9: Exposures

(*continued*)

Table 3.2 Continued

Session Note	Session Description	Measures	Client Handouts	Client Activities	Homework Forms
C5	Session 8–17			In-Session Exposures (*until all items on hierarchy competed*)	A9: Exposures
C5	Session 18–19: Being Your Own Therapist	YBOCS-II Severity Scale A4: DOCS Other Applicable Self-Report Scales	A10: Guidelines for Normal Behavior	Devise Own Exposures	A9: Exposures
C6	Session 20: Final Session		A11: Relapse Prevention	Review Test Scores Follow-up Plan	

Basics of Exposure and Response Prevention

Following the assessment and the building of the hierarchy the therapist should have a good idea of how to activate obsessions in the client. For instance, from Annette's hierarchy (see previous discussion), she might begin by looking at pictures of children in a magazine or images the therapist has printed out from the Internet. A good working relationship with the client is important because it is incumbent on the client to be open about what will cause the distressing activation of the obsession. This is particularly important in S-OCD since frequently what seems like an activating cue may actually be a type of checking or reassurance. For instance, a male client with seuxal-orientation themed OCD, looking at a magazine for gay men may be a way of checking for the lack of arousal.

When conducting exposures in session, the therapist should guide the client through the exposure during the session. The therapist should model doing the exposure whenever possible first and demonstrate that they are not worried or harmed (Röper, Rachman, & Marks, 1975). When the client does the exposure, the therapist should ask the client for their SUDS score every five minutes and write it down (use session note C5: Progress Note with Exposure). Generally, the exposure should continue for 30 to 60 minutes or until the client's SUDS has decreased by at least half. If the exposure is too easy (i.e., it does not evoke a SUDS above 50 or the client habituates after only a few minutes), the therapist may alter the exposure to make it more challenging.

Sometimes clients will object to specific exposures because they will note that they already encounter that situation all the time in real life, and so exposure won't help. For example, someone with pedophilic-themed OCD may argue that looking at pictures of children won't help because they do that all the time to ensure they are not a pedophilic. But the difference here is that the exposure purposely will not include compulsions, which in this example would be checking for signs of sexual arousal while looking at such pictures. In fact, the exposure may even include looking at children's pictures while chanting, "I am turned on by kids." So exposures may not always be items that are avoided, rather they can be activities that have been used for compulsions, but repurposed as exposures.

After an item from the hierarchy has been successfully confronted in session with a therapist, the client then practices self-exposure to the same item as daily homework (see section on Homework in this chapter for more details). This allows the client to practice completing the exposures independently and promotes greater generalization across various environments. Once mastered, the client faces the next progressively more distressing object or situation in session with the therapist. The client learns (a) that the feared consequence will not occur, (b) to better tolerate anxiety, and (c) that anxiety diminishes over time even without performing compulsions. As the client progresses up the hierarchy, each next item becomes a bit easier.

Ritual Prevention

The ritual or response prevention component involves instructions for the client not to engage in compulsions or rituals of any sort since clients frequently perceive that their rituals prevent the occurrence of their feared outcome. Stopping the rituals will help clients learn to break the association between their rituals and their obsessional concerns. Typically, rituals have a functional relationship with the obsessional thought (i.e. "Washing my hand after shaking hands with a male will remove possible semen residue and prevent me from becoming pregnant" or "Saying a prayer three times will prevent me from going to hell after an intrusive sexual thought"). Many times this functional relationship is logical (e.g., sitting with one's back to a play area in a fast food restaurant), alternatively rituals have a magical flavor (i.e. "If I wear the color blue to work, I will not become gay"). At times, clients cannot articulate any negative outcome that is prevented by performing the rituals; rather, the performance of the ritual "just feels right." In this case the function of the ritual is to reduce anxiety or discomfort, and the disastrous consequence is psychological, such as falling apart.

Similar to obsessions, rituals in S-OCD can take many forms. As noted previously, a frequent S-OCD ritual is reassurance-seeking. The client may seek reassurance from friends and family members, the therapist, or engage in self-reassurance. Response prevention would involve the client not indulging in self-reassurance or in seeking reassurance from others when exposed to stimuli that provoke distress related to S-OCD. The therapist should point out to clients when they are engaging in a ritual to help increase awareness of the behavior. Once it is clear that the client understands that their behavior is a ritual, the therapist may respond with an exposure statement that may exacerbate the client's distress. Typically, this is either a statement of uncertainty (e.g., "I don't know if you are a pedophile") or an encouragement to increase the anxiety by affirming the obsession (e.g., "I am starting to think you really are a pedophile"). For example, a male client states that he inadvertently looked at a passerby's backend and wonders if he looked because he is gay. The therapist can encourage the client to affirm the obsession by saying, "I looked because I *am* gay."

Individuals with S-OCD also typically engage in a variety of mental rituals. One ritual may involve thinking positive thoughts to reverse the distress of negative ones. A client may also review or check their memories for times when they did not have S-OCD concerns as a form of self-reassurance. Response prevention would require the client to not engage in these mental rituals during exposures and in general. Because these rituals cannot be seen in-session by the therapist, it is important to check in with the client about whether or not they are engaging in rituals during exposure exercises.

Clients who have been practicing covert rituals for some time may believe it is impossible to simply stop. Therapists should emphasize that change is a process and that they should simply do their best. As clients continue to work at it, they will become better at resisting. Clients may also have difficulty distinguishing obsessions from mental rituals. Clinicians can help identify mental rituals by determining the mental processes that the client employs after having an obsessive thought. Another way to teach clients how to distinguish obsessions from mental rituals is to ask them the function of their thoughts: obsessions increase anxiety, while rituals are designed to reduce anxiety. This can help clients understand that they can have thoughts that cause anxiety but should refrain from the thoughts that are meant to decrease anxiety. It may be helpful to have clients substitute their mental rituals with exposure statements to prevent them from engaging in those rituals. If a client does engage in a mental ritual, the clinician can have the client re-expose themselves to the anxiety-provoking stimulus to cancel the effects of the ritual. One thing not to do is to teach the client to use self-statements, like "That is my S-OCD," to reframe their covert rituals, since such statements can then become mental rituals. Instead, the clinician should teach the client to use an exposure statement that targets their core fear (e.g., "I must be deviant!").

Clients with S-OCD may also engage in overt behaviors in response to their obsessions. For example, someone with sexual orientation fears may watch same-sex pornography and opposite-sex pornography to compare levels of sexual arousal to ensure they are "still straight." They may increase their levels of sexual activity to "prove" that they are not LGBTQ, or they may surf the Internet to find reassurance that their sexual orientation won't change. This again highlights why the function of the behavior, rather than the topography (i.e., what you see) is so important. Response prevention for clients with these overt compulsions involves stopping such behaviors and not overcompensating for perceived possible deficits (Williams, Slimowicz, Tellawi, & Wetterneck, 2014).

Spoiling Rituals

Clients may report that they sometimes perform rituals out of habit or that they are aware of their involvement in a ritual only after it was completed. It is important to teach clients how to discredit or "spoil" rituals, no matter whether they occur willingly, spontaneously, or automatically. Spoiling will help clients continually break the association between ritualizing and feeling a sense of relief. The following script may be used to teach this concept to a client:

> An important component of your treatment was to gain greater understanding regarding the association between rituals and relief. Namely, that this association is broken through ritual prevention (stopping compulsions). Your brain learns that you no longer need to perform compulsions to reduce your anxiety. Instead, the passage of time allows anxiety to go down naturally while resisting the urge to ritualize. If you happen to give in to that urge hereafter, then I want you to reverse the effect of that compulsion by doing something called "spoiling." When you spoil, you're attempting to bring back the anxiety that was temporarily reduced by the compulsion.

After providing the client with an introduction to spoiling, provide several examples related to their own obsessions and compulsions to model how it works. For example, if a client with P-OCD obsessions takes an alternate route on his way to the store to avoid an elementary school, he may spoil the compulsion by turning the car around to intentionally pass by the school. In another example, if a client with impregnating obsessions washes their hands after they accidentally touched a handrail, then they may spoil the compulsion by immediately touching the handrail and resisting the urge to wash again.

Ritual Monitoring

Implementing ritual prevention involves a detailed analysis of all compulsions or rituals performed by the client, and so typically clients are asked to keep daily logs of all rituals performed. The therapist uses these logs initially to identify the rituals that need to be stopped, and, as treatment progresses, the log is used to identify areas of difficulty that need more therapeutic attention. Completing these logs will also allow the client to develop greater awareness of the frequency of daily rituals and to identify patterns in their behavior.

The therapist will demonstrate to the client how to use the Compulsion & Avoidance Monitoring Log. Provide multiple copies of the form, as the client is expected to fill out one log daily between sessions. The following is a sample narrative that can be used to describe the log:

> One of the methods I will use to track your progress is through daily logs. You will use the Compulsions & Avoidance Monitoring Log to report each time you perform a ritual. On the left side of the form, you will notice the table is divided by 30-minute increments. As soon as you complete a ritual you should log the event on the form. In the first column, you will report the situation, activity, or thought that may have occurred before you started the ritual. For example, [use an example the client shared during the assessment]. You can be brief in your description of the activity in this first column. In the next column, rate the intensity of your distress in this situation using the SUDS scale. You can use your SUDS anchors to estimate your level of distress. Next, write a description of the ritual in a few words. For example, [use an example the client shared during the assessment]. Finally, log the amount of time you spent completing the ritual in the last column.

The completed Compulsion & Avoidance Monitoring Logs are reviewed with the client at the beginning of subsequent treatment sessions. Review the forms for accuracy and provide feedback as needed. It is helpful to compare the information collected on the daily logs to what was reported during the assessment. It is not uncommon for clients to report rituals on their self-monitoring forms that were not discussed during the assessment. Discuss the accuracy of their reported SUDS ratings compared to their previously determined anchors. Some clients may overestimate the intensity of their anxiety in the beginning stages of treatment. Review time spent on rituals and make note of patterns or discrepancies. After a review of the logs, the client is provided with blank copies again and given the assignment to record rituals daily between sessions.

Sometimes clients state they cannot use the log because their OCD is so severe that they are constantly doing compulsions, and so they would be spending all day writing. In such cases, it might be best to have clients start with recording for a specified time period each day (e.g., 7–9 pm at night).

If a client arrives to a session with incomplete homework, the therapist should troubleshoot any problems or setbacks related to noncompliance or resistance. Reasons will vary for incomplete self-monitoring, but it is important to assist clients with practical strategies that will increase motivation and compliance with the treatment plan. No matter what strategy is used to increase motivation, the therapist should re-emphasize the importance of completing daily logs in the progression of the treatment plan. Additional tools and strategies are referenced in the Troubleshooting section for resistant clients.

Once the ritual prevention is well-established, clients can stop using the monitoring forms and just note any areas of difficulty to discuss at the next session at the bottom of their Homework Forms. Generally, we stop using the Compulsion & Avoidance Monitoring Log by Session 8, unless the client is still having a great deal of difficulty at that point. That being said, if the client is still engaging in many compulsions by that time, treatment may not be progressing well and an expert consultation or higher level or care may be warranted.

In Vivo Exposure

Exposure is the cornerstone of Ex/RP treatment, with in vivo exposure reliably shown to reduce obsessions and related anxieties. This technique involves repeated and prolonged confrontation with situations that cause OCD-related distress. Exposure sessions may last anywhere from 30 minutes to two hours. The primary goal is for the OCD sufferer to remain in the situation long enough to experience some reduction in distress and to realize that the feared consequences are unrelated to the compulsive response. A common analogy that is used for sufferers is jumping into a swimming pool in which the water feels cold at first but soon there is a shift to the water feeling warmer. With repeated exposures, the peak of the distress as well as the overall distress decreases over sessions. With repeated exposure, the OCD sufferer will habituate to their distress. Thus, the client habituates to upsetting stimuli in two ways, within the session and between sessions. More recent research (Craske, Treanor, Conway, Zbozinek, & Vervliet, 2014) had found that within session habituation is not necessary to achieve between session symptom reduction. However, it is recommended that an individual's distress has gone down by at least 50% before stopping the exposure, to facilitate a calm and collected end to the session. Consider that OCD sufferers who are highly distressed at the end of the session may be reluctant to complete homework or even to return for more sessions! When an exposure session ends without sufficient habituation, debriefing and recovery support is necessary.

After mastery of a given exposure has been achieved (as demonstrated by between-session habituation and no ritualizing), a more challenging item is selected for exposure. It is important to note that the actual achieved SUDS levels will vary depending on the context of the exposure and the modification of elements of the exposure. Modifications to exposures should occur as needed to ensure that the targeted SUDS level is reached (generally at least 50 to start for in-session exposures).

Out of Office Exposures

In vivo exposures may require flexibility in terms of the treatment setting, as it may be hard to evoke certain obsessional worries in the office. For that reason, it is sometimes more useful and practical to conduct exposures outside of the office, where the client is having most of their problems. This could be in the home, but other exposures might take place other venues, such as a playground, gay bars, or strip clubs.

When considering out of office exposures, you will need to maintain a balance between benefit to the client and how you may affect others in the environment. For example, asking a man who has fears of being a pedophile to go alone to a public park or fast food restaurant play area to closely stare at playing children may be a viable exposure, but it may also cause alarm for parents and even put the client in jeopardy of getting into trouble. The following are examples of things *not* to do for public exposures. For someone with pedophile-themed OCD: walking up to parents with their children at a playground and declaring oneself to be a pedophile or commenting on one's desire to kidnap or harm them. This may cause the parents and children undue stress and even lead to them calling the authorities. For someone with sexual orientation-themed OCD (SO-OCD), approaching someone you believe or actually know is gay and bringing up their sexual orientation publicly may not be a good idea. Unless you know the person has "come out" to everyone and is comfortable talking about this topic in all settings, you may be revealing something they don't want known or that they prefer not to discuss with you or in the presence of others. For someone who feels that they may act out on a sexual impulse to another adult, you should not ask them to approach strangers and state they are a rapist or that they want to do something sexually inappropriate to them. Similar to the earlier examples, this may be traumatizing to the other person and be even considered an actual criminal offense. Another example of a possible problem exposure might be to encourage a woman who has bestiality fears to grab a stranger's dog at the park. It may be more appropriate if the client asks the owner first and then approaches the dog in a courteous and safe manner. We hope that these examples seem like common sense, but we do see some creative, but overzealous exposure ideas that we think need to be rethought before being acted upon. See Chapters 5 and 6 for suggestions of safe and appropriate exposure examples.

As noted previously, the therapist should also consider home visits when situations or places in the home are a focal point for OCD symptoms. This allows the therapist to observe the home environment and the client's functioning in it as well as provide coaching for exposure exercises in that environment. During the home visit, the therapist should note areas of concern to address with the client. For example, one client was terribly avoidant of a particular room in the house where there was a computer that had been used by another person in the home for pornographic viewing of online materials. She was afraid that by touching the computer, desk, or nearby items, she might come in contact with semen that could impregnate her. In her case, exposures included eliminating avoidance, spending time in the avoided space, and even using the computer in question without any rituals during or after use.

Imaginal Exposure

In some cases, it is not possible to construct an in vivo exposure to a client's fear, and in these instances an exposure can be done in the imagination. Situations especially appropriate for an imaginal exposure are those in which a client fears changing in a fundamental way (i.e., having a change in sexual orientation or becoming a serial killer), causing a distant catastrophe (i.e., starting a chain of events that results in harm coming to unknown people), or that the outcome of failing to do a ritual is far in the future (i.e., going to hell or dying from AIDS).

To conduct an imaginal exposure, the therapist and client develop a detailed narrative scene together based on the client's obsessional theme. A key to this exposure is that narrative is consistent with a "worst case scenario" for that particular obsession. For example, for someone who fears acting on an unwanted impulse, brushing up against someone's buttocks might have a different worst case scenario than imagining acting on an impulse to rape someone. (Although, it should be noted that "worst case scenario" is not necessary synonymous with "most difficult imaginal exposure ever." We still want the difficulty level to be about 50 SUDS.) The story will describe a catastrophe befalling the client and/or loved ones as a direct result of the client's failure to perform compulsions. The therapist might first recount the story aloud and then have the client do the same, ideally in the present tense to make the events seem more real. SUDS levels are taken at various points throughout the narrative (i.e., every five minutes) to assure that the story is evoking enough anxiety to be productive. The exposure is typically recorded to facilitate repeated listening as homework. See Chapters 5 and 6 for imaginal exposure examples.

Imaginal exposure is effective when it evokes the same sort (i.e., type and amount) of distress in a client as the actual obsession and avoids any form of self-reassurance or other ritualizing. A person with OCD typically fights to suppress the obsession because of the thought–action fusion process. However, suppressing the obsession and the associated emotional response will ironically strengthen the obsession in intensity, duration, and frequency (Clark, 2004). By repeating the unwanted intrusive thoughts in the form of a distressing narrative, the person with OCD begins to habituate to the emotional distress. By making an audio recorded script of the client's obsession, to be listened to over and over again, it allows clients to expose themselves to scenarios that can't be experienced in vivo. Most smartphones have voice recorders that have built in looping functions. There are also free apps that can be downloaded for this purpose as well as free software that can be downloaded to personal computers. This may take a bit of technology research, but any problems can usually be easily solved. Be sure to always test your technology before trying it with a client.

Since the goal is to tap as close to the core fear as possible, we usually include specific language in the script that indicates that the feared consequence happened because the client deliberately chose not to do compulsions. Within the script, it is important to not include parts that might function as neutralizer, intended to suppress the intrusive thought. For example, someone with P-OCD may write a script that describes going to a playground and exposing themselves to children. This would be done in the most graphic detail that is possible for the client to tolerate. Part of the script might be that the client is arrested and taken to jail. This would be useful if being taken to jail is a part of the obsessional fear (as opposed to disappointing friends and family, feeling out of control or responsible for hurting someone, going to hell, or another negative consequence). However, for some people the consequences of the feared scenario may function to suppress the obsession such as, "I better not do this or I will be taken to jail!" since it is common for people with OCD to use a punitive thought control strategy to suppress their thoughts (e.g., "It would be a relief to be in jail so that I can't get to any children to harm them") to address their perceived lack of control. Additionally, it is important to exclude worries and ruminations from scripts (Box 3.1), since including these can constitute "practice" worrying and

---

Box 3.1 Three Types of Distress: Obsessions versus Worries versus Ruminations

- **Obsessions** are unwanted, typically about stimuli or thoughts in the present, specific to a few fears, contain more visual images, and typically linked to feelings of fear or disgust.
- **Worries** are more future-oriented, diverse across most areas of life, less visual, and may be wanted at times (to allow one to prevent bad outcomes or show caring).
- **Ruminations** are typically past-oriented, related events that have actually occurred, are less visual, and typically linked to depression.

ruminating. However, the important point is that the narrative script elevates the client's distress adequately to promote habituation and tolerance.

In a hierarchical way, as the client habituates to the imaginal exposure, newer more distressing narratives may need to be developed. Through the exposure the client develops a different and more functional relationship to their intrusive thoughts. In other words, by encouraging the client to relinquish control of their intrusive thoughts by intentionally having them, they begin to re-evaluate the meaning of the obsession and develop a greater tolerance for having obsessionals.

There are several techniques for using imaginal exposures. A client may write a scenario in describing an event based on the obsession and then read it repetitively. Likewise, the client may record the scenario and listen to it repeatedly, which is more effective than simply reading it. Visual aids can be useful such as a picture of a cue for the thought (e.g., picture of an animal for bestiality obsessionals, picture of a person that represents the target of the obsession). The client can write the imaginal as part of a pretend diary, good-bye letter, or tell-all confession. A more novel technique is the use of chromatic drawing in which a client is asked to use colored pens or pencils to draw their obsessional content in a story board fashion (Hart & Fountain, 2007). This is intended to add a visual component to the exposure to evoke a stronger emotional response.

Some clients are stunned at the very idea of doing an imaginal exposure. They say that these horrific thoughts and images are already looping in their brains with wild abandon, and they want to think about the subject matter less and not more. They may also be apprehensive because of beliefs in the increased probability that the obsession will become true, that a moral principle will be violated, or that thoughts will become grossly out of control. We explain that an imaginal exposure can be likened to a horror movie. The first time you watch it you may be very frightened and jump every time a shadow appears on the screen. But what would happen if you watched the movie again? Would you be as scared? What about after five times? After 20 times? Once you have seen the movie enough times, it will no longer frighten you. You know the exact scene where the bad guy pops out of the closet with the knife. The blood that looked so gory starts to look fake. The movie starts to get boring. An imaginal exposure works exactly the same way. After listening to the story repeatedly, it actually gets boring. When the client is bored with the imaginal, it is time to move to a more challenging one.

Homework

Homework is a critical part of the treatment process. It is very important for clients to understand that their OCD will not be successfully treated by just coming to sessions regularly; rather being free from OCD will involve a major lifestyle change that will require daily discipline and practice. Generally, we find that if clients are unwilling to do the homework they are not great candidates for treatment since the type of work they do for homework will eventually become their new way of managing their OCD.

At the end of each session, we review the homework clients are to do each day. Generally, the homework will be the very same exposures conducted in session, or a close variation. We may also include the previous homework assignment as well if those exercises are still causing significant anxiety. Homework for a typical outpatient client is expected to take about an hour; however, if the client has more time available to work on exposures (i.e., unemployed or in a residential center) more time can be allocated to homework. Clients should understand that the more homework they can do, the faster they will get better. Clients can stop an exposure early if their SUDS goes down to 10 or less (i.e., they are bored). The therapist will write the homework to be completed on one of the homework sheets. Options include the Daily Homework & Task Sheet, Daily Homework Sheet, Weekly Homework Sheet, or Exposure Homework Plan Sheet.

Selecting a particular homework sheet over another will be based on the specific tasks the individual is expected to complete between sessions. The Daily Homework & Task Sheet is suitable for clients who are not only asked to do daily exposure, but who were also instructed to work on specific avoidance patterns or types of ritual prevention. This form may also be used to remind clients to bring certain items back to their next session to complete an exposure. The Daily Homework Sheet, Weekly Homework Sheet, and the Exposure Plan Sheet are all different formats for reporting similar information. All three of these forms have tables the client will use to report their SUDS rating at the start of the exposure, their highest SUDS rating during the exposure, and their rating at the end of the exposure, except for the Exposure Plan Sheet. This form allows the client to report their SUDS rating in 5- and 10-minute increments.

An important point is that understandably clients generally don't *want* to do homework. As a result, asking a client "What do you want to do this week?" may be met with resistance, so the therapist should have a clear plan. Initially clients may be resistant to homework, which is why it is important that the therapist is able to generate concrete ideas, especially in the early stages of treatment. Clients with OCD are very anxious, which may interfere with their ability to think creatively about possible exposures. In the long term, clients develop their own homework rather than having it assigned to them. The very word *homework* may generate resistance, and other words may be used (e.g., *challenges, exercises, self-directed exposures*). However, we find that young people are usually fine with calling it homework as the concept readily maps on to something familiar that they are already engaged in within an academic context.

Often clients will have difficulty completing homework and may show up for sessions without their homework sheets. Completing homework is an important indication that clients will be able to adhere to treatment guidelines once therapy is over and that they are dedicated to the treatment process. After exposures are initially assigned, we typically schedule a check-in call to ensure there are no problems with homework. That way we can adjust the assignment on the fly if it turned out to be too difficult. If clients arrive at session without having done their homework, we will spend some time troubleshooting to determine why homework wasn't completed and problem-solve around making sure it will be done next time. If the next week homework is still not completed, we typically increase the structure provided by helping the client to schedule specific blocks of time when homework will be done. If the client is still unsuccessful, then we will arrange to call the client at the beginning of the scheduled times to ensure they are starting the homework. If this is not successful, the next step would be for the client to come into the clinic to complete homework at scheduled times. We have an empty room that can be used for this purpose that clients can use at no charge. Keep in mind, however, it is important to not be judgmental or punitive when clients are not willing or able to do their homework. As noted, taking a problem-solving approach to getting it done can be useful. It can also be helpful if the therapist shares some of the responsibility when the homework process doesn't go as planned. Also see Chapter 8 on troubleshooting if homework refusal is a problem.

While the just described recommendations should work for a typical outpatient client, there are many intensive outpatient program models that can implemented by practitioners who are able to give a lot of time to one client. One such model would include daily appointments per week with the therapist to set and review homework and troubleshooting, while trying to complete approximately five trials of five separate exposures each day. This method can take up to two to four hours per day depending on the length of the exposures, but can also help address those with stronger avoidance or severity issues by getting more practice with the techniques. We also offer this treatment in an intensive format that involves two weeks of daily treatment. This model includes two 60- to 90-minute sessions per day, one session with the therapist and a second with an assistant to help with homework completion and out of office exposures. The assistant role is perfect for practicum students and trainees to help them learn the treatment techniques, while also providing additional support for clients.

It is very important to check the client's homework at the start of each session. If the therapist forgets to review last week's homework, it can be problematic as the client may be left feeling that their efforts are not important. Asking about previous homework at the beginning of the session shows that you as a therapist recognize its importance, and discussing it can help consolidate learning from the Ex/RP experience. It also prevents avoidance of discussing OCD-related problems.

Inhibitory Learning: Is Habituation Necessary?

Despite the demonstrated effectiveness for Ex/RP for the treatment of OCD, the explanation for how it works is not completely clear. Specifically, does habituation have to occur? Evidence of habituation does not always predict good outcomes over time, and some people do have successful outcomes in the absence of habituation during Ex/RP (Arch & Abramowitz, 2015). The goal of Ex/RP is extinction learning, and that has been traditionally believed to occur when a fear is activated and prolonged until fear reduction, which promotes extinction. However, new research based on principles of learning theory have advocated for the importance of "inhibitory learning." Rather than the association between the activation of fear and the response being broken or erased, inhibitory learning promotes the learning of new competing nonthreat responses that become easier to access through prolonged and repeated exposure. Considering Ex/RP from this perspective, repeated exposure is the strengthening of newer nonthreat connections so that they are easy to remember and retrieve (Jacoby & Abramowitz, 2016). See Chapter 6 on associating splitting for novel cognitive techniques that can be used to break S-OCD mental connections.

An important aspect of inhibitory learning is developing a tolerance to the older threatening response. A useful metaphor we used previously is physical exercise. Just as one can develop increasing strength through lifting weights, a person struggling with intrusive thoughts can develop a resistance to the thought (i.e., by not reacting to the compulsion) while the new nonthreatening thought gets stronger. As a person lifts a weight, the resistance becomes less, and the person can increase the amount of weight to be lifted.

For example, Bill has intrusive thoughts of exposing his genitalia in the presence of children at a playground. Through inhibitory learning, children at a playground becomes a stimulus with two meanings. The obsessional meaning in which the presence of children at a playground is associated with expectations of anxious repugnant feelings and an inappropriate act that is neutralized by ritualizing and avoidance. The second meaning is acquired through repeated exposure that being present at the playground does not lead to the feared response. In other words, a playground with children is just a playground with children with a neutral meaning—or even a place of value in where Bill can take his children to play. Both meanings may remain in memory but the new inhibitory learning gains increasing strength to inhibit the original fear.

How is this inhibitory learning obtained? Inhibitory learning theory has several components (see Craske et al., 2014, for a review), although just two will be reviewed here. The first is expectancy violation. This component is based on the principle that new learning occurs when there is a discrepancy between an expectancy and an outcome, also a key component in the concept of surprise. Expectancy violation occurs when someone intentionally violates the relationship between what happens when an obsession is activated and a ritual or avoidance is prevented. In Bill's case, he expects that if he has a sexually intrusive thought at a playground, then he will be at risk to do something sexually inappropriate. Going to a playground, activating his intrusive thought, and staying there will violate his expectation of something bad happening. This shifts the emphasis from fear or distress reduction to a learning process as to whether the outcome occurred or the experience was as bad as expected (e.g., "I can be at playground and act appropriately" to "I can be tolerant of uncertainty"). It is important that after each exposure session that the client reviews what they learned from the expectancy violation. Another principle in inhibitory learning theory includes deepening exposures through presenting multiple cues, such as

Bill listening to an imaginal exposure about molesting children in a playground and then going to a playground right after. His exposure could be further deepened by asking him to listen to his imaginal exposures while at the park watching the children play.

Cognitive Therapy

Can You Reason with OCD?

As previously noted, a certain amount of unwanted intrusive thoughts are considered normal, and generally these thoughts, although disturbing to most, are dismissed as exceptions to their normal stream of thought. We call them "garbage thoughts"—random, bizarre, meaningless thoughts that tend to float in an out of one's head at random. However, if these garbage thoughts are assessed as overly significant then the resulting distress leads to efforts to suppress or the urge to engage in compulsions to reduce the intensity of the distress. Cognitive therapy for OCD aims to change the automatic thoughts and beliefs that contribute to and maintain the misinterpretation of the obsessional experience. The Obsessive Compulsive Cognitions Group (1997) categorized the various belief domains that are commonly found in individuals with OCD. These domains include overestimation of threat, intolerance of uncertainty, inflated sense of responsibility, overimportance of thoughts, and overcontrol of thoughts. In addition to these established belief domains, other dysfunctional beliefs can be found that are not exclusive to OCD, such as a person's belief in their inability to tolerate distressing emotions (Smith, Wetterneck, Hart, Short, & Björgvinsson, 2012).

A primary reason why CT for OCD was developed was to help people with OCD change the way they perceive, interpret, and attribute meaning to these unwanted thoughts or cognitions. In the first stage of CT, clients are taught to identify the unwanted intrusive thoughts as obsessions and the rituals as compulsions. Instead of ritual monitoring, as described in the previous section, the client keeps a daily diary of obsessions, called a *thought record*. In the thought record, clients write down their obsessions and the interpretations associated with the obsessions. Important details to record may include what the client was doing when the obsession began, the content of the obsession, the meaning attributed to the obsession, and what the client did in response to the obsession—usually some form compulsive thought or behavior.

At the start of each session, the therapist reviews the thought records with the client with an emphasis on how the obsession was interpreted. Using reasoning and Socratic questioning, the therapist helps the client gently challenge their obsessive-compulsive beliefs. This helps the client to identify the type of cognitive distortion, such as a client's ability to tolerate uncertainty (e.g., "I have to check!"), an exaggerated sense of responsibility (e.g., "I must never think a harmful thought!" or "I am bad person for even thinking such a thing!"), or fears that thinking something negative will make it come true (e.g., "If I have this thought, then it will come true!").

So, can you reason with OCD? Yes and no. Often the mistake is made in attempting to reason with the content of the obsession. Reasoning with a client as to whether they are pedophile is not likely going to be useful and even counterproductive. In other words, CT for OCD targets modifying the *how* a client thinks about the content of their obsessions. For example, clients may learn that they are able to tolerate more uncertainty than they think or that failing to control their thoughts does not lead to increase danger. Similar to inhibitory learning theory, clients frequently are asked to challenge their beliefs by testing thoughts contrary to their OCD beliefs.

Testing New Beliefs: Behavioral Experiments

Once clients are able to identify their obsessions and compulsions as symptoms of OCD, the therapist initiates *behavioral experiments* to underscore the problems with following their OCD beliefs surrounding cause and effect. These behavioral experiments are similar to but not the same as exposures. For example, a client compulsively says, "I am only attracted to my husband" in response to unwanted intrusions about males that she encounters throughout the day, because she believes that without the mental mantra, she may make a sexual advance on a male peer. In other words, she may believe that she might act on the intrusive thought if she doesn't neutralize her obsession with the compulsive saying. Or, she might not believe that she would act on it but feels overwhelmingly guilty and immoral for having an intrusive thought at all. Furthermore, she may believe that if she doesn't block the thought or neutralize it, her intrusive thought may run rampant in her mind. A series of effective exercises could be: (a) asking her to test her beliefs by resisting her mental compulsions, (b) intensifying her behavioral response by saying to herself, "I don't love my husband," and (c) intentionally bringing on the thought in the presence of other males including her peer. By doing this she can challenge several OCD beliefs at once. For instance, she challenges the belief that she can't tolerate uncertainty and that she doesn't have to control her thoughts, and then she can modify her beliefs in the overimportance of thoughts by learning the difference between having a thought and believing a thought.

For best results, the client and therapist should together write down their predictions of the feared result before doing the behavioral experiment. Then, after doing the exercise, the therapist can note that despite letting go of her mental compulsions and deliberately thinking the bad thoughts, she did not actually make a sexual advance on her boss that day. The therapist and client refer back to the predictions and compare the feared outcome with the actual results. Over time, the client learns to identify and re-evaluate beliefs about the potential consequences of engaging in or refraining from compulsive behaviors and subsequently finds it easier to eliminate compulsions (Williams, Powers, & Foa, 2012).

Dropping Concealment Experiment

Many people who experience S-OCD will hide the content of their obsessions from everyone, even those in their closest inner circle. People with S-OCD often fear that if they tell someone, that person will think about them the way they think of themselves—that they are perverted or dangerous. Concealing obsessions can be conceptualized as a maintaining factor for the disorder. For example, a S-OCD sufferer may believe "the only reason my husband hasn't abandoned me is because he doesn't know about my twisted, graphic, perverse thoughts." Dropping concealment is a behavioral experiment where patients are asked to tell someone close to them about content of the obsessions and then learn from the outcome (Newth & Rachman, 2001).

If a client is willing to disclose their thoughts to another important person in their lives, it provides a wonderful opportunity for both disconfirmation of their feared outcome and increased closeness and support from their loved one. Before conducting this experiment, clients should be asked about their expectation of the other person's interpretations of their unwanted sexual thoughts. For example, does the client expect the other person to share their own catastrophic interpretations? Does having a sudden unexpected thought of touching a child automatically make one a monster? Does having a same-sex sexual thought mean that divorce is inevitable? In almost all situations, the other person is not distressed by the information and may even be dismissive of it. However, be sure to get as much information as needed about the target of the behavioral experiment in advance. This experiment should only be attempted if the client has a close person who is noncritical and understanding that can be supportive in the process. If it does not seem likely that the dropping concealment experiment will succeed, it should not be conducted. The goal is for the person to get feedback from others that the obsessions are not a reflection of their character in the eyes of those closest to them.

In rare instances, the person who is given the information will react in a critical and negative manner. If so, the therapist and client need to deal with the emotional fallout of this outcome, and therapists should prepare for this in advance with clients. For this reason, Newth and Rachman (2001) encourage all clients to disclose to more than one person to avoid the possibility of such an unfortunate reaction from a single person that might then be generalized to everyone.

After a successful behavioral experiment, you should process the experience with the client. You can ask questions like (Newth & Rachman, 2001):

- How did the person respond when you told them?
- Were they as bothered by your thoughts as you are?
- Did they avoid you because of what you shared?
- Did their behavior towards you change in any way?
- Did they show signs of being fearful of you?
- Do they seem concerned about you being alone with particular people (e.g., children or attractive people of the same sex?)
- If their behavior toward you hasn't changed, what can you conclude about the significance that person attaches to your thoughts?

In summary, concealment of obsessions in S-OCD is common but easy to miss and should not be ignored in treatment. Dropping concealment can be quite beneficial when judiciously applied because it introduces disconfirming information and helps clients arrive at new interpretations that can be helpful in reducing the disastrous meaning they tend to attach their S-OCD. However, it should be noted that this exercise is only appropriate for people who have been hiding their S-OCD thoughts from others. It is not appropriate for situations in which the person repeatedly tells others about their thoughts for the purposes of getting reassurance. In such a case this exercise will only strengthen the OCD.

Acceptance and Mindfulness Approaches

Acceptance- and mindfulness-based approaches emphasize taking an open nonjudgmental stance toward the awareness of any and all inner experiences. Mindfulness entails being in the present moment with the willingness to experience unwanted and distressing thoughts and feelings. Acceptance, as opposed to resignation, is the willingness to experience distressing experiences and accepting them as they are—inner mental events and not realties. Additionally, in contrast to tolerance, acceptance is not about gritting one's teeth and just resigning to having to continually deal with awful unwanted experiences. Rather, it is compassionately making space for these human experiences as they occur without giving undue attention to them or fighting against them. These approaches do not emphasize altering or eliminating unwanted thoughts and feelings; rather, this approach encourages the individual to accept such inner experiences as a necessary and inevitable part of the human experience.

Acceptance and Commitment Therapy for OCD

In ACT, the goal of treatment is to increase psychological flexibility. Psychological flexibility is the willingness to consciously and fully experience the moment, without judgment or evaluation, while behaving in accordance with one's chosen personal values (Hayes, Pistorello, & Levin, 2012). It is being able to adapt to changing situational demands by effective use of mental resources, considering different perspectives, and managing competing needs and values (Kashdan & Rottenberg, 2010). ACT attempts to increase psychological flexibility, with the ultimate goal of increasing values-consistent behavior, through six theorized processes: (a) cognitive defusion: the ability to interact with inner experiences nonjudgmentally and not overidentify with them; (b) acceptance: willingness to experience mental and emotional events without avoiding or struggling against them; (c) flexible attention to the present moment: the ability to connect with the present in a voluntary and focused way; (d) self as context: the ability to not overidentify with conceptualizations of one's self; (e) values: directions in life that are individually chosen and that guide one's actions; and (f) committed action: choosing long-term patterns of behavior that that are in line with one's values (Levin, Hildebrandt, Lillis, & Hayes, 2012). Treatment with ACT targets all six of these processes in an attempt to increase psychological flexibility.

ACT aims to help clients to create a new relationship with obsessive thoughts and distressing emotions through encouraging clients to notice that a thought is just a thought and anxiety is simply an emotion to be felt with no inherent meaning. "Private events" such as emotions, physical reactions, and thoughts are to be experienced through observation rather acted upon as reality. Like the inhibitory learning approach, ACT targets the promotion of new learning as opposed to emphasizing habituation and the elimination of symptoms. This difference is an emphasis since all therapists want to see their clients in less distress and have reduced maladaptive behaviors. However, in ACT, the aim in the forefront is to broaden the range of possible valuable, worthwhile, or even necessary responses while experiencing the intense distress that comes with OCD. In this sense, ACT could be considered additive rather than eliminative in its approach to treatment.

Exposure therapy is approached in a manner that is consistent with, and topographically similar to, traditional Ex/RP. Yet, in ACT, exposures are done within the context of a client's stated values and distress reduction is de-emphasized. Because of this, SUDs are not used during exposure exercises, or at the very least they are not used as a way to evaluate progress. Rather, acceptance (often described as "willingness" with clients) is used to guide exposure. Using the example of the sleeping monster from the previous section, the client is not encouraged to intentionally wake the sleeping monster in an effort to "fight" or conquer it. Instead, clients are taught to identify valued actions and commit to move down a path toward these values, but where the monster also often resides. The commitment in this case is to move down this path for an agreed upon amount of time while practicing engaging in an open, willing stance toward the monster, no matter how big or scary it may seem. Success is therefore measured by whether there was movement toward the value and whether the client practiced willingness by not attempting to fight, change, or avoid the monster (i.e., use compulsions) for the specified time period. Likewise, the client's distress level, amount of obsessive thoughts, and physical sensations are not used as markers of a successful exposure exercise, reinforcing to the client the benefits of engaging in a defused, accepting stance toward these private events. Clients learn that engaging with OCD in this manner allows them to live the life that they want to live, whether or not the monster is present. Moreover, they learn that the monster, despite its scary appearance, has no real power to control how they choose to engage with the world.

Imagine a man with P-OCD who has obsessive thoughts about becoming aroused by children and feels apprehensive and unmotivated to engage in treatment. One component of ACT treatment might include exploring his values in an attempt to foster psychological flexibility and increase willingness to engage in exposure exercises. It is important to remember that in ACT values are distinct from goals. If goals are well-defined, accomplishable objectives along an unending path, values are the path. Values are a direction, not a destination. For example, one might identify education as a value. This could include a desire to learn new things, personally challenge oneself, and improve writing skills. Notice that these concepts are not achievable per se, whereas goals along this path, such as earn a degree, read a book, or attend a class, are. Thus, values tend to be broad domains such as family, relationships, career, recreation, healthy lifestyle, spirituality, etc.

A simple exercise to explore values is to imagine oneself far in the future and look back on your life. This man with P-OCD might be asked to visualize his 90th birthday party in detail. Who would he like to be at this party (it can be anyone whether it fits the timeline or not, such as parents or grandparents)? Where would it be located, and how would it be decorated? Then he would be asked to choose one person from the crowd of attendees who is very important to him and imagine that they offer a toast to the crowd in his honor. What would he like for this person to say about him? What kind of life did he live? What impact did he have on those around him? What was his life about? He would then be asked to do this for one or two more people at the party. What would they say about the life he led? An exercise like this can be useful to help people step outside of their short-term desires to control their OCD and the expectations that others have for them and identify with their own values. Often individuals with OCD have become so consumed by efforts to deal with their symptoms that they have lost sight of, or not adequately explored, what is truly meaningful to them.

It can be helpful to ask something like, "if you didn't have OCD, you had all of the money in the world, and you had every material thing you could ever want, what would you do with your time?"

Following this exercise, this man has identified family to be a significant value for him. In his case, an exposure could be attending a family event where children may be present. Since being supportive and nurturing via family participation are chosen personal values, he will perhaps be more willing to make space for his intrusive thoughts, anxiety, and other distressing emotions that are likely to be present at the family event. Before the event, he would be asked to make a commitment based on how long he will be there (e.g., 10 minutes, one hour, etc.) or on a specific task that he will accomplish (e.g., serve dessert to the children) while practicing willingness. As an indirect values-guided exposure, he may commit to go to a fast-food restaurant where children may be present. He might say that he doesn't even like fast food and question the value of being able to go to such a place. What would be explained from an ACT framework is that this commitment allows him to practice willingness skills that can be used to engage in more obviously values-consistent events such as attending family events or taking his children to activities.

ACT has been demonstrated to be a viable evidence-based approach to anxiety and OCD-related disorders (Bluett, Homan, Morrison, Levin, & Twohig, 2014). For OCD, a randomized controlled trial has been conducted that demonstrated that ACT was superior to a progressive relaxation control group (Twohig et al., 2010). Although at this point it is not clear that ACT combined with Ex/RP is more effective that Ex/RP alone, there may still be some important benefits (Twohig et al., 2018). A preliminary study with adolescents has also been conducted (Armstrong, Morrison, & Twohig, 2013) as well as an ACT-based parent facilitation of OCD treatment for children (Barney, Field, Morrison, & Twohig, 2017). The ACT approach also maps onto the inhibitory learning model in a few ways. First, it encourages spontaneity of exposures and even allowing an exposure to increase in difficulty prior to habituation. This requires an increase in acceptance and overall psychological flexibility. In addition, more recent protocols of inhibitory learning encourage a focus on more positive aspects of one's life—a values-based shift away from one's negative attentional bias and toward wanted or positive biases. It's not as simple as a carrot-and-stick approach but makes intuitive sense to us and many of our colleagues that while focusing on potential threats and sitting with distress is effective for habituation or extinction to occur, it does not necessarily focus a client on defining and developing a meaningful life, truly, a life worth living.

Mindfulness Techniques in OCD

In recent years, focused effort has been made to assess the effectiveness of mindfulness and acceptance-based strategies in the treatment of OCD. Mindfulness can be used during exposures to help individuals take a nonjudgmental stance toward themselves when they continue to perform compulsions even when they are trying not to; this may help to reduce shame or self-judgment during a difficult process of change.

In the treatment of OCD, a mindfulness approach would involve changing the way clients relate to their inner experience. Individuals with S-OCD have unwanted thoughts and use behavioral strategies to avoid the anxiety related to these thoughts. In mindfulness, this avoidance is called *experiential avoidance*, and it involves efforts to change the content, amount, or sensitivity of challenging private events, such as cognitions and emotions, even though these efforts result in actions that are inconsistent with an individual's values and goals. Experiential avoidance can be thought of as the opposite of ACT's concept of acceptance. Experiential avoidance is clearly a key issue in the treatment of OCD, as many compulsions are used to avoid certain thoughts and feelings. Furthermore, mindfulness approaches can help target the thought–action fusion that occurs in OCD, when a person believes that thinking about an occurrence makes it more likely that it will actually happen. This relates to the ACT concept of fusion, in which thoughts are so intertwined with external experience that an individual cannot discriminate between the two.[1]

---

[1] Fusion occurs because words can be stimuli and therefore can acquire stimulus properties or functions. These properties/functions can transfer (or more accurately be shared) when one stimulus in a relational network is changed based on the function or properties of another stimulus in the network and the relation between them. Therefore, if stimulus A has the function of eliciting autonomic arousal and is trained in a derived relationship with stimulus B, then the presentation of stimulus B will also elicit autonomic arousal. These relationships are regulated by contextual cues. Examples of contextual cues may include nonarbitrary features of the stimuli involved in the relational network or they may involve stimuli encountered during the relational process of developing a relational network. For example, if someone were presented with a nickel and a dime and asked either, "Which coin has more mass?" or "Which coin has more worth?" the answer would differ based on the context of the question (i.e., worth or size) and the arbitrary (i.e., value) or nonarbitrary (i.e., size/weight) features of the coins. The transfer of many stimulus functions has been extensively documented including simple discriminative control, ordinal functions, conditional stimulus control, contextual

When people are in a fused state, their momentary obsessions are the only thing that guides their behavior. For example, an individual who has an S-OCD thought and is not fused with this experience might simply notice this for what it is: an internal experience produced by a combination of their environment and neurons firing in their brain and nothing more. Conversely, someone who is fused with this thought might label the experience as "bad" or "unhealthy" and therefore feel compelled to engage in strategies (i.e., compulsions) to avoid this experience. Fusion interferes with a person's awareness, which can lead to a cycle of constantly dealing with obsessions in the short-term without realizing that it comes at the cost of more long-term values-focused behavior that provides one with meaning and purpose.

Additionally, mindfulness encourages clients to cease their struggles with their thoughts and accept that experiential avoidance strategies are only helpful in the short term. This helps clients manage their unwanted thoughts by letting go of their struggles, which, in OCD, takes the form of compulsions. Specifically, for SO-OCD, acceptance and mindfulness can help manage the unwanted thoughts of becoming LGBTQ. Learning to accept the S-OCD thoughts as part of their experiences allows individuals to better tolerate these thoughts and subsequently reduce compulsions in the service of increasing values-directed behavior. This also makes it easier to engage in exposure exercises. Moreover, mindfulness is helpful in teaching individuals to not engage in evaluations, judgments, or appraisals of their thoughts. People with OCD tend to spend too much time scrutinizing their thoughts, which is counterproductive. This is specifically important in the treatment of S-OCD because of the current stigma toward people who are attracted to children or who identify as LGBTQ. Reducing the negative appraisal of unwanted thoughts surrounding S-OCD helps clients reduce the distress caused by these thoughts and, more important, helps them better engage in actions that they find meaningful and improve their quality of life.

---

control, and conditioned reinforcement and punishment. Although those examples only refer to operant functions, respondent or classically conditioned functions have also been documented to transfer within relational frames. For a more in-depth reading on the topic, see Hayes, Barnes-Holmes, and Roche (2001).

Relapse Prevention

One of the main objectives in OCD treatment is teaching the client to become their own therapist. Therefore, the client must acquire skills that enable them to monitor their obsessions and compulsions, spoil rituals, create their own exposures and carry them out independently, and limit reassurance-seeking behavior (Hiss, Foa, & Kozak, 1994). It can be useful to tell clients that recovery is a lifelong process that requires proactive commitment to what was learned in treatment.

Similar to most therapies, treatment is often tapered with increasingly longer periods of time between sessions. Clients being seen twice weekly may extend to once-weekly sessions for two weeks so that the clinician can monitor adherence to the treatment plan between sessions. Shorter sessions are warranted if exposures no longer need to be done in session. Spread any remaining sessions out over two weeks—or once monthly—to provide feedback on completed exposures and to ensure that the client is managing the occasional lapse or moments of high stress. Some client conditions may require a slower tapering while others may only need a three- or six-month booster session to maintain treatment gains.

One indication that a client is ready to reduce or even stop treatment is if they are routinely designing and executing effective exercises (e.g., exposures) on their own. In the final weeks of treatment, the client should be instructed to try out some of their own ideas for exposure and return each session to report on progress and receive additional feedback. The therapist will ensure the client's ideas contain all the necessary components of a constructive exposure. For example, a client with P-OCD reports that they sat on a bench at a nearby park for five minutes. The therapist's feedback should include instruction to the client that teaches them to adequately raise their SUDS by staying seated on the bench for a longer period of time so that they can experience a natural reduction in anxiety. Although the client's exposure was incomplete, they should be given praise for generating an idea that could be effective with just a few changes. The therapist may also brainstorm possible scenarios during the remaining sessions and help the client practice conducting exposure via role plays.

Another indication that a client is ready to reduce or even stop treatment is if the person is routinely spoiling rituals when they occur. For instance, if a client with P-OCD changes a television channel to avoid seeing children, they would be expected to automatically change the channel back. Clients who are approaching the close of treatment will be spoiling compulsions regularly to maintain progress and prevent relapse.

Clinicians should also use results from an objective measure as an indicator to determine when treatment could end. For example, if results on the YBOCS and DOCS show that the client has fallen within the subclinical or mild range of severity, then the client is likely ready to move to a new stage of treatment. Other instruments measure constructs across various life domains that may be indicators of readiness to end treatment. For example, the World Health Organization Quality of Life–BREF (WHOQOL-BREF) can measure improvements in quality of life, the Acceptance and Action Questionnaire–II (AAQ-II) can demonstrate growth in psychological flexibility, and the Sheehan Disability Scale can show changes in functional impairment in three life areas: work/school, social life, and family.

A discussion with the client about potential stressors will help them to prepare for the onset of unanticipated obsessions (McKay, 1997). Clients are likely to experience an increase of symptoms during times of high stress. Use examples from their own life to illustrate times when stress affected their overall well-being. Perhaps there were moments during their treatment when stress was high and they noticed an increase of symptoms. Clients are encouraged to respond to these obsessions using the skills they acquired during treatment (ritual prevention, exposure, mindfulness, etc.).

OCD can manifest in many different ways, so it is important to teach the client how to recognize when it is appearing in one of its various forms. For example, a client with pedophilic obsessions panics at the sudden onset of bestiality obsessions. One useful way of describing this phenomenon is comparing it to the arcade game Whack-A-Mole. The participant uses a mallet to hit toy moles popping their heads out of holes at random. Once a mole is struck, others appear in random areas of the surface, making it difficult for the participant to keep up with the hurried pace. Once they feel like they can manage one obsession, another one shows up.

Instruct clients how to discern subtle attempts by their OCD to catch them off guard. The following script may be used to teach this concept:

> Imagine that your OCD is having a hard time letting you go, although you've made it clear that you don't want it hanging around anymore. Like a clingy ex, you've even gone so far as to block OCD's number from calling your phone. However, OCD has some unfinished business it insists on discussing with you, so it starts calling you from unfamiliar phone

numbers to trick you into answering and engaging in an argument. Not knowing it's your OCD, you answer and it starts yakking! You are so annoyed and upset that you argue back. Before you know it, OCD's got you hooked and you are having the same old arguments. Hang up the phone! Don't let OCD trick you into returning to that bad relationship.

Teach clients to be vigilant of their OCD's attempts to fool them into a spiral of obsessions by re-emphasizing the skills they have successfully utilized thus far: namely, to resist the urge to perform compulsions, practice nonavoidance of feared situations, and use exposure to face their fears.

Help clients to understand that lapses—a partial return of symptoms—are merely setbacks and are to be expected. Setbacks are explained as normal reactions to anxiety that may be overcome through using the skills learned in treatment (Hiss et al., 1994). A full relapse—a return of symptoms and level of functioning prior to treatment—is less common and can be prevented with early intervention. Clients are instructed to call their therapist for a "tune-up" if they are finding a lapse difficult to manage. A lapse does not have to turn into a relapse! Box 3.2 highlights tips for therapists.

Review the *Relapse Prevention* Handout (Appendix A, Handout 11) with your client prior to the completion of treatment. The handout emphasizes several strategies that will help them to monitor stress, be reminded of important psychoeducational features of their OCD treatment and to practice nonavoidance on a regular basis. Discuss the difference between lapse versus relapse and instruct the client to contact you if needed.

Box 3.2 Relapse Prevention: 5 Dos & Don'ts for Therapists

1. DON'T save discussion of relapse prevention for the end of treatment.
   Relapse prevention should be incorporated throughout treatment and clients should be regularly reminded of the following:
   - Intrusive thoughts can increase and decrease throughout treatment and may come back after treatment.
   - Intrusive thoughts, alone, are not indicative of relapse—everyone has intrusive thoughts.
   - Intrusive thoughts may be trigged by life stress, which is normal.

2. DO educate about the role of compulsions in relapse.
   OCD symptoms are best managed by resisting compulsions and by not engaging in avoidance.
   - It is good to notice if/when obsessions return, but clients should also be aware of their RESPONSE to the obsessions.
   - Clients should be aware of and refrain from engaging in compulsions in response to distress.
   - Clients should be encouraged to continually and actively challenge themselves to confront distressing situations and not avoid.
3. DO challenge clients to take an active role in setting up their own exposures.
   As treatment progresses, clients should be encouraged to act as their own therapist by:
   - Suggesting homework assignments.
   - Designing their own exposures.
   - Looking for opportunities in "real life" to confront anxiety, as opposed to avoiding.
4. DO use the last two sessions to further discuss relapse prevention.
   At the end of treatment, clients should receive education on relapse prevention in greater detail:
   - Review successes and how far they have come in treatment.
   - List helpful strategies that were used to achieve gains in treatment.
   - Develop a plan for client to independently address any remaining challenges.
   - Explain the difference between a "lapse" and "relapse":
     - Lapse—a partial return of prior symptoms.
     - Relapse—a return to symptoms and level of functioning prior to treatment.
5. DO encourage clients to contact the therapist if a lapse or relapse occurs.
   Clients should have a plan in place prior to ending treatment with regards to what to do if they experience difficulty.
   - Clients should be encouraged to contact therapist for help, even if they are experiencing a lapse (does not have to be a full relapse to get help).
   - Intervention during a lapse can be effective in preventing a full-blown relapse.

Session-by-Session Outline for Ex/RP

The treatment protocol is detailed in the following text, as a session-by-session outline to help guide therapists in adhering to the Ex/RP treatment protocol (adapted from Foa, Yadin, & Lichner, 2012; Yadin, Lichner, & Foa, 2012) as outlined in Table 3.2. Note that the consultation and assessment sessions are described in detail in Chapter 2. Handouts referenced below are in Appendix A, measures are in Appendix B, and therapist notes are in Appendix C.

Consultation: (use Session Note C0: Consultation)

- Collect Relevant Self Report Measures
  - DOCS (A4)
  - Others, as needed, such as the SORT (A2) and AOIS (A3)
- Explain OCD and Symptom Dimensions
  - Define obsessions and compulsions.
  - Describe symptom dimensions.
- Explain the OCD Cycle
  - Use examples from client's presenting problem to teach the cycle.
  - Illustrate two associations targeted in the treatment of OCD.
- What to Expect in Ex/RP
  - Discuss the assignment of daily homework and active involvement in treatment strategies between sessions.
  - Basic description of exposure and response prevention.
- Assign Homework
  - Provide the Family Accommodations Scale (FAS) to client to give to any family members involved in rituals (if applicable).
  - Provide Handout 1 on *OCD Symptom Dimensions* and Handout 2 *the OCD Cycle*.

Assessment 1: (use Session Note C1: Assessment & Diagnosis Form)

- Review Homework
  - Answer client's questions related to the consultation, if needed.
  - Review results from the Family Accommodations Scale.
- Intake Questionnaire
  - Gain a deeper understanding of client characteristics that may influence treatment using the C1: Assessment & Diagnosis Form.
- Psychopathology Assessment (MINI)

- Assess for co-morbid disorders.
- Identify overlapping symptoms across other conditions (worry related to OCD vs. generalized anxiety disorder, harm obsessions vs. suicidality, OCD anxiety vs. panic symptoms, etc.).
- Assign Homework
  - Self-monitoring of rituals (give Handout 3a *Compulsion Monitoring Log Instructions* and Handout 3b *Compulsion Monitoring Log*), not to include their SUDS ratings yet.
  - Provide Handout 4a *Understanding S-OCD* handout (Yadin et al., 2012).

Assessment 2: (use Session Note C2: Case Formulation Part 1)

- Review Homework
  - Answer questions or comments about reading assignments.
  - Review self-monitoring.
- OCD Assessment (YBOCS-II)
  - Make sure the client understands the difference between obsessions and compulsions prior to starting the assessment.
  - Determine severity of client's OCD.
- Review Format of Ex/RP
  - Discuss how assessment information is used to inform the treatment plan.
  - Remind the client there will be at least one more session before exposure begins.
- Assign Homework
  - Self-monitoring of rituals, not to include their SUDS ratings.

Session 1: Treatment Planning—Setting the Stage (use Session Note C3: Session 1—Case Formulation Part 2)

- The Basics
  - Describe the plan for the session, explaining that it will consist largely of gathering more information about the client's specific symptoms and laying the foundation for the treatment approach.
- Review Homework
  - Review the reading *Understanding S-OCD* with the client and answer any questions.
  - Review self-monitoring of rituals.

- Administer the quiz for *Understanding S-OCD* Handout 4b (if developmentally appropriate).
- Psychoeducation
  - Provide correct and factual information about relevant sexual issues (reference Handout 7: *Unwanted Sexual Thoughts in a College Sample*).
  - Provide a thorough explanation for the use of exposure and response prevention treatment, specifically its aim to disrupt the associations that feed OCD (reference Handout 2 *The OCD Cycle*, as needed).
  - Guide the client to make a link between their obsessions and compulsions.
  - Note the connection between core fears, triggers, obsessions, and compulsions on the *Case Formulation II* form.
- Roadmap to Treatment
  - Outline the treatment plan to the client, including when you will build the exposure hierarchy (Session 2), when exposures will begin (Session 3), and the homework schedule (daily).
  - Acknowledge that treatment may at times be taxing but also emphasize that substantial time and effort are necessary for excellent outcomes.
  - Allow time for any questions the client may have.
- Self-Monitoring and Homework
  - Provide the *Compulsion Monitoring Log* worksheet and accompanying instructions to client and review the instruction sheet.
  - Assign the *Compulsion Monitoring Log* as homework to be completed daily and brought to the next session.
  - Assign the reading Handout 5a *OCD and Unacceptable Thoughts* as homework (Williams, 2011).

Session 2: Treatment Planning In-Depth (use Session Note C4: Session 2—Treatment Planning)

- Review Homework
  - Review self-monitoring worksheets, providing clarifications and making corrections as necessary.
  - Discuss the *OCD and Unacceptable Thoughts* handout and answer any questions.

- Administer Handout 5b, the quiz for *OCD and Unacceptable Thoughts* (if developmentally appropriate).
- Review the Rationale for Ex/RP
- OCD Symptom Information Gathering
  - Introduce the SUDS and refer to Handout 8 to instruct the client on how it is to be used.
  - Set SUDS anchor points (0, 25, 50, 75, 100).
  - Ask the client to describe specific situations, thoughts, and images unrelated to OCD that cause distress and have them rate their SUDs for each.
- Create a Treatment Plan
  - Using the OCD symptom information previously collected in the *Case Formulation I and II Forms*, select items for exposure based on client report of SUDS ratings.
  - Build the exposure hierarchy.
- Commitment
  - Revisit the conversation on the time and effort necessary for treatment and garner an agreement from the client toward that end.
  - Emphasize the importance of complying with the exposure plan (both in session and at home) and the rules for ritual prevention.
- Homework
  - Continue self-monitoring of rituals using the *Compulsion Monitoring Log*, this time including SUDS scores.
  - Have the client read Handout 6a, *Understanding CBT for OCD*.

Session 3: Embarking on Exposure and Response Prevention (use Session Note C5: Psychological Progress Note with Exposure)

- Review Homework
  - Review the *Compulsion Monitoring Log* with the client, providing clarification and making corrections as necessary.
  - Review *Understanding CBT for OCD* and answer any questions.
  - Administer Handout 6b, the quiz for *Understanding CBT for OCD* (if developmentally appropriate).
- Client Explanation of OCD Model
  - Ask the client to describe the model of OCD and how it applies to their treatment.

- Have the client provide the rationale for using exposures and ritual prevention.
- In-Session Exposure
  - Recall the exposure plan, guided by the hierarchy, and do an initial exposure exercise.
  - Therapist should demonstrate exposure to client before asking client to do it.
  - Do a second exposure in session, if time permits.
- Prepare for Exposure Homework
  - Explain the importance of practicing exposure independently between sessions.
  - Assign homework based on the exposure(s) conducted in session.
  - Ensure the client is familiar with how to use the exposure *Homework Form* (Handout 9) to track their progress.
- Ritual Prevention
  - Provide specific instructions for ritual prevention.
  - Write down a list of compulsions that the client should resist doing.
- Homework
  - Continue self-monitoring of rituals using the *Compulsion Monitoring Log* with SUDS scores.
  - Assign the agreed upon exposure practice homework using the appropriate *Homework Form* (Handout 9).
  - Schedule a time to call to check on progress before the next session.

Sessions 4–17: Exposure and Response Prevention (use Session Note C5: Psychological Progress Note with Exposure)

- Review Homework
  - Review the *Compulsion Monitoring Log* and, if necessary, bring attention to any problems with ritual prevention.
  - Go over the *Homework Form* to evaluate success with exposure practice homework.
  - Troubleshoot any difficulties with homework.
- Review Progress
  - Make time to review the client's progress and ask the client to share any changes, struggles, or obstacles they have noticed.
- In-Session Exposure

- Use the hierarchy as a guide to systematically continue with exposures in session (1–3 per session).
- Therapists should model all exposures before client attempts them.
- In-session exposures can be stopped once client has successfully completed all items on hierarchy.
- Homework
  - Assign the agreed upon exposure practice homework using the *Homework Form*.
  - The client is to continue keeping the *Compulsion Monitoring Log* for review in the next therapy session (can stop after Session 8).
  - Write down a list of compulsions that the client should resist doing.

Sessions 18–19: Being Your Own Therapist (use Session Note C5: Psychological Progress Note with Exposure)

- Review Homework
  - Go over the *Homework Form* to monitor success with exposure practice homework.
- Review Progress
  - Review the hierarchy to ensure mastery of all items.
  - Assess Progress
  - Re-administer the YBOCS-II Severity Scale
  - Re-administer the DOCS and other relevant self-report measures
- In-Session Exposure
  - Ask the client to identify any areas of lingering difficulty.
  - Invite the client to devise their own exposure for managing the obsession.
  - Conduct the client-devised exposure during the session as needed.
- Provide Handout 10, *Guidelines for Normal Behavior*, and review with client (Yadin et al., 2012)
- Homework
  - Advise the client to devise their own exposures for daily homework based on any current concerns using the *Homework Form*.
  - Ask the client to make note of any areas of difficulty.

Session 20: Final Session (use Session Form C6: Final Session Form for OCD)

- Review Homework
  - Review the *Homework Form* to monitor success with exposures.
  - Review before and after test scores
- Provide Handout 11, *Relapse Prevention* and review typical causes and signs of relapse
- Make a follow-up plan, e.g. schedule for follow-up appointments or phone check-ins

4

Association Splitting

A Cognitive Technique for Reducing Obsessions

Terence H. W. Ching, Steffen Moritz, and Lena Jelinek

The Semantic Network Conceptualization of Obsessions

The semantic network conceptualization of intrusive thoughts in obsessive-compulsive disorder (OCD) is an exciting new approach to understanding and treating this condition. This approach is based on research coming out of the cognitive psychology tradition. As such, semantic network models can be useful for better understanding how the brain works, including what is happening during the experience of sexual obsessions in OCD (S-OCD).

In brief technical terms, a semantic network is a group of concepts linked to one another in one's memory. These concepts can be activated via their meaningful associations with each other when any one or more of such concepts are initially activated (McDermott & Watson, 2001; Roediger, Balota, & Watson, 2001; Roediger & McDermott, 2000). The way concepts in a semantic network are subsequently activated is called *spreading activation* (Anderson, 1983; Anderson & Bower, 1973; Anderson & Pirolli, 1984; Collins & Loftus, 1975). When applied to OCD, obsessions, including those of a sexual nature, can be viewed as exaggerated activations of linked concepts within a tightly knit OCD-relevant semantic network (Moritz, Jelinek, Klinge, & Naber, 2007). To make this more clear, however, let's explore the relevant ideas in simpler and less abstract terms.

One key aspect of the semantic network approach are meaningful associations, or connections, between the linguistic constructs (i.e., words, phrases, or sentences) in one's thoughts (Reisberg, 2001). In the brain, these associations are organized as cellular interconnections in the areas responsible for memory. Another important aspect of this approach is that communication between concepts within the semantic network occurs via spreading activation (e.g., McNamara & Altarriba, 1988). In other words, one concept or thought activates another via the association between them, and so on and so forth. Attempt the following questions as quickly as possible to get a better understanding of spreading activation: "What is the color of a polar bear? What is the color of a snowflake? What is the color of a lab coat? What does a cow drink?" You probably answered the first three questions with "white." If, however, you spontaneously answered the last question with "milk" instead of "water," you have just experienced the phenomenon of spreading activation of concepts related to each other. This happened because "milk" was preactivated, or warmed up (think of this process as pre-heating the oven), via its meaningful associations with "white" (the answer to the first three questions) and the word "cow" in the last question. "Milk" therefore became more accessible as a response to the last question than "water," prompting a wrong response. In the following, we shall explore additional principles that are necessary for a comprehensive understanding of semantic networks relevant to OCD.

First, the associations in a semantic network are largely learned (i.e., dependent on past experiences), and often develop and increase in intensity when thoughts and events occur together more and more frequently. For example, we think of the color green when we look out at a meadow, or the color blue when we look up at a clear sky. Owing to shared experiences in any particular culture, people tend to produce very similar associations. For example, people in the United States will typically associate the word "celebrity" with "Brad Pitt" or "Beyoncé," or other famous actors or singers. At the same time, however, specific learning experiences come into play for any individual. A professional tennis player is probably more likely than the average person to associate the word "love" with "zero." In a similar vein, individuals with OCD will have certain idiosyncratic and exaggerated associations due to their experiences with their obsessions and compulsions. Specifically, these individuals process ambiguous concepts that are related to a wide variety of other concepts almost exclusively in the context of their OCD-relevant concerns, rather than also connecting the ambiguous concepts to other neutral, OCD-irrelevant concepts. For example, a sufferer of sexual orientation obsessions will be more likely to associate the word "gay" with their fear of their sexual orientation changing (and subsequent perceived societal rejection and total loss of life satisfaction, etc.), rather than a positive association with the word "happy." Likewise, a person with obsessions about pedophilia, when seeing a bathtub, is more likely to associate that with their fear of molesting their children during their bath (and subsequent rejection by friends and family, as well as incarceration, etc.), rather than a more neutral cognition like taking a nice, warm, relaxing bath at the end of the day. For individuals with S-OCD, these OCD-relevant associations operate in a biased direction, in an intense, catastrophic, chain-like manner, making the alternative associations much weaker than their S-OCD-relevant concerns. There is, in fact, some scientific research demonstrating these observations. Jelinek, Hottenrott, and Moritz (2009) developed an association task that required participants to generate associations for OCD-relevant, negative, and neutral cue words that were either ambiguous or unambiguous. Results indicated that participants with OCD generated significantly more negative, OCD-relevant associations than healthy controls, thereby supporting their hypothesis of biased, negative semantic networks in OCD. Jelinek, Hauschildt, Hottenrott, Kellner, and Moritz (2014) used the same association task in a follow-up study examining biased OCD-relevant semantic networks in OCD patients. As expected, OCD patients generated more negative and OCD-relevant associations to cue words than healthy participants, replicating findings in the previous study. Furthermore, the OCD relevance and emotional valence of these associations improved after cognitive-behavior therapy (CBT) in the OCD patient group. In other words, the strength of biased, negative semantic networks was weakened in these OCD patients.

Second, the development and maintenance of associations can occur either automatically or through practice and rehearsal. For example, when we first learn to drive a car, we consciously look out for red traffic lights as a sign to brake and stop. This association eventually becomes automatic to the extent that we brake and stop the car naturally when we encounter a red traffic light. Similarly, automatic, intrusive associations are a commonplace occurrence for everyone upon encountering certain situations (e.g., thoughts of an upcoming test whenever you walk past the designated exam hall, or having a certain song stuck in your head whenever you enter the gym). Most people pay little attention to these associations, so they do not have much strength. However, in the case of S-OCD (as well as other forms of OCD), the additional, frequent conscious intent to elaborate their S-OCD-relevant thoughts ("Am I going to turn gay?" or "I must be a pedophile!") unfortunately maintains the biased, exaggerated associations characteristic of their obsessions. Additionally, the subsequent performance of compulsions in an attempt to reduce the distress caused by one's obsessions paradoxically strengthens (i.e., negatively reinforces) these S-OCD-relevant associations (see Heyman, Mataix-Cols, & Fineberg, 2006).

Third, the denser a semantic network (i.e., the more associations a particular semantic network contains), the lower the chances of activating any specific association upon encountering a triggering word or thought. This is because activation energy has become more thinly spread out along the various associations in the network. The opposite is true too; the fewer associations there are in a semantic network, the more likely any specific association becomes activated. Such is the case in S-OCD: Activation energy becomes concentrated along a sparse number of biased associations in the S-OCD-relevant semantic network. This also explains why individuals with sexual orientation-OCD almost exclusively associate the word *gay* with their fear of their sexual orientation changing and why, for example, people with pedophilia-themed obsessions are plagued by thoughts of molesting minors whenever they walk past a playground.

In the next section, with these principles in mind, we'll introduce a novel cognitive technique for reducing obsessions that evolved out of the semantic network approach to OCD.

What Is Association Splitting?

In line with the principles laid out in the semantic network framework of obsessions, Moritz and colleagues developed the cognitive technique of *association splitting* to combat the biased OCD-relevant associations commonly found in individuals with OCD (Moritz & Jelinek, 2007, 2011; Moritz & Russu, 2013). It is very important to note that the technique was not developed as a stand-alone treatment for OCD. Rather, it is meant to complement, instead of substitute, standard psychotherapies (e.g., CBT).

Association splitting operates according to the *fan effect* in a semantic network (Anderson, 1974; Reisberg, 2001). What this means is that association splitting weakens associations with any particular concept in an OCD-relevant semantic network by increasing the number of competing associations with that same concept (i.e., *fanning out*, or distributing, activation energy among a greater number of links). Because the practice of association splitting redirects spreading activation away from established associations in an OCD-relevant semantic network to additional, new links with OCD-irrelevant concepts, OCD-relevant associations are weakened over time, while OCD-irrelevant ones are strengthened. At the symptom level, obsessions (and subsequent compulsions) are thereby reduced.

Association splitting is a basic, two-step process. First, one must create OCD-irrelevant associations in the semantic network, which allows for a limited amount of activation energy to be divided more thinly across the different connections in the network. Because these OCD-irrelevant associations also tend to be emotionally positive, the negative emotions affiliated with OCD-relevant associations are simultaneously interfered with, which reduces urges to perform related compulsions. Second, if the new, OCD-irrelevant associations are consistently practiced, they tend to become stronger in intensity (just like a muscle that grows stronger with training) than the OCD-relevant associations, which are consequently neglected and weakened.

Take, for example, the nonpathological case of a child learning the meaning of the word "fruit." At first, he might associate it strongly with the word "apple," if he was frequently fed applesauce. However, later on, as the child learns other meanings for "fruit" as his parents feed him other fruits more regularly, he might generate alternative associations (e.g., "pear," "orange"), therefore making the initial connection with "apple" less dominant. In the context of sexual obsessions, the steps are the same. A person with pedophilia-themed obsessions may, at the onset of such obsessions, exaggeratedly associate the words "child" and "playground" with the concepts of "molestation" and "pedophile," as opposed to alternative associations with "joy" and "happiness." The goal of association splitting is then to first expand the semantic network in question with alternative, nonpedophilia-relevant associations that compete with pedophilia-relevant associations for activation energy, and subsequently practice nonpedophilia-relevant associations to strengthen their intensity to a higher level than the pedophilia-relevant ones. This, again, occurs via the voluntary redirection of activation energy to the nonpedophilia-relevant associations, which happens during the practice of association splitting. With association splitting, OCD-relevant associations (and therefore obsessions) are weakened because activation energy now diverts more strongly to OCD-irrelevant associations.

Findings from a study conducted by Ching, Goh, and Tan (2015) support the two-step process of association splitting. In that study, contamination-relevant, negatively valenced, and neutral word lists each consisting of 10 words semantically related to an unpresented word (i.e., the critical lure) were presented to an unscreened sample of 142 Singaporean college students (106 females and 36 males). Previous studies using similar lists have indicated that people tend to falsely recognize critical lures (i.e., wrongly saying that unpresented words were previously presented in the lists). For each list, participants were instructed to either process the meaning of each word in a relational or item-specific manner. The relational semantic processing instructions had participants think of the meaning of each word that related it to other words in the same list and was intended to simulate an obsessive processing of the words in question. On the other hand, the item-specific semantic processing instructions required participants to think of a unique meaning or creative use of each word that differentiated it from other words in the same list. This was intended to simulate the technique of association splitting as applied to the words in each list. Results indicated substantially lower rates of false recognizing critical lures (contamination-relevant and otherwise) with simulated association splitting, compared with simulated obsessions. Therefore, this was evidence that limited activation energy had been divided more thinly along the additional OCD-irrelevant associations created during simulated association splitting, as the technique purports to do.

Association Splitting: A Case Description

Hottenrott, Jelinek, Kellner, and Mortiz (2011) presented a case description of a 46-year-old female receiving inpatient CBT services (e.g., in vivo exposure) for severe contamination OCD (e.g., obsessions about getting infected by germs, disgust in response to perceived contamination, fear of transmitting contamination to others, as well as washing compulsions performed for an average of almost eight hours per day). Association splitting was administered as an adjunct treatment over six 60-minute sessions following initial moderate reduction in OCD symptoms with exposure therapy. The following summarizes how association splitting was implemented with the patient.

In the first association splitting session, the theoretical background of the technique was explained. A good understanding of the theoretical fundamentals was seen as essential for the correct application of the technique. At the end of the session, the therapist handed the association splitting manual to the patient, with instructions to read it thoroughly to consolidate knowledge.

At the beginning of the second session, the patient was asked questions about how association splitting worked to demonstrate understanding of the theoretical background of the technique. The therapist and the patient then spent the session exploring and accurately summarizing the cognitions and concepts at the core of the patient's contamination-related obsessions. The patient was then assigned homework to write down as many positive or neutral noncontamination-relevant associations to the core OCD concepts/cognitions as possible for the next session.

In the third session, the therapist reviewed the homework assignment, troubleshooting where necessary (e.g., clarifying that generated associations were indeed positive or neutral and not linked semantically to her core obsessive fears about falling sick, feeling disgusted, or contaminating others). The therapist also sourced for a few example pictures to illustrate the new noncontamination-relevant associations that the patient had generated, collating all of this visually on a worksheet. Near the end of the session, the therapist reviewed how the technique should be practiced with the patient (i.e., picking a core contamination-relevant concept and saying it either aloud or in her mind, then connecting it to new contamination-irrelevant associations in the same way, and/or imagining these associations in her mind with the respective visual images). The rules of association splitting were also emphasized (e.g., practicing it for a maximum of 10 minutes per practice and never using association splitting practice as a compulsive ritual to neutralize obsessions about contamination, etc.).

For the entirety of the fourth session, the patient practiced the technique, first as guided by the therapist and the worksheets and then alone for a few of her core obsessive cognitions/concepts. The next two sessions dealt with more core cognitions, creating more worksheets as appropriate, and practicing association splitting for each worksheet, making sure to adhere to the guidelines for practice. The last association splitting session summarized treatment gains with the technique, as well as how the patient can independently incorporate association splitting exercises as a self-help tool into her everyday life.

Similarities and Differences between Association Splitting and Other Approaches to Treating OCD

It may be useful at this point to explore the similarities and differences between association splitting and other approaches to treating OCD. For example, one may point out that association splitting exercises seem analogous to exposure and response prevention (Ex/RP) procedures. In other words, much like how clients in Ex/RP are exposed to OCD-relevant stimuli and instructed to refrain from acting upon triggered anxiety and compulsions, clients practicing association splitting come into contact with words at the core of their obsessive cognitions and are instructed to engage in rehearsing non-OCD-relevant associations, instead of performing rituals. While a valid observation, the elements of Ex/RP are found in other cognitive techniques as well (e.g., cognitive restructuring). Indeed, the reverse is true; Ex/RP can have an effect on obsessive cognitions (e.g., obsessive beliefs), even if this is not the specific focus of the treatment. It is apparent that these mechanisms of action are largely intertwined in most CBT procedures. The key difference therefore lies in the rationale that therapists convey explicitly to clients for the treatment. In association splitting, the core rationale is to redistribute limited activation energy over non-OCD-relevant associations so as to weaken OCD-relevant associations (i.e., obsessions) over time. On the other hand, in Ex/RP, the core rationale, traditionally, is to habituate to anxiety during exposure to threatening actual or imagined stimuli over time.

Another therapeutic approach is pertinent in this discussion. Based on an extensive basic research program on human language and cognition termed *relational frame theory* (RFT), acceptance and commitment therapy (ACT; described in Chapter 3) represents a new wave of cognitive-behavioral procedures that conceptualizes psychopathology in a different manner (Hayes, 2004; Hayes, Luoma, Bond, Masuda, & Lillis, 2006; Hayes, Levin, Plumb-Vilardaga, Villatte, & Pistorello, 2013; Twohig, 2012). According to RFT, at the heart of normative human cognition and behavior is the ability to learn to construct relational frames. In abstract terms, one can learn that stimulus A is smaller than stimulus B (and that B is larger than A) in a particular context. If one learns that B is also smaller than stimulus C (and that C is larger than B) in the same context, then one can respond to A as something that is smaller than C (and that C is larger than A) in that context. Responses to A, B, and C according to implicit rules about their relations to each other in a particular context thereby represent a relational frame.

Psychopathology then, according to RFT/ACT, is primarily conceptualized as psychological inflexibility, in which there is poor or absent control over the application of relational frames across contexts, leading to impairment in the ability to voluntarily persist in or change behaviors in adaptive, valued ways. For example, a client suffering from obsessions of sexual harm toward infants will tend to experience contact with infants as dangerous and immoral, regardless of the context (see Masuda, Hayes, Sackett, & Twohig, 2004; Twohig, 2009; Twohig, Hayes, & Masuda, 2006). In a psychologically inflexible manner, objects that come into contact with infants (e.g., baby wipes, baby cot beds, nursing bottles, toys, etc.) will then acquire the function of being dangerous, and contact with such objects will be construed as indicative of personal moral failure, again regardless of the context.

As such, the general goal of ACT is to increase psychological flexibility, and it has been shown in several studies to be helpful in treating OCD (Bluett, Homan, Morrison, Levin, & Twohig, 2014; Swain, Hancock, Hainsworth, & Bowman, 2013; Twohig, Plumb-Vilardaga, Levin, & Hayes, 2015). It is important to note that ACT differs fundamentally from CBT procedures in that ACT emphasizes changing how one becomes aware of and relates to thoughts, feelings, and sensations, as opposed to changing the contents of such psychological phenomena as in CBT. Thus, if a client thinks that they are an immoral person because of their pedophilia-themed obsessions, instead of correcting the validity of that thought as in CBT, ACT will help the client relate to that thought in a more adaptive way while not modifying its content. This is achieved via six core processes, which include acceptance and cognitive defusion (e.g., repeating a feared word over and over again until it loses its meaning, to demonstrate to the client that fear responses to the meaning of the word need not occur across all contexts).

From our previous discussion, it is obvious that association splitting is much more aligned with conventional CBT tradition than "third-wave" approaches such as ACT. Superficially, there seems to be an abstract similarity in the idea of *relations* as crucial to semantic network models and RFT. However, in the former, this entails the more specific domain of biased semantic associations, while in the latter, as applied clinically, this refers to the broader idea of inflexible application of relational frames across contexts (e.g., generalizing fear responses to previously innocuous contexts). Furthermore, association splitting is dissimilar to RFT/ACT in an extremely important aspect: The goal of association splitting is to change actual content of biased semantic networks by emphasizing non-OCD-relevant associations (i.e., a strong CBT rationale), while the goal of RFT/ACT is to change how individuals relate to the content of their thoughts. By emphasizing this key difference between association splitting and ACT processes, we therefore hope to highlight the incremental utility of incorporating association splitting, alongside ACT processes as mentioned elsewhere in this book, as part of a holistic, multitheoretical therapeutic approach for OCD.

Research Evidence for the Efficacy of Association Splitting

There have been several other studies conducted by Moritz and colleagues to examine whether association splitting works to improve OCD symptoms.

In the first of these studies, Moritz et al. (2007) tested the efficacy of association splitting for reducing OCD symptoms according to an Internet-based, self-help intervention protocol. Specifically, the researchers posted invitations to participate in the study on two Web forums specially created for individuals suffering from OCD. Thirty-eight registered forum users with self-reported OCD were recruited for an online survey, which consisted of the Maudsley Obsessive Compulsive Inventory questionnaire (MOCI; Hodgson & Rachman, 1977), the Yale–Brown Obsessive-Compulsive Scale-Self-Report Version (Y-BOCS; Goodman et al., 1989; Steketee, Frost, & Bogart, 1996), and the Beck Depression Inventory (BDI; Beck, Ward, Mendelson, Mock, & Erbaugh, 1961). The association splitting manual (Moritz & Jelinek, 2007) was then emailed to participants upon completion of the survey, with regular check-ins about the implementation of the technique. Three weeks later, participants were emailed a link to complete another online survey containing the same measures, with a response rate of 84.2%. Results demonstrated that the association splitting technique was very helpful in reducing OCD symptoms. Intention-to-treat analyses indicated that 33% of participants reported substantial subjective symptom relief from association splitting, as well as significant symptom decline of 35% or more on the Y-BOCS. Per protocol analyses showed a treatment response rate of 42% for participants who responded to the postintervention survey. Analyses of supplementary questions further indicated that 77% of participants felt that the association splitting technique was easy to apply to their OCD symptoms, 93% easily comprehended the association splitting instructions, and 86% expressed interest in continuing to practice association splitting order to cope with their OCD symptoms. However, there were a few limitations to the study. For example, there was no control group for definitive randomized clinical trial comparisons. Additionally, no diagnostic interviews were conducted to verify participants' self-reported OCD status and specific OCD symptom dimension(s) (e.g., how many participants suffered from sexual obsessions). Lastly, long-term assessments of maintenance of symptom improvements are also needed.

Moritz and Jelinek (2011) conducted a subsequent replication study, with several improvements. First, invitations to participate in the study were posted on more recruitment outlets (e.g., specialized Internet forums for individuals with OCD, online OCD support groups, and the websites of international, not-for-profit OCD organizations). Second, to participate, participants had to fulfill the same prerequisites as the original study, as well as provide documented proof of having received a diagnosis of OCD by a healthcare professional. Third, participants were randomly assigned to either the association splitting intervention or waitlist control group. At first, 66 participants were recruited for the baseline online survey consisting of the Obsessive-Compulsive Inventory-Revised (OCI-R; Foa et al., 2002), the Y-BOCS, and the BDI. Twenty participants withdrew prematurely from the study at this stage; therefore, the remaining 46 participants were equally and randomly assigned to either condition (ns = 23). The association splitting manual was emailed to participants in the association splitting condition immediately upon completion of the baseline survey, and any questions about the application of the technique were promptly clarified via email. Four weeks later, participants were emailed a link to complete the postintervention online survey containing the same measures, with a response rate of 74%. Similar to the previous study, association splitting was shown to be efficacious in reducing OCD symptoms: There was a 25% decline in scores on the Y-BOCS (especially on the obsessions and resistance subscales) with medium to strong effect sizes in the association splitting group, compared with the waitlist control group. Association splitting also had a positive impact on BDI scores and scores on the OCI-R obsessions subscale. Importantly, these findings were obtained with completers who, at the outset, tend to suffer from more severe OCD symptoms than noncompleters. Subjective opinions of the technique in the association splitting group were also generally favorable, with 82% of participants expressing interest in continuing practicing the technique in the future. However, an important limitation of the study was the high dropout rate in the association splitting group, especially compared with the control group. The researchers speculate that this was either due to a lack of symptom improvement, the tendency for males (majority of noncompleters) to drop out, or lower OCD symptom severity among noncompleters, which possibly present as risk factors for noncompliance with protocol. Notably,

OCD symptom dimensions were not examined separately in the analyses. Therefore, at this point, it is not known whether association splitting was efficacious in reducing, say, sexual obsessions alone, or more than any other symptom dimension.

Rodríguez-Martín, Moritz, Molerio-Pérez, and Gil-Pérez (2013) investigated the efficacy of association splitting for reducing thought suppression in a small, nonclinical community sample in Cuba. Forty-nine participants (mean age = 35.67 years, SD = 10.79) who met inclusion criteria (i.e., classified as "healthy" by the Cuban National Health Care System, experiencing regular unwanted intrusive thoughts, and not having received psychological or medical treatment for mental health issues) were randomly assigned to the association splitting (18 females, 8 males) or waitlist control group (18 females, 5 males). The White Bear Suppression Inventory (WBSI; Wegner & Zanakos, 1994) was used to assess changes in thought suppression after a two-week interval. Additionally, the association splitting manual was modified to suit the needs of nonclinical individuals in the association splitting group. For example, there was more psychoeducational information on intrusive thoughts and their prevalence in the general population, as well as the paradoxical effects of thought suppression. Association splitting instructions were also tailored to target intrusive thoughts instead of, more broadly, OCD. Results indicated that association splitting significantly reduced thought suppression with a large effect size, compared with the waitlist control group. Analysis of supplementary responses on difficulty to get rid of unwanted intrusive thoughts also revealed that only participants in the association splitting group reported a significantly easier time getting rid of such thoughts after the intervention. Furthermore, participants in the association splitting group reported benefits, on average, just six days after implementing the technique, and all participants in the association splitting group viewed the technique as effective. Although the sample was a nonclinical one, the participants endorsed unwanted intrusive thoughts, as well as counterproductive means of coping with these thoughts (i.e., thought suppression), all of which are risk factors for the development of OCD. Therefore, these findings were still relevant to the question of whether association splitting might be helpful for addressing OCD symptoms and related maladaptive coping strategies. However, the contents of these unwanted intrusive thoughts were only broadly classified into "family issues," "couple issues" and "other issues." Once again, the findings do not tell us whether association splitting was helpful in specifically reducing unwanted sexual intrusive thoughts.

Jelinek et al. (2014) investigated whether incremental improvements in OCD-relevant semantic networks would be observed with association splitting (compared with computerized cognitive training) as an add-on intervention to standard CBT for OCD. Seventy patients with OCD were recruited from several mental health clinics in Hamburg, Germany. These patients were randomly assigned to either the CBT-plus-association splitting or a CBT-plus-computerized cognitive training group. CBT consisted of 15 individual sessions. Each add-on intervention consisted of six 50-min sessions over three weeks (two sessions per week), which began one to two weeks after admission into treatment, alongside CBT. Participants receiving association splitting as an add-on intervention were guided with the manual on how to apply the technique to their obsessions, while participants in the other group underwent a cognitive remediation program that addressed the different cognitive domains (e.g., attention, memory). Thirty-six participants were additionally recruited for the healthy control group. In the association task presented to all participants at baseline and posttreatment, participants were instructed to generate up to five associations to standardized OCD-relevant, negative, neutral, and idiosyncratic cue words. Associations were then categorized based on OCD relevance and emotional valence. Results indicated posttreatment improvements in biased semantic networks in OCD patients pertaining to idiosyncratic cue words, particularly for those receiving association splitting as an add-on intervention. Specifically, in the CBT-plus-association splitting group, there were increases in neutral and positive OCD-irrelevant associations, as well as decreases in negative OCD-irrelevant associations. These changes were expected, given the underlying mechanisms of association splitting. Although these findings were highly encouraging in their support of the efficacy of association splitting for targeting biased semantic networks in OCD broadly, there were still several limitations. For example, the researchers cite the absence of a formal examination of interrater reliability for classifying associations. There were also no clinical control or CBT-only groups. Additionally, OCD symptom heterogeneity was high in the OCD patient sample, and although cue words relevant to sexual obsessions were included in the association task, the associations that participants generated were analyzed only according to general OCD relevance. As such, it was not possible to infer the efficacy of association splitting for improving semantic networks relevant to sexual obsessions.

Very recently, we conducted our own investigation into the efficacy of association splitting for improving biased semantic networks and symptoms specifically relevant to sexual orientation-OCD (SO-OCD) in college students (Ching & Williams, 2018). SO-OCD symptoms can involve unwanted thoughts about sexual activities contrary to one's sexual orientation, and/or fears about one's sexuality changing (Williams, 2008; Williams, Crozier, & Powers, 2011; Williams, Slimowicz, Tellawi, & Wetterneck, 2014). As discussed in previous chapters, the doubt and anxiety from perceived judgment by others often lead to compulsions, which include reassurance seeking and checking for physical/sexual arousal, particularly around members of the sex contrary to one's established sexual preferences (Williams, Tellawi, Davis, & Slimowicz, 2015; Williams, Wetterneck, Tellawi, & Duque, 2015). Not much research has been conducted on the treatment of SO-OCD symptoms, which is especially alarming given the substantial prevalence of SO-OCD concerns (e.g., 10% of treatment-seeking individuals; Williams & Farris, 2011). To test whether association splitting works for SO-OCD symptoms, 120 undergraduates (82 females, 38 males) from a large Midwestern university were randomly assigned to either the association splitting or waitlist control group. Criteria for inclusion were being 18 years or older and mental health treatment naivety. In the initial session, participants completed baseline measures of SO-OCD symptoms using the Sexual Orientation Obsessions and Reactions Test (SORT; Williams et al., 2018), sexual obsessions using the Sexually Intrusive Thoughts Scale (Wetterneck, Siev, Adams, Slimowicz, & Smith, 2015), and thought suppression using the WBSI. Participants also completed an association task in which they generated associations to SO-OCD-relevant, negatively valenced, and neutral cue words. Those in the association splitting group received a version of the association splitting manual modified for SO-OCD concerns. Four weeks later, participants were contacted to complete the same measures and association task, yielding a 100% response rate. Generated associations were classified into predetermined categories based on SO-OCD relevance and emotional valence. Results indicated statistically significant reductions in both SO-OCD-relevant associations across levels of emotional valence, as well as negative SO-OCD-irrelevant associations, only in the association splitting group. These were accompanied by statistically significant increases in positive and neutral SO-OCD-irrelevant associations. Furthermore, there were statistically significant decreases in SO-OCD symptoms, sexual obsessions, and thought suppression only for participants in the association splitting group. Therefore, association splitting appears to work in reducing SO-OCD symptoms and thought suppression in an unscreened sample of college students. However, future research with diagnosed SO-OCD patient samples needs to be conducted to determine whether symptom improvement can be maintained for this particular OCD symptom dimension. Nonetheless, these findings are encouraging in that they provide support for the use of association splitting in targeting a particular subset of sexual obsessions.

Why Use Association Splitting?

Even though there is substantial evidence showing that association splitting works in reducing OCD symptoms, the question remains as to why this technique should even be used to complement effective CBT programs that are already available for treating OCD. In the following, we'll explore the practical advantages of association splitting for overcoming various barriers to treatment, which enhance its clinical utility when used to complement face-to-face CBT for OCD.

Financial difficulties, the lack of affordable healthcare and related subsidies, as well as poor accessibility to OCD treatment in rural areas or developing countries are a few of the obvious barriers to treatment that make simpler methods such as association splitting a viable (and sometimes the only) alternative to conventional face-to-face therapy (e.g., Marques et al., 2010). Additionally, individuals sometimes report disruptions in daily functioning due to OCD symptoms without necessarily meeting full criteria for a diagnosis of OCD, which leads to nonreimbursement by insurance companies for psychological services (Fullana et al., 2009). Furthermore, some therapists may have reservations about treating individuals with OCD or even refuse to treat them outright due to prejudiced and surprisingly stigmatic views about their poor cooperativeness and/or responsivity to therapy (Hand, 1991). Association splitting, as a self-help tool, will likely be helpful in these cases in providing some symptom relief at no financial cost.

An additional significant barrier to treatment is stigma about mental illness and mental health treatment. OCD symptoms, particularly those of a repugnant and/or sexual nature, are frequently concealed and underreported due to shame and embarrassment (Newth & Rachman, 2001) and/or the fear of involuntary hospitalization (Glazier, Wetterneck, Singh, & Williams, 2015). Unacceptable/taboo forms of OCD also tend to be improperly assessed and treated, in turn increasing clients' mistrust of psychological services (Moritz, Timpano, Wittekind, & Knaevelsrud, 2013), as well as their fear of being wrongly diagnosed with relatively more stigmatizing labels (e.g., "schizophrenia" or "pedophilic disorder"; Glazier, Calixte, Rothschild, & Pinto, 2013). In other cases, the improper treatment of repugnant and/or sexual obsessions may unintentionally escalate clients' fear of losing their friends and loved ones due to perceived societal judgment and punishment. The client may even internalize an inaccurate illness identity (e.g., an individual with pedophilia-themed obsessions erroneously believing that he is really a pedophile), leading to actual rejection by others, as well as potential legal repercussions.

More important, the issue of stigma intersects with considerations of ethnoracial minority clients' different cultural backgrounds (Glazier, Wetterneck et al., 2015). For example, compared with non-Hispanic Whites, African Americans endorse more negative attitudes about mental illness, feel a stronger need to conceal symptoms of mental disorders, report greater fears of discrimination by treatment providers, are more likely to mistrust the mental health profession, and are less likely to know where to seek help (Williams, Domanico, Marques, Leblanc, & Turkheimer, 2012). African Americans also tend to believe that conventional, face-to-face mental health services are designed with the needs of non-Hispanic Whites in mind, with little consideration of their particular socioeconomic difficulties and limited access to treatment (Alvidrez, Snowden, & Kaiser, 2008; Thompson, Bazile, & Akbar, 2004). Furthermore, prevalent pathological stereotyping of African Americans as criminal and sexually predatory or deviant (Williams, Gooden, & Davis, 2012), combined with their unique presentation of OCD symptoms, elevate African Americans' fears of being misunderstood and misdiagnosed in face-to-face treatment (Williams, Elstein, Buckner, Abelson, & Himle, 2012). This is particularly relevant in cases in which Black individuals suffer from sexual obsessions. It is therefore no wonder that only 40% of African Americans with any kind of OCD report these concerns to a physician (Simmons et al., 2012), and only 60% of African Americans with severe OCD receive treatment (Himle et al., 2008), compared with 93% of all Americans with severe OCD (Ruscio, Stein, Chiu, & Kessler, 2010).

Similarly, Latino/Hispanic Americans, particularly Latino/Hispanic American men, tend to view mental illness and mental health services negatively, compared with non-Hispanic Whites (e.g., Hampton & Sharp, 2014; Nicolini et al., 1997). This is perhaps due to immigrant cultural values such as *spirituality* (i.e., ascribing mental illness to supernatural causes) and *fatalism* (i.e., that the environment, instead of the individual, controls one's life outcomes; Kouyoumdjian, Zamboanga, & Hansen, 2003). Other gender-specific cultural attitudes include those of *machismo* (i.e., hypermasculinity) and *caballerismo* (i.e., chivalry and defending the weak; Arciniega, Anderson, Tovar-Blank, & Tracey, 2008), both of which discourage Latino/Hispanic American men from admitting mental illness and seeking help in face-to-face psychotherapy (Saez, Casado, & Wade, 2009). Additionally, disproportionately more Latino/Hispanic Americans are uninsured, compared with rates among non-Hispanic Whites, thereby severely limiting their access to necessary specialty treatment (Alegría et al., 2002). Therefore, this might be why less than 9% of Latino/Hispanic Americans with a mental disorder seek help from mental health services (Wetterneck, Little, Rinehart, Cervantes, & Burgess, 2010).

In Asian Americans, socioeconomic difficulties, poor or lack of health insurance coverage, and stigmatic attitudes against mental illness and mental health treatment are also relevant barriers to treatment (e.g., Cheon & Chiao, 2012). However, Asian Americans have to grapple additionally with positive, model minority stereotypes about themselves as intelligent and academically successful (Son & Shelton, 2011), which may ironically be a source of distress and deter endorsement of mental illness and help-seeking from mental health professionals (Leong, Kim, & Gupta, 2011).

In light of these barriers to treatment, it makes sense to use association splitting as a cost-free, readily available, adjunct tool for individuals with OCD, particularly those of an ethnoracial minority status, who might not report, seek, or receive proper treatment for such concerns (see Moritz, Wittekind, Hauschildt, & Timpano, 2011). Engaging in association splitting also communicates to clients that their OCD is not omnipotent and unchangeable (cf. the cultural attitudes of spirituality and fatalism in Latino/Hispanic American clients). Rather, the cognitive model based on simple learning principles described within the manual should educate clients that their associations are learned and do not stem from an "inner evil" and that these associations can be voluntarily redirected and changed to some extent, thereby motivating clients to challenge the power that they perceive OCD has over them.

Finally, for clients who do enter CBT for OCD, there is a strong theoretical chance of symptom improvement, given encouraging evidence from randomized controlled trials for the effectiveness of CBT and/or psychopharmacotherapy (see Franklin & Foa, 2011). Nonetheless, several obstacles may occur during the therapeutic process in actual clinical practice. For example, the current gold-standard technique of Ex/RP is associated with less-than-optimal rates of treatment adherence in practice, due to the client's unwillingness to engage in exposure to feared stimuli and/or the therapist's lack of training and experience in administering Ex/RP (Kulz et al., 2009). Ex/RP may also be less successful in treating obsessions, compared with compulsions (Moritz et al., 2007). Furthermore, other conventional techniques such as behavioral experiments may be challenging or even unethical to construct and implement (Moritz & Jelinek, 2011), especially when the individual suffers from sexual or otherwise morally repugnant obsessions. In light of these issues, association splitting again presents as a useful, complementary technique in the initial help-seeking phase to boost chances of successful subsequent treatment in face-to-face therapy (Moritz et al., 2013). As the first step in a stepped-care model for OCD (Mataix-Cols & Marks, 2006), association splitting can also be useful in correcting patients' misconceptions about their symptoms and psychotherapy in general, thereby motivating them to seek more intensive treatment from a mental health professional. This can be helpful especially for individuals reluctant to seek help, who would otherwise not receive necessary psychotherapy for a long time (Besiroglu, Cilli, & Askin, 2004).

A Step-by-Step Walkthrough of the Association Splitting Technique: How Therapists Can Guide Clients in Their Practice

The association splitting self-help manual (Moritz & Jelinek, 2007) is available online at the following URL: https://clinical-neuropsychology.de/manual_association_splitting_english/ or from the authors. There are several translated versions available, including in English, French, German, Italian, Russian, and Spanish. The manual can be downloaded and printed if necessary, prior to using this technique.

The association splitting technique was developed for individuals who suffer from obsessions in any of the major OCD symptom dimensions of contamination concerns, responsibility for harm, symmetry or ordering concerns, as well as unacceptable thoughts with sexual, religious, or violent themes. The technique might not be suitable for individuals who perform physical or mental compulsions without awareness of their triggering obsessions. This technique might also be less helpful for individuals with low insight, that is, those who do not acknowledge that their obsessions are absurd, exaggerated, and irrational. It is important for therapists to be aware of these potential limitations for their clients before getting started.

The manual contains information about what a semantic network is, as well as the learning principles that contribute to the network. Although written in a layperson's fashion with several diagrams included to aid comprehension, therapists can still go over the respective contents with their clients to clarify questions. Therapist involvement is also helpful in maximizing treatment adherence, since previous studies of related self-help treatment methods for OCD have documented poor outcomes due to low motivation to complete out-of-session intervention exercises (see Schneider, Wittekind, Talhof, Korrelboom, & Moritz, 2015). There is also psychoeducational information about the prevalence of intrusive thoughts and how individuals with OCD appraise such thoughts differently (e.g., the influence of obsessive beliefs and related appraisals), as well as information on maladaptive coping strategies (e.g., thought suppression) that ironically reinforce obsessions. Very often in CBT for OCD, similar psychoeducation is conducted to normalize the client's intrusive thoughts, prior to introducing the proposed treatment plan (e.g., Ex/RP). This information in the manual is therefore helpful for clients to gain greater clarity about their symptoms, as well as knowledge about the maladaptive ways in which they may be coping with their obsessions.

In the following, to conclude the chapter, we will conduct a simplified, step-by-step walkthrough of how to practice techniques that will be helpful for therapists and their clients, with a modified focus on sexual obsessions. To facilitate association splitting exercises outside of therapy sessions, therapists can also provide clients with a copy of the handout with tips and reminders that we have prepared to accompany this chapter (see Appendix A, Handout 12).

Step 1

Clients practicing the technique should seek out a quiet place with a relaxed atmosphere. The environment should not contain any triggers for the client's OCD concerns. For example, the client with pedophilia-themed obsessions should not practice the technique in situations (e.g., at the playground) or near objects (e.g., the baby cot in the next room) that may trigger their OCD concerns. For therapists guiding clients through association splitting practice in sessions, objects (especially Ex/RP stimuli) that might trigger clients' OCD concerns should be removed from the therapy room. Importantly, the client should not be experiencing obsessions or compulsive urges at the time of practice. Therapists should check in about this prior to practicing the technique with clients.

Step 2

Clients should then write down individual words that are most representative and almost always present in the contents of their obsessions. For example, the client with sexual orientation OCD may write down the words "gay," "sex," "straight," "orientation," etc. Tables 4.1 and 4.2 provide nonexhaustive lists of examples of possible words for a limited variety of sexual obsessions. Clients who find it difficult to generate representative words can look at these examples for ideas. Therapists may also use these examples to help clients in coming up with representative words, in addition to generating idiosyncratic words relevant to the contents of sexual obsessions identified in therapy.

Step 3

After generating representative words, clients should select *at least two words for each obsession*. Clients can decide whether or not they want to include more than two words for each type of obsession. Therapists can assist clients in these decisions.

Table 4.1 Possible Representative Words and OCD-Irrelevant Associations for Sexual Orientation Obsessive-Compulsive Disorder

Examples	Possible Representative Words	Possible Associations—Be Creative!
1. Concerns about your sexual orientation changing 2. Avoiding same-/different-sex individuals 3. Checking your sexual arousal around same- vs. different-sex individuals 4. Seeking reassurance that your sexual orientation is not changing	gay straight orientation lesbian bisexual closet confused identity sex penis	gay → day (rhyme); gaze (rhyme); happy; Gaylord Focker from Meet the Parents (film); etc. straight → straight flush; eight (rhyme); third straight win; straight from the heart; date (rhyme); etc. orientation → Oreo cookie (emphasizing a syllable); North, South, East West; freshman year; meditation (rhyme); etc. lesbian → amphibian (rhyme); Arabian (rhyme); Serbian (rhyme); Colombian (rhyme); etc. bisexual → biennial (rhyme); bilingual (rhyme); bidirectional (rhyme); intellectual (rhyme); etc. closet → wardrobe; clothes; Home Depot (company); Telco (letter-dropping, letter rearrangement/company name); deposit (rhyme); etc. confused → Dazed and Confused (film); amused (rhyme); defused (rhyme); etc. identity → driver's license; The Bourne Identity (film); entity (rhyme); etc. sex → biology; Malcolm X (rhyme/person); checks (rhyme); decks (rhyme); etc. penis → Venus (rhyme); genus (rhyme); pens (letter-dropping); etc.
5. Questions about your sexual orientation (e.g., "Am I going to turn gay?")	→	When such threatening thoughts come to mind, don't counter them. Instead, associate them with obviously absurd or unanswerable questions, such as: How many trees are there in the world? Who will win the next NFL championship?

Table 4.2 Possible Representative Words and OCD-Irrelevant Associations for Obsessions about Infidelity, Pedophilia, or Incest

Examples	Possible Representative Words	Possible Associations—Be Creative!
1. Concerns about cheating on your significant other, or fears about actually being a pedophile or committing incest 2. Avoiding others (adults, children, relatives, etc.) for fear of committing infidelity or pedophilic or incestuous acts 3. Checking your sexual arousal around others (adults, children, relatives, etc.) 4. Seeking reassurance that you are not guilty of infidelity, pedophilic acts, or incest	*confused* *sex* *penis* *cheater* *baby* *incest* *molest* *child* *rape* *sin*	*confused* → *Dazed and Confused* (film); *amused* (rhyme); *defused* (rhyme); etc. *sex* → *biology*; *Malcolm X* (rhyme/person); *checks* (rhyme); *decks* (rhyme); etc. *penis* → *Venus* (rhyme); *genus* (rhyme); *pens* (letter-dropping); etc. *cheater* → *Cheetos* (rhyme); *heater* (letter-dropping); *Don Cheadle* (actor); etc. *baby* → *Baby* (Justin Bieber song); *Bambi* (Disney film character); *bay* (letter-dropping); etc. *incest* → *insect* (letter rearrangement); *indeed* (emphasizing a syllable); *c'est la vie* (emphasizing a syllable); etc. *molest* → *unless* (emphasizing a syllable); *mole fries* (emphasizing a syllable); *most* (letter-dropping); etc. *child* → *O-O-H Child* (The Five Stairsteps song); *chia seeds* (emphasizing a syllable); *chill* (letter substitution); etc. *rape* → *drape* (rhyme); *grape* (rhyme); *ape* (rhyme); etc. *sin* → *sine* (mathematical symbol); *cosine* (mathematical symbol); *tin* (letter substitution, rhyme); etc.
5. Questioning yourself about whether you are guilty of infidelity, pedophilic acts, or incest	→	When such threatening thoughts come to mind, don't counter them. Instead, associate them with obviously absurd or unanswerable questions, such as: *How many flowers are there in the world?* *Which country will have the most golds in the next Olympic Games?*

Step 4

After clients have selected representative words that they want to target for each obsession, they should write down *at least three new associations to each word* that are neutral or positive. In other words, these new,

OCD-irrelevant associations are not fear-provoking, and would branch out of the constraints of the respective OCD-relevant semantic network. These new associations should also make sense and can be words, phrases, sayings, rhetorical questions, etc. that rhyme and/or connect in meaning, perhaps even as an associative chain moving out of the respective OCD-relevant semantic network. Importantly, while generating new associations, clients should avoid those associations that deny or otherwise run directly counter to their obsessions (e.g., "infant" → "I would never touch an infant inappropriately!"), because there are no alternative meanings or themes involved. These counterassociations tend to backfire, much like thought suppression, ultimately reinforcing their obsessions. Instead, the goal should be to build up alternative meanings when generating new associations. Clients are encouraged to be as creative as possible and to introduce humor into their new associations wherever possible, because the positive emotions that accompany such associations will help in combating the negative emotionality of established OCD-relevant associations. Tables 4.1 and 4.2 show nonexhaustive lists of example associations that therapists and clients can use for inspiration. Attaching vivid visual images to newly generated associations is also helpful in the practice of association splitting, since imagery encourages the formation of strong associations. Internet search engines (with the appropriate search filters) provide a rich source of pictorial stimuli that clients can memorize as visual images to accompany their newly generated OCD-irrelevant associations.

Step 5

Once clients have generated a sufficient number of OCD-irrelevant associations, they can begin their association splitting practice. First, clients should start by picking a word that they have selected to be representative of their obsessions (e.g., "gay") and saying it either out loud or in their mind. Shortly thereafter, clients should connect this word to the different OCD-irrelevant associations that they have previously generated by saying these associations out loud (e.g., "day," "gaze," "happy," "Gaylord Focker"), and/or imagining it in their mind with related visual images. Experiencing these new associations in multiple perceptual modalities will strengthen them. Once this is done, clients should move on to the next word that they have selected to be representative of their obsessions (e.g., "sex"), and repeat

160 SEXUAL OBSESSIONS IN OBSESSIVE-COMPULSIVE DISORDER

the same general process of connecting it to another set of OCD-irrelevant associations (e.g., "biology," "Malcolm X," "checks," "decks") that they have generated for it. This should continue until all of the representative words are targeted and connected to their respective OCD-irrelevant associations. Each practice session should last a maximum of 10 minutes. Therapists can help facilitate this process with clients, especially for their first few practice sessions. The construction of an association splitting diagram will also provide a concise reference for ease of practice. Figure 4.1 shows an example diagram that could be constructed for a client with SO-OCD concerns. Similar diagrams can be constructed for other sexual obsessions. It is important at this point to reiterate that association splitting practice sessions should not be conducted when clients are experiencing obsessions or compulsive urges. The goal of association splitting is to divert activation energy

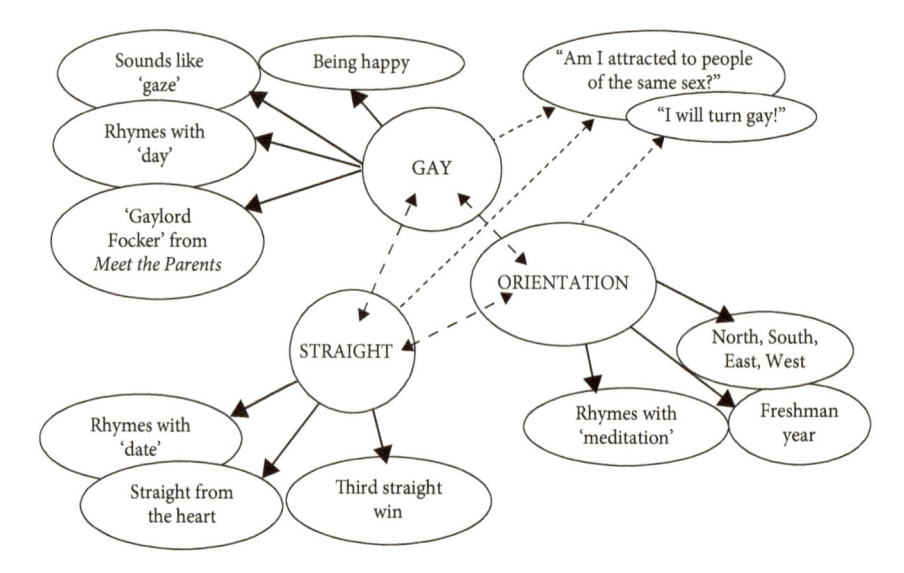

Figure 4.1 A simplified diagram of sexual orientation obsessions ("Am I attracted to people of the same sex?" or "I will turn gay!") involving the core concepts of "gay," "straight," and "orientation," as connected by thin, dashed arrows. New, neutral, and positive associations branch out via thick, solid arrows. The thickness of the arrows shows the strength of the association flow. Association splitting builds strong neutral and/or positive associations leading away from the core concepts of one's obsessions, which weaken the strength of the OCD-relevant semantic network. Eventually, sexual orientation obsessions should subside with consistent practice of the association-splitting technique.

away from core OCD concepts to OCD-irrelevant associations to weaken the OCD-relevant semantic network and reduce obsessions. Therefore, the practice of association splitting itself should not become a compulsive ritual or means of neutralization in immediate response to the experience of obsessions. Indeed, doing so will ironically reinforce perceptions of obsessions as threatening. Therapists should engage clients in an ongoing discussion about the appropriate function of association splitting, correcting any misapplication of the technique as soon as possible. Additionally, it is important for clients to check the direction of their associations as leading *out* of the OCD-relevant semantic network (i.e., "gay" → "day," "gay" → "gaze," "gay" → "happy," etc.), instead of the other way round (i.e., "day" → "gay," "gaze" → "gay," "happy" → "gay," etc.).

Step 6

Clients should continue practicing association splitting daily for as many times during the day as possible, referring to their association splitting diagram if necessary, until their obsessions are weakened and lose their power to trigger compulsive rituals. Although reductions in unwanted intrusive thoughts have been found as early as six days after initiating association splitting practice (Rodríguez-Martín et al., 2013), clients should be advised to continue their practice for durable intervention gains. Therapists can monitor their clients' progress with weekly check-ins about the effects of association splitting on their obsessions. Any difficulties in practicing the technique should be addressed in a collaborative fashion. For example, new OCD-irrelevant associations may need to be created if the previous ones are too difficult or unwieldy to implement. Regardless, clients should recognize that the technique might be difficult to practice at first but will likely become easier as the new associations are strengthened over time.

5
Treating Sexual Orientation Obsessions

Jenifer A. Viscusi and Monnica T. Williams

Case Example of Sexual Orientation Obsessions

Case Introduction

Leo (not his actual name) was a 37-year-old, non-Hispanic White male, unmarried and with no children. He lived with his girlfriend, with whom he had been in a relationship for about three years. He had earned a bachelor's degree in computer science and worked as a computer engineer at local state university. He was raised Catholic but identified his religious affiliation as agnostic.

Presenting Complaints

During his initial meeting, Leo stated that he was worried about being gay and being perceived as gay by others, despite the fact that he had neither been attracted to nor engaged in sexual activities with other men. His biggest fear was that he would blurt out sexually explicit phrases about being gay or begin to have desires to engage in sexual acts with men around him. His fear of blurting was particularly strong at work, at times where he was surrounded by men, and in quiet situations, such as listening to presentations or at staff meetings. Leo feared that if he blurted such obscenities that he would lose his job, face extreme humiliation, and experience social rejection. In addition to the fears of blurting, he had constant fears that he had perhaps been gay his entire life and his relationship with his girlfriend was really just an effort to repress his "true self." Leo believed that others could potentially pick up on cues from his body language and his tone of voice that would cause them to determine that he was really gay. The idea of judgment from others was particularly distressing, because he worried that they would "figure out" his identity before he was ready to determine it for himself. He also feared that, should he be gay, he would deeply hurt his girlfriend and that his friends and family would ridicule him for not "knowing himself." He imagined himself being rejected by both the LGBT community, as well as the heterosexual community, which he believed would result in him being alone and isolated for the rest of his life.

Leo was presented with the diagram illustrating various symptom clusters of obsessive-compulsive disorder (OCD; *OCD Symptom Dimensions*; see Appendix A, Handout 1) and asked to indicate which of the categories he felt was representative of his greatest concerns. He selected the category labeled "Unacceptable/Taboo Thoughts," which was associated with symptoms of "Ruminating, Mental Review, Reassurance, Checking." He was then given the next diagram, which further expands "Unacceptable/Taboo Thoughts" into additional categories. He agreed with the therapist that his worries were represented by the category labeled "Sexual," which included worries about "Sexual Orientation, Pedophilia, and Rape." Leo was surprised and relieved to find that his sexual orientation worries fit into an existing category, and he felt some increased optimism that he could be effectively helped.

The therapist also reviewed *The OCD Cycle* handout with Leo. He demonstrated a good ability to identify his primary compulsions and avoidances. He recognized that he constantly reviewed his interactions with men (primarily at work) to determine if he had blurted obscenities, and he also replayed the situation to mentally check the reactions of others to determine if there were any clues to suggest that he had said something inappropriate or if their body language indicated that they thought he seemed gay. For example, after leaving a meeting, Leo would try to remember everything that he had said, and then he would imagine the expressions of his co-workers. He then would evaluate the meaning of any noteworthy body language that he remembered from the meetings. Leo also reported avoiding speaking in groups and being alone with men, especially if he thought they were attractive. Leo described listening to the sound of his own voice and evaluating his vocabulary, tone, and vocal inflection to decide if it was "gay" or "straight."

Leo initially reported that his symptoms were most impairing at work, as he was limited in not only his interactions with colleagues, but also in theextreme anxiety he felt each work-night in anticipation of meetings and interactive projects. He shared with his therapist that he was holding back many important ideas and information from his team, due to his fears of blurting. He also believed that his potential for growth was limited, since he was not able to lead meetings and was unable to participate in important department decisions, such as interviewing candidates for employment. Although this was not immediately apparent to Leo, his symptoms were causing impairment in his social and romantic functioning as well. He was avoiding participating in many social activities, such as getting coffee alone with a male friend, and even when he was out with friends, he experienced extreme anxiety and discomfort during the interactions. Leo typically remained withdrawn from conversations and thus felt isolated, even in groups. He constantly felt that others were judging him as gay. With regard to his romantic relationship, Leo was physically and emotionally distant from his partner, due to fears that he would eventually have to break up with her for a man. While Leo was open with his partner regarding his OCD symptoms, he also frequently confessed all of his obsessive worries with the hope that she would reassure him about his sexual identity. He also would ask her if she thought others had looked at him strangely, or if she thought he sounded "strange" when speaking.

History

Onset and Treatment History

Leo began to notice symptoms of OCD in his late 20s, when he found himself frequently feeling anxious about being gay, despite the fact that he had no desire to have sex with men. He first entered treatment at the age of 30, working with a male psychologist. His therapy included being assigned reading from books about anxiety and practicing meditation and mindfulness. But these approaches were not helpful. He experienced a worsening of symptoms and felt additional distress by having to spend sessions with a therapist who was a male, and so he quit therapy after a few months. Leo reentered therapy four years later and specifically selected a female therapist, and he worked with her for approximately one year. He described the treatment as "talk therapy" and, despite regular participation in therapy, continued to experience a worsening of his OCD symptoms. Leo remembered feeling frustrated that the therapist would not engage in conversations about sex with him, and thus he felt as though he was unable to process his confusion surrounding healthy sexual behavior. Neither therapist ever diagnosed Leo with OCD.

Family Mental Health History
Leo has an older sister who was also in therapy but he was unsure of the reason for treatment. He suspected that she was getting help for an anxiety disorder. He did not believe that anyone else in his family had mental health issues.

Trauma History
Leo denied any instances of experiencing or witnessing physical, sexual, or emotional abuse. He did recall witnessing and experiencing bullying in high school. He had been called "fag" and "homo" on a few occasions and often witnessed his friends being called similar names.

Family/Social History
Leo described his childhood as "good" but noted that his parents did not communicate well with one another. He felt most connected with his mother, and described his father as "aloof" and "judgmental." Leo has an older sister (41 years old) from whom he reported being "estranged" and stated that they never got along, even as children. His parents divorced when he was 18 years old, and his father remarried and had another daughter (16 years old). Leo stated that he felt very close to his half-sister and considered her a source of support. Leo believed that he had always made friends easily and that, despite his anxiety, he has maintained relationships with his male friends.

Sexual History
Leo was raised in a Catholic home and attributed this to the reason the conversations about sex and sexuality were "nonexistent." He learned about sex from listening to peers at school but felt self-conscious about the topic matter and never actively engaged in these conversations about sex. At age 13, Leo experienced a spontaneous erection while in the presence of a male peer during a sleepover and has harbored confusion, guilt, and shame surrounding the incident ever since. He reported his first sexual activity at 16 years old with a girlfriend, which resulted in her getting pregnant and subsequently terminating the pregnancy. Leo recalled feeling guilt and shame from her family, and while he did not feel shamed by his family, he was told to never talk about it and never processed the abortion with anyone.

Assessment

While sexual obsessions are a well-known symptom of OCD, each individual is different with regard to specific symptom presentation, so it was important to understand the context surrounding Leo's case. To best inform the proper treatment plan for Leo, he was given several assessments to help identify his obsessive-compulsive symptoms, evaluate the severity of symptoms, and identify the internal and external stimuli that triggered his obsessions and compulsions.

Leo and his therapist spent the majority of his second and third visits dedicating time to understanding both internal and external stimuli for his obsessions and discussed some of the details surrounding his thoughts, images, and urges. They also identified his primary behavioral responses to his distress, including his avoidance strategies. When asked to describe situations in which he worried about being attracted to other men and blurting out homosexual obscenities, Leo stated that it happens mostly at work when he is one-on-one with a male co-worker or in groups. He was worried that he was attracted to co-workers and that others would think so as well. Leo was also extremely concerned that he would blurt out inappropriate words or phrases that would confirm his homosexual desires to himself and everyone around him.

Leo did not take any psychotropic medication prior to or during treatment. As part of a comprehensive assessment, he was also screened for other mental health issues, including mood, personality, psychotic, and anxiety disorders. Results from this screening indicated heightened anxiety and panic, but it was believed that the results were reflective of symptoms related to OCD.

Upon intake, Leo was given several self-report and clinician-administered measures to assist in establishing his current functioning. These assessments are described in more detail in Chapter 2 and several are available in Appendix B. The measures Leo received and his scores are listed as follows:

> Yale–Brown Obsessive-Compulsive Scale, Second Edition (Y-BOCS-II) is a clinician-administered scale that measures the severity of obsessive compulsive-symptoms in adults. It also provides a severity rating scale to determine subclinical to clinical impairments in functioning.

Leo's initial score was 23, which was indicative of clinically significant impairment from OCD symptoms in the moderate range.

The Dimensional Obsessive Compulsive Scale (DOCS) assesses OCD symptom dimensions, in multiple areas. Leo obtained a total score of 10, which was comprised solely from the symptom dimension regarding unacceptable thoughts. Supplemental scales, which are not included in the DOCS total score, indicated that Leo also experienced sexually intrusive thoughts (9), but denied any concerns with violent thoughts or immoral and unscrupulous thoughts.

The Beck Depression Inventory (BDI-II) is a self-report measure that assesses the prevalence and severity of depressive symptoms. Leo obtained a score of 8, which is indicative of minimal symptoms of depression.

Beck Anxiety Inventory (BAI) is a self-report measure that assesses the prevalence and severity of anxiety symptoms. Leo obtained a score of 15, which is indicative of mild anxiety.

The MINI International Neuropsychiatric Interview 6.0 (MINI) is a structured diagnostic clinical interview designed to assess for psychiatric disorders in adults. The interview revealed past disturbances and symptoms of major depressive disorder and past symptoms of mania (irritability). Upon intake, it was suspected that the symptoms of mania were likely related to depression and possibly related to past substance use, as Leo endorsed having used marijuana regularly during the period of time in which some of his excessive irritability occurred. Leo's interview also indicated current risk for panic disorder (with agoraphobia), current OCD, and current alcohol dependence. It was believed that his panic symptoms and anxieties were not truly indicative of a diagnosis of panic disorder with agoraphobia, rather that they were reflective of anxiety from OCD.

Case Conceptualization

Leo's symptom presentation and maintenance can best be understood with a cognitive-behavioral conceptualization. While intrusive and unwanted thoughts are a common experience for most people, Leo assigned strong meaning to his thoughts and erroneously believed that merely experiencing a thought would carry certain, unwanted consequences. When he realized that he thought another man was attractive, he believed that it must mean he is gay, and the thought of being gay triggered his fear of blurting out sexually explicit content around other men. Leo's own thoughts contributed to his worry that others would label him as "strange" or "gay," based on his body language or speech. The thought of being gay, blurting out sexually explicit content, or being labeled as "gay" by others was highly distressing to Leo because he values his heterosexual understanding of his sexual identity and his reputation, both of which he believed would be jeopardized if his fears were to have come true.

Leo attempted to limit or suppress his unwanted thoughts whenever he could to avoid feelings of extreme distress. He either avoided situations that triggered thoughts or engaged in behaviors to temporarily reduce his intense worry. Leo avoided interacting with men that he thought were attractive in efforts to avoid thoughts of homosexuality and worries about blurting out something inappropriate. For example, he did not talk to men at work unless it was absolutely necessary; he avoided work meetings and remained isolated from others. When avoidance was not possible, Leo's compulsions were to constantly monitor the behaviors of others for clues as to whether or not they thought he was gay and monitoring his own voice and body language for the way he looked and sounded. After such situations, Leo managed his anxiety by engaging in more compulsions, such as mentally reviewing the encounter for evidence of blurting. He also reassured himself by mentally reviewing his past sexual encounters to convince himself that there was no evidence he had been gay his whole life.

Despite Leo's best efforts to limit exposure to triggering situations, his unwanted thoughts persisted, and he was finding the anticipation of each workday nearly unbearable. Avoiding males and avoiding speaking reinforced his belief that he was not blurting because he was not speaking; he never learned that he could worry about blurting yet still speak and not blurt. However, since complete avoidance was not possible, Leo still experienced blurting fears and began to rely heavily on his reviewing rituals. He thought that if he could remember every detail of every encounter, then he could feel secure. As he reviewed, the time it took to fully cover every detail increased, and because he kept thinking of things he may have missed, it took longer and longer to satisfy his worries. Leo maintained his OCD cycle by experiencing an intrusive thought, engaging in avoidance or review, and feeling temporary relief until the next time.

Course of Treatment and Assessment of Progress

Leo was self-referred to treatment for assessment of OCD. Despite never having been diagnosed, he suspected that he may have OCD after reading several articles on the Internet about homosexual obsessions and OCD (H-OCD). He researched clinicians in his area but was unable to find treatment centers within a few hours of his house, so he explored online options for treatment. He was initially evaluated during an intake session by a doctoral-level clinician (MW). Subsequent assessment and treatment was conducted by a master's-level clinician (JV, supervised by MW).

Treatment Session 1
The first session was dedicated to psychoeducation regarding OCD, including a review of symptom dimensions, compulsions, and maintenance of the disorder (the OCD cycle). Leo was instructed to read a handout on OCD (*Understanding S-OCD*) and begin monitoring and logging his compulsions. Time was also spent gaining a fuller understanding Leo's specific presentation and how his thoughts and behaviors were maintaining his symptoms.

Also discussed was the rationale for treatment using exposure and response prevention (Ex/RP). It is extremely important for clients to not only understand how OCD works but also why Ex/RP is considered the gold standard for behavioral intervention. An understanding of treatment is more likely to engage the client in the treatment and gives the client a foundation for understanding why it is important to participate in exercises and complete homework, particularly when the instructions from the therapist may seem counterintuitive or difficult to complete.

The OCD cycle was maintained primarily by two components: (a) negative, irrational appraisal of unwanted thoughts and (b) behavioral responses, which were performed in efforts to remove the anxiety that the thoughts caused. Like many individuals with OCD, Leo interpreted his thoughts to hold particular meaning with power to evoke certain, negative consequences. For example, he interpreted that a mere thought that another male was attractive meant that he was certainly gay and that he would act out sexually toward the man. He was unable to consider the possibility that we can find others attractive without sexually acting out and was unable to consider that a thought does not have the power to redefine our sexual identity. As a means of protecting himself from his worst fears from coming true, Leo engaged in many behavioral responses (e.g., checking, reviewing, avoiding) to temporarily reduce his distress from the obsessions. It was explained to Leo that performing the compulsions, though providing temporary relief, was maintaining OCD because he was developing an incorrect association between his thoughts and actions. He was incorrectly learning and reinforcing a belief that to not have sex with men, he must avoid them. The therapist further explained that while we cannot necessarily control the content of the obsessions that come to mind, we can control our behavioral response to the thoughts, images, or impulses.

Through Ex/RP, the therapist guides the client through situations that trigger upsetting thoughts, images, or urges, and while the distress is present, the client is instructed to not engage in compulsive behavior. Rather, the client is asked to sit with the anxiety, which will eventually subside over time. The reason for Ex/RP is to have the client experience the natural decline in distress, as well as collect evidence that the worst fears do not come true, even without performing compulsions. With repeated exposure over time, the thoughts and images become less disturbing. It is not to say that the client will find the obsessions pleasant or desirable (and this is not the goal of treatment), but rather the obsessions will lose their power and the client will function without debilitating distress and without performing compulsions. Freedom from the distress of obsessions allows for individuals to act according to values and thereby make decisions based on their values instead of fear.

In addition to psychoeducation about OCD, the therapist explained sexuality and the general differences between arousal from fantasy versus fears. Leo expressed feeling very inadequate in his understanding of healthy sexual development and was hesitant to accept that sometimes heterosexual individuals can be aroused by individuals of the same sex or sex between individuals of the same sex. He constantly reviewed his experience as an adolescent boy (spontaneous erection in the presence of a same-sex peer) for "evidence" of his homosexuality.

Treatment Sessions 2 and 3

These sessions were used to review Leo's rituals and establish an exposure hierarchy for treatment. Leo had completed compulsion monitoring each day between sessions. His primary obsessions were about being attracted to male colleagues and worries about blurting. In monitoring his rituals, Leo recognized that he practiced many strategies to avoid being around co-workers, including declining coffee breaks and not speaking in groups. He also reported replaying scenarios, such as team meetings, over and over in his mind to check if anyone had reacted in a way that indicated that he had blurted something inappropriate. He also noticed himself constantly surveying the body language of others to "decode" their expressions for signs that they thought he was gay. His avoidances were used as the basis for developing his hierarchy, based on his score on the Subjective Units of Distress/Discomfort Scale (SUDS; Wolpe, 1969).

Leo's SUDS was developed in a collaborative effort between he and the therapist during session. The therapist explained that the first goal was to establish anchors on a scale of stressful situations that would be on a scale from zero to 100 with zero being perfectly calm and 100 being the highest level of distress. The scale was meant to represent situations that were *not* related to OCD, because the scale would serve as a reference for comparison for situations that were related to OCD when developing the exposure hierarchy. Leo and the therapist established four anchors on the scale: zero (no distress; e.g., lying on a beach), 25 (mild distress; e.g., practicing for a big game), 50 (moderate distress; e.g., getting in a fight with his girlfriend), 75 (significant distress; e.g., coming home to find his house broken into), and 100 (extreme distress; e.g., finding out that his dog was dead after suffering).

Once the SUDS was complete with situational examples, Leo and the therapist came up with ideas for exposures, which were specifically targeted to Leo's reported obsessions (homosexuality, blurting, evaluation from others, etc.) With each exposure idea, Leo was asked to estimate the anxiety he would expect to feel in the given situation (knowing that he would not be able to perform compulsions) using his customized SUDS as a reference. Leo's hierarchy (see Table 5.1) was organized from most distressing to least. The least distressing exposures were the starting point for treatment.

By the third session Leo and his therapist had established a treatment hierarchy to begin exposure work; however, Leo expressed ongoing difficulty in understanding certain aspects of sexuality, particularly with regard to healthy sexual development for adolescent males. While he understood that his OCD symptoms were entangled in his experience as a boy, he felt at a loss for what actually was normal for other boys and thus had difficulty fully accepting aspects of treatment that treated his fears as irrational. The first exposure was postponed to dedicate additional time to more psychoeducation about sexuality and allow time for processing his guilt and shame around the childhood incident.

Table 5.1 Leo's Hierarchy

Exposure	SUDS
Telling two or more men that he is gay and describe sexual acts to perform (e.g., blow jobs)	75/100
Go to a gay bar and ask for someone's number	75
Blurting "I am gay" to group (males and females)	75
Stranger telling you that you sound gay	65
Starting a conversation with an attractive male stranger	65
Talking to group of people about nonsexual topics	60
Telling a female stranger that he is gay and describe sexual acts to perform (e.g. blow jobs)	60
Going to a gay bar	50
Participate in online support group for gay men	50
Talking to a stranger in a "gay" way (defined by Leo as effeminate voice, high pitched tone, flamboyant hand gestures)	50
Keep session intake paperwork in home (w/guests in house)	50
Striking up conversation with male about "male stuff" (e.g., tools, trucks, motorcycles)	50
Participate in real-life support group for gay men (without speaking)	50
Blurting "I am gay" to therapist and one male	50
Keep intake paperwork in home (w/o guests)	40
Posting picture of self with attractive male to social media	40
Make a videotape of session (for therapist's supervision)	40
Watch a video of self	40
Volunteer for a gay rights organization	40
Hang out in male bathroom (conducting imaginal exposure beforehand)	40
Talking about a picture of naked male	35
Wear a progay shirt	35
People staring at you without clarification of what they are thinking	30
Type and email sexually explicit stories about being gay/homosexuality to therapist	30
Offer co-worker a coffee	30
Striking up conversation with male stranger	30
Blurting "I am gay" to therapist	30
Use words, "totally" and "like" in conversation with others	30
Therapist saying that you sound/seem gay	25
Typing/texting/saying things to therapist about being gay/homosexuality	25
Talking about a picture of a male model in a sexual manner	25
Writing a story about blurting out that I'm gay	25
Wearing gay pride bracelet	25

(*continued*)

Table 5.1 Continued

Exposure	SUDS
Writing "I am gay;" "I will tell everyone that I am gay"	20
Creating/reading a story about talking to a group of men who think you are gay	20
Sending emails specifying codes (H, B, S)[a]	20
Saving treatment intake paperwork to desktop	20
Take a selfie with another male (not in work setting)	20
Looking at naked male	15
Posting progay articles to social media	15
Writing the words "gay" or "homosexual" on paper	10
Looking at a picture of a male model	10
Watch videos about "don't ask, don't tell" policies	10

[a] Leo initially used codes on his Ritual Monitoring sheet to identify the theme of a particular ritual (H=homosexuality; B=blurting; S=surveillance). The codes were used in response to surveillance fears of someone hacking his computer and publishing the contents of his ritual monitoring forms.
Note: SUDS = Subjective Units of Distress/Discomfort Scale.

Leo's homework was to read material provided by the therapist about sexuality in the adolescent male and to continue to monitor and log his rituals.

Treatment Sessions 4 and 5

Leo completed his ritual monitoring each day and read the educational materials provided. He came prepared to session with several questions and insights related to his own sexual history that he wanted to discuss. For example, Leo did not know that spontaneous erections were normal experiences for males, nor did he know that children of the same sex sometimes experiment with each other as part of heterosexual development. Leo was extremely tearful during the session. When asked about his emotions, he stated that for the first time he has felt safe in discussing sex and processing his confusion. He also reported feeling saddened by a sense of lost time, due to how much OCD had consumed his thoughts and behaviors.

Processing thoughts and emotions, along with reviewing educational materials allowed Leo to establish a baseline "truth" for sexual health and development, which helped him to better recognize irrational OCD fears. The remainder of Session 4 was spent reading some of the materials that he found triggering and practicing accepting the unwanted thoughts. For example, when he read that boys get spontaneous erections, he had a thought that being aroused around a boy when he was younger meant that he was gay. As an exposure, he agreed with the thought, and said, "Yes, that means I like men and am gay." He also resisted mental review of the incident and told himself, "I could review, but I am not going to." For homework, Leo read the triggering aspects of the literature daily and resisted compulsions.

Due to heavy demand at work, Leo knew that he would not make the second session that week, so a 30-minute phone session was scheduled for Session 5. He reported habituation to homework and decided to read materials in a public place to increase distress again, since being in groups triggered his blurting obsessions.

Treatment Session 6

Starting with Session 6, exposures were conducted using either in vivo or imaginal exposures. In vivo exposures were focused on blurting out explicit, phrases associated with men and homosexuality, surrounding himself around gay men (e.g., participating in an LGBT support group, visiting a gay bar), as well as exposing him to worries about surveillance (e.g., sending therapist homoerotic emails; videotaping a session for therapist's supervision). When in vivo exposures were not possible, imaginal exposures were used to recreate situations that could not be conducted in person, such as blurting out sexual fantasies about a co-worker or imagining the consequences of such blurting. The first exposure was conducted for approximately 35 minutes, where Leo blurted out feared phrases to the therapist (e.g., "I like penises," "I am gay," or "I want to give oral sex to men").

SUDS ratings were monitored to gauge Leo's distress during exposures. During the 35 minutes of exposure, Leo's SUDS peaked at 50 and dropped off at 10 by the end of the exposure. For his homework, Leo was instructed to continue to read the sex education materials and blurt out the things he was afraid to say. He also was instructed to continue monitoring rituals and challenge himself to not avoid male co-workers during the week.

Treatment Session 7

Leo completed his ritual monitoring form and reported habituating to his homework. He also was successful in agreeing to take a coffee break with a male co-worker and remaining around others in meetings. During session, Leo was instructed to look at a picture of a male co-worker, whom he thought was attractive, and say sexually explicit comments to the picture.

Leo was very distressed at the start of the exposure (SUDS 60), but then ended the 30-minute exposure at a 20 on the SUDS. For homework, Leo was instructed to continue saying sexually explicit comments to pictures of male co-workers and imagine it was happening in a meeting or in front of others.

Treatment Sessions 8 to 10
Leo continued to complete all of his daily homework and reported a significant reduction in his mental review and reduced his avoidance of co-workers. He reported feeling a reduction in his daily anxiety and noted a decrease in his worries about blurting. Leo was then instructed to not avoid speaking when around others. Exposures maintained a focus on his sexual obsessions while incorporating some fears about being watched. Leo sent homoerotic emails to the therapist, without deleting the email and without checking the destination address more than once. He reported fears about being aroused by the emails, and the therapist reminded him that some arousal, due to the sexual nature of the content, is to be expected.

In Session 8, Leo also asked for some time to discuss the concept of sexuality on a continuum. He identified a compulsion of taking online tests of sexuality, which assign a number (1–5), with 1 being completely heterosexual and 5 being homosexual. He recognized the compulsion and stopped but felt that he needed more education. Leo and the therapist discussed what he had learned about categorization of sexual identity, societal expectations, and how his views and beliefs were informed by his experiences. Leo also discussed in detail that which he found arousing versus his fears. He determined that he did not find men attractive but understood that sometimes gay porn was arousing because it made him think of sex with women; he reported enjoying transgender porn for similar reasons, though experienced more shame with this fantasy. Leo confirmed that his fears around homosexuality were about possibly being gay (which was distressing because he was not aroused at the thought of sexual activity with men) and others' perceptions of his sexual identity. We amended the hierarchy to reduce pornographic images and added exposures that would leave his identity ambiguous to others (e.g., going to a gay bar) or exposures that focused on him being gay (e.g., participating in gay support groups; imaginal exposures about the consequences of being gay).

Leo's Imaginal Exposure (Session 11)

The other evening I had an encounter with a male at a bar. He and I decided to go back to his house, after a few drinks, we both felt comfortable enough to lay naked together in bed. I spent the night, and throughout the evening we made out and gave each other blow jobs and really enjoyed ourselves. After having sex with him, I realize that I like having sex with both men and women, and now I know that I have never really known who I am. All of my relationships are now ruined and stunted from growth.

After getting back home, my girlfriend already heard that I had been at a man's house for the evening and immediately broke up with me. She was crying and screaming, "I cannot believe you are gay! You have ruined my last couple of years. I guess this is the end." I am left by myself, not only without a support system but also questioning my sexuality. I know that since she left on such bad terms, she has already told all of our friends that I spent the night at a male's house, who I picked up at the bar.

I saw on Joey's (a co-worker; not his real name) instant messenger that he was talking to Jackie (another co-worker; not her real name)—he said, "Did you hear Leo is gay?" Jackie replied, "Ha ha ha, no surprise there. We have been laughing about this for as long as we have known him. This type of uncertainty makes me uncomfortable, I am not going to hang around him anymore." Joey said, "I agree."

As I am still questioning my sexuality, my father had spoken to my sister and she told him that I did not know myself and that I was homosexual and that I don't realize it. My dad told her to not tell anyone else, because this was so embarrassing for the family. Once he found out that she had told everyone, he stopped talking to me about important things and distanced himself from me.

In an effort to understand my sexuality, I try to have relationships with men and women, but I get no reassurance from those relationships because they are superficial. I am not connected with anyone and cannot really take any strides to know myself better. Before I know it, I am an old man, who is not attractive to anyone. I end up old, alone, and confused. Why did I stop resisting these urges? I've wrecked my whole life.

Treatment Sessions 11 to 15

Leo had eliminated nearly all avoidance of speaking around others and described feeling "empowered" by being able to speak whenever he wanted.

He still reported difficulty in surveying body language of others, since reading body language is part of natural communication. Leo was instructed to "spoil" any reassurance he gained from his interactions by telling himself that he missed a cue from the other person and that people indeed think he is gay.

Leo identified (in session) a new compulsion to check his zipper when walking, due to a fear that his zipper was down and he was exposing himself in public. Leo was able to identify obsessions surrounding this trigger and committed to stop checking.

Exposures for Sessions 11 to 15 were still focused on homosexual obsessions and involved Leo rereading his homoerotic emails from previous sessions, listening to imaginal exposures about co-workers realizing he was gay, and participating in online support forums for the LGBT community.

Treatment Sessions 16 and 17

Prior to Session 16, Leo had been participating in online support groups as part of his homework. He felt much less distressed than he originally anticipated with the assignment and reported feeling differently toward sexuality. During the session, Leo remarked that he believed participating in the online forums helped him not only face fears about being perceived as gay but also helped him learn more about what others experience with regard to sexual identity. He stated that he understood how sexuality could be more on a spectrum as opposed to simply binary.

Session 16 included an exposure with a female confederate, whom Leo told he was gay, and then he described his sexual attraction toward men. He began the exposure with SUDS of 60, and after about 25 minutes, he ended the exposure with SUDS of 15. Session 17 involved a similar exposure with a female confederate, except in this session, the confederate laughed at Leo and affirmed many of his negative thoughts and worries (e.g., people do think he seems weird). Between sessions, Leo was instructed to intentionally engage in conversations with others and not avoid speaking when uncomfortable.

Treatment Session 18

Between sessions, Leo had intentionally engaged in conversation with others and in groups. He reported feeling better about his interactions and was successful in agreeing with fears before speaking, when distress was at its highest. The session was dedicated to readministering the YBOCS-II, re-evaluating the remaining items on his hierarchy, and discussing his desire for sexual exploration, which arose since entering treatment. At his initial assessment, Leo's YBOCS-II score was 23, but after 16 treatment sessions, his score was at 13, which was in the borderline clinical range and highly indicative of improvement. His hierarchy was adjusted slightly, because he now thought that going to a gay bar would be less distressing than speaking to a male confederate about homosexuality.

Leo reported feeling a need to explore his own sexuality and stated that he believed he never was allowed to examine his curiosity and desires due to his strict Catholic upbringing and interference from OCD symptoms. He and the therapist talked about making choices based on values and desire and how those choices are different from engaging in activity as a compulsion.

Treatment Session 19

Leo went to a gay bar and had conversations with the bartender and other patrons. Since therapy had been conducted via telehealth, the therapist was unable to attend the bar with him, so the therapist and client were in communication via phone and text messaging to monitor SUDS, thoughts, and compulsions. The exposure was approximately 40 minutes long, and Leo's SUDS were highest at 10 minutes (SUDS 50) and were lowest around 35 minutes (SUDS 20). Similarly to Leo's experience with the online forums, he reported gaining insight into sexuality, realizing that the exposure helped him challenge some of his assumptions about gay men that he did not know he had (e.g., that he would feel threatened by or preyed upon by gay men).

Just prior to entering treatment, Leo had enrolled in an outdoor climbing class through the local university. Shortly after starting treatment, he learned that the class was planning a weekend-long climbing excursion that was scheduled to take place several weeks into the course. When Leo first learned of the excursion, he decided to not commit. He was interested in attending; however, the class was made up of mostly males, and at the time, his OCD was quite severe. He was afraid that the experience would be ruined due to fears of blurting and sexual obsessions from OCD (S-OCD). During this session, Leo informed the therapist that he decided to attend the climbing excursion, which was to take place between Sessions 19 and 20. He stated that he had decided to commit to the excursion as part of practicing nonavoidance, and he believed he was able to manage any obsessions that may arise with the skills he had learned in therapy. As part of his homework, he was instructed to engage in self-led exposures that included engaging in conversation with the other men and not avoiding situations that may trigger OCD (e.g., showers, changing rooms).

Treatment Session 20
Leo reported having enjoyed his trip over the weekend. He engaged with others and reported feeling very little anxiety throughout the weekend. He resisted compulsions to review situations and did not avoid situations that would have typically triggered OCD. During session, Leo completed the last exposure on his hierarchy by engaging in conversation with a male confederate about being gay and liking men. His SUDS score was highest at the beginning (SUDS 50) and reduced to 10 SUDS after 30 minutes.

Leo and the therapist discussed his progress, and, based on his improvement, they decided to reduce the frequency of sessions for the following week from two 90-minute sessions to one 60-minute session. . He was also encouraged to devise his own exposures as homework.

Treatment Session 21
Leo engaged in daily, self-led exposures between sessions and reported feeling "free" from blurting obsessions. He had scheduled himself to lead an information session at work, which would require him to speak at length to a group of co-workers, who were nearly all male. Leo stated that he wanted to engage more with others and felt more "open" in interactions with others, both at work and at home. The second half of the session consisted of psychoeducation about relapse prevention and plans for termination.

Treatment Session 22
Leo reported maintaining gains from his last session and had been regularly conducting self-led exposures through his daily life activities. He also described that he ended his romantic relationship of three years. He described the break-up as "best for both parties," and described them as "best friends." He and the therapist discussed the role of stress and OCD symptoms and reviewed relapse prevention strategies. Leo was able to explain relapse prevention back to the therapist and demonstrated insight into the distress he may experience as a result of the breakup. He also discussed benefits of the breakup, one of which was exploring relationships with others, without OCD being "in the driver's seat."

Complicating Factors

While Leo demonstrated good insight into his symptoms and an ability to understand treatment rationale quickly, he was limited in his knowledge of human sexual development and health. Lack of knowledge created a barrier to recognizing some of his fears as irrational, since he truly did not know what was reasonable or healthy. He had always thought of sexuality as binary, had not discussed sexuality with anyone, and had never considered the idea of sexuality on a continuum or the sex and gender norms of our society. He also had begun to explore different genres of pornography and was bothered that he found some of the content arousing, such as transgender porn. With sex education and processing of his fears versus his fantasies, Leo was eventually able to recognize OCD fears and make choices about sexual behavior based on these values and not fear.

Leo also had some irrational fears about surveillance and being watched by others. He knew that his fears were irrational, but since his therapy was conducted via the Internet (see the following discussion), he was initially hesitant to fully disclose information. We were careful to have engaged in responsible and ethical practices regarding confidentiality and security but were able to use the format of our sessions for exposures and treatment of his irrational surveillance fears.

Access and Barriers to Care

Leo was limited in treatment options due to the lack of access to clinicians who specialize in Ex/RP treatment for OCD. His closest options were approximately two hours away from his home, which was not feasible. Leo received treatment from our clinic through teletherapy sessions, which were conducted twice per week via a secure, Web-based platform.

Leo may also have been delayed in seeking treatment due to the sensitive nature of his obsessions. He may have had worries about being misunderstood or misdiagnosed, especially since he had been in prior treatment, which he reported to be unhelpful.

Follow-Up

At the close of the last session, a 60-minute follow-up session was scheduled for two weeks later. Leo continued to report success in managing his OCD symptoms and continued to engage in self-lead exposures and resisted avoidance. Another 60-minute follow-up session was scheduled for two weeks out, as Leo thought he may need additional support, due to his recent change in relationship status. At the second follow-up session, he reported feeling increasingly confident at work and even approached his boss about leading an information panel at work. He reported continuing to manage OCD and stated that though he still experiences some intrusive thoughts, he is not impaired by anxiety. A termination session was then scheduled for eight weeks later. Leo maintained his gains from treatment and was able to continue to progress at work. He was able to explain strategies for relapse prevention, was able to explain the importance of continued, self-led exposures with everyday situations, and gave examples of how he incorporated them into his life. For example, he no longer avoided speaking in groups, he did not avoid men whom he deemed attractive, and no longer spent time reviewing his interactions with others.

Treatment Implications of the Case

It is important that clinicians are familiar with sexual orientation obsessions as a part of OCD, as symptoms can be easily misunderstood for other problems, such as sexual identity issues, leaving the person potentially misdiagnosed and, therefore, mistreated (Glazier, Wetterneck, Singh, & Williams, 2015). Additionally, the explicit and sensitive nature of the topic may be extremely difficult for some individuals to confront, which can lead to guilt and shame with regards to their unwanted thoughts and behaviors. Although there is limited research on the treatment of sexual obsessions, cognitive behavioral therapy with Ex/RP is a highly effective approach for those with sexual obsessions.

Recommendations to Clinicians and Students

In this case study, Ex/RP was successful in treating unwanted sexual thoughts as part of OCD treatment. Based on current research and understanding of sexual obsessions in OCD, this dimension should be treated in a similar fashion as other, more common dimensions, such as contamination. It is important to remember that since sexual obsessions are a less discussed and a less researched topic than other OCD symptom dimensions, clinicians may not as readily recognize the symptoms as a presentation of

OCD. The obsessions can easily be confused with other mental health issues, such as a crisis in sexual identity or even aspects of paranoia. In the case of Leo, his OCD symptoms caused him to question whether or not he had been living his entire life in denial of being gay. His symptoms also made him hyperaware of what others were thinking, which made him extremely attentive to his behavior and the behaviors of others. It is very important that the content of obsessions are fully examined, as with any other dimension of OCD, so that the presentation can be understood in context and so that the treatment plan can be appropriately targeted. Further, it is important for clinicians to understand the covert compulsions associated with sexual obsessions. If the compulsions cannot be readily seen, they may be overlooked. The client may not even be aware that mental behaviors, such as mental review, are compulsions, so it is important that the clinician is familiar with common compulsions or rituals associated with sexual obsessions in OCD. To identify such compulsions, the clinician may need to explicitly ask about these behaviors.

Shame and stigma are notable barriers to treatment for OCD (Glazier, Wetterneck, Singh, & Williams, 2015). The clinician should be sensitive to the fact that the content of obsessions may be a source of guilt or shame for the client. It may even be the first time the client is giving details on their thoughts. While the clinician should not be afraid to examine the content, exploration should be done in a compassionate manner, and the discomfort that the client may be feeling at the time should be validated and normalized as needed. Failure to recognize the potentially delicate nature of the discussion could lead to bad rapport and negatively impact treatment.

In Vivo Exposure Suggestions

The following discussion provides some examples of in vivo exposures that clients can do to address S-OCD. Keep in mind that not all of these examples will be anxiety-provoking or relevant for every person with this kind of OCD. Therapists should first ask clients how anxious they anticipate they would be to do these exposures before putting them on the hierarchy. If the SUDS is very low, then there may be no need to assign it, unless the therapist has reason to believe that the reported SUDS is an underestimate. It should be noted that these exposures are written for people who are worried about turning from straight to gay, but several can be adapted for the reverse scenario—which is uncommon but does occur. These ideas are meant as a starting point and are in no way comprehensive. Therapists should feel free to use their imagination to devise exposures that best fit the client's fears and are doable in session and/or for homework.

1. *Wear a gay pride bracelet*: This is can be an effective exposure for people who worry about others thinking they are gay. There are many different types of rubber gay pride bracelets that are relatively inexpensive, and these can be ordered online. We keep a stash of these bracelets at our clinic in many different colors and styles. A knitted rainbow-patterned bracelet is also a good option. Clients should start by wearing the bracelet in session until they feel comfortable. This can be expanded to wearing it around the office, then at stores or malls, and then at school or work. This may not be an appropriate exposure in every setting. For example, if a client has a legitimate concern for their safety in certain settings connected to others thinking they may be gay, then the exposure should not be done in those settings.
2. *Write and/or read phrases about being gay*: Sometimes client have trouble agreeing with the thoughts of being gay, and they may have difficulty even saying things like "I am gay," "I like vaginas," or "I want to have sex with women/men," especially at the beginning of treatment. Having a client write out and read such phrases can be helpful for individuals who are afraid to even utter such words. Depending on the client's expected distress with the exposure, the therapist could start the exposure by simply writing a single word (e.g., "gay," "penis," "lesbian") and work toward writing sentences. As the client habituates, the exposure could be made even more challenging by writing words and phrases on pictures of penises, nude or barely clothed models, or pictures of gay individuals engaged in sexual activity. Therapists should explore the distressing aspects of the exposure, as sometimes clients are equally distressed by reading aloud as writing, while other times a client may find one mode of expression more distressing than the other.
3. *Wear clothing that feels "gay"*: Sometimes people with S-OCD avoid certain clothing or fashion because they are afraid that others will think they "look" gay. Together, the client and therapist can explore what styles of clothing the client determines a "gay look." It is important that the therapist not assume what the client thinks looks gay,

since clients' individual assessment of what seems gay is subjective and unique to their own perception. However, some ideas for men may be to wear a shirt that is a traditionally feminine color (e.g., pink, purple), wear shirts or pants that are tight, or wear short-shorts. Women may benefit from wearing clothing that is traditionally masculine, such as baggy pants, athletic shorts, or baggy polo shirts. Similarly to wearing a gay pride bracelet, the client should start by wearing the clothing in session and gradually expand to wearing the clothing out in public.

4. *Hot guy/girl rating game*: Rating people of the same sex with regards to attractiveness can be a good exposure for clients who are afraid to find members of the same sex attractive. There are several games available online (e.g., "Hot or Not") that can be used to ask the client to evaluate members of the same sex based on physical appearance. Pictures that are evaluated as "hot" can be further discussed with regards to the physical qualities that make the person "hot" and why the client might find the person attractive. When we have clients do this exposure, we tell them that they have to rate everyone on a restricted scale (7–10) to make the exercise more challenging.

5. *Watch LGBT pornography*: This exposure can be very effective for triggering fears of arousal toward the same sex. Therapists can utilize free pornography websites to find videos of sexual encounters involving the same sex as the client and should select some appropriate material in advance of the session. The therapist and client should watch the videos together in session, and then the client should be instructed to view the videos for homework. This exposure should be conducted after the therapist believes that the client has an accurate understanding of human sexuality, as clients may actually become aroused during the exposure. It is important that psychoeducation regarding sexuality includes the understanding that we are prone to becoming aroused at sexually explicit content (images, videos, thoughts), and arousal is not indicative of sexual identity or preference. Clients who report becoming aroused should continue the exposure but should not check for arousal or assign meaning to any indication of arousal, as this is a compulsion. If clients have religious objections to pornography, erotica can be used instead.

6. *Talk to a confederate about leading a "gay lifestyle"*: Talking to a confederate can be helpful for clients who are worried about what others

will think or how others will judge them. The client should introduce themselves as gay and talk about how much they enjoy having sex with members of the same sex. The therapist should choose a trusted confederate to engage in the exposure and incorporate any qualities that may provide additional exposure for the client. For example, if the client is a female who is concerned about being attracted to other women, the confederate could be a woman who could be instructed to be a little flirty with the client. If a client fears being laughed at, the therapist could instruct the confederate to laugh at the client when they talk about lifestyle and sexual identity. Some clients may be worried about secretly being judged by others as gay. In this case, a confederate can be instructed to remain silent or give neutral feedback to the client, so that the client must sit with the uncertainty of how the confederate is reacting to the discussion.

7. *Watch "coming out" stories online:* Several videos can be found online (for free) of individuals who have shared about their "coming out" experience. Exposing clients to coming out videos can be helpful for clients who frequently worry about being gay and have constant doubts. Clients can find similarities between their persistent doubts and the real-life stories of individuals who came out as gay. During the exposure, the therapist can help clients recognize ways in which they are like the person in the video and expose fears associated with being gay. This exposure could also serve as a good foundation for an imaginal exposure in which the client writes their own coming out story, full of all the feared consequences of being gay and coming out. The therapist should identify good exposures for this exercise ahead of time, in advance of the session, to ensure they are appropriate for the treatment plan.

8. *Watch movies with gay story line or love scenes* (e.g., Brokeback Mountain, Milk, Dallas Buyers Club, etc.): When clients with S-OCD are avoiding triggers of gay obsessions, it might be helpful to introduce LGBT-themed content through movies or TV shows. This exposure can be helpful for many different clients and may create distress for a variety of reasons: fears of becoming gay from being exposed to content, worry about arousal from intimate scenes, or fear that they may suffer the same consequences as the characters (e.g., rejection, AIDS, etc.), just to name a few. Depending on the client's predicted distress, it can be helpful to start with a specific scene in a movie and gradually work toward incorporating larger segments for viewing. Conversely,

there may be specific scenes that are too distressing to start with but can be worked toward viewing over time. For homework, you can pick an appropriately distressing clip to watch over and over.

9. *Go to a gay bar or club*: This can be really helpful in exposing a client to uncertainty and ambiguity about sexual orientation, because when a client goes to a gay bar, they assume others are gay, and it may be assumed by others that the client is also gay. The client and therapist should plan to go together, and, if needed, the exposure can be conducted with a gradual increase in the difficulty of the exposure. The client and therapist can first simply sit in the parking lot of the establishment and work up to going inside, to talking to bartenders and other patrons, or even to getting the phone number or email address of someone of the same sex. The graduated exposures may be done in one session or over a few different sessions.

10. *Participate in an LGBT support group:* Not only does a support group place the client in an environment in which it is assumed that they are gay, but it also can offer exposure to some fears that clients may have about the consequences of a gay lifestyle (e.g., stigma, discrimination, etc.). When clients attend the meetings, they should be encouraged to participate as a member of the LGBT community. Some clients may be anxious about participating in a group, so it may be helpful for the client and the therapist to come up with a "story" or "scenario" ahead of time that the client will use when participating in the group. There is no need for the client to be dishonest about their orientation, as they can identify as an "ally" or "questioning," if asked. It is recommended that the therapist and client also properly research the group prior to attending, as it is important that the group is appropriate to meet the needs of the client, as some groups may be geared toward a specific part of the community that does not apply to the client's goals for the exposure (e.g., family groups, trans-only groups, lesbian groups if the client is male).

Sample Imaginal Exposures

Included here are some actual imaginal exposures we have drafted for use with our own clients or that have been graciously provided by therapists in our clinics (with identifying information changed, of course). Student therapists have told us that these sample imaginal exposures are especially useful for clinicians trying to improve their treatment of S-OCD and the variety of obsessions that occur. You can use these verbatim with a client or customize them to your client's situation. Generally, it is better to customize them for maximum impact, rewriting them in the client's own way of speaking; however, if a given story is adequately anxiety-provoking to be used as-is, then the story should not be customized (other than changing the names used in the scenario) until the client has habituated somewhat (exposure causing 40 or less SUDS).

Imaginal Exposure 1: Realizing I'm a Lesbian

One of my friend tells me that she met the perfect guy for me and wanted to see if I was willing to be set up. My friend, who is in a relationship herself, has always been there for me to listen to my dating ordeals. She knows how picky I really am and has heard that dating for me can be a bit scary (although I never really let on how anxious I get while dating or how much of an effort I feel it requires on my part). She never really knew of a guy that would be right for me, until now. She said he was friends with one of her co-workers, his name was Joshua, he was tall (over six feet tall) and was built well (had enough meat that I wouldn't feel like the dominant one in the relationship). She said he had an amazing personality and could win over a room with his smile. He was in business and did well for a living but wasn't a workaholic and didn't have the attitude that most NY guys had who were in I-banking. He was Jewish, but not overly religious; he went to a great school (or so she thought) and was athletic, and she felt that we shared similar interests. She kept saying, "This is definitely the one for you; I can feel it you will totally be into him; he is perfect. What type of person wouldn't want to be with him?"

I tell my friend thank you for thinking of me and to definitely give him my number. On the outside I appear so thrilled, eager, and excited, but deep down I am starting to feel a little off. I can't really voice this fear to anyone really (besides my best friend maybe—who gets that dating for me is not the easiest), but this guy seems so good that even she would think what is wrong with you for not being so excited. It is a lot easier to talk to my friends about dating issues when the guy doesn't seem all that amazing, but in this scenario I know I am going to like him, and if I don't, then something is seriously wrong with me and I will feel forced into liking him.

He seems so great on paper and so great the way my friend described him, but I automatically think, what will I find wrong with him? Yes, he sounds great, but I still don't feel overly excited to go out with him. A normal girl would think "Yes, finally, weddings bells, yay happy ending"; instead, my mind starts racing when I think about the date. Will I even like him? Will I be attracted to him right away? If I'm not attracted to him immediately, what does it mean? How will I even know if I like him? I just go on this date because that is what is expected of me. I just go to appease my friend. What if I am just going so that no one will wonder if I am into guys or not? And what if the reason why I am so apprehensive and the reason why I feel so forced into going is because secretly I am gay? I will admit it seems like less of a chore than other dates have been on the past—when I know off the bat that the guy is not that attractive or went to a bad school or something—but I have to admit I still feel wary, and I still don't feel any sparks or massive amounts of excitement and that scares me.

Although part of me almost hopes and wishes that he never contacts me—that is the perfect excuse for why I can't date him (if he never calls or reaches out), the other part of me wants to see if he will and if he will even like me and want to go out on a date. One week goes by and I don't hear from him. My friend keeps asking if I've heard, and I can feel good in saying, "Nope, not yet. What is his deal? I hope this isn't a sign of his communication and follow-through skills." Already I am starting to build the case against him, either consciously or subconsciously thinking of reasons why Mister Perfect may not be so perfect after all.

A few days later I wind up hearing from Joshua. I am curious to get to know him better, and we make plans to meet up at a wine bar (my favorite type of place for a first date) for the following Thursday. I always to try plan my dates at least one week in advance so that I have some time to put it out of my mind—I almost feel that it's like putting off the inevitable. As Thursday starts to get closer and closer, all of my friends (and especially the friend that set me up with Joshua) seem to get more and more excited for me. They all tell me to go in and just have fun and let loose a little bit (wish they knew how much I'd love to take their advice, but how hard it is for me to do so). I am still not all that excited, I am more nervous and really anxious as the date gets closer. The day of I start to feel really sick after lunch at work. My stomach starts to hurt, and I get a wave of dizziness and nausea. I go home from work and get ready (I follow my tried-and-true predate routine: I shower, put on more make-up, reiron my hair, change clothes, etc.) I try to pump myself up, but when I look in the mirror I start to ask myself a number of questions and get a feeling of uneasiness once again. As I'm looking at myself getting all pampered for a date, I wonder is this really me? Why am I putting in all this effort? I'm pretending to be someone I'm not. Am I pretending to be like all other girls who have a predate getting-ready routine? Am I just going through the motions, because it is evident that I don't have much feeling attached to anything. As I am leaving my apartment for the date I start to think, OK maybe one date isn't so bad, but then I think OMG one date for most people would turn into more than one date. The purpose of dating is to continue the process and find some guy to settle down with. I almost think of it as a burden I need to keep doing and engaging in. I start to feel less normal with every passing minute here.

I arrive at the bar and before I walk in I do my best to clear my head and clear my thoughts. I see Joshua waiting for me in the entrance way, and immediately I can understand why my friend set me up with him. He is really attractive, like probably the hottest guy I have gone out with ever and one that I have always envisioned going out with. We grab a seat and order glasses of wine. While I am trying to listen intently to what he has to say my brain starts to veer off and I can't help but think, "I am just playing a role. I am just asking him the right questions because that is what I think I should do. I am sitting this way because this is how girls sit who are on dates." A passing thought goes through my head of do I even want to be here. I come back to reality and back to the conversation, and Joshua starts asking me about myself and what I do, and I answer him back but I keep feeling this out of body experience that I am not really myself; I truly don't feel comfortable or in my element. My mind then starts to wander and think hmmm . . . if I'm not comfortable would I be more comfortable if a girl were sitting across from me instead? I immediately then start to notice the table of girls sitting next to me and think, hmm . . . one of those girls at that table that I'm more attracted to than Joshua?? I realize I am very attracted to one of the girls at the nearby table who looks especially pretty. She is tall and has a great presence about her. She seems confident and comfortable and has an incredible bikini ready body. She sees me looking at her and looks over at me with a smile. While Joshua is in the restroom, she comes over to me to ask how the date is going, and there is an instant spark. As Joshua comes back from the bathroom, I get up and slip a piece of paper into her hand with my number on it. As I return, she slips a piece of paper right back at me—we have exchanged numbers.

For the remainder of the date, I am not able to focus on Joshua. He really does seem like a great guy, and we are laughing (but it is more forced than genuine on my part, like I'm playing the role of being the perfect heterosexual girl to date), but I keep thinking about the attractive young woman who gave me her number.

Joshua is a polite guy and offers to walk me home. It is winter, and I am shivering and cold and keep my hands in my pocket—again he is cute, but I don't feel the urge to be physical with him at all. In fact, that feeling alone brings up a lot of discomfort for me. We get to my apartment, and we have one of those awkward wrapping up of conversations. I lean in for a kiss on cheek and hug, and he takes me and kisses me. I start to analyze the kiss, while we are mid-kiss, I start to think, am I into this? I do not like kissing him. I will never like kissing a guy or ever feel like I could sit there and kiss one for hours on end. I keep having thoughts of secretly wanting to kiss a girl instead, but I try to not focus on that in the moment.

We say goodbye, I go upstairs, text him before bed to thank him for a great night and say "We should do that again soon"—while secretly I have decided that I will NOT go on that second date. Joshua is the perfect guy, and I do think a great guy for anyone, but I don't feel head over heels and realize that I never want to be with a man. What is wrong me? As I imagine trying to be with the girl at the bar, something inside of me feels panic but also happiness and relief. The truth is finally coming to the surface. I don't have to pretend anymore. I am a lesbian. I will give her a call. It scares me, but I know that it is the only way I can be happy.

Imaginal Exposure 2: Gay Coming Out Story

Back in high school I was terrified about people thinking I was gay. I would see other guys in the hallways, and I would think about whether or not I found them attractive. If a friend mentioned something about being gay, I would constantly wonder if I was gay too or if they were talking about me. Even when I became much older these, thoughts really bothered me. Years later, I began dating a girl named Pauline. Things were great. I even lost my virginity to her, but still something was not right. These thoughts just would never leave me alone. I went to seek professional help for these stubborn worries, and I was diagnosed with OCD. The therapist had me doing all sorts of exposures to try and get rid of the worries that I might be gay and the therapy was going fine. She had me looking at pictures of gay men and watching movies with gay people. Eventually, I started realize that I was not anxious about looking at these things. I actually liked it. Luckily, the pictures my therapist found me became more graphic. I was looking at pictures of men standing together naked touching each other in sexual ways. I realized that these images really turned me on sexually. I knew that Pauline would be hurt by this realization, but I also knew I had to stop living a lie. I had to find out what it would be like to touch another man's penis the way the guys in the pictures were. I have been having images of this in my head any way, and the therapy has taught me to embrace these images, so I took it all the way.

Without Pauline knowing, I met up with some of the gay guys I had been avoiding, and we went to a gay bar. Surprisingly I was not anxious at all. As time rolled by, I realized that I was becoming more and more comfortable being with and around gay people. When the outing first started, I was bothered by the fact that Pauline thought I was somewhere else, but after an hour or so I realized she was not even on my mind. I was talking with these guys, standing close to them, and became flirtatious with a few of them. It felt so liberating to finally be having an evening not ruined by thoughts of being gay. I came to realize this entire time I had been running away from my true self. The more I hung out with this one particular guy, the less and less I felt for Pauline. Especially since this guy looked a lot like the Hollywood actors I've always been attracted to. Finally, I decided that me and my boyfriend would take things to the next level. We went back to his place, and we had sex. I was nervous about it since this would be my first sexual encounter with a man but now that I can do it—I can honestly say I have never felt that way in bed with a Pauline. It's not that I never loved Pauline, but now I know that she could never satisfy me sexually the way a man can. I have accepted the idea that I am gay, and while it used to make me sad to think that I could miss out on having a life with Pauline with children, I see now that if I allowed myself to go down that same path I would also wonder about what it would be like to be gay. Now I can forget about all that because I was not living the life I was meant to live. I am now in a relationship with a man that satisfies me in ways a woman never could, and I will never go back. I ended up leaving Pauline after all because it was not right to hold her life up waiting on me to decide what my sexual orientation is. I am so glad I went into treatment because if I had not gone through that, I would have never gotten used to the idea of being with men. Right now I just want to have fun and meet as many guys as I can, but eventually, I hope to meet the right man that I can settle down with for the rest of my life.

Imaginal Exposure 3: Lesbian Coming Out Story

It was last November when Garret and I took a trip to San Francisco that I started realizing that I am turning gay. At first I felt uncomfortable in the city because it's the "gay" city, but then a voice inside me told me that it's not the city but my sexuality that's making me uncomfortable. My sexual desire was diminishing for my husband, and I thought it was because I was pregnant. However, when Garret and I went shopping at the Gap, I felt really uncomfortable looking at women. First I ignored the uncomfortable feeling, but then it was too strong to ignore so I had to face it. I started trying to avoid certain situations because I knew that if women were there, especially Asian women (which I find particularly attractive), I would get uncomfortable. Eventually, I became tired of avoiding this uncomfortable feeling so I had to face the fact that the discomfort was just me trying to deny that I had turned into a lesbian. Being married was definitely going to put a strain on this new lifestyle I knew I needed to try, but I decided to deal with that later. I fancied the girl behind the cash register. I looked at her name tag—her name was Erika. She was tall, blonde, with blue eyes. I couldn't take my eyes off of her. She was stunning. I realized the feelings I was experiencing were feelings I had never felt for my husband! She was wearing a short skirt with a low cut shirt. Garret was trying to find pants, and I was looking at Erika. I was happy Garret was distracted by his shopping so that I could spend more time looking at Erika.

All I wanted to do was put my hand under her skirt and on her boobs. I never felt that same rush of desire for my husband. I knew I wanted to follow my impulses and put my hands all over her, but Garret was around so I didn't want to do it in front of him. So I told him that I wanted to go looking at some clothes in another part of the store, but I was really planning on meeting Erika. This is what we did: I touched her breasts, I kissed her nipples, I put my face between the two breasts, and then I went further down to her private parts, which I caressed and then I kissed with passion. Erika was one lucky lady. She got wet, and she was so happy. Garret hadn't realized what I was doing. I hope he had not called my name or anything because I certainly would not have heard him. At that moment all that

I wanted to pay attention to was Erika. Probably he thought I was looking at the women's dresses. But nope—I was turning into a lesbian while I was expecting his first child. I felt bad, but that's life. What I need to do is tell him the truth so that he can find someone new before it's too late. That way I can go on with my life and be who I really am instead of faking.

Imaginal Exposure 4: Sexual Identity Problem

I have been plagued with doubts about my sexuality for many years, and I felt a strong need for absolute certainty about my sexual identity. To this end, I would constantly check myself with gay porn to see if I would enjoy the sexual acts that were being performed. I wanted to make sure that that I was not feminine in any way and that I would not enjoy being kissed by another man, or penetrated, or dominated. If ever I felt like this was the case, I would go back and look at the porn again until I was sure I was *not* enjoying it. I spent many hours checking and reassuring myself. Finally, I came to accept that these doubts were caused by the OCD, and I decided to stop checking myself. But I kept having this nagging thought that I just might like it. Because I stopped checking myself, I didn't realize that over time my sexual preferences started to change.

I didn't even know this was happening to me, and it wasn't my OCD after all. My feelings of attraction and sex drive all started to expand. I still had all of my competitive drive, and I still liked sports, but I found I was also watching the TLC channel and *Kate Plus 8*. I started to love my job at Kohl's, folding and arranging the towels by color. I found myself feeling attracted to both men and women. Over time, I realized that I was not strictly masculine or feminine on the inside. I started having sexual experiences with both males and females at different times. Even though I was having sex all the time, I couldn't decide which I liked more because I liked them both. I enjoyed being close to women, and the look and feel of their bodies made me aroused. But I also liked the good looks of a well-groomed man and the feel of being sexually dominant over him. Both kinds of sex appeal to me, but I can't ever figure out what I like more.

I had a girlfriend that I liked very much, but she just wasn't enough for me. I kept feeling the urge to be with men because sex with her was not good enough. I would spend my Fridays with her and my Saturdays masturbating to gay porn and loving it, or sometimes even having sex with a guy. Of course, this ruined my relationship with my girlfriend, so I didn't bother finding a new one.

I should never have stopped doing my checking. If I had seen it coming, I could have stopped it. Now I will never know if I am straight or gay. I seem to be stuck somewhere in between with no place to go. Sometimes I think I'm gay and other times I think I'm straight, and other times I feel bisexual. The fact is that sometimes I like having sex with men, but other times I don't. I often decide that I prefer being with women, but then the urge to have sex with a male gets so strong I give in to it.

Although I always thought I would reclaim my heterosexual identity, it never happens. My life never improves or launches to the next level. I lead an average life, except for my sexuality, which is hopelessly screwed up, and I can never find a place where I am satisfied or happy. Wondering about my orientation continues to bother me all the time, and I have a bad sexual identity problem. My life is completely wasted, and I never figure out what was wrong with me. People think I am just a loser.

Imaginal Exposure 5: She-Male

It has been many years since I have been worried that I was secretly gay, that my attraction to women was somehow less than other men, that whatever I feel for women was much less than what other guys feel. I now realize I am gay. I've been told I have H-OCD, but it was never that; it was that I really want the bodies of men. It began when I started getting help for my H-OCD and I stopped doing any and all compulsions that I performed to ensure I was straight. As I stopped those compulsions, it revealed my true gay nature. Women no longer attract me. All those times I masturbated to lesbian porn and got aroused by women was just a fluke, some strange kinda of arousal due to the sexual nature of the images but I was never really into them. Stopping the compulsions was the key; once I stopped them my gay identity was revealed. It was so scary but it felt right. I knew I wanted guys and penis all along. I am scared but happy to admit to it and finally start living my gay life. I no longer will engage in sex with women, and now I realize that all along I never was attracted to them and was never turned on by them.

It was myself holding me back from truly enjoying a gay life and gay sex. I started going to gay bars and picking up hot guys. Man, it was an awesome experience. The first time I kissed a man while touching his penis was the most thrilling thing I have ever done—the rush and happiness I felt was unthinkable. I just wanted to take his clothes off and see him naked. I kept doing this stuff with so many men of different shapes and sizes, and it was the best most pleasurable thing I have ever done. I cannot believe it was ever in doubt, I am so turned on by their smell and taste and look and shape.

I've always wanted a man. I want to kiss a handsome man more than anything now and don't want to have sex with women again. All those times I was afraid I was attracted to men, it means that I really was and just afraid to admit it. All those times I noticed good-looking guys and thought that those guys were handsome, it meant I was gay all along. No straight man can think another man is handsome. I am liberated. I can live my gay life like I was meant to all along.

Then strangely something happened. I started to develop a strong attraction to she-males, the really feminine ones. How could I not? They had the sweet sexy shape and taste of women with the added bonus of a penis. This I found was even better than men. I loved she-males. They were so sexy with their curves and breasts and nice big penises—they had the best of both worlds. I couldn't wait to touch a she-male penis while I kissed him/her all over. When I finally got my she-male lover's pants off, it was amazing. That is why I was so confused about my sexuality. It was because all this time I needed a woman with a penis, something with a woman's body all over but with a big male penis and balls. I'm so sad and depressed and upset that those childhood times when I was turned on by naked vagina were a lie, and now I am not turned on by vaginas at all. I am sad and depressed that I will never have kids, so all I can do is take solace with my she-male lover. It isn't what I wanted—I wanted have sex with women and their vaginas, but that is not my life. I like she-males and I like to have penis, and so it will never be any other way.

Imaginal Exposure 6: Attracted to Penis

So since I was 15, I have always been concerned with whether I am attracted to my own penis. I have spent a lot of time avoiding looking at my penis in fear that I will think it is attractive, which would mean that I am attracted to a penis, which must mean I want to be with men and that I am gay. If I were gay, it would ruin my life, because everything I have experienced and dreamed of having one day will be completely out the window and destroyed. I have always dreamed of having a beautiful wife and kids, with a farmhouse and a family for my parents to enjoy. Lying in bed each night with a woman who you knew loved you and wanted you next to them. I went through several compulsions physically in regards to touching my penis and looking at it to monitor my feelings toward it. I have always worried that liking how mine looks and feels will result in enjoying how other attractive guys' looks and feels. I feel like I may be attracted to certain penises in the right situation and avoid stress and my own body in fear that it will trigger these uncomfortable thoughts.

These thoughts scare me and are very irritating and annoying because this could mean I am gay. I even get extremely emotional to the point of crying because of them. I decided after several years of being mentally tormented to go to a treatment facility and see a doctor in regards to what I am experiencing. After going through treatment and the Ex/RP program, I continued to have the thoughts of thinking my penis (and an image of the same type of penis) was attractive. We even did exposure therapy by having me look at my own penis for 30 minutes and overcome these ritual thoughts. These thoughts include me looking at my penis and imagining someone else having one that I thought was attractive and knowing that I like how mine feels and looks that I would enjoy theirs and would like to be with them intimately—imagining if I would enjoy touching or kissing it and monitoring my thoughts and feelings, gauging if I was into that. It upset me that the treatment wasn't working. I thought if I came here that I would figure out that these thoughts were irrational and not that they truly meant I was gay. I am upset and feel like I have wasted my time and that I have been gay all along. After several sessions, I realized that the treatment was not working. I would do these exposures during treatment and realize that I really liked looking at my own penis and how it feels and this means that I do find penises attractive.

I really tried my best to go through the treatment, but the thoughts just kept coming, and I finally realized that Dr. Williams had misdiagnosed me with OCD and that I really must like penises and therefore other men. I discontinued treatment and decided explore the gay lifestyle. These thoughts being in my head cause me to not enjoy sexual intimacy with women as much as it felt in the past. I tried one last attempt to have sex with my girlfriend, and I spent the whole time analyzing how her body looked and if I was enjoying it enough, while the image of an attractive penis is in my head. I was unable to perform with her and decided that this further proves my theory that all I can think about is a penis. I realized I could like the idea of being with someone who has a penis like I do. I couldn't believe that this was finally happening. I hated to break her heart, but these thoughts were not going away. I still had images of attractive penises in my head, and knowing this was my last option or attempt to figure these thoughts and feelings out led me to the conclusion that since these images are in my head constantly, and I am not grossed out by them, that I am attracted to men. I realized that I am attracted to my penis, and since it is similar to everyone else's that I indeed was attracted to the male penis and thus would be better off having relationships with other men instead of women.

On top of that I see now that I am not aroused sexually by women because I was not able to perform with my girlfriend. I have decided to stop fighting the urge to be with women and find a man I can be in a loving relationship with. I ended up breaking up with my girlfriend, because I realized I was no longer attracted to her sexually; I needed to be with men instead. After several months of searching for the right guy, I finally found someone who I love spending time with and enjoy sexually. I wish I wouldn't have spent so much time with one woman after another and just gave in to these feelings years ago. If I would have known how happy I could be with a man, I wouldn't have wasted so much time. The thoughts I had been having have finally gone away, and I know it is because I have finally done what I needed to do from the start. I needed to realize that I am gay. Now that I do, I am happy with my life this relationship I am in. Earlier, I said I have always dreamed of having a beautiful wife and kids, with a farmhouse and a family for my parents to enjoy, lying in bed each night with a woman who you knew loved you and wanted you next to them. But now I can have all of that with a man, and I am OK with that. This all happened because I tried to get help for OCD and stopped checking myself. If only I had kept checking, I might have been able to keep myself from becoming gay.

Imaginal Exposure 7: Gay at Work from a Banana

I walk into work Tuesday morning and begin preparing the store to open by 6:00 AM. That leaves me 45 minutes to get everything done. My OCD warns me that today is going to be awful. It is the day that I will finally be forced out of the "closet."

The conditions are perfect for something to go wrong. First, Mike is opening with me this morning. Second, the truck will be here after the morning rush. Finally, Jake is stopping by later to evaluate our store on the new operating standards. This must be what all gay people go through.

I sit at the manager's desk and begin taking a look at the numbers from last night's crew. As I'm logging into the computer, I see that my night manager, Skye, left some food out on the desk. It is a half-eaten sandwich and a banana. I examine the banana and notice that it resembles a penis. It is long, hard, and has only a slight curvature. I feel hot right now, like I'm about to start sweating. What if I grab it and start stroking it? What if I suck it?

Somehow I manage to force these thoughts out of my head and log in to the computer. I am looking at the numbers from last night, but that banana stares at me like it wants to be held. I pick up the banana and feel slightly aroused. Just then Mike walks into the office area to clock in and start his shift. He sees me with the banana but only says, "Good morning." I put the banana away and hid it under some papers. I know that he saw me. He's going to tell everyone at the store that I'm holding a banana and I'm gay.

I try to focus on my work, but my heart is beating so fast right now. Am I really gay? Mike pops his head into the office to ask me for a hand with some boxes of meat. I get up quickly and wonder if I'm going to start staring at his butt or crotch as we walk to the back of the store. He's in front of me, so I notice his butt—just like any other gay person would. He bends over to pick up a box, and I freeze. I am staring at him while he's bending over. His butt looks so tight and firm. I control the urge to run into him or to touch him, because I don't want to freak him out. He turns around and asks me if I would help him. I'm sure he saw me checking him out. He probably feels awkward around me now. We finish stacking the boxes, and he casually heads back to the kitchen to do his other preparations. He's probably worried that I have sexually harassed him and does not know what to say.

The food truck arrives and I go and tell Mike. I say, "Mike, meet me at the rear." Wait! Why didn't I say "back" instead of "rear?" Did I tell him to meet me *in* the rear? He still follows me to the door, but he hasn't said a word to me since this morning. As we unload the food and bring it into the store, I find myself frozen again. I am watching Mike like a hawk. He sees me, and I act like I'm looking somewhere past him off in the distance. What if I start fingering him? If I'm gay, then I just won't be able to control my actions.

As Mike finishes up with the truck order, Jake arrives. Jake is looking better than ever. I can tell that he is successful and probably has no trouble with dating. I think he is handsome, and just having that thought totally confirms that I am gay. He shakes my hand. I cannot seem to find my words. I mumble a sort of greeting, and he asks me to follow him into the office. On my way in the door, I overhear Mike speaking with the truck driver. Just as I walked past them, I hear the truck driver whisper, "Is he gay?" I act like I did not hear that, and I follow Jake to the office.

Jake is sitting at the desk with his legs uncrossed. He places his bag down and notices that there is something underneath it. He reaches under the stack of papers and pulls out the banana. He is holding it in a way that looks like a man holding an erect penis. Sure enough, I get aroused. I try not to think about it, but my impulses are taking over. With my shirt tucked in, it was hard to conceal the growth beneath. Jake looks over and sees the boner. He stands up and screams, "You pervert!" Mike opens the door and says, "I knew it!" He tells Jake that I've been staring at him sexually all day. Jake shakes his head in disbelief and says, "That's it. You're fired for sexual harassment." He tells me that he will make sure that I do not get a job in this town ever again.

I am definitely gay. I am a pervert, and I let my impulses get the best of me. I should not ever have touched that banana. Life as I know it is over.

Imaginal Exposure 8: Born Gay

Although I have been living like a straight person, all my life I have secretly wondered if I might actually be gay. One of my earliest childhood memories is playing with dolls, and I remember a Snow White doll that was one of my favorites. I loved her silky dress and smooth black hair. I remember from the time I was a very small child that I liked arts and hands-on crafts. While the other boys were out on the playground, climbing monkey bars and kicking balls, I was making colorful crafts with the girls in my classroom. As I got older, I saw that most of the other boys liked sports, but I was afraid to play sports with them until third grade. I didn't want to get hurt. I knew there was something different about me, that I was more feminine than the other boys, so pushing myself to play sports was a good way to fool them into thinking that I was just like them. As the years went on, I did more and more sports and even fooled myself into thinking I enjoyed it.

I realize now that there were other signs that I was not really like others. I hated it when my dad came home. I wanted to spend my time only with my mom and be just like her. I didn't relate to my dad at all because we were so different. So, I never got what I needed from him psychologically to develop into a proper male. I missed the lessons on masculinity, so my development as a male was stunted. And the fact that I didn't want to be around him was proof that I was not like him.

One day when I was in fifth grade, I was watching a music video with John Mayer. He was dressed in a bizarre feminine outfit covered with ruffles while making wild sensual movements. I realized that I was attracted to this and felt myself getting an erection. Finally, in a moment of utter panic, it all made sense. I was completely gay. I realized I was not interested in females at all. I only wanted to think about other dudes. Rather than accept this fact, I buried it and tried to deny my true orientation. I dated girls and had sex with many of them to try to convince myself I was really straight. For a while, I even believed it was true. When other people made fun of gay people, I joined in to make it look like was not one of "those people."

Over the last two years, the worries about my sexual orientation became worse and worse. I couldn't cope with the inner distress and turmoil. I was finally diagnosed with OCD. I got treatment for the OCD, but the worries never completely went away. As I reflect on my life now, I realize that the real issue was not OCD. I really am gay. I have always been gay. This is why I can't stop thinking about guys. I was born gay. There is nothing I can do to change this. Although I have a girlfriend and I force myself to go through the motions, it will not change who I really am inside. I am homosexual. I like dudes. I really like dudes. Even though I deny it to the whole world, I cannot run away from it.

I have heard many stories of men who lead double lives. John Travolta, Will Smith, and Tom Cruise, and how they have gay sex on the side and yet still keep their lifestyles that they currently have. I can be just like those other guys. And really, because I can have gay sex on the side in addition to the life that I already have, I decided to go onto the Internet, look at pictures of hot men, and masturbate to them. And then I will find a man to hook up with. Once I have done this, I can truly be sexual with men, have gay sex on the side, and still have my girlfriend at home (even though I don't really like sex with her a much as I will with dudes). I really am a closeted homosexual who needs his life as it is. I am just like those guys on gay.com who hook up with other gay men in their free time.

Before I had feared that this was severe internalized homophobia and not OCD. And as I started to go through with the treatment, all I wanted to do was prove, one way or another, that I was not gay. As I was going through with the treatment, I realized that I did have was severe internalized homophobia and not OCD. I really truly did desire to be sexual with other men, but I was just afraid of doing it because of what my family and friends would say and how they would look at me. I just needed to come to grips with this and stop trying to prove this and analyze that. I am happy that I can finally admit this, at least to myself, and I will die a gay man.

Imaginal Exposure 9: Lost My Attraction to Women

I am a man who has always been excited and aroused only by women. I have never had a problem in this area and consider myself very good in bed. Over the last few years however, I have been having issues getting an erection. It started slowly, but it's been getting worse over time. Even more troubling is that I have been having these images of penises in my head! I don't know where they came from or what to do about them. In addition to these thoughts, I've had images of receiving and performing oral sex on men. At first these thoughts came only now and again, but over time they became increasingly worse to the point that I am constantly distracted by them.

Through reading an article by psychologist Dr. Monnica Williams, I came to understand this was all caused by OCD, and I started getting treatment. I stopped checking to make sure I was still turned on by women. However, after much time, money, and effort the treatment was unsuccessful. I was so hopeful to finally get help, but it seems there is really no help for me. I continued to have these images pop into my head whenever I was around men. Not only that, the images occurred when I was watching TV, relaxing, and even having sex with my girlfriend. The pictures occupied every waking hour of my day, and there was not a moment that I was free of them.

I found that over time I started to lose my interest in women. I was no longer excited or aroused by them. Even the most stunningly beautiful women failed to produce any arousal in me. I felt absolutely nothing. My girlfriend would do all sorts of sexual activities to get me turned on, but none of it worked any more. I would get an erection for 30 seconds, but then put on the condom and my erection just died. My sexuality was slipping away. Every night my girlfriend went to sleep disappointed, and I felt increasingly like a failure. I went to many parties, and every woman in the room seemed plain and uninteresting. I didn't feel anything. As badly as I wanted to, I could not get an erection to women any longer. My penis was now my enemy.

It was not right for me to hang onto my girlfriend when I was unable to please her. She lost respect for me and said I was not a real man. I was constantly embarrassed by my problem. She started having sex with other men behind my back. I knew one of the men she was sleeping with, and she said that he was better in bed than I was. She wanted to break up and just be friends. No women were interested in being with me because I was now impotent. I couldn't even look at pictures of them because it reminded me of how miserable I had become. I could not have sex with women any more. My penis would never get hard again. I had to give up women forever. Because I couldn't have sex, I lost my manhood. I don't feel like a man anymore and probably never will.

I had become asexual, and soon I lost my confidence in general. Something about my maleness made me good at what I do, but I started to doubt everything about my ability. Once my sex drive was gone, people no longer looked up to me as a leader at work. I started to make mistakes and worried too much about what they were thinking about me. I could no longer function on the job because I didn't believe in myself.

Imaginal Exposure 10: Better Gay

I always considered myself straight, but as the years went on, I started to notice subtle signs that I could possibly turn gay. Although many doctors and therapists told me that these thoughts are symptoms of OCD, I was never quite reassured. I have been battling the worries with many rituals, like checking to see if I am still aroused by women, convincing myself that I am truly straight, and mentally reviewing my past for proof that I wasn't gay. I have also been avoiding so many gay things, such as movies and TV shows with gay characters, like Elton John, and anything that reminds me of my sexual orientation—news articles, you name it.

I thought at first that by doing these things, I was winning a mental battle, but I soon came to realize that these behaviors only helped me to cope with the upsetting OCD thoughts. I was not winning a mental battle but giving into the OCD and fueling it with its compulsions. I said to myself, "Fuck it, I'm not letting the OCD rule my life anymore." I stopped doing compulsions and avoiding things. I decided to live my life and it felt fucking great. I fell in love with the perfect woman, we got married, we had two beautiful kids. I had fucking beaten it!

Then the trouble started. The reality was that I have been hiding my gay tendencies subconsciously all my bloody life, and when I stopped the compulsions, it was finally there free to surface. One day I became intrigued by pictures of men that are built and fit: David Beckham and Gareth Thomas. They really started to turn me on, and I liked it. I started admiring pictures of Gareth Thomas with his shirt off and fantasizing about his tattoos and his build. Eventually sex with my wife was shit. I needed something ELSE—I needed to try something sexual with a man.

I thought for a long time what it might be like to have sex with a man. Finally, one day I went to a gay bar, and it just felt right. I saw a sexy guy at the bar, and I knew I had to have him fuck me. Once we did it, I finally felt whole and knew he was truly the love I have been searching for all these years—not just the sex but the emotional part as well.

I tried to lead a double life for the sake of my wife and the kids, but my marriage and life that surrounds it became a sham. I mean, my wife is a great person, and although I enjoy her company, I realized that I am not truly in love. I love her like a friend but not a life partner. It was hard to tell her the truth, but she deserved to know. l broke her heart and caused SO much humiliation for her, myself and my kids. I'm gay. I moved away and lost my family and friends because I needed to complete my life change. I couldn't live here or have the friends I used to because I had to come out of the closet. But it's OK, because now I can really be who I am—I can finally be gay and proud of it.

You would think I don't fit the stereotypes of a gay man—I play rugby, I swear, and I drink booze. Just look at Gareth Thomas. He captained the British Lions, played for Cardiff and Toulouse, and he turned out to be gay. He had to break his wife's heart, so I guess I am in good company.

It turns out that I never really had OCD; I knew it all along. I wasted so much money on those fuckin doctors. The gay obsessions were my subconscious breaking through. I stopped taking the medication because now I am facing the truth. I will, however, have to deal with the misery I have caused others and the humiliation. My wife filed for custody of the kids, and she won because (let's be honest) I didn't oppose it. I never see them any more except on Christmas, and I can tell they don't really like me, and they don't accept my lifestyle. But it's OK because now I can have sex with all the dudes I want. That is what really, really makes me happy.

Imaginal Exposure 11: HIV Positive

I had been dealing with thoughts about being gay for a very long time and doing all sorts of behaviors to make sure that I was not actually turning gay. This included jacking off to straight and gay porn and comparing the those and constantly checking myself for signs of sexual arousal around attractive men and women.

Through the course of getting treated for my OCD, I realized that I was not gay and that all of these things I was doing were compulsions. I stopped doing all the rituals and just decided to live my life and let go of the worries. I would stop being vigilant for signs that I might change my orientation. My wife was very glad that I stopped doing all the rituals, but I continued to have pesky doubts that I might actually be gay. Even though I loved her, I realized I was not turned on by her anymore. I kept having dreams about being with men, and although I hated the dreams at first, eventually I started enjoying them.

I decided to go to a gay bar to see if I would enjoy being around gay men. One night when my wife was out with the kids, I went to nearby gay club to see what I might find. Inside there were a number of very good-looking men, kissing everywhere. There was one guy in particular with an athletic build and dark hair. I couldn't stop looking at him and realized I was really turned on by his good looks. He bought me a drink and then later followed me into the restroom where we had gay sex.

I realized that this was the part of my life I had been missing all along. I didn't want to be a family man any more. I didn't want to be a husband or a dad. I wanted to submerge myself in the gay lifestyle. I moved out of my home and went to New York City where I could live in the Village. My wife was very shocked an upset. She urged me to think about it for the sake of kiddos, but I just couldn't stop myself. I left it all behind and filed for divorce. I started going to gay clubs every night and meeting a new man each time. We would do all sorts of crazy gay sexual activities, and I enjoyed everything.

My parents were ashamed of me and told me that I should not have left my family and should go back. I can't help it if that is just who I am.

They should accept me, but they don't. They stopped inviting me home for Christmas because each time I came with a different guy.

Honestly, I don't blame them. I became very flamboyant, wearing tight yellow shirts and tight khaki pants. People who see me know I am gay from 10 miles away. I wear my hair spiked up, and on Sunday nights I go in drag to a gay karaoke club and sing Madonna songs and sip tropical drinks. I love to hang around for the best booty contest. Those guys are hot.

Because I was so busy hooking up with every guy in the Village (mostly gay but some straight too), I didn't even think to use a condom. I shouldn't have been surprised to discover I was HIV positive, and I also got Hepatitis C. I can never go back to my family now, but that's OK because I don't want to. My kids are now 17 and 13, but I never see them. Eventually I settled in with another guy who also has HIV. I forget I ever had a family and laugh at the idea that I once thought I was straight. It was all worth it.

Resources

For additional recommended reading for treating clients with sexual orientation fears, readers are directed to the following articles:

- Williams, M. T., Crozier, M., & Powers, M. B. (2011). Treatment of sexual orientation obsessions in obsessive-compulsive disorder using exposure and response prevention. *Clinical Case Studies, 10,* 53–66.
- Williams, M. T., Davis, D. M., Tellawi, G., & Slimowicz, J. (2015). Assessment and treatment of sexual orientation obsessions in obsessive-compulsive disorder. *Australian Clinical Psychologist, 1,* 12–18.
- Williams, M. T., Slimowicz, J., Tellawi, G., & Wetterneck, C. (2014). Sexual orientation symptoms in obsessive compulsive disorder: Assessment and treatment with cognitive behavioral therapy. *Directions in Psychiatry, 34,* 37–50.

6

Treating Pedophile Obsessions

Chad T. Wetterneck and Erin C. Nghe

Case Example of Pedophilic Obsessions

Case Introduction and Presenting Complaints

Sondra (not her actual name) was a 26-year-old, non-Hispanic White female, who was married with a toddler at home. She lived with her husband of five years and son, and she was a full-time mother after giving birth. She had an associate degree, and prior to becoming a mother, she had worked as a teacher's aide at her church's school for four years. She identified as "very religious" and Mormon by faith. She and her husband's family lived in the neighboring area, and she had strong ties with others in her religious community.

Sondra's presenting complaints were about three main sexually related obsessions that had overtaken her life in the past year. In her words, she was "unable to be the person I want to be. I can longer be a mother or helpful family member. I can no longer lie to loved ones and my (religious) community. I can no longer function in the ways I had imagined I would like to lead my life." In addition, she reported that she had seen three different therapists in the past nine months, one of which was an obsessive-compulsive disorder (OCD) specialist, and she did not feel much hope that she could get better.

History

Onset and Treatment History
Sondra was referred to us by a member of her church who was a counselor by profession. He had suggested she go to therapy approximately nine months earlier, which she did, leading to the three failed therapy attempts before coming to our specialty clinic. Sondra was smiling throughout much of the

initial consult but indicated that she felt silly and ashamed of thoughts and was tired of avoiding them and not addressing them in a helpful manner. She was not able to discuss her concerns very openly with her friend who was the counselor, or her first therapist, but was able to outline three main concerns in our first session and said, "I guess I have OCD, and most of my thoughts are uncommon even for that condition. They all are about sex and my religion." She went on to explain that she was always aware of and monitoring any thought that could be sexual so that she would know how much spiritual counseling she would need from her church leaders to maintain good standing with her faith. She believed thought monitoring was quite normal, but it became much more challenging after puberty, once she began dating her now husband, and again after childbirth.

Shortly after reaching puberty, Sondra was aware of distressing thoughts about acting out on "inappropriate" urges. She had intrusive images, commonly while meeting with church elders or teachers, in which she thought she might spontaneously hug or kiss them before they could stop her. She never acted on these urges and considered herself as needing extra religious guidance to deal with her impure thoughts. While she was mostly confident that she had the urges in check, she wondered if she would ever be able to fully trust herself, commit to a relationship with only man, and if he could trust her if he knew what she was thinking.

Sondra continued to have thoughts primarily about church officials when a man named Eric, who would end up becoming her husband, courted her at age 17. She felt a great deal of love toward Eric early in the relationship but feared that she would act inappropriately with another man during the courtship. She also began to have strong thoughts toward Eric—while they had hugged, held hands and kissed during the first six months, she also had images of jumping on him and rubbing against him in a sexual manner while alone and in public places. She developed a lot of shame around her thoughts and wondered if she could even remain in her church.

After less than a year, Eric mentioned something related to marriage, and she immediately suggested they get married. While he was pleased and surprised, she admitted to us that she felt confused about whether her thoughts were based on love or something less pure and concluded that she would be safer around other men if she would permanently commit to Eric. She now was able to realize that she actually did love Eric, but for a few years, she questioned her true intentions with him. She also stated that she never initiated sexual activity with him.

Another distressing area for Sondra was her thoughts about seeing her own body without clothing. As her body changed during puberty, she began to be more aware of her sexual "urges" and so avoided looking at herself without clothes on, either directly or in a mirror. She felt seeing the "sexual parts" of her body would lead to more thoughts about sex. While she began dating Eric, she noticed a particularly distressing thought about her own sexuality—what if she had a sexual thought while seeing her own body? Does that mean she was attracted to herself and therefore bisexual? She was confused as to how she could be bisexual—she only considered herself to be sexually attracted to men, even though she tried not to think about that. Although she rated this as the least distressing of her fears, she said this fear increased when Eric would make positive comments about her body or even her appearance in general. His appreciation of her physical or other areas of beauty (including her personality) usually triggered thoughts about whether she could be bisexual.

Sondra shared her most distressing fear, which happened to be the most recent unwanted thought to develop. She said, with her head hanging low, and her typically smiling face turning somber, "I'm afraid I am going to act on urges to sexually abuse my son. Maybe other children too." Sondra said she knew from her previous therapist that this was an "OCD thought," but it felt too real and too painful to ignore. Now it seemed unbearable to add this to her tireless work in controlling all other aspects of her sexual thoughts and urges. She first had the thought when her son was only a few months old. She was changing his diaper in the middle of the night, and he began to urinate on her and all over the changing table and surrounding floor. She put her hand out over his penis to prevent more mess from the urine and touched it. In the next few seconds, she felt as though his penis twitched and thought she noticed an awkward facial expression. He began crying, and she completed his diaper change and rocked him back to sleep. She could not sleep, however. Although it was relatively dark in the room, she could not stop thinking whether or not he had reacted to his penis being touched and the hard-to-make-out facial expression. She wondered, "Did I touch him in a way that made him feel some pleasure, and did he smile a bit? No, that's crazy; babies don't have smiles this early or for that type of feeling . . . do they?" She continued to obsess about whether she touched him too hard or inappropriately and whether he was actually making a facial response related to that. She questioned whether he began crying before or after she touched him and whether she hurt him by touching his penis.

Sondra was plagued by these thoughts. Every time she changed him after that she wondered more about what happened, what type of person she was, and if he would be permanently damaged from her inappropriateness. She began watching him for more signs or cues associated with pleasure or being hurt while changing him. She avoided his genital area except when there was fecal matter present and began to have her husband do more and more of the changing or asked him to keep her company while she changed him so as to not be alone with her baby. She asked her husband to bathe him more regularly, and eventually he did all the bathing.

Sondra wanted to breastfeed her son for at least 9 to 12 months but found that she was monitoring his reaction to sucking on her breast. She realized that she had previously looked away from him after he successfully latched because she did not like seeing her own breasts, but now watched him for any sign that could indicate stimulation. She also felt incredibly stressed trying to monitor her own thoughts and bodily reactions to seeing him nurse and also seeing her own breasts. She told Eric that she wanted to switch him over to formula a few weeks later, and he reluctantly agreed.

The avoidance of changing diapers alone, bathing her son, and breastfeeding eventually led to Sondra not wanting to be around her son alone at all. She even had difficulty holding him without feeling anxious. She remembers a family gathering happening shortly thereafter, and her relatives brought over many of their own small children. She had the thought, "Maybe it was possible that I would harm my sister's and my in-laws' children as well." It was at this point that she decided to discuss her most recent fears with a church elder, and he consulted with a church member (who was the counselor) and they (thankfully) told her to seek therapy.

Sondra was able to share the details of her previous treatments. The first therapist she saw was a community mental health counselor. The counselor was not religious, and he may have even alluded to being somewhere between agnostic and an atheist. Sondra had little confidence that he could understand how important her faith was to her. He also admitted that he was not a specialist in working with people who may or may not be experiencing inappropriate desires to touch small children but that he "would do the best he can." Due to her desire to change and her fear that perhaps she was a "disgusting human being who should not be around children," Sondra forced herself to two more sessions with the therapist. Although we do not like to pass judgment on other therapy or therapists without knowing all of the details (which is near impossible to have when you only have one reporter of the experience), we believe that this counselor should have at least offered to help her find a referral due to his lack of awareness of her condition and the available evidence-based methods to treat it. It was clear he did not consider her presentation to be OCD-related—and unclear whether he believed she could be a pedophile. Nevertheless, he attempted to "assess her risk" to acting on her thoughts, which led to an increase in her fears.

Sondra was heartbroken as she considered her options. Within a few weeks of ending her therapy she began searching on the Internet for "cures for sexual thoughts," which led to articles or sites that discussed "cures for pedophilia." While initially discouraged by what she read, she did run across a post on an Internet forum about sexually related thoughts caused by an anxiety disorder. Some of what was written sounded remotely similar to her own thoughts. She wondered, and prayed, that her thoughts about her son could be due to a different type of condition. She searched online for providers covered by her insurance that listed anxiety as a specialty. She remembers being astounded and somewhat hopeful that 10 out of 20 providers listed anxiety as a specialty. She also noted that most of them had between 8 and 15 specialties listed and interpreted this as a sign they were experts in many things. Unfortunately, that was not the case. Her next therapist was very willing to see people who had stress or anxiety and offered a number of eclectic tools to relieve these feelings, recommending reducing stressful activities, and adding yoga, massage, other regular exercise, sleep hygiene, oils and guided imagery exercises. When not in close proximity to her family, Sondra felt better for a small period of time while engaging in these activities, but she also noticed that her fears were not diminishing overall, and she was still not able to engage with her family, loved ones, or religious community as she had before her son was born. Her therapist was part of a monthly professional consultation group, and she brought up Sondra's case in a de-identified manner to her peers. One of the group members was an OCD specialist and recommended that she consult with her patient to see if she had OCD.

Within a week Sondra had switched to the OCD specialist. She felt a mixture of hope and felt like this was her last chance at getting better. She wondered if other people in therapy had to get to a third therapist to recover or if she was "extra crazy." The OCD specialist was very knowledgeable and seemed more direct, asking straightforward questions about her thoughts and how she responded to them—it was a little scary at first, but

Sondra recognized that she was becoming a little less nervous to discuss her concerns. Within a few sessions there was a treatment plan with an exposure hierarchy full of things of which she questioned her ability to complete.

The specialist set a timeline and mapped out/reviewed Sondra's progress every two sessions (meeting once per week). Sondra did her first exposure—writing out the word "pedophile" repeatedly with the specialist present. She could barely bring herself to spell it out, thinking about a future exposure in which she would write, "I am a pedophile." But she did. She did a few times until her anxiety came down. She was both relieved and confused that seeing herself write the word did not lead to high levels of anxiety after doing the fourth exposure.

Sondra was assigned three to four exposures to do each day between sessions. She tried to do all of her therapy assignments the next day but did not make enough time to do so. Each day after, her adherence to homework got worse and avoidance built up. She tried making changes in her schedule, and the specialist suggested bringing in her husband (who now was aware of 90% of her obsessions), and he came in to learn and to support her. The specialist tried many helpful improvements to increase Sondra's chances of completing her therapy. She taught Eric how to best support the work without being too reassuring, conducted more in-session exposure work with Sondra, reduced the level of exposures, and suggested time management and planning strategies. Sondra's specialist also suggested stimulus control reminders to begin working at home and, in the end, finally set some contingencies about needing to complete enough homework to remain in therapy. Eventually, Sondra was not able to meet these requirements. She was encouraged to come back to the specialist at a later time, when she felt capable of fully engaging in the treatment. The specialist also offered to refer Sondra to another specialist; Sondra chose the latter and came to our clinic.

As a result of her previous therapy experiences, Sondra felt she was beyond help. She did not know why this time would be any different and had only a little confidence that we even knew what we were doing. Based on this, we felt that we had to take a slightly different approach to the beginning of therapy.

Family Mental Health History
Sondra stated that recently she had learned a lot more about her family history and that her knowledge of it was much greater than when she saw her

first therapist. Her mother was always worrying, which she thought was normal, but, in hindsight, her mother's anxiety prevented her from enjoying life. She had a grandfather who most likely had post-traumatic stress disorder, as he was previously in the military and had been involved in combat. Other than that, Sondra was unaware of any other mental health diagnoses in her family.

Trauma History
Sondra reported no history of physical, sexual, or emotional abuse. She had attended school with a number of students who had different religious backgrounds or who were most likely atheists. Some of the latter students intermittently teased her throughout middle school, and her parents simply told her to ignore them and that their fates were most likely already decided.

Family/Social History
Sondra was the second child of five and grew up with her biological parents, who had been married for 29 years, and four siblings. She stated that she had a "fulfilling" childhood, learning and playing mainly with members of her religious community and developing strong bonds with many people. Her parents were firm and vigilant to make sure she and her siblings followed Mormon spiritual teachings and values. Being a respected, yet humble member of the community was heavily emphasized. Sondra learned from her siblings' mistakes and how they were punished and rarely did anything remotely wrong or requiring discipline. Three of her siblings were married, and between them they had seven children between the ages of 4 months and 11 years old. Her husband had three siblings, and she was an aunt to another four children between the ages of two and eight on his side. Family and community were valued over all else.

Sexual History
Sondra was raised in the Mormon faith, and she admitted that her family or community members did not speak much about sexual topics, except to reinforce that intimacy occurred between a man and woman who wed and desired to have a family. She heard a lot of talk from peers in school, mostly those she did not spend time with, whom she considered to be obsessed with dating and not having their priorities straight. She did not date anyone prior to her husband and, given her early fears after puberty, felt most comfortable avoiding any discussion related to sexual intimacy or even talking

to male peers outside of her community (and many of those within as well). Between her religious upbringing and her fears, she had well-defined beliefs about what was right and wrong regarding sex, with no gray area.

Assessment

Sondra had previously taken some standard assessments while working with the last OCD specialist. We did have access to them, but they were also taken three months prior to working with us so we readministered all measures and added in a few extra ones specific to our conceptualization of an alternative approach to treatment. Her results are listed in the following discussion. Several of these measures used can be found in Appendix B, with more information about them in Chapter 2.

Yale–Brown Obsessive-Compulsive Scale (Y-BOCS) is a clinician-administered scale that measures the severity of obsessive compulsive-symptoms in adults. Sondra's score when beginning therapy was a 29, which was comparable to her score at intake (27) with the previous therapist. This placed her in the severe range.

The Dimensional Obsessive Compulsive Scale (DOCS) assesses OCD symptoms in various categories. In addition to the standard four subscales, Sondra was administered three additional subscales that split up the unacceptable thoughts factor into violent, sexual, and scrupulous content. Her subscale scores were as followed: Contamination—6, Harm—8, Symmetry—2, Unacceptable Thoughts—16, along with Sexual Thoughts—15, Violent—2, and Scrupulous—10. We discussed the various elevations with Sondra, and she indicated that most of her concerns endorsed in the Scrupulous, Harm, and, Contamination areas were driven by her sexual obsessions and the behaviors she utilized to control herself and to prevent harm to others.

The Beck Depression Inventory (BDI-I) is a self-report measure that assesses the prevalence and severity of depressive symptoms. Sondra's BDI score was a 22, which indicated moderate levels of depression. She had previously scored a 14 when she began seeing her previous therapist. We considered this a significant increase in her depression.

The Behavioral Activation Depression Scale–Short Form (BADS) examines areas of activation and avoidance. Sondra scored a 12, with low endorsement of engaging in pleasurable activities and high levels of avoidance of daily tasks.

The MINI International Neuropsychiatric Interview 6.0 (MINI) is a structured diagnostic clinical interview designed to assess for psychiatric disorders in adults. In addition to a diagnosis of OCD, Sondra also met criteria for major depressive disorder. Her mood was quite depressed most days, she did not engage in pleasurable events nor get pleasure from events once thought pleasurable and had a host of other symptoms (sleeping too little, not having much appetite, difficulty in concentrating, and feeling hopeless). She did not endorse any suicidal thoughts, even though she questioned whether her family and the world would be better without her.

The Valued Living Questionnaire (VLQ; Wilson, Sandoz, Kitchens, & Roberts, 2010) is self-report questionnaire we frequently give after discussing a patient's values in many areas of life and define what type of person they would like to be in multiple domains. The VLQ asks for respondents to rate the importance of values in 10 domains: marriage/intimate relations, parenting, other family relations, friendships, employment, education/training, recreation, spirituality, citizenship/community, and physical well-being. It also asks how consistently the person has lived their life according to these values in the past week. Her initial scores are reported in Table 6.1.

Sondra's scores indicated that there were a number of very important areas in her life, and yet she did not feel as though she was moving toward her values with much regularity (based on a total score of 28 for consistency with her values).

Table 6.1 Valued Living Questionnaire Scores

Value	Importance	Consistency
Marriage	10	3
Parenting	10	1
Other Family	10	4
Friends	8	4
Work	5	3
Education	5	3
Recreation	5	2
Spirituality	10	4
Community	10	2
Well-Being	8	2

Case Conceptualization

Sondra's symptoms and course of dysfunction were conceptualized through a cognitive-behavioral approach. She had a strong sense of what was right and wrong and believed that her actions and thoughts were a representation of who she was and how God viewed her. Her sexual OCD (S-OCD) thoughts, although unwanted, meant that God was aware of how imperfect and dangerous she could be, and this led to her developing as many mental and overt behaviors (i.e., rituals) as possible to counteract her sexual thoughts. Unfortunately, the temporary relief provided by the rituals reinforced her beliefs that rituals and avoidance were keeping her safe and keeping others safe from her.

To that end, Sondra's avoidance had reached such high levels that she was disengaging from almost all previously rewarding experiences. She distanced herself from her husband emotionally and physically, rarely interacted with her child without others present, and avoided family and community/religious events where she might be "unsupervised" around children or alone with a male member of her church. Work and chores that she used to do around the home and for others in her extended family and community were neglected. Not surprisingly, this extended dip in rewarding activities and accumulation of work resulted in her feeling quite depressed. As we have discussed throughout this book, OCD and depression are common comorbid conditions, and in most cases, patients will develop OCD first and then experience increasing levels of depression as rituals, avoidance, and life in general shrink to only attending to one's fears.

The combination of depression and fear had hijacked her previous attempt at therapy. Hopelessness was the main reason she was stuck doing low-level exposures, despite seeing some reduction in fear during sessions with her previous therapist. She also thought, "What was the point of even trying?" if she was already viewed by God as unable to refrain from these terrible sins.

Course of Treatment and Assessment of Progress

Sondra came to our clinic already knowing that she had OCD but now was seriously depressed and even more convinced that her treatment would be unsuccessful, because she had already seen someone considered an expert.

She was now going to start working with another psychologist who claimed expertise (CW). She completed an initial intake (CW) and then worked with a master's level clinician to complete the MINI.

Treatment Session 1
Despite already seeing someone with experience in OCD, we treated Sondra very similar to any other new client in Session 1. Even though we were going to deliver the same foundational principles of exposure and response prevention (Ex/RP) that she received with her former therapist (albeit with some variations in approach), psychoeducation was important to repeat with Sondra. Psychoeducation is important to cover with any repeat clients, as it gives patients more opportunities to hear similar information a second time, delivered in a confident expert fashion, thereby reinforcing previously learned concepts and possibly providing additional analogies to provide new perspectives. Early in the session Sondra stated that she knew the model of OCD and it did not need to be repeated. When we asked her to share her understanding of the model, and how it worked, she had about 50% of the explanation correct and admitted she did not have all the answers, which allowed us to fill in the rest of the information. She understood that she viewed her thoughts as if they were actually actions in her view (and in the eyes of God) and that her preventative actions (rituals) were designed to keep her and others safe (thereby reducing her feelings of anxiety and disgust). While she stated that her rituals "used to work," she acknowledged that nothing seemed to work anymore.

A second reason for repeating activities such as psychoeducation is that not all clinicians deliver it the same way or as thoroughly as needed. This applies to all aspects of treatment. Many patients that have seen someone they thought was using Ex/RP but yet are unable to share a recent exposure or even describe an exposure hierarchy. Even after months of treatment, some clients never engage in this type of work.

Sondra was given a good overview of OCD, normalization of sexual thoughts in all people, and even how religion can influence one's symptoms by her previous therapist. We asked her to state what she remembered and filled in any needed areas, while also reminding her that we might not be as clear about it in the future, to avoid giving unnecessary reassurance. She was familiar with that concept as well and agreed that it was an issue for her.

Sondra came in 20 minutes early to complete self-report measures, and we also completed the Y-BOCS during the latter half of the session, after discussing psychoeducation. Her main fears, ranked from most distressing to least, were (a) she would molest her son, end up in prison, and her family would reject her; (b) she would molest her family or community member's children, if left unsupervised; (c) due to having perverse sexual thoughts, she would not receive any type of salvation in the afterlife; (d) she would become bisexual, and her husband would leave her; and (e) she would sexually assault a church elder and be kicked out of her community. She endorsed a number of rituals including avoidance (e.g., bathing her child, changing diapers, touching children in general, seeing herself nude, looking at children in general, averting her eyes from other's chest and groin areas, maintaining five or more feet between her and male church members), excessive information-seeking about "cures" for S-OCD and treatments for changing pedophiles and sexual orientation, excessive praying for strength and forgiveness, and checking her body for inappropriate "arousal" reactions. In addition to more common signs of arousal, Sondra also felt an accelerated heart rate could be due to arousal, which was quite challenging as her heart rate elevated frequently due to anxiety.

Sondra was asked to keep track of her rituals each day using a "ban book." She was not instructed to stop ritualizing between now and the next session but rather to record how often she engaged in a particular ritual (by placing a check in her book on the appropriate page after each time she performed a ritual or "submitted" to a fear). She had been asked to do something similar in her previous treatment and found it hard to remember to do. We simplified the procedure by changing from a regular notebook to a pocket-sized notebook that was easier to carry. Given that Sondra stated she did not remember to record her rituals very often, we advised her to set four different alarms on her phone that would go off every four hours while she was awake to prompt her to think about and record what recent rituals occurred.

If Sondra chose not to engage in a ritual, she was asked to record her ability to "resist" as well and to note the situation in which she was able to resist. We used the first week of data from ritual monitoring as a baseline (occasionally we will use the first two weeks, but not in Sondra's case) as a way to chart progress. We divided the number of *resists* by the total of *resists* plus *submits* for each area to obtain a percentage. We then set goals for number of *resists* as a percentage and noted whether there was change based on the overall number of occurrences.

During, and more thoroughly at the end of, the first session we assessed Sondra's confidence in her ability to commit to the treatment. Her expectations for success were low, and she pointed to her experience with the previous treatments as evidence. Based on her circumstances, we decided to make a few changes to the treatment. First, we asked if she was willing to commit to two sessions per week, to which she agreed. We felt this session frequency, which is in line with evidence-based protocols, would help maintain treatment fidelity. Considering the 167 hours that separate most weekly therapy sessions, it was important to decrease that gap for Sondra as a way to reduce opportunities for rituals and increase the level of support. We also suggested that there might be a way to focus on things she wanted in life, rather than trying to control or reduce unwanted experiences. This statement was intriguing to her, and she stated that she would be open to a new approach.

When Sondra asked for more information on the new approach, we stated that we would have to discuss it in more detail during the next session. She seemed a little confused and expressed that the sooner she knew the new path, the sooner she might get better. We again declined to give more information, and she scheduled the next appointment. The lack of elaboration was strategic. Sondra was already doing anything she could to avoid or neutralize her thoughts and needed something to increase her hope. Letting her leave without allowing her enough information to turn it into some control strategy that she might misuse or completely dismiss would help maintain hope and perhaps provide some "fresh mental space," free from the previous experiences of failing treatment.

Treatment Sessions 2 and 3
Sondra returned later in the same week. She stated that she had thought a lot about the possibility of a different type of treatment working but could not figure out what it would be. She even reported an increase in online information-seeking, hoping to find an obscure treatment that might align with her limited information. Sondra was anxious but also excited about a potential alternative.

We explained that most people come into therapy because they are troubled by thoughts or emotions that they do not want to have. We try all sorts of things to escape or avoid these experiences and have limited success, and eventually many of us come to therapy. Part of what we should learn in therapy is that we have two basic strategies for living with our experiences; simply put, we can choose to accept or we can choose to change (and sometimes we will employ aspects of both strategies). We have to learn about acceptance and change strategies, and similar to the serenity prayer, we have to determine when each should be used. Now, occasionally when we are trying to escape, avoid, or otherwise change our experience, we may do something that is fulfilling (rather than only relieving). This may be a time in which we are, intentionally or unknowingly, moving toward a *value*.

As described in Chapter 3, and in line with the approach of acceptance and commitment therapy (ACT), we defined what we meant by a value and distinguished it from a goal, explaining that it is not tied to any external contingencies or rewards from others and can be selected (and changed) without having any experience with a particular value. We also noted that she may already be pursuing her values but might only be pursuing a limited number of them or over pursuing some while neglecting others. We began looking at each domain listed on the VLQ and asked her to consider, "What type of person would you like to be in this area of your life, regardless of whether you feel as though you have acted this way before or not?" Sondra provided a beginning list of values in her core domains (defined as those she rated most high on importance) that she thought would be internally meaningful to her—descriptions that would shape her behavior regardless of who was watching or what others would say. Sondra stated that the idea of values was very much in line with what she considered to be her religious conviction and faith. She drew a parallel to maintaining a course of conviction to religious principles, despite others laughing or debasing her beliefs and religion-based actions. We discussed the similarities and stated that she was free to pick her own values, even if they were different than her religion's views. Sondra picked the following values in her core areas (see Table 6.2).

Sondra was able to choose many of her values with little help, which is atypical for most of our patients. Many require seeing lists of values or answering broad questions ("If you could do anything you thought was important in any of these areas, what would it be?") and then linking to specific concepts of values. Following the principles of ACT, we discuss values without any judgment or personal bias, and we try not to tell anyone what they should or should not value. However, in Sondra's case, she had a hard time coming up with values for well-being and could initially only describe "being selfless" as her value. We did suggest that being selfless is more in line with other domains of values, *and* we suggested a few values that we have found particularly useful for OCD patients (and that are inversely related to OCD severity; Wetterneck et al., 2013) when doing Ex/RP and

Table 6.2 Highly Important Domains and Values Descriptions

Domain Area	Values Description
Marriage	Loving, caring, nurturing, understanding, practicing patience, faithfulness, practicing honesty, being respectful
Parenting	Loving, caring, nurturing, teaching, understanding, practicing patience, protecting, practicing honesty
Other Family	Loving, caring, nurturing, teaching, practicing patience, being respectful
Friends	Loving, caring, nurturing, helping, practicing acceptance
Spirituality	Sharing her faith with God and others, being selfless, nurturing
Community	Helping, sharing her faith, being selfless, being respectful
Well-Being	Being courageous, being self-compassionate, being respectful

having taboo sexual thoughts—namely, being courageous and being self-compassionate. Sondra was willing to "try on" these new values.

Instead of designing an exposure hierarchy based on fears, we started to design a values hierarchy based on actions in the service of values for each domain where she had stopped doing and/or wanted to start doing. Sondra was able to list a number of activities that were in the service of a value and rank them from least to most challenging. From this work, we developed seven separate hierarchies of valued actions. We provide examples of some of her domains of desired valued actions in the tables that follow.

We noted that every values-based action was going to require Sondra to move toward courageousness. We also highlighted that Sondra valued protecting her son but how she may be placing a disproportionate amount of effort toward this value at the expense of others in this domain. Given that Sondra reported many rituals when interacting with her son (e.g., praying for strength to do him no harm, to keep her free from sexual thoughts/urges, for God to protect him if she tried to molest him), we applied a broad rule of refraining from rituals while participating in valued actions while fear was present. We added the designation "while fear was present," because we wanted Sondra to be able to pray for other reasons and not feel as though the treatment was meant to distance herself from her religious community or relationship with God. These are illustrated in Table 6.3.

In terms of *values-based exposures in the spiritualty and community domains*, we combined these areas. Even though Sondra viewed them as possessing separate values, she desired to become more involved with her

Table 6.3 Values-Based Exposures in the Parenting Domain

Valued Action	In the Service of...
Bathing her son alone	Caring, being courageous
Bathing her son with a family member present	Caring, being courageous
Changing her son's diaper and applying rash cream as needed	Caring, loving, being courageous
Holding/soothing her son	Caring, loving, being courageous
Reading to her son prior to his nap and at night in his room with limited lighting	Nurturing, teaching, loving, being courageous
Reading to her son during the day in an open, lighted area	Nurturing, teaching, loving, being courageous
Kissing her son on the mouth before bed at night	Loving, being courageous
Kissing her son on the cheek	Loving, nurturing, being courageous
Giving her son a long hug	Loving, nurturing, being courageous
Giving her son a quick hug	Loving, nurturing, being courageous
Playing with toys with her son on the floor with others around	Caring, teaching, nurturing, being courageous
Playing with toys with her son on the floor without others around	Caring, teaching, nurturing, being courageous

spiritual community and saw the two areas as interwoven most of the time. Even her relationship with God typically involved worship with others and guidance from others. During this values-based actions, Sondra understood that she needed to refrain from common rituals (e.g., maintaining more than five feet of distance at all times while sitting or standing with someone, averting eye contact for more than one second, allowing herself to look at clothing and shoes of others [to counteract only looking away or above one's neck area], and praying for strength from God), as shown in Table 6.4.

In the area of well-being (Table 6.5), Sondra identified a number of self-care activities that she had avoided for many years (e.g., washing her breasts or genitals or grooming/shaving areas of her body) and some that she had only recently omitted as she became more depressed and scared. A few of the activities were suggested to her by the therapist as she tried to accomplish most of her grooming without looking at areas of her body (e.g., she did not want to look down at her underarms when she shaved them because she would also view her breasts), and this was not always safe or functional.

Table 6.4 Values-Based Exposures in the Spiritual/Community Domain

Valued Action	In the Service of . . .
Volunteering to assist teaching spiritual lessons to groups of children	Sharing her faith with God and others, being selfless, nurturing, being courageous
Volunteering to assist teaching spiritual lessons to groups of adolescents	Sharing her faith with God and others, being selfless, nurturing, being courageous
State a positive to someone about their actions or appropriate attire	Nurturing, being courageous
Shake hands when greeting others	Nurturing, being courageous
Acknowledging and talking with other members of the religious community, one-to-one	Sharing her faith with God and others, being courageous
Attending religious community events with family while other children are present	Sharing her faith with God and others, being selfless, nurturing, being courageous
Attending religious services	Sharing her faith with God and others, being selfless, nurturing, being courageous
Meeting with male church elders to discuss spiritual concerns	Sharing her faith with God and others, being selfless, being courageous
Saying prayers for others without her needs	Sharing her faith with God, being selfless, nurturing, being courageous

Toward the middle of her third session we decided what types of valued-based exposures she would try over the next three to four days prior to our next session. She had a number of community events she would have attended in the past that she knew she wanted to attend in the future. To aid in her practice, we began to practice a few values-based actions during the session. Sondra engaged in conversation with her therapist in closer proximity (moving from 10 feet to 6 feet away) while maintaining eye contact. She also practiced smiling when he said something complimentary about her efforts. Sondra was able to comply with the actions and recorded them on her values-based exposure form. She was then instructed to attend two community events and attend a one-to-one meeting with the church elder who served as her spiritual advisor.

It should be noted that during the second session, Sondra signed a release of information for her therapist to discuss relevant parts of her treatment plan with the church elder she trusted the most. It is very important, when possible, to contact a person the patient respects in her religious

Table 6.5 Values-Based Exposures in the Well-Being Domain

Valued Action	In the Service of...
Washing her breasts with a wash cloth	Being courageous, self-compassionate, and respectful
Washing her breasts without a wash cloth	Being courageous, self-compassionate, and respectful
Shaving her underarms or other areas while looking at them	Being courageous, self-compassionate, and respectful
Washing her genitals and anus with her hands	Being courageous, self-compassionate, and respectful
Washing her genitals and anus with a wash cloth	Being courageous, self-compassionate, and respectful
Washing other parts of her body	Being courageous, self-compassionate, and respectful
Looking at herself clothed in a mirror	Being courageous, self-compassionate, and respectful
Brushing her teeth in front of a mirror	Being courageous, self-compassionate, and respectful
Combing her hair in front of a mirror	Being courageous, self-compassionate, and respectful

tradition so that principles of treatment can be understood as helpful rather than as an attempt to make someone less religious, lose their faith, or doubt more. In this case, the church elder was familiar with some of Sondra's OCD challenges, which led to a productive conversation about how he could support her. The therapist was also able to ask questions to fill in some gaps he had about their religion. When meeting with a patient's clergy and community for the sake of obtaining support with the patient's treatment goals, it is important for these kinds of interactions to be bidirectional in terms of having openness and wanting to learn. While most of the people we have contacted are very interested in helping fellow members, it can be disrespectful to feel as though only one professional needs to learn from the other. There are times when a church official is not open to supporting OCD treatment that changes a member's type or frequency of interaction with the community or higher power or is not willing to hear or read education about mental health concerns. In these instances, we try to find another respected church member who could be consulted, even if that person is not in the same geographic region. Sometimes, facilitating a discussion between this person/member and the patient is needed, after a release of information is obtained. This type of enlistment of help is crucial for many patients, and if one is going to be an expert OCD clinician seeing a diverse range of patients, therapists would be well-served to have access to a priest, rabbi, imam, minister, parson, etc. who is familiar with cognitive-behavioral therapy (CBT) for OCD.

Treatment Sessions 4 and 5
By sessions 4 and 5, we noticed that Sondra's level of "buy-in" to the treatment became increasingly evident, which we attribute to a few things:

1. It was a source of motivation to connect Sondra's exposures to value-based actions, where she had to attend religious events, interact more with her family, her friends, and the community. Sondra developed a sense of awareness around being able to do things in treatment with us that she had not been able to previously do with her former OCD specialist. Though she would not admit it without prompting because of her bashfulness, being able to do these things gave her a sense of pride and hope.
2. Incorporating her religious leaders into our sessions created a sense of trust between her as the client and us as clinicians. Because religion was such a big part of her life, naturally there was skepticism while working with her first therapist who professed to be an atheist. Once Sondra realized that we were not only interested in learning about her religion from her perspective (and how it impacted her OCD) but also willing to work side by side with her religious leaders, this created more openness on her part, as well as a curiosity to see how their involvement could actually be a part of her journey toward wellness. This also made her feel understood and provided a sense of comfort.
3. Having a trustworthy rapport with her clinicians, developing awareness around her ability to approach treatment, increased motivation, increased pride and hope, all improved her outlook and slowly decreased her level of depression. The more Sondra's level of depression decreased, the more she felt capable of taking on some of the more difficult exposures.

Sondra was then able to begin movement to work in multiple areas on her values hierarchy. She was asked to pay special attention to what she noticed in terms of unwanted and wanted thoughts while engaging in values-driven exposures that were completed for homework and on the low to moderate end on her hierarchy. Sondra noticed that several thoughts came up including:

- "Community members and friends will discover that I interact with my son sexually if I play with him in their presence."
- "I must be a really bad mom since I'm not even capable of playing with my son without others monitoring us."
- "It is pointless to have others monitor my interactions with my son because I'll somehow end up touching him inappropriately when they look away."
- "Saying prayers for others is useless because I'm no longer in good standing with the religious leaders or God, because of all of the bad thoughts that I have."

Sondra also discussed how these cognitions resulted in anxiety and uncomfortable emotions that she occasionally tried to suppress. It was her impression that the suppression of these emotions was innate. This allowed us to engage Sondra in more of the key principles of ACT, specifically in the areas of acceptance and being present. Utilizing ACT in conjunction with Ex/RP in session better equipped Sondra for the self-led exposure homework outside of our sessions. Teaching Sondra strategies for not giving meaning to her thoughts and teaching her how to not judge her thoughts proved to be very helpful. For most clients with OCD, negative and scary thoughts are followed by running emotionally and sometimes even physically. This in essence is avoidance. In Sondra's case, she thought that if she allowed herself to be around male church members and leaders, for example, that maybe she would have a sexual thought and act on that thought. She was also concerned about what feelings might come up as a result of her thoughts. We decided to delve further into ACT with Sondra to teach her how to refrain from giving meaning to those thoughts. Through psychoeducation on ACT's principle of defusion (described in Chapter 3), we helped Sondra reframe her connection to her negative thoughts. We began by teaching her how everyone has thoughts that may feel negative and explained how she had been engaging with her negative thoughts through avoidance of church and social settings. We revisited how avoidance maintained the cycle of OCD as we had discussed early on in her treatment and began to set the framework for relating to her thoughts differently. In teaching her about *defusion*, we educated her in the following ways:

1. Everyone has thoughts that they personally deem as unacceptable.
2. The thoughts may or may not be true (exposure statement) but how placing judgment on the thought and classifying herself as a bad person as a result of the thoughts and feelings was not effectively using an exposure statement and essentially making an assumption that there was truth to her thoughts/feelings.
3. We also discussed the idea of acknowledging and accepting that she may not be able to control which thoughts come up but how she controls whether she responds to the thought by staying home from church on Sunday because of a fear (compulsion) or going to church (exposure) and sitting with the discomfort of not only being unaware of whether she'll act on her thought but also going out of a willingness to face her fears head on.

Finally, in addressing Sondra's natural tendency to give meaning to her thoughts/fears, we compared those thoughts to our initial discussion on values. We inquired about whether responding to her thoughts by avoiding church or changing her son's diaper was setting her up for having a greater quality of life with her family and with her community. She was almost able to immediately recognize that doing a compulsion through avoidance was not helping to move her toward being a better mom, wife, and friend to those in her community; rather, it was pulling her away from all of those things.

Sondra also found it helpful when she learned how to stop fighting the feelings of discomfort after every scary thought. Instead of pushing away or trying not to think about possibly being an inadequate mother, friend, spouse, or Christian, she started to learn to accept and truly experience the discomfort in her body from all of those thoughts. When this technique was coupled with Ex/RP, she realized that even the act of suppressing the feeling in her body was a form of avoidance, which would only bring back her OCD thoughts even stronger. Of course, this was a difficult task to practice inside and outside of our sessions, but she determined that it was worth it if it meant that she was drawing nearer to her values.

Treatment Sessions 6 and 7

At the beginning of session 6 we readministered Sondra's measures and spent time with her to review her progress. We repeated these measures so that we could keep track of her growth and the areas in which she needed more support, but the goal was to also keep her abreast of these improvements so that she stayed motivated and engaged in the treatment. As aforementioned, when Sondra started with us she was in the severe range, with a score of 29 on the Y-BOCS. By Session 7, her severity score had dropped to a 23, in the moderate range, which indicated that the treatment was working. In addition, her total score for living her life consistently with her values went from a 28 to a 40. Sondra was pleased with her results, and so were we. Because of this, we grew more and more confident in her commitment to therapy while in session and her level of commitment to homework outside of our sessions together.

A few difficulties did arise in initiating some of the work with respect to her religious beliefs and meetings with her religious leaders. We discovered that out of habit and, most times unknowingly, when Sondra attempted some of the values-driven exposures that involved interacting with her religious leaders, she sometimes sought or received reassurance from the church leaders even without prompting. We learned that Sondra received reassurances like, "You've come so far in your treatment, but you've always been in good standing with us. This isn't your fault" or "God loves all of his children, and he has not turned his back on you, so you don't have to worry about not being in his good graces."

We were glad that Sondra inquired about whether it was okay to receive these kinds of reassurances from her leaders. It provided insight into her sense of awareness and desire to participate in the treatment in the most effective manner. It also allowed us to offer her and her religious leaders support in these areas. We were able to provide this support by planning an in-person meeting with Sondra and one of her church leaders. During this meeting, we practiced some of her exposure work in front of the elder, so that he was able to see how easy it was for reassurance-seeking behaviors to emerge and how to best address or respond to these behaviors in a way that felt kind, yet helpful. We taught the church elder to make statements and ask questions like, "Sondra, it sounds like you're looking for some reassurance here, is that something you're supposed to be doing?" or "Sondra, I'm sorry it seems that you're having a hard time right now, but if I respond to that question, that would mean that I'm providing reassurance and that wouldn't be helpful for your treatment." Once Sondra's leaders had a clearer understanding of what might be reassurance-seeking behavior and what constituted providing reassurance, they were committed to working with her in a more helpful manner. We also taught Sondra to not ask for reassurance, and by practicing these techniques with her religious leaders, it provided a context for what to look out for and how to better censor her dialogue in this setting.

Treatment Session 8

Session 8 focused on preparing Sondra for valued work at a large family gathering where she would be taking care of most of the smaller children alongside one of her siblings. Sondra expected that there would be approximately 10 to 15 children at this gathering. Understandably, the thought of doing this created anxiety, but the number of children increased Sondra's anxiety even more. We prepared Sondra for this experience by working with her to create an imaginal exposure that involved her serving as caretaker at this event. While reading the imaginal out loud during our session, Sondra was also asked to share some of the thoughts and emotions that came up for her.

While Sondra had some reassuring thoughts like, "At least my sister will be there to make sure I don't hurt any of them," and "I can't possibly hurt all of them; there are too many!" Sondra almost immediately recognized her reassuring statements and utilized exposure statements to spoil the reassurance. We also pointed out how her OCD voice grew louder after her reassuring thoughts. She also had thoughts like, "But what if I sexually engage even one of them when my sister is distracted by caring for another child?" We helped Sondra respond to that voice through acceptance, and by encouraging her to use exposure statements like, "I will hurt, inappropriately touch, and sexually engage with one or many of the children that I care for that day" and "I am disappointing God by thinking about touching the children in sexually inappropriate ways." This was yet another teaching moment on how avoidance and compulsions inevitably end up making OCD even worse and how she could gain mastery over her fears by confronting them.

Because the family gathering was scheduled to be an all-day event in one venue where Sondra was responsible for the children all day, we highlighted how the event could feel like an all-day exposure. This discussion helped manage Sondra's expectations. As a way to balance out her anxiety and not feel pushed into situations that appeared to be at the top of her hierarchy, she was encouraged to gradually interact with the children, while maintaining awareness of her emotions with each interaction. We encouraged Sondra to have a conversation with her sister about how she would approach the time with the children. Sondra agreed and said that this would help her sister to be aware of how much she would be involved so that she wouldn't feel that Sondra wasn't pulling her weight.

We encouraged Sondra to start out by entering the room, talking, smiling, and joking with the children. Next, she would give a child high-five and then progress to rubbing their hair and cheeks. This would then evolve into having a child sit on her lap, and, if she felt capable, her goal by the end of the day was to hug a child goodbye and change the diaper of one of the younger children. Sondra was asked to also be mindful of any avoidance, where she might assign her sister a task because of anxiety or fear. We provided Sondra with examples of how this could come up while working with her sister that day and ways to counteract these behaviors if they arose.

Treatment Sessions 9 and 10

At the beginning of Session 10 we repeated Sondra's measures, reviewed her results, and progress with her, as well as processed the details of her family gathering. Her score on the Y-BOCS was a 21, and her consistency with her values was a 50. She beamed with a glow of excitement as she shared how she was able to get through the family gathering without avoidance. Sondra said that while at the gathering she was able to connect a few dots from what she learned in our initial psychoeducational sessions when doing the exposures with the children. Sondra explained that though she had some anxiety and even had thoughts arise while serving as a caregiver that day, she saw in a more powerful way (compared to other exposures) how habituation really worked. "I had no choice but to stay in the situation and eventually habituate because I had decided that I wasn't going to let OCD win that day," she shared.

After this experience, we were able to build further off of Sondra's success with her family gathering. She started to unreservedly embody the *committed action* principles within ACT. She decided that she wanted to tackle initiating more contact with her peers and the relatives that she didn't see as often as her immediate family and family of origin. Sondra acknowledged some apprehension and concerns about what family members were thinking after not seeing her for so long. Because her religious community and family were tight-knit and overlapped, she was certain that many of them were aware of her issues. Sondra said that although these thoughts and concerns didn't exactly feel like obsessions, she thought that using exposure statements could prove to be helpful, as they could easily become obsessions.

To address those concerns, we worked with her on *defusion* principles again. Our first step was to show Sondra how to reframe her concerns about her relatives' perceptions by exploring whether she was giving weight to their perceptions. We explored how uncertainty could be used with her concerns. We also discussed how acceptance, utilizing uncertainty, and not attaching value or truth to those concerns didn't mean that the emotions attached to the thoughts would necessarily diminish. Sondra agreed to visit her acquaintances and family while practicing what she had been learning in treatment. She suspected that she might have some fear or panic while interacting with male relatives or friends, out of concern that she might think about them sexually. She also suspected that when interacting with the women that she would have fears of them gossiping about her issues and rumors being spread about her "sexual sins." We investigated how even calling her thoughts sins was placing judgment and giving importance to her thoughts. Additionally, we facilitated dialogue around shame, because it was clear that shame was a driving force and a theme that impacted Sondra in several areas in her life. After Session 10, Sondra felt more prepared to make these visits and expressed how she was willing to "risk it," if it meant getting her life back.

Treatment Sessions 11 and 12
Sondra's momentum within the treatment plan allowed us to continue to move up her hierarchies. With her consent, we invited her husband Eric to Session 11, so that we could begin to focus more heavily on valued work in the area of her own body and marriage. Sondra had developed more confidence in her ability to overcome her OCD anxiety, so she felt it was an appropriate time to work on her issues with her body and her relationship—two important areas that went hand in hand.

We started out by assessing Eric's level of understanding of Sondra's condition and inquired about ways or areas in which he had seen Sondra improve. Eric shared how Sondra had made significant strides in her interaction with church leaders, her willingness to be around family and friends, and even some improvement in her engagement with their son. He admitted that he was glad to be a part of the session, because he was especially interested in improving the dynamics in their marriage. Eric discussed how it was difficult to see Sondra incapable of giving attention to the physical aspects of her own body and revealed that he had hoped that the session would show them how to improve in their physical and emotional intimacy.

Eric shared how he had stopped giving Sondra compliments a long time ago, because of how it triggered obsessions for her. He believed this created emotional distance in their relationship, because he felt that complimenting her physical beauty and aspects of her character were ways to affirm his love and appreciation of her. Learning more about the specific details related to offering compliments was an excellent segue into providing him with more instructions on how to navigate Sondra's compulsions. It was pointed out that every time he refrained from giving Sondra a compliment, that he was helping Sondra engage in avoidance. Eric was aware that Sondra was not allowed to do compulsions while in treatment but never viewed his actions as supporting her OCD. We discussed how doing so was accommodating Sondra's avoidance and that avoidance was functionally the same as a compulsion.

Sondra and Eric also discussed how OCD had impacted their physical intimacy. Sondra said she felt guilty when they engaged in sexual activity, as it made her concerned that she was "giving into lust." She feared that this would seep into other areas of her life and cause her to act on those feelings with other people, specifically children and religious leaders. She was aware of how her actions impacted her marriage but confessed that there were parts of her that felt she was protecting herself and others from harm. Avoiding physical interactions with her husband prevented her from spiraling out of control, which meant that she would not accost someone sexually. Avoiding compliments from her husband meant that she wouldn't have sexual thoughts about others or question her own sexuality. This was also why she avoided looking at her body parts in the mirror and while bathing.

Even while talking in session, Sondra was able to identify how all of this was avoidance, and though it was scary, she was willing to practice receiving compliments from her husband in-session upon our recommendation. We started slowly by having her husband compliment her hands, hair, smile, eyes, and attributes of her character. We felt it was important that we not immediately address things related to what Sondra might perceive as the sexual parts of her body because of how easily embarrassed Sondra became in previous sessions. Sondra became flushed on more than one occasion during this exposure, and we worked on practicing mindfulness and acceptance, which required that Sondra hold space for her feelings of discomfort. We practiced naming those feelings of discomfort so that she could get used to naming her feelings without placing judgment on her feelings. We also helped Sondra find the exposure statements that felt most appropriate for this particular exposure. For homework, we encouraged Sondra and her husband to practice the same exposure but also encouraged them to increase the level of anxiety by having her husband transition into describing other parts of Sondra's body. We also encouraged Sondra to start working on looking in a mirror again, by first practicing looking in a small hand held mirror, where she couldn't see the rest of her body. Our hope was that the mirror exercise would help initiate her into the future sessions, where she would be required to look at her whole physical body in the mirror.

It was important to have Eric a part of Sondra's sessions for several reasons. Eric was able to see Sondra engaging in exposures and the effectiveness of the exposures first hand. He was also able to see how Sondra's anxiety decreased over time while doing exposures and how reassurance looked in a clinical setting. This helped to reinforce his level of understanding of Ex/RP and how he should respond to Sondra's inquiries for reassurance. We also discussed how Eric had been assisting Sondra with her compulsions by discontinuing his compliments. "All along I thought I was helping her, but now I see that I have been unfortunately perpetuating the OCD." We all made a verbal agreement that Eric would no longer hold back the compliments. We decided a behavioral contract would be useful for Eric and Sondra, so that in case there were any questions while they were at home, that they had something to refer to in writing. The contract not only included behavioral modifications regarding Eric's compliments about dressing nicely, hairstyles, and smile but also modifications for continuing to engage with their son. Eric and Sondra also agreed to continue to utilize Eric during Sondra's exposure homework that involved compliments to various parts of her body, which were slightly more anxiety-provoking than Eric's day-to-day compliments about her hair, etc.

Treatment Sessions 13 and 14
Sondra continued to maintain a noticeably higher level of engagement with her son and family. We instructed her to do more "spontaneous-valued work" in those areas in Session 13. Even if something wasn't necessarily on

one of her hierarchies, we discussed how she should always look for creative ways to do exposures throughout the day with her family. She started to learn that finding more impromptu, unstructured ways of engaging in her treatment increased her feelings of accomplishment. It also meant that Sondra was getting closer and closer to reclaiming the life she once enjoyed.

At the beginning of Session 14, we repeated Sondra's measures and reviewed her results and progress. After our last session where we focused on always finding ways and reasons to do exposures, she reported taking a number of calculated, valued moves that she had not considered before or discussed with us in previous sessions. This was reflected in her Y-BOCS scores. By Session 14 Sondra's score was a 16. Her consistency with her values was a 62. She continued to feel proud, although she was embarrassed to freely share this. Even with her consistent progress, per Sondra, she continued to struggle with the idea of accepting her body and needing to have a sexual approach with her husband. She and her husband did make an effort to practice the homework where she received compliments, but she felt that this, along with having to look at her face in the mirror, had serious implications and felt riskier than other valued moves.

Assuming that Sondra wanted positive change in these challenging areas, we decided to employ motivational interviewing (MI) to dig deeper into her concerns (see Rosengren, 2009, for a review). We thought using MI would nicely compliment the ACT techniques in which Sondra was already familiar (Zuckoff, Balán, &, Simpson, 2015). We felt that doing so would help reconnect her to "the why" of all of the hard work that she had already accomplished so far and help reaffirm the competencies in her own skills. We explored some of the following questions:

- What would giving in to these fears mean for the longevity of your marriage?
- How might stopping now impact all of your previous valued work?
- What might be some things that may require acceptance with regards to being more sexual with your husband?
- When it was hard to perform anxiety-provoking exercises in the beginning of starting treatment with us, what were the strategies you used to approach your fears that might also help you move forward now?

Processing these questions together helped Sondra re-examine her thoughts and her emotions. At the end of the discussion, she thoughtfully pointed out that the questions made her reflect on whether she really wanted change in all areas or only in the areas that "felt easy" by now. She acknowledged that none of the values-driven exposures felt easy in the beginning and stated that she started to grow accustomed to addressing the fears that involved spending time with other people because she had been feeling isolated from her community for so long. After the MI, she questioned whether she was placing more value on being connected to her religious community than the family inside her own home. We appreciated the insightful questions that she began to ask herself. We encouraged her to continue asking herself similar questions, as she deemed appropriate, but to do so while balancing, not placing judgment, on whatever the answers were to those questions.

Treatment Sessions 15 and 16
Sondra, her husband, and our team all agreed that working on her ability to face her body parts on her own would be a better transition into approaching her sexual nature with her husband. During Sessions 15 and 16, and after both sessions for homework, Sondra purposefully practiced various exposures in the well-being domain. She gave special attention to washing her body, looking at her body in the mirror, and shaving while looking at her body, all while doing exposure statements that addressed her anxiety.

We asked Sondra to be on the lookout for avoidance of thoughts while grooming. Sondra was asked to not push back any sexual thoughts that arose while looking at her body. We taught her to begin welcoming her sexual thoughts while in preparation for her shower, before shaving, looking in mirrors, and to continue doing so while in the midst of her exposures. We encouraged Sondra to practice statements like:

- All of my sexual urges are rapidly approaching as I prepare to look at my breasts and genitals in the mirror.
- Looking at my breasts while bathing means that I want to have sex with my church leader.
- The sexual thoughts that I'm having while looking in the mirror mean that I am sexually attracted to both men and women and that I will act on these feelings.
- My sexual urges mean that I am out of control and that I am not favorable in God's eyes.

Even stating something like "I am having sexual thoughts right now" created anxiety for Sondra. This statement in particular is what she decided to hold onto as a method for practicing mindful acceptance whenever she felt the urge to emotionally or mentally withdraw while in the middle of an exposure. It was her way of simply naming her actions without placing judgment. We also found it helpful to generate a discussion on her religious beliefs in conjunction to doing more work around shame, as it was clear that these exercises in particular produced feelings of guilt and shame that she felt stemmed from her religious background.

Treatment Session 17

At the beginning of Session 17, she repeated her measures and then was provided with the results (Y-BOCS = 13; consistency with values = 70). We also began to take a long-term outlook on the rest of the treatment. Sondra and the therapist both agreed to move to biweekly sessions for the next three sessions and reassess her at that time. It was also important to incorporate Eric into Session 17 to start incorporating him into her exposures. His involvement was also necessary as sessions were going to be more spread apart, and they would be doing more exposure homework together.

During this session, we increased the anxiety from her well-being exposures, by having Sondra look at herself in a full-body length mirror, while her husband sat next to her. We encouraged Sondra to focus on the different parts of her body while making some of the aforementioned exposure statements, and also saying things like, "I am a sexual being," "I have sexual urges," or "I enjoy sex." Sondra was nervous about these particular exposures because of her husband's presence and our presence. Despite this, she made the suggestion to push herself a bit more by holding her husband's hand while also making these statements in the mirror.

After successfully tackling holding her husband's hand in the mirror, we asked that she do the same while at home but to gradually increase the difficulty. Sondra was assigned to do more of these exposures by looking in a full mirror and making the statements while being held by her husband. She could then progress into making these statements in the mirror without clothes, while also being held by her husband. Both Eric and Sondra shared ambivalence, excitement, yet a willingness to see what progress could be made by the next session. With Sondra's permission, we invited her husband to participate in future sessions, as he and Sondra felt appropriate. We asked that they both report back at the midway points between sessions, to give updates on their progress. This appeared to help them both maintain focus and challenged them to move toward the direction of their values and treatment goals.

Treatment Sessions 18 to 20

For Session 18, Sondra and Eric entered our office with a more positive outlook for how the treatment helped to improve their interactions at home. Sondra said that it had been challenging to look at her naked body while her husband held her but said that she was habituating more and more each day. Eric stated that even though they weren't necessarily engaging in sexual activities, that it felt good to begin rebuilding their intimacy through his participation in her homework. Even if intimacy within the marriage wasn't Sondra's only, or main goal—rather it was one of her many goals for treatment—it was really important to both Sondra and Eric, and Eric was especially grateful that it was being addressed. Sondra appeared to be pleased with her own progress and noted that it was also gratifying knowing that Eric was benefiting from her improved mental and emotional health. She was happy that she hadn't continued to allow her fears to control her and was eager to address scarier tasks that would improve the marriage. Sondra admitted that she was grateful for Eric's participation in her homework. Where his presence was once a source of discomfort, she now considered it to be a comfort.

During Session 19, we asked Sondra and Eric to engage in a discussion about the things that they like about each other's sexual body parts. At this point they had already practiced complimenting character strengths and neutral body parts like hands, hair, and eyes. It was difficult for Sondra to hear these things, and she thought it was weird to receive and make these compliments in front of a therapist. However, the session felt hopeful, light, playful, and less somber than previous sessions. For homework, Sondra and Eric were asked to build upon this exercise by engaging in a sexual conversation with each other, while Sondra looked in the mirror with clothes on. Once she habituated, their next activity was to do the same thing without clothing.

When Sondra visited us during Session 20 we readministered the Y-BOCS and provided her with the results (see Table 6.6). By this time, her Y-BOCS score went from a 29 at the beginning of treatment to a 9, and her consistency with values went from a 28 to an 81. We were all elated. We determined that Sondra would only need two more sessions and that

Table 6.6 End of Therapy Score for the Valued Living Questionnaire

Value	Importance	Consistency
Marriage	10	9
Parenting	10	8
Other Family	10	9
Friends	8	9
Work	5	7
Education	5	5
Recreation	5	8
Spirituality	10	9
Community	10	9
Well-Being	8	8

they could be one month apart. We were all on the same page about Sondra targeting various tasks within all of the domains. Sondra thought it would be especially beneficial to do more exposures involving her son and her husband. However, her goal was to always be mindful of doing exposures from all domains daily, so as not to regress in any of the domain areas.

Complicating Factors

A number of factors complicated Sondra's treatment including her previous treatment experiences, comorbid depression, and a lack of familiarity by the therapist of her specific faith. It's not uncommon to have to validate and remoralize a person after receiving previous treatment that was not helpful. In Sondra's case, she did work with a professional but the dosing she needed, the tweaks to the approach, and her level of depression prevented benefit in that venue. Given the frequency of OCD leading to significant depression, other techniques (from MI, ACT, and behavioral activation) may need to begin prior to or simultaneously to Ex/RP. In addition, when working with a client whose religious or spiritual views are not well-known by the therapist, it is imperative to find a trusted person in that faith to assist in therapy (preferably someone in that person's denomination who can assist in spiritual advice).

Follow-Up

Sondra and the therapist scheduled two follow-up sessions, one for a month out and the other tentatively for a month after that. She reported that she was consistently doing exposures and moving toward her values and was even making a game out of finding spontaneous exposures and values movement. Her scores reflected this as well (Y-BOCS = 7; values consistency = 84). Sondra was actively involved in all areas of her life. She took care of her son and all of his needs without the assistance of anyone else while her husband was out of the house working. She also became reengaged with all of the community and religious events that she desired.

We decided that we should have Sondra call a few days before the next appointment to determine if she needed to meet or if we wanted to delay the last meeting. She stated this was acceptable, called before the next meeting, and reported that she was doing quite well and challenging herself with spontaneous exposures while moving toward values whenever a situation presented itself. We decided to reschedule for another month out and repeated this process three times as she continued to say she was doing well. We never did have a final session but did receive a holiday card seven months later indicating she was doing well, and her smile in the photo with her immediate and extended family attested to this.

Treatment Implications of the Case

Sondra's case is similar to many in that she had previous therapy that was not suited to deal with symptoms and goals. What was unusual was that she had previous Ex/RP and did not see much benefit. However, we did consider that these attempts occurred in quick succession and while she was fairly depressed; therefore, having more contact and an approach that meshed better with her own personal (and religious) values was needed.

We do not believe we would have had success with Sondra (or at least not as much) without offering and then involving members of her religious community both directly and indirectly with the exposure work. This seemed to temporarily be anxiety-reducing and created a window of opportunity for the treatment to really begin with reduced ritualizing and avoiding and for feeling supported closer to her home and community environment.

While it may have served at times as reassurance, it's important to recognize that as long as rituals (such as reassurance) are becoming less frequent, the therapy is moving in the right direction, and most people with severe OCD cannot simply stop all rituals and avoidance early in treatment.

Recommendations to Clinicians and Students

We believe this case illustrates how using Ex/RP without consideration of other critical factors would have likely lead to treatment failure. It's always important to consider the recent and distant context of the patient's experience with therapy and that they may have actually had experience with the gold-standard treatment for OCD (or oftentimes told they were doing CBT and/or Ex/RP when they were not). Finding out what had and had not worked for them in terms of therapy, dosage, knowledge, understanding, acceptance of their condition, the recommended treatment model, engagement in adjunctive CBT techniques, and resources in the client's home and community environment gave us the best chance for success with Sondra.

The integration of ACT principles in Sondra's treatment combined nicely with her motivation and goals in life and who she wanted to be as a person. It gave her something to look forward to other than simply reducing symptoms and most likely served to relieve or discredit some of the shame she experienced from OCD symptoms. Most of our clients are already thinking about symptoms too much upon entering treatment, and therefore a focus on moving forward and becoming who they want to be can be appealing and also a realistic "destination" as opposed to saying, "You will no longer have symptoms of OCD." For people that have experienced OCD for most of their lives, that does not tell them what their life will look like.

The typical way we introduce values work into Ex/RP is while giving the rationale and developing a treatment hierarchy. We say,

> Now that you are beginning to understand how we will alter your experiences with anxiety/disgust/shame related to OCD, we also want to help you move toward things that are important to you and that you want to be in life. We want you to consider that while you are changing your relationship with your feelings, you don't have to wait to determine what

type of person you want to be in important life areas. We can help you define what you value now, even if you can't fully behave in a way in accordance to these values at the present. We want you to begin taking steps in that direction early on, and therefore we will develop exposures that serve two purposes—providing you with an opportunity to experience change within your relationship with your feelings through habituation, *and* provide you with the experience of moving toward being the person you want to be—what that looks like is up to you. We will give you examples of what values are, and ask you to choose some and move forward exploring them, whether or not you believe you can 'have' them depends on how you determine to view this.

This is important to say because many people with OCD have obsessions regarding causing harm to others (e.g., as a pedophile, not controlling urges, or being careless or contaminating them), and have a hard time accepting moving toward values about caring and connecting with others. We also explain that how they view this can be reframed (through cognitive restructuring) but also note that their perspectives can only be shaped based on their willingness or level of engagement in the cognitive restructuring activities.

Also, values can help keep people focused on tangible benefits of doing high emotion-eliciting exposure work. We have worked with a number of people who have had OCD for such a long time that they felt as though they would not know who they are without it. The symptoms were so consuming, often from an early age, that OCD had become their personality per se, and they missed a lot of opportunities to learn about values and develop skills to support efficacy in these areas. Looking forward to values is not meant to be a ritual to distract one from unwanted emotions but rather allowing one to recognize desired actions—what most people would call positive experiences—while in the midst of seemingly needing to be aware of every cue that indicates danger is near.

In Vivo Exposure Suggestions

We next provide some examples of in vivo exposures that clients can do to address pedophilia-themed S-OCD (P-OCD). We have placed these in order from (typically) least difficult to (typically) most difficult, but keep in mind that not all of these examples will be anxiety-provoking or relevant for every person with this kind of OCD. Therapists should first ask clients how anxious they anticipate they would be to do these exposures without rituals before putting them on the hierarchy. If the Subjective Units of Distress/Discomfort Scale (SUDS) score is very low, then there may be no need to assign it, unless the therapist has reason to believe that the reported SUDS is an underestimate. These ideas are meant as a starting point and are in no way comprehensive. Therapists should feel free to use their imagination to devise exposures that best fit the client's fears and are doable in session and/or for homework.

In Vivo Exposure 1: Repeatedly Say and Write Out Pedophilic Fears

For some clients, the anxiety from pedophilic fears are so unnerving that even verbalizing their fears or seeing the word *pedophilia* on paper is overwhelming. The act of saying or repeatedly writing out these fears causes clients to address their fears head on. In this instance, we often start slowly with our clients by having them say or write the word *pedophile* on paper or a dry erase board in our office. As they begin to habituate to saying the word and looking at the word, they can increase this anxiety by saying and writing out things like, "I am a pedophile," "I like kiddie porn," "I am a pervert," or "I am dirty and creepy." Clients will discover that their anxiety decreases, which will then support therapists in facilitating a discussion on how saying or writing out these things doesn't necessarily make them true.

Therapists can build on this exposure by having clients say and write out similar statements in a public setting on paper. Of course, therapists should take into consideration client confidentiality and ensure that writing out or saying these statements in public will not, in fact, put the client at risk of facing negative consequences. The therapist can do this by visiting parks in advance or intentionally choosing parts of child-friendly areas that are somewhat secluded. The therapist can slowly begin this exposure outside the office setting by initially having the client make the statement in the car with the windows rolled up, then with the windows rolled down, and then outside of the car in a more secluded area of a park where children are playing. Clients may be concerned that strangers might be able to see the statements that they're writing or overhear the verbalized statements. Though the therapist has done their due diligence in ensuring that the client is safe and can't be overheard, they would not provide reassurance for the client around this fear but instead work with the client on using an exposure statement about the concern.

In Vivo Exposure 2: Pedophile for a Day

When working with clients on this exposure, the client and therapist can initially start out by developing a list of physical characteristics, clothing, body language, verbal language, and behaviors that the client perceives to be that of a pedophile. If clients have difficulty with this task, they can be encouraged to recall their previous exposures that involved watching pedophilic movies. Once a list is developed, clients can also rank these items based off of which behaviors and clothing would create the most anxiety for them, if they were asked to do these things in a public setting. Therapists can then have clients embody these characteristics based on where they would fall on a client's hierarchy. Clients would then be asked to walk through public areas "acting like" a pedophile, wearing clothes and holding objects that make them feel as though others would perceive them as a pedophile. This can include dressing like an adult child, passing out candy or bubble gum, carrying a pinwheel, or other toys like stuffed animals. Some clients might believe that wearing an overcoat with shorts, a V-neck t-shirt with visible socks and shoes seem like pedophilic behavior. You might also have the client wear questionable clothing with sayings or words related to fears of pedophilia, like "I'm Creepy." Some of these items may have to be special ordered, but the sky is the limit on what could be perceived as a pedophile.

In Vivo Exposure 3: Become a Child Magnet

Clients with P-OCD not only have internal fears about being a pedophile but also have concerns that others will perceive them as a pedophile. An exposure that can help clients address this obsession is visiting and sitting in high-traffic areas that are frequented by children. This can include places like Chuck E. Cheese's, amusement parks, neighborhood parks, or playscapes at child-friendly restaurants like McDonald's. Clients can initially begin these exposures with their therapist, depending on where it falls on their hierarchy. When working on this in session with the therapist, clients should be encouraged to wear bright, child-friendly clothing with cartoon characters on it, or bring objects of interest to children like balloons, toys, and pets. Clients can also bring popcorn or cotton candy and even wear a clown's nose! Once clients habituate to being in those areas, they should then look for excuses to engage the children and their parents in conversations while in these environments. Ideally engaging in conversations will evoke concerns of whether a parent is suspicious of their behavior and, in turn, increase the client's anxiety. As the client's anxiety increases, therapists can work with clients on exposure statements that create uncertainty around whether or not a parent actually perceived them as a pedophile. Clients should also visit similar settings as homework, once they are outside of the session.

In Vivo Exposure 4: Diary of a Pedophile

This exposure could be completed with the therapist or as an exposure homework assignment. Clients would be asked to drive to and park in front of a school or playground and pretend they are a pedophile who is planning what it would be like to kidnap a child or a couple of children. The client should keep a diary of the kids they are watching. This would include the gender and race/ethnicity of a child, a description of the child's physical attributes like eye and hair color, why they are specifically drawn to this type of child or why they chose one child over another, the color clothing and shoes the child has on, and what color items the child might be holding, like a backpack. The diary entry would also include information on how they plan to lure the child into their car and what they plan to do with them. It is likely that clients will share their concerns about someone discovering their diary and the possibility of being arrested. Therapists would encourage clients to use exposure statements as these fears arise.

In Vivo Exposure 5: Talk to Others about Your Love of Children

As aforementioned, much of the anxiety that clients have stems from how adults (strangers and acquaintances) perceive their actions and whether their actions "seem pedophilic." The anxiety generated from these thoughts likely result in clients going to extremes to prevent feeling the discomfort of being perceived this way. A compulsion that has been seen in our clients is the refusal to discuss anything pertaining to their affinity for children. One way to address this specific concern is by doing exposures where clients are asked to talk in detail about their love for children in front of strangers and acquaintances. It is likely that the least familiar the client is with the individual, the more anxiety the client will have while discussing children. Clients should be descriptive in their language about their love for children. Some of the following statements can be helpful in giving your client ideas on generating anxiety-provoking dialogue about children:

- Children are the best hug givers (or huggers). I just love how their tiny arms are so comforting and make you feel like the world is a better place.
- Kids are great at keeping us youthful. I especially enjoying playing games with them like hide and seek and doctor. They're so imaginative and that makes me feel good.
- There's nothing better than making a child happy by giving them gifts, candy, and toys. Most people really enjoy doing so on Christmas day, but I find ways to give out candy and toys to kids even when there isn't a special occasion and sometimes even to strangers' kids. It's so rewarding to see them light up from someone thinking that they're special.
- I love volunteering at organizations that are focused on giving back to children. I especially enjoy mentoring programs where you get to have one-on-one quality time with them. Sometimes those organizations even let volunteers have sleepovers with their mentees.

Therapists can initially have clients practice these conversations during therapy sessions, initially with the therapist and then with a confederate. Once clients have habituated to having these conversations in the office, they can then practice having them for homework with varying people in their spheres. The level of the exposure and anxiety generated from the exposure will vary depending on the person they talk to.

In Vivo Exposure 6: Personalized Pedophile Profiles

The US Department of Justice has created a national sex offender database, which allows individuals to research whether there are any sex offenders living in their neighborhoods. Therapists can have clients look up pedophiles based on the zip code of their client's home address or based on the area where the client is receiving OCD treatment. Clients should be asked to look at the pedophile on the computer, touch the screen with the pedophile's face, and even kiss the pedophile on the computer's screen. It is likely that clients will have more anxiety when looking at pictures of sex offenders in their own neighborhood. Therapists can also print a picture of the pedophile and have the client place the picture in their pocket and walk around the office and outside the office with the sex offender's picture in tow. Additionally, a printed picture of a pedophile could be used in conjunction with a confederate. Therapists would ask the client to pretend the sex offender is their friend and have a conversation about their friend with the confederate. Clients should be descriptive about the kinds of activities that they enjoying doing with the sex offender and make up qualities that they like about their friend. Furthermore, if the therapist feels it is relatively safe, they could drive to an area near the child sex offender's home, park several houses away from the home, and walk several blocks up and down the sex offender's street, ensuring that they and the client actually walk past the sex offender's home. Clients can also print out 7 to 10 pictures of pedophiles and complete a poster board project with the sex-offender pictures, while including their face on the board, next to the sex offenders.

In Vivo Exposure 7: Look at Pictures of Nearly Naked Children

Individuals with P-OCD often believe that they must avoid looking at things like child swimwear ads at all costs out of fear that the act of looking at the ads intrinsically means that they are a pedophile. They also fear that they will become aroused. Therapists can address this by having clients look at swimsuit ads from clothing stores online and in magazines. The therapist should check in with the client to assess their fears and feelings of sexual arousal. If the client reports any sexual arousal, the therapist can respond with an exposure statement, such as "Of course, this turns you on, since we both know you are really a pedophile."

If using online images, prior to sessions, therapists should identify several potential images at a range of difficulty levels and then print them out. We have a color laser printer in our office just for this purpose. Rather than just staring at the images, therapists can build upon this exposure by having clients write stream-of-consciousness pedophilic statements on the ads themselves, like "This kid is really sexy!" Since the act of generating material and writing it out occupies the mind, it is also a good way to prevent mental ritualizing during the exposure. This exposure can be intensified by having clients look at these ads in public settings for homework. During the summer, therapists can take clients to local swim clubs or neighborhood pools to watch children who are taking swimming lessons.

In Vivo Exposure 8: Participate in Physical Contact with Children

The client should be instructed to initiate physical contact with their own children or child relatives (e.g., hugs during greetings and saying goodbye, wrestling/tickling child, giving high-fives, thumb wrestling, piggyback rides standing or while you are crawling). Reading stories to children is a perfect exposure, because you have a great reason to plunk them right on the client's lap. If that is too anxiety-provoking, they can start by just reading to the child while sitting next to the child and work up to the lap in a later session. If the client does not have easy access to children, they should be instructed to think of other ways children can be accessed, for example, by offering to babysit a friend's child or volunteer for nursery duty at a local church. This specific exposure should not be skipped, as will be important to facilitate recovery.

In Vivo Exposure 9: Bathing/Changing Diapers

If your client has a baby or toddler, these exposures are a great place to start. The client should be instructed to change the diaper or wash the baby without ritualizing, being sure to clean all areas without attempts to minimize touching. Sometimes clients will want to have a partner nearby to reassure them that they have not done any inappropriate touching. This should be considered ritualizing and therefore disallowed. Ideally, the client will do this as homework without any adults present to ensure the safety of the potential child "victims." If this exposure is too overwhelming, it can be graded in difficulty, with the help of the client's partner. The client can start off washing the child's hair alone, for homework, then next week move up to washing the body, and then eventually add the child's genitals to the washing regimen.

In Vivo Exposure 10: Pedophile Cinema

It is not uncommon for P-OCD clients to be sensitive to movies with pedophilic content. For some clients, watching the movies invokes thoughts of becoming like the characters they see depicted. Therapists can be creative about the various ways to find pedophilia storylines, including biographies, crime stories on *20/20* and TV shows like *CSI* and *SVU*. Some movies that may be helpful for evoking this anxiety include: *Gone Baby Gone* (2007), *Antwone Fisher* (2002), and *The Woodsman* (2004). Therapists can also utilize YouTube and Netflix, as well as literature, to find material that will be helpful for these exposures. While watching pedophilic movies in session, the therapist should encourage the client to be vocal about which scenes are disturbing. Some clients may have anxiety during the scenes leading up to a kidnapping, while other clients may be more disturbed by the scenes that show the child with the pedophile. Knowing which scenes create more anxiety allows therapists to be able to find future content for exposures. Additionally, having clients verbalize the scenes that bring up fears or anxiety, allows the therapist to understand how to formulate exposure statements that are specific to each client's needs. The most anxiety-provoking scenes can be assigned as homework for rewatching. An alternative to this assignment could be reading stories on these topics. Clients might read such books in a café or other public space to increase anxiety, or even better, a space frequented by children.

In Vivo Exposure 11: Provocative Child Music Videos

Provocative child music video exposures involve watching music videos that portray children as adults, where they are encouraged to display adult-like behavior, like dancing in a way that is perceived to be provocative or wearing high heels and revealing clothing. This is a topic that has been controversial to the general public and excellent for P-OCD exposures. Sia's "Elastic Heart" and "Chandelier" are some of our favorites as they feature a little girl dancing in a flesh-colored leotard. When asked to watch these videos, feelings of disgust are often generated for P-OCD clients. Clients may want to turn their heads during certain scenes but should be discouraged from looking away, as this is an avoidance. Client may also report feeling physically sick or nauseous or verbally express dissatisfaction when viewing these videos. Therapists should validate each client's physical discomfort while maintaining that clients stay present in their exposure while utilizing exposure statements. In the example of the young girl dancing in a flesh–colored leotard, clients may think that the girl is being violated by the man she is dancing with in the video. Rather than reassurance, therapists would aid clients in creating uncertainty around whether or not the child is, in fact, actually being violated or otherwise exploited.

Sample Imaginal Exposures

The following are some actual imaginal exposures generated by our therapists and clients (with identifying information removed, of course). You can use these verbatim with a client or customize them to your client's situation. Generally, it is better to customize them for maximum impact and rewrite them in the client's own manner of speaking, but if they are anxiety-provoking enough to be used as-is, then they should not be customized (other than changing the names used in the stories) until the client has habituated to some degree (exposure causing 40 or less SUDS).

Imaginal Exposure 1: Becoming a Pedophile: Attracted to Girls

In September, I first started having worries about being attracted to little girls. I started doing a lot of checking and thinking to make sure that I was not sexually attracted or becoming a pedophile. I started looking at all sorts of people—women, men, boys, and girls—to make sure I did not like the feelings I got. As long as I didn't feel any arousal, I knew everything was OK. In the process of getting treatment, I learned that the worries were all part of my OCD. I needed to resist the compulsions before I could get better, so I decided to stop doing the checking and stop ruminating. I resisted the urges to check and ruminate, and after a while the urges went away. I felt better and over time stopped worrying that I might be attracted to girls.

But because I decided to stop checking myself, I didn't realize that I was slowly developing a sexual preference for children. The fact that the anxiety was gone really meant that I liked all of those thoughts and feelings. These latent urges had been hiding under the surface all the time and were finally free to emerge unchecked. Deep down, I had always been attracted to children, and I had only been denying it. OCD turned out to be a horrible misdiagnosis. My real problem was pedophilia, along with an eroding conscience.

I starting enjoying fantasies about doing sexual acts with children, especially girls aged 6 to 10. I would spend hours at a time staring at pictures of little girls and wishing I could have sex with them. After a while I wasn't interested in my partner any more. I was only attracted to my niece Rayne and her nine-year-old friends. I would spend my waking hours fantasizing about having sex with each one of them. After a while, fantasy wasn't good enough. I started to invite girls down into my basement, where I would take pictures of them without clothes on. I then starting having sex with the girls and would buy their silence with candy and threats. Pictures weren't enough; I started making my own home movies of my activities. I would then upload these movies to the Internet where I would share them with others. Other pedophiles started sending me the movies they had made, and eventually I could find everything I wanted online by trading the movies I had taken of Sarah and her friends.

The police tapped my computer and found me out. They came to the house, arrested me, and seized my computer. It was a public humiliation. I was written up in the newspaper and lost my job. My partner couldn't even look me in the eye. He immediately left me and cut off all communication. I didn't care because I just didn't love him anymore. My conscience was completely eroded away at this point.

As it turned out, I wasn't the person everyone thought I was. I was fooling everyone and was really a warped sociopath. These secret desires were now out in the public, and there was nothing I could do about it. I was hopelessly lost, and I had failed myself. I should have never stopped my checking. I changed into the person I feared and hated.

Imaginal Exposure 2: Attracted to Boys

For a long time I have been worried about having an attraction to little kids and failing God. I kept worrying about children and wondered if I could ever become a pedophile. I was checking and rethinking to make sure that I am not attracted to kids. In the process of getting treatment, I learned that the worries were all part of my OCD. I needed to resist the compulsions to get better, so I decided to stop doing the checking. I felt better and over time stopped worrying that I might be attracted to children.

Because I decided to stop checking myself, I didn't realize that I was slowly developing a sexual preference for children. These latent urges that had been hiding under the surface were finally emerging. My personality was changing.

I started enjoying fantasies about doing sexual acts with children, especially boys aged 10 and younger. I would spend hours at a time staring at pictures of little boys and wishing I could have sex with them. I imagined touching them and undressing them. I could see myself grabbing a young boy by the hand and sitting him next to me. I saw myself reaching down to work my hands up from his knee to his thigh. I could feel the softness of his skin, especially as I worked my hand in to the middle of his legs. I begin to undress him in my mind, removing his shoes and socks first. I would then slowly take off his shirt. I would leave the bottoms for last because it was the most exciting part. Then I would go all the way. I would repeat these actions in my mind.

After a while I wasn't interested in my wife any more, but I was increasingly attracted to my son and his six-year-old friends. I would spend my waking hours fantasizing about undressing them and having sex with each one of them.

After a while, fantasy wasn't good enough. I started looking at child pornography on the Internet. I could find everything I wanted online. I was masturbating to the images many times per day. I had become a complete pervert. I started spending time in online chat rooms where young boys would gather. I pretended I was a kid so they would chat with me. I would then ask what they were wearing. This all made me very sexually aroused. I decided I was no longer attracted to my wife and instead loved looking at young boys on the Internet. I eventually decided to file for a divorce. I thought it would be easier for me to live alone. I found my own apartment because I wanted to bring young boys home. As soon as I found my own place, I returned to the Internet. I joined different pedophile chat rooms and met "new friends." I started swapping notes with my "new friends" to learn new ways to meet young boys. I would spend hours on the Internet chatting with them trying to gain their trust. I felt like I was in *heaven* spending all this time in the chat rooms with little boys. They really loved me.

As it turned out, I wasn't the good man everyone thought I was. I was really a heartless, twisted pedophile. I used to think I would feel guilty if I actually molested a child, but I didn't. I should have never stopped my checking, since I had become the person I once despised. I started saving up money to take trips to Bangkok where I could spend time with children openly and legally. Since it wasn't against the law, there was nothing wrong with it. In the end, I lost my family, moved to a country where I was free to meet young boys, and was free to molest children. I love being a pedophile.

Imaginal Exposure 3: Fear of Therapy Exacerbating Pedophilia

I have always been afraid that I might be capable of hurting my daughter. I was afraid that by getting too close to her I might be capable of molesting her and that I am a pedophile. The fears became so real that I started avoiding changing her diapers and bathing her. I wanted to keep her safe from me because I knew that I might assault very quickly and that nobody would see this. I would ask my wife for reassurance to make sure that I had not hurt my daughter. I knew that my daughter was too young and innocent to know what was happening to her so I needed to be supervised at all times. Soon I became resentful of the fact that I even had a daughter, and my wife decided I needed to enter treatment. I was so scared to stop doing all the things I felt were keeping my daughter safe from me. I was changing diapers and watching movies about pedophiles. I was instructed to wash my daughter and touch her private parts. This terrified me, but, as my therapist predicted, it all became easier. One of my main concerns was that I would get an erection while being in the presence of my daughter or while changing diapers, but I was told to just agree that I might get one and that I might like it. Everything had become so easy that I had no problem saying I hoped I got an erection and that I would like it. But then, something went wrong, and I really did start getting erections during diaper changes. I really did start to enjoy getting erections, but this was not bothering me. Everyone was praising me for doing all the diaper changes and for starting to wash my daughter all alone but little did they know that these activities were sexually gratifying for me! I used to be scared to have her in my lap, but now I welcome the times she jumps in my lap because I know I will enjoy every minute of it. My wife sees me smiling a lot more and thinks it is because the treatment I am receiving is working and that I no longer think I am a pedophile, but really I am happy to be getting so much pleasure. This is the worst possible outcome because now I know I am a pedophile, and this is not socially acceptable. If I get caught, I will go to jail for a long time. If I were in India, I would probably be hanged if people found out I was molesting my daughter. If my wife finds out, she will divorce me and take my daughter away. I would have no job, and my family would be so disappointed and embarrassed they would disown me. I wish I had never gone to treatment. If I had kept doing my compulsions, I never would have realized what I am! Now I have to live the rest of my life hiding the fact that I am sexually aroused by my daughter. I am not sure how to do this. When she gets older, it will be harder so I have to just enjoy the time I have now while she is too young to know that I am molesting her.

Imaginal Exposure 4: Fear of Specific Fetish with Children's Feet

It is difficult for me to acknowledge that I have yet another peculiar problem. While I've accepted the fact that I am likely a pedophile and a danger to society and while I've undergone treatment to address that issue and all possibilities that may stem from it (my likelihood of molesting, my attraction to little girls' sexual organs, etc.), I am also likely a "foot-sniffing" pedophile. While foot fetishism is completely "normal" when it involves two partners above the age of consent, mine has, of course, been perverted to encompass the broad category of prepubescent and early pubescent females as well. Now, I would probably not find the feet of an adult like myself attractive at all.

Likely because I've spent so much time with my younger sister, my brain has been bombarded of thoughts wherein I leap at her feet and viciously and passionately smell and lick them. Maybe if I was normal these thoughts would disgust me, but I can't get them out of my head. There must be something wrong with me. Their presence, especially whenever I take a breath, is incessant and so must mean that I would like to act out my fantasy.

I am afraid because these "sexual" organs are often exposed—not hidden like breasts and vaginas by clothing. My constant contact with bare feet prompts many unsolicited thoughts, and my fear is that I will act on them. If I succumb to that temptation, I will likely also have forcible intercourse. The trifecta of evil deeds would be complete if I were to worship a young girl's foot, molest her groin, and violate her breasts. These exposures only render me more likely to commit these acts. If I had continued dealing with everything by myself this never would have happened, but now it is most probable that I will snap and seek out children as only a dirty, foot-sniffing pedophile could.

Imaginal Exposure 5: Fear about Finally Snapping and Acting on Images and Fears

I have been plagued with terribly upsetting thoughts about becoming a pedophile. Things got so bad for me that I began avoiding being around or even looking at children all together. My fear was that exposing myself to kids and related disturbing sexual material might change something inside of me; it might make me likely to snap and become what I never want to become: a pedophile! I even had some panic attacks about this. Life became so tough for me that I decided to go to treatment in hopes of figuring out that these thoughts and images were something I could get rid of. While searching online, I found there was a type of OCD where people have obsessions about becoming a pedophile. I was so excited to call and book an appointment at this clinic. While in treatment, my therapist told me I would be facing all of my fears and that these thoughts and images would soon fade away. I began doing all these exposures where I would look at pictures of children with bathing suits on and I even wrote a story about becoming a pedophile. I have been watching shows about pedophiles. I was very nervous about allowing myself to be exposed to these materials because I knew this could change me forever, but I continued. As my therapists told me, my anxiety did decrease, but then my worst fear began to happen. As my anxiety decreased, my interest in all things involving children increased. The obsessions I have while looking or listening to an exposure might say "You like that, Rebecca. You want that to happen!" I began to realize that this might be true. I was right all along. My personality and values have been warped. I knew if I kept exposing myself to these things I would eventually change into a pedophile. Now I see that the fear and anxiety I felt is what kept me from snapping and becoming a pedophile! I have become a danger to children now that I have become comfortable around them. My therapists made me spent time alone with children, and now I think that this is all I want to do. I have become someone who will snap and do pedophilic acts toward a child. I have to hold all of this in right now but when I return home, I know that while at the bus station, I will snap. Everyone I know at the bus station will look at me with sheer horror and confusion as to why I snapped. They will think, "What on earth happened to Rebecca that brought her to this?" and they will wonder "Has she ALWAYS been this way?" Rebecca has become a wolf in sheep's clothing. Rebecca has turned into a twisted, perverted person and has no business being among good people in society. Rebecca's younger sister and brother will discover that she has become a pedophile and a creeper. Rebecca's sister will be glad that she discovered the truth about Rebecca before she had children. Rebecca will lose all her family and friends because she snapped and became a pedophile. Rebecca wonders what exact thought or feeling caused her to snap and become a pedophile. Rebecca wonders if she didn't snap but always had being a creeper inside of her.

Imaginal Exposure 6: Chuck E. Cheese Is Pedophile's Amusement Park

I was starving and was thinking pizza sounds good today! I called my friend and was like where do you want to go? She told me let's go to Chuck E. Cheese for old time's sake. So within a little while we were on our way to

Chuck E. Cheese. It was like being a big kid again. Once we got in, we ordered our pizza and went to go sit down. I decided to go look at the video games. Once I got there, I noticed there were children all around me. There were kids running by all over the place. I felt kids running by passing against my legs, running behind me touching me as they ran by, and I was enjoying it. Suddenly, as a child was running by I felt my bottom go out a little and suddenly felt the child go by and felt them brush up against me. Did I just put my butt out on purpose to feel a child on me? Yes, I did it on purpose to feel aroused. Even just thinking about the shape of pizza made me think of vaginas and get even more aroused. Then I started feeling wet/hard and saw a child running toward me, and all of a sudden my pelvis went out, and I humped the child, and the child looked at me scared and ran off. I was horrified. I went back to the table sweating and feeling super guilty as my friend told me excitedly, "Pizza's here!" I am a pedophile because I enjoyed all of it, every minute.

Imaginal Exposure 7: Molesting My Relatives

It was a nice day, and my relatives were coming for a visit. And my niece and nephew were coming to visit for the Thanksgiving holiday. We were getting ready for the holiday so we decided to make some cookies with just the girls. While working on the cookies, my niece said she had to go to restroom, and her mom asked me if I could take her. So I told my niece, "OK, let's go to the restroom. Come with me." I told her, "Here's the toilet paper, and if you need anything, I'll be right outside the door." But then she asked me if I could stay and help her. So I closed the door, and I helped her pull down her pants and her underwear. Next I grabbed her and picked her up and sat her on the toilet. She used the restroom, and she said, "Wipe me, wipe me!" So next I took some toilet paper, and I started wiping her, but all of a sudden I felt aroused when I saw her bottom and her vagina. After that I felt that I was wiping her aggressively and was putting a lot of pressure on her bottom and genitals. I also squeezed her chest. Before I knew it, she yelled, "Ow, you're hurting me." I stopped and started panicking. I did this on purpose; I hurt her. I can feel that I'm aroused that must mean that I wanted to do this. She's going to go and tell her mom. This makes me a child molester. So, after cleaning her up she went back to help her mom and the other ladies. Later the evening her mom came up to me and told me very angrily that her daughter had told her that I had hurt her while taking her to the bathroom and asked how could I do such a thing. I know my life is officially over, I am a horrible, horrible person and a sick person.

Imaginal Exposure 8: My Son Is My Victim

I came down to Kentucky to get treatment for what I thought was OCD. I had been having all these horrible thoughts about molesting my son, and I was afraid and anxious all the time because I was scared that I was a pedophile and that I would hurt my son. The intensive treatment lasted for seven full days. They had me doing all kinds of exposures. I wrote down all the thoughts I had been having over and over again, and I also looked at pictures of kids that looked a lot like my son. At first I was very anxious, but eventually the exposures got a lot easier, and after treatment I realized I didn't have OCD. I was truly a pedophile from the beginning. All the thoughts I had been having were just manifestations of things I really wanted to do to my son and to other people. I used to dread changing his diaper because I feared touching his penis too much and touching his thighs and butt more than I actually needed to, but now I realize I enjoy touching my son in every way imaginable. As his mother, nobody would ever suspect that I am doing these things.

I have been molesting my son since he was born, but nobody ever knew it. I always did it when nobody else was around, so they would never know. The best thing about having a child so small is that he could never tell anybody anything. All he can do is lay there and allow me to do whatever it is I want to do to him. One of the images I used to have before I realized I was a pedophile was that I might squeeze his penis or mess with it more than I should, but now that I have accepted the fact that I am a child molester, I do it, and I enjoy it. I now realize that I had had these sexual feelings even when I was pregnant with him but never told anybody. I am so glad I never revealed these feelings or else I would not be able to play out my fantasies with my son. I was really excited when I found out that I was pregnant, so I would have my own child to molest and not have to rely solely on other peoples' children when I had the opportunity. I did it every day, multiple times a day, since I enjoyed it so much. I am convinced nobody will ever catch me. He is still very young so I figure I have a very long time before he could actually start telling anybody what his mom has been doing to him since birth.

I am so glad that I came down to Kentucky and went through all these exposures because now I see that molesting kids is exactly what I've wanted to do from the start, and these exposures allowed me to see that what I am doing is not so bad after all. That is what the physical sexual feelings have been telling me all along. The sensitive nipples and feelings in my vaginal area means that I am sexually stimulated or may be easier to "excite." In fact, I could see myself moving on to another child in the future since I see that molesting children is really not hard to do. I will have to choose very carefully though since other kids are not as accessible as my own. The last thing I would ever want is to get caught because then I would not be able to be who I really am.

Imaginal Exposure 9: Praying for Forgiveness

I am SURE that I have crossed "the line." I have molested my son. I told myself repeatedly that I wasn't going to do it again, but I just couldn't control myself. It's almost like I'm being possessed or something. I got these really graphic photos of kids from off the Internet, and I keep looking at them, fantasizing about what I could do to them. I felt guilty about downloading the pictures, so I deleted them, but I went back on the Internet and downloaded them again because I just couldn't help myself. I went to the park earlier today to scope out some prospects, and I brought my pictures with me so I could use them along with the kids that were there. I was trying to keep my back facing away from the other moms, so they couldn't see what I was doing. To make it worse, I stuck my child molester photos in Cole's diaper bag, so I would look like I fit in with everybody else. I tried to get rid of the guilty feelings, but I just couldn't shake them. I kept analyzing my feelings and thoughts and concluded that I had crossed "the line" again despite my best efforts not to. I had tried to find the point where I should "stop," but I couldn't figure it out, and I just did everything that my mind told me to do because Dr. Williams had told me not to avoid things and allow the thoughts to be there. Simone at first had said that there wasn't a line, but then, she had given me an example of what crossing the line was. How could I go home to my husband and act like a good wife? How could I look my son in his innocent eyes and tell him that I loved him?

I don't like the fact that I am so easily sexually stimulated. At first, I had avoided things that provoked the feelings, but then I just let whatever happen, happen. I feel bad for doing this, but I just couldn't help it. I prayed that God would take away the urges/feelings, but for some reason, He chose not to. I just don't understand. Why would God allow me to be a mother and have these horrible, inappropriate feelings/actions? Maybe God wants me to be a pedophile, but then I realize that I am just trying to rationalize who I really am. The "real me" just keeps coming out, no matter how hard I try to control myself. I don't really feel like going to church anymore, because I feel like God has abandoned me. I feel like I am all alone. I keep asking for forgiveness for my sins, but since I continue to keep doing it, I wonder if God really has/will forgive me? Even if He forgives me, that won't make me a good mother again. It's already too late for that. I have messed up too much. My son would be better off without me and so would my husband. I plan on divorcing my husband, so he can marry somebody better than me and giving up my son to my mom so he can be raised right. Hopefully, he doesn't remember all the things that I have done to him, since he is so small.

Imaginal Exposure 10: Babysitting Gone Bad

I came to the OCD clinic in September, and I began seeing Betsy for the assessment. I always thought that even thought it might be P-OCD, that my thoughts were way worse than anyone else and that Betsy wouldn't be able to help me. For the first time, I felt like I was finally in a place that understood me.

We completed all the paperwork, began talking about P-OCD and the OCD cycle and how treatment would work. We started with our first exposure, "toddlers and tiaras." After discussing the thoughts with Betsy, I felt better until the next week when they came back in another form. I began doing homework on my own and noticed that I was beginning to feel a little better and that using exposure statements made some of my anxiety decrease. The next week, we began watching a pedophile movie called "Unthinkable Acts."

I realized that I could try this again on my own. I began making a list of possible exposures and things I could do to face my fears alone. I decided I really wanted to get better so although I didn't want to do it. My first exposure would be to babysit Bella. I knew Laura probably wouldn't let me watch her, so I offered to give her and her husband Armando a night off. The night went pretty well, I was using exposure statements and noticed that they were helping. She asked me to help her in the bath, and I figure this would be another exposure and maybe help really get rid of my OCD. Inside the bathroom, she asked for my help, and I felt very little anxiety. I wondered if I was aroused, but again used an exposure statement and agreed with the thought and felt better. She got out of the tub, naked, and began lifting up my dress. I lifted my leg up onto the bathtub, and she began performing oral sex on me. It felt so amazing, unlike anything I had ever experienced with my husband or anyone before. I felt so aroused and good that I began touching her nipples and vagina. I didn't know if she liked it, but I still couldn't help myself. After a few more minutes, I stopped and told her to never tell anyone. I knew this was so wrong, but it felt like I couldn't stop myself. I began asking my sister-in-law if she needed a babysitter for Bella weekly. I knew Laura thought it was strange, but I felt addicted to touching Bella. One weekend, Bella wanted to have a slumber party, and Laura asked me to watch her and her friends because she was ready to have the baby any day. This was the perfect opportunity for me. Once all the girls went to bed, I woke Bella up and brought her into my bed. I had her straddle me and began feeling up and down her body. I stuck my fingers into her vagina really hard, and I knew it probably hurt her. I didn't care and couldn't seem to stop myself. It felt so good, we both were naked and I was so aroused by her and what I was doing to her. Once again, I told Bella not to tell anyone.

After the slumber party, Bella began to act different, and I was really nervous that I would get caught. Laura began to accuse me of doing something to Bella, but I kept denying it. I was stressed out all the time, wondering if anyone would find out, and if Bella would tell what happened.

Imaginal Exposure 11: Caught in the Act

I am feeling much better after treatment. Kara and I decided to elope and get married before we have a big ceremony. While planning that, we ended getting pregnant, and Kara was beautiful and so big, and I loved it. While she was pregnant, I started having pedophile thoughts again, and this time it wasn't OCD. This was real, and I was a pedophile. So when Kara had the baby, it turned out to be a little girl, and it made me so aroused. We named her Tina, a really sexy name. One day when I was changing her diaper, I decided to try and molest her and so I put my finger in her pussy, and I ended up liking it. I then decided I wanted to lick her pussy, and I did and it tasted good. As soon as I looked up Kara was right there in my face, and she punched me in the face and told me to leave or she would kill me. Kara never stopped crying, and she never stopped telling me how much she hated me. She cried for hours until the police showed up. She also found out that for years I had been molesting our son Marshall and raping him, and I had sucked his penis. Kara said that she hoped I lived the loneliest life anyone could ever possibly have. She never once thought I would ever do that to our only two children and that made me so upset. I never wanted to hurt anyone including Kara, and this ruined my life forever. Kara pressed charges against me, and so I spend the rest of my life alone in a six-by-six cell. I loved Kara, and this ruined my life forever. From then on, I still found myself really aroused, and I masturbated to the thoughts of molesting my little girl and my little boy Marshall, too. I couldn't stop because I really, really like the thought of molesting them so much.

Resources

For additional recommended reading for treating clients with pedophilic fears, readers are directed to the following article:

- Bruce, S. L., Ching, T., & Williams, M. T. (2018). Pedophilic obsessions in obsessive compulsive disorder: Assessment and treatment with exposure and response prevention. *Archives of Sexual Behavior, 47,* 389-402.

7

Relationship Issues

Monnica T. Williams, Jenifer A. Viscusi, and Chad T. Wetterneck

Impact of Sexual Obsessions on Relationships

Sexual OCD Can Impair Relationships

Humans are hardwired to connect with others. From birth, we innately attempt to attach to caregivers, and as we grow, we expand our attachments through friendships and romantic relationships. The quality of connection we feel toward others, our cultural group, and humankind as a whole is important for overall quality of life and life satisfaction. When we are connected with others, we feel understood and safe. Physically, we connect with others through hugging, kissing, and sexual activity; emotionally, we connect through exchanging personal experiences, ideas, and feelings.

Perhaps not surprisingly, obsessive-compulsive disorder (OCD) is quite harmful for relationships, which impacts not just the afflicted but also those who want to be close to them. While this may seem intuitive, it is important to understand why and how this happens, so that treatment can be optimized within the fullest context of the illness. Research has begun to examine OCD beyond the cognitive and behavioral symptoms to include the interpersonal challenges inherent in the experience of OCD, which produce both direct and collateral damage to interpersonal functioning and relationships (Riggs, Hiss, & Foa, 1992).

OCD can make a person feel distracted and distressed by everyday life, which can, in turn, make it harder to connect with others. Preliminary research suggests that people with OCD have difficulty interpreting visual cues and responding to spontaneous social cues, as compared to nonafflicted individuals, and these difficulties increase with symptom severity (Tumkaya et al., 2013, 2014). It can require a great deal of mental attention and energy to manage the constant and repeated obsessional worries encountered throughout the day. In addition, there may be a host of time-consuming mental compulsions (e.g., counting or praying), which can also be extremely distracting, drawing attention away from everyday social interactions such as conversations.

Sexual obsessions experienced by sufferers may seem to prey on every person that is encountered in daily life, which can make it very difficult to be around others, let alone engage in meaningful conversation or experiences. Intrusive images of violent sexual acts, worries about sexually violating children, or worry about being attracted to the "wrong" sex may be triggered by a simple social experience like going to a coffee shop or out to dinner. As men, women, and children are everywhere, so are the triggers for sexual obsessions. Since the natural response is to fight the thoughts, the only solution imaginable may be to isolate or avoid others as much as possible to prevent interactions that cause distress. It goes without saying that developing or maintaining interpersonal relationships is virtually impossible in isolation.

The withdrawal and avoidance that accompanies OCD can produce particularly negative effects on intimate relationships, affecting both partners. Not only is it difficult for the partner with OCD to manage symptoms, but the nonafflicted partner may also feel isolated and disconnected, which can create a void resulting in emotional and sexual dissatisfaction. Many times, the partner with OCD may feel tremendous amounts of guilt and shame surrounding the content of sexual obsessions, due to the fear of being misunderstood or rejected, so that person may go to great lengths to hide what they are experiencing. Sex may be limited or avoided altogether, as it may trigger unwanted thoughts or time-consuming compulsions, such as washing rituals.

Though an understandable attempt at self-protection, covering up or minimizing OCD creates a situation in which the partner with OCD is left to manage an unrelenting condition alone, and potential support from a partner is lost. Further, the nonafflicted partner is likely to notice the withdrawal behavior but may misattribute it to a personal deficit or an unrelated issue if the OCD is kept hidden. Left untreated, OCD within a relationship can quickly erode the core components of emotional support, sexual pleasure, and emotional intimacy.

Understanding the Fears Behind the Obsessions

Understanding fantasy is extremely important in the treatment of OCD, and while it can be an intimidating topic, an understanding of sexual desire will shape the content of exposures in treatment. We recently treated a male patient, with obsessions about being gay. He spent as many as eight hours per day worrying about his sexual identity and roughly the same amount of time performing compulsions in efforts to gain certainty. His worries significantly impacted his daily functioning to where he could not participate in activities, such as going to the gym or attending work functions, for fear of triggering his obsessions. He identified as heterosexual and was in a committed relationship with a woman but had persistent fears about an attraction to men. He experimented with his sexual behaviors and watched gay pornography in an attempt to better understand his sexuality. In working with his therapist (JV), he was able to identify that he found pleasure in both men and women. The OCD was feeding off the fluidity of his sexual identity, and through compulsions, he was trying to definitively label himself "gay" or "straight." Through working together, we learned that his fears regarding homosexuality were not surrounding sexual activity with other men; rather, he was afraid of the *consequences* of a homosexual or bisexual lifestyle. Originally, when we made his hierarchy of items for exposure, we included looking at erotic pictures of naked men and watching gay pornography. As we progressed, he disclosed that he enjoyed looking at the images and was turned on by them. The exposures were not tapping into his fears, which meant that the hierarchy needed revising!

Treatment was then designed to target his fears regarding the consequences of being bisexual, which were primarily surrounding the emotional damage he may cause his girlfriend, consequences according to religious beliefs, and the fear of losing familial and social support. While the idea of sex with men was pleasurable, the potential consequences were not only incongruous with his values but also terrifying, due to irrational and exaggerated core fears. He deeply loved his girlfriend; so being unfaithful to her (with a male or female) was the opposite of his values, and he was ultimately concerned that he would cause irreparable damage that would prevent her from ever finding happiness. He also valued his family and friends, so the idea of losing them was terrifying, and while he had many rational fears of being rejected, many of his fears were irrational. For example, he was afraid that he would act on his intrusive, sexually violent thoughts (despite no history of criminal behavior) and would be sentenced to life in prison, where he would engage in sex with another male inmate, contract AIDS, and then die. Furthermore, his value of security in the afterlife was jeopardized, as he was convinced that he was destined to burn in hell for eternity should he act on his obsessions.

When confronting the OCD within a relationship, it is important for partners to know that the sexual obsessions the patient experiences are *not* fantasies. This means that the idea of acting out sexually with someone of the nonpreferred gender or a child, for example, is horrifying, not pleasurable. Misunderstanding the fundamental concept that the worries, fears, and images represent the *opposite* of the individual's values and desires is what leads to misunderstanding and stigmatization of the afflicted person. In fact, this is a major barrier to seeking and receiving proper treatment.

With the help of the therapist, partners can be further educated in the symptoms of sexual obsessions and compulsions. The patient can work toward learning to share appropriate aspects of their OCD experiences with a partner and increase the amount of support and communication at home. Sexual dysfunction and avoidance can be addressed in treatment, to weed OCD out from the important, intimate aspects of a relationship.

Bringing a partner into therapy can be extremely scary for patients, especially when the topic of sexual obsessions is on the agenda. It is important that the therapist and patient discuss ahead of time the purpose of including a spouse, and they can decide what details are necessary to share to achieve the goal of support, without leaving the patient feeling overly exposed. I (JV) worked with a man, who came to the clinic for intensive outpatient treatment of OCD, which included persistent, violent sexual thoughts. He was not only afraid of acting out sexually with men, but at times during treatment, he also worried that he would rape me or act out in an violent sexual way toward me during session.

He and his wife arrived to treatment together, both from a very small, rural community that was primarily made up of members of the Mennonite faith. Their religious values were very conservative with regard to sex and sexual activity, and talking openly about sex was not commonplace for either of them. The private manner in which they regarded sex in general made the content of his obsessions not only taboo but also incredibly shameful and scary. After a few initial sessions, we understood that he was getting reassurance from his wife by evaluating his sexual interactions with her and asking her for reassurance about his sexual identity. He also confessed many of his distressing thoughts to his wife for assurance that he would not incur religious consequences for having the thoughts.

In working with the patient, we agreed that his wife could be helpful in not giving reassurance, but she would need to be first educated on OCD, and she would need to understand how his OCD impacted him. We did not go into details about the content of his obsessions, but rather spoke in general terms. He had control of how much content he shared, and I provided educational information, as well as emotional support to the couple as they processed information and the approach to treatment. Once the wife understood what to look for, she was able to recognize when her husband was seeking reassurance and compulsively confessing. Additionally, explanation of the treatment helped her get comfortable with not accommodating her husband's OCD, even though it was counterintuitive to her traditional role as a wife. Finally, having involved her in treatment provided him with additional support during homework exposures and creating his own daily exposures as they transitioned from intensive treatment back to their daily life in their hometown.

Family Accommodations

Watching a family member suffer from OCD can be incredibly painful. The amount of anxiety that arises from obsessive-compulsive symptoms can cause visible distress to the afflicted person, which can be agonizing to witness. It is only natural that when we see someone we love in pain, we want to alleviate the suffering any way possible. Almost as if to capitalize on our inherent compassion, OCD has a way of convincing family members that the afflicted loved one must perform the compulsions to avoid disastrous consequences or experience personal suffering. So frequently we hear the words, "I have to . . ." when family members describe their interactions with the patient. The truth is that while the accommodation of compulsions may seem helpful at the time, it actually strengthens the OCD cycle (Van Noppen & Steketee, 2009).

Out of what is meant to be love and support, family members may tolerate excessive behaviors or adjust schedules to allow for elaborate routines; they may offer continued reassurance against distressing or taboo worries; family may take over performing duties or activities around the house that prove to be stressful for their family member with OCD. In addition to wanting to alleviate suffering and maintain relationships, it may simply seem easier for the family to accommodate. Research on family accommodation shows that a majority of family members accommodate OCD at least weekly, with an overwhelming majority of families providing some form of accommodation daily (Gomes et al., 2014).

In the short term, family accommodation can be perceived as helpful. After all, assisting with responsibilities or offering repeated comfort can help prevent conflict, save time, or soothe high anxiety. One study found that family members endorsed higher levels of relationship satisfaction while accommodating, despite feeling an increase in burden (Lee, Steinberg, Phillips, Hart, Smith, & Wetterneck, 2015). It appears as though the short-term consequences of accommodations may be rewarding or done out of compassion, but how long can a relationship or family system sustain accommodating the OCD before other members of the family begin to suffer? As is well-documented, the relief from rituals is temporary. It is only a matter of time before the next obsession triggers another compulsion. This is because the link between the obsessive fear and the compulsive behavior is not actually functional, and the rituals provide a false sense that the behaviors prevented fears from coming true. Since the pattern is cyclical, the more the family accommodates, the more frequent and stronger the demands for accommodation will be in the future.

As the burden on the family grows, the stress on the family system as a whole can become strained or even unsustainable. The satisfaction reported in relationships has been strongly linked with family accommodation, suggesting that as accommodation for a partner increases, over time, the nonafflicted partner feels less satisfied in the relationship (Boeding et al., 2013). Relationship satisfaction is important not only for daily interactions, but it is also important for the maintenance of overall quality of life and sexual satisfaction in a relationship.

Effective treatment for OCD includes sessions dedicated to educating patients on how OCD works and how the OCD cycle maintains itself. This type of therapeutic education should also involve partners and family members when possible. Educating both the patient and the support system can offer insight to a cohesive and comprehensive treatment plan, as aspects of the treatment that require resisting of compulsions may seem counterintuitive. Family can learn how to offer love and support while not accommodating rituals, which can be particularly important in the beginning of treatment when the patient may require additional support.

Family Counseling and Interventions for Sexual Obsessions

How OCD Affects Partners

Unfortunately, very little research has focused on how OCD affects those around the affected individual, especially their spouses. Preliminary studies involving married couples in which one spouse suffers from OCD indicated that the partner with OCD suffers not only from the stress of OCD symptoms but also from significantly lower levels of self-compassion, as compared to the nonafflicted spouse. Afflicted partners were also more likely to avoid painful private events, such as experiencing negative emotions. Despite the internal turmoil, individuals with OCD reported feeling greater satisfaction within the marriage, as compared to the nonafflicted spouses. Interestingly, spouses with OCD felt more satisfied with their relationship as whole, and they also reported greater satisfaction with their spouse (Tellawi, Viscusi, Miller, Williams, & Chasson, 2015). It appears that those with OCD may be interpreting family accommodation as emotional support for their illness.

More work is needed to provide information that would be most helpful for therapists assisting couples experiencing difficulty with this disabling disorder. For example, it would be important to better understand how OCD severity may impact marital satisfaction and the mental health of the nonafflicted partners. It would also be important to better understand why there is such a difference in marriage satisfaction between spouses with and without OCD, such as perceived support, sexual satisfaction, and role of family accommodations.

Helping Partners Understand

What can you tell partners of people with OCD? We usually explain that people with OCD don't do compulsions because they want to, but because they are terrified of what will happen if they don't. The compulsions are often misguided attempts to keep loved ones (like the partner) safe from harm. The more they can empathize with that struggle, the better they will be able to demonstrate compassion, communicate efficiently, and show caring.

With working with partners and caregivers, you must not only ask them to reduce and eventually stop accommodating, but also tell them how to interact in a functional way with the OCD individual. Focus on the positive attributes of the client and encourage the partner to provide praise for any attempt to resist OCD symptoms. It is important for partners not to scold, criticize, or participate in their loved one's OCD rituals. For partners who want to be proactive, we suggest that they read some good books about OCD or join the International OCD Foundation to get support from other people who have been there. They can encourage their partner to stay in treatment and offer to go to therapy too. When they are feeling very frustrated because of the OCD symptoms, partners can motivate themselves by saying things like, "Am I going to let my spouse's rituals ruin our marriage, or am I going to find strength to be supportive and compassionate so that we can have the marriage that we have always wanted?" (Bach & Williams, 2013). This is not easy, and sometimes when a person's spouse has OCD, that person may need their own supportive therapist to cope with the situation.

When couples are being treated for OCD, it might be helpful to involve the partner in a more comprehensive manner, especially if the couple is particularly close, if the OCD includes obsessions about the partner or if the couple is part of a collectivistic ethnic or religious group. It may even be helpful to involve siblings and older children, who are in regular contact with the patient, since OCD rituals and family accommodation may be far-reaching within the family system. Research demonstrates that partner and family involvement in OCD treatment can be effective, not only in the decrease of OCD symptoms but also in improving interpersonal dynamics within the family (Maina, Saracco, & Albert, 2006; Thompson-Hollands, Abramovitch, Tompson, & Barlow, 2015).

There are many different methods that are effective for treatment with the involvement of partners and families. Options include, but are not limited to, family members' regular attendance of several individual exposure and response prevention (Ex/RP) sessions in addition to attending support groups for family members with loved ones with OCD and family or partners attending a few individual sessions or even participating in couples Ex/RP. However a patient and therapist decide to involve family, it is important that the involved individuals receive quality psychoeducation regarding the obsessive-compulsive cycle, as well as a strong understanding for the treatment rationale. It is also extremely important that partners and family members work with the client and therapist to understand the targeted accommodation behaviors.

Changing behaviors within the family system can be challenging for both the patient and the partner. After all, the rituals and accommodation can become engrained within the relationship, and despite best efforts, partners may continue to participate in rituals. Sometimes the partner is not always fully aware of accommodating behaviors, or they may even feel that they are being cruel toward their loved one, especially if the client is distressed. Including the partner in therapy can be instrumental in providing further education, emotional support, and encouragement for both the client and the loved one during the adjustment of eliminating rituals. In general, the involvement of supportive family members in individual OCD treatment is helpful for overall symptom reduction in the patient, but even if family cannot be regularly involved in treatment, research suggests that the quality of family involvement may be more important than the quantity. To be most helpful, the therapy time spent with the family should offer a strong foundation in psychoeducation about OCD, treatment rationale, and an understanding of targeted behaviors in treatment (Thompson-Hollands et al., 2015).

Once treatment is underway, before the partner is brought into session, the therapist and client should discuss ways that the loved one can be helpful in providing support without accommodating compulsions. The client is likely able to identify specific ways in which their partner in involved in compulsions, and as treatment begins and compulsions are resisted, it will be helpful for the client to ask their partner to not do their rituals or to not enable their rituals anymore. While this step can be very difficult for the client, it can also be very empowering, as the decision for the partner to stop compulsions comes from within the client, as opposed to an external mandate, which can feel punitive or punishing. The therapist should support the client by kindly, yet firmly, asking the partner to not participate in rituals. We usually plan to have a session with the partner shortly after starting exposures to give the client the opportunity to ask their partner not to accommodate the OCD any more with the therapist present to boost the sense of accountability and ensure clarity of the message. The client might say something like, "Thank you so much for supporting me through my struggles with OCD all of these years. The best thing you can do for me now is to stop offering me reassurance when I seem confused or upset about my sexual obsessions. Although I might feel better in the short term, I have learned that getting reassurance from you only makes the OCD stronger." The therapist can then follow up the statement with encouragement, positive reinforcement, and clear strategies to help the partner stop accommodating.

Involving partners in sessions will give them an opportunity to gain expertise in supporting their loved one by offering coaching and learning how to support to the client during difficult times without accommodating compulsions. For example, if a patient struggles with confronting a situation that would typically be avoided, the partner should not say, "Stop those compulsions. You are really screwing up your treatment and driving me nuts!" Instead, words of encouragement should be offered, such as, "You can do it. I am here with you to help fight the OCD." Or, if a patient is seeking reassurance, "It sounds like OCD is really bothering you right now, and you want reassurance. I want to support you and your treatment, so I can't reassure you, but I know you can get through the anxiety you feel right now." The partner can also help by encouraging and supporting daily homework. However, it is important that the therapist first ascertain from the client what sorts of behavior surrounding homework would feel supportive. For example, some clients would like reminders from their partners to do homework, but others might perceive this as nagging. So it is important that effective helping with homework is perceived as both helpful to the client and useful to the partner.

As therapy progresses, the partner can take an even more active role in helping with the OCD treatment. If supporting the client in resisting compulsions and completing homework is effective, the therapist should arrange another session to discuss how the partner can be more involved. For example, to help with ritual prevention, if the client asks for reassurance, instead of the encouraging statements just described, the partner can respond with an exposure statement. If the client says, "I just had a mental image about same-sex behavior. Is that sinful?" The partner can respond by saying, "It sounds awfully sinful to me. Who knows, maybe you will go to hell for that thought." Of course, a good sense of humor is essential to this process, and the client must understand in advance that their partner will saying these things to help in the recovery process.

To help directly with exposures, the partner can participate in many constructive ways. For example, a partner might look at nude pictures or videos with the client and encourage the client to focus on genitals or other distressing areas while saying things like, "You probably want to have sex with that person," or "You are probably getting aroused right now!" If direct involvement with exposures is uncomfortable for the client or partner, the partner can be helpful by offering words of encouragement during an exposure, such as, "I am proud of you!" and "You can do this! Great job!" It is important for the encouragement to be ideographically reinforcing for the client, so asking in-session for the partner to make these statements toward the client and getting feedback on the effectiveness (or suggestions for what they want to hear) is helpful. The partner can also learn to coach the client through an exposure (much like the therapist would do in session) by asking about levels of distress, encouraging the tolerance of distress without performing compulsions, and helping the client remember that the distress subsides over time.

The idea of participating in a loved one's treatment may seem invasive or daunting and perhaps may even cause concern that involvement in treatment may cause additional distress to the nonafflicted partner. Preliminary research indicates that not only are intimate partners involved in couple's OCD generally not negatively affected by treatment but also that couple's treatment can provide benefit to the relationship as a whole, particularly with regards to constructive communication (Belus, Baucom, & Abramowitz, 2014). Through participation in couples treatment, the client and partner can learn to share perspectives and emotions with regards to the impact of OCD symptoms and troubleshoot difficult situations that exacerbate OCD symptoms. Treatment can encourage couples to confront OCD as a team, which promotes constructive communication and collaboration between the couple.

It is important to remember that while OCD is frustrating and exhausting for the client, it can also be frustrating and exhausting for the family member(s). Even with education and involvement in therapy, partners and family members may still feel a pull to offer accommodation to avoid fights or save time. Patience can run thin, especially when frequent demands for accommodation are made, which can lead to critical comments toward the client or even an increase in anxiety or sadness in the supportive family member. While such feelings are natural, critical comments toward the client can lead to an increase in compulsive behavior, which can be counterproductive to treatment, and can be further damaging to interpersonal relationships within the family system (Amir, Freshman, & Foa, 2000). Family frustration should be acknowledged in family-involved treatment, and strategies for disengaging should be discussed if family is feeling frustrated or overwhelmed when trying to offer support. Arguments between partners should be strongly discouraged during the treatment process. If the partner offers supportive statements as described earlier and the client becomes upset with the partner, getting physical space is important. The partner could be instructed to tell the client that they will need to move to another room to prevent the OCD from creating an argument between them. When the situation escalates or the partner feels as though they are about to act on frustration or anger, this is a cue to leave the situation and thereby prevent a direct confrontation. In addition, you can offer separate sessions for partners if they just need space to vent and get additional support for the difficulties of living with OCD.

Differences in Views about Mental Illness

We have encountered various scenarios where families have been more of a hindrance to a client's process than an encouragement. Sometimes families don't believe in mental illness or that their loved one has OCD. Other times, they believe the mental illness is real, but they don't believe in the treatment. There are also challenges when relatives enable clients by providing reassurance or perform rituals for the client. Though they feel they are being helpful, their actions are, in fact, worsening the OCD symptoms. The following is a case example of how we addressed these challenges as they presented themselves when working with one client whose spouse didn't believe that the client, his wife, had a real issue.

The client, we'll call her Velma, was a 35-year-old woman with checking OCD. The client had fears of burning down her home with household appliances, and her fears began taking a toll on her marriage because of the amount of time she spent worrying and asking her spouse for reassurance. The client's husband felt that her fears were unreasonable because he believed she should simply go check the appliance and be able to logically see whether or not it was turned off. Her husband was not aware that the act of checking the appliance was a compulsion that would worsen the client's OCD and that telling the client that he double-checked the appliance and that everything would be fine was actually reassurance. When the client entered treatment, her spouse didn't understand why it was necessary to pay for treatment when (a) the client should be able to simply look and walk away confidently knowing just like he was able to and (b) he didn't believe in mental illness because he had no exposure to anyone with mental illness in his family. The client's experience with mental illness was the complete opposite, however, as she had several relatives with bipolar disorder and substance abuse disorders. Whenever we meet with our clients, we provide family members with an accommodation scale to assess for unhealthy patterns so that we can address these behaviors early in the treatment plan. For this particular client, it was necessary to have a family session with her husband so that we were able to dispel myths about mental illness, OCD, how treatment works, and develop a strategy to best support the client, her spouse, and both of them as one unit. We learned that the treatment sessions were an area of contention because the client's checking carried over at work where she checked appliances in her office out of fear of causing damage to the building and its customers. This eventually led to the client working part-time, so there was an additional financial strain on the family to meet household expenses and pay for treatment. The spouse also had concerns about the validity of the treatment, as it was his impression that the client's concerns had worsened since entering treatment.

Conducting psychoeducation on the OCD cycle and how treatment works helped to ease some of the husband's doubts. Exploring the previous attempts that they had made to address the clients' concerns helped them to see that if she could, in fact, just stop, then she would have done so already and there would be less stress within the marriage. Educating the family on how carrying out checking compulsions for the client and how providing reassurance exacerbated the symptoms was also enlightening for them as they realized that the client's symptoms worsened as a result of doing more compulsions while in treatment, rather than the treatment itself not working. With education, support, and ideas to better care for their marriage, they were able to see light at the end of the tunnel and work together to carry out the overall treatment plan.

A second example of how others may misperceive mental health concerns occurred with one of the first OCD patients seen early in the therapist's career (CW). Prior to coming to treatment, a man was having obsessions about raping his wife and others. He eventually told his wife about it prior to finding out he had OCD. His wife was taken aback and would no longer sleep in the same room as him. She ended up participating in therapy with him but prior to that also mentioned to her parents that he had OCD and shared some of the obsessional content. They asked her what that meant, and she tried to explain his obsessions. Her parents called the police immediately and tried to convince their daughter to get a divorce. It was essential in this case for anyone who learned about the symptoms to also be educated on OCD at the same time to avoid strong reactions based on a lack of understanding. In this case, the last time we heard from the client, it may have been too late to save the marriage.

Cultural Issues

Most research focused on OCD and family therapy has been conducted in Western cultures, and less is known about how effective family involvement might be in treating OCD in Eastern cultures. Since Western cultures tend to emphasize independence, family accommodation may negatively impact the family system more than in collectivist cultures, due to familial and societal expectations for individual contribution and functioning (Thompson-Hollands, Edson, Tompson, & Comer, 2014). Additionally, the degree to which emotions are expressed within a family or culture may also impact the usefulness of family involvement in OCD treatment. Limited research suggests that cultures that are more emotionally expressive may more readily demonstrate anxiety and frustration, which may do more harm than good when trying to support the patient. Examples of this include disappointment with not being able to comply with all treatment instructions, refraining from all rituals, inability to do exposures even beyond those assigned in therapy, slower than expected symptom reduction, or inability to regain previous functioning and/or learn life skills thwarted by OCD during normal developmental periods while doing better in treatment. Family members of cultures that are less emotionally expressive may be better able to put their own frustrations and anxieties aside during treatment, which could facilitate faster positive results. Thus, in working with more emotionally expressive cultures, it may be more beneficial to first work through the family members' anxieties and frustrations prior to involving them in treatment (Steketee & Van Noppen, 2003).

Conversely, people from more expressive cultures may be able to provide greater encouragement, affection, and enthusiastic support for improvement during the treatment process. Mehta (1990) found that outcomes for East Indian patients were improved when cognitive-behavioral therapy was administered according to a family-based model, taking into consideration the centrality of the patients' family in this particular cultural group.

Among ethnic and cultural minorities, family tends to be a primary means of support and is often the informal outlet for mental health concerns within these communities. Thus, clinicians should make an effort to integrate family into the treatment as described in this chapter to bolster the therapeutic alliance and gain support for treatment in the home (Williams, Sawyer, Ellsworth, Singh, & Tellawi, 2017). If family are not supportive of Western mental healthcare, this may pose an obstacle for successful completion of treatment. Thus, understanding the client in their cultural context is essential.

Sexual Problems: Sex and Anxiety Don't Mix

Most people don't connect OCD and sex, but many people with the disorder are having struggles in this most important and intimate area of life (Aksaray, Yelken, Kaptanoglu, Oflu, & Özaltin, 2001). We are not talking about people who have sex over and over again, compelled by a need to achieve technical sexual perfection. In fact, OCD is more likely to result in a sex life characterized by lack rather than repeated memorable performances. Here are a few ways that OCD can interfere with sexual happiness and drive couples to the brink of frustration.

Impregnating Obsessions

Some people with OCD worry excessively about becoming pregnant or impregnating others. Women with this sort of OCD may engage in repeated washing to remove any traces of semen they may have encountered unknowingly during the day. They may avoid swimming pools and public restrooms out of fear that such places put them at risk of pregnancy. Males with this type of OCD may resist touching objects or others out of fear that a random lone survivor sperm might be transferred to an unsuspecting female victim through something as innocuous as a handshake, leading to unintentional pregnancy. One of our patients made his girlfriend take pregnancy tests every week, just to be sure he hadn't impregnated her—despite the fact they had stopped sexual activity many months ago due to his extreme obsessional fears. As you can imagine, people with pregnancy obsessions stay as far away from sexual activity as possible.

Sexual Orientation Obsessions

People with sexual orientation-themed OCD are generally not attracted to people of the same sex emotionally or physically but are nonetheless hypervigilant for signs of possible same-sex attraction. This hypervigilance typically extends to sexual activity, where sufferers may be obsessively monitoring their feelings of arousal to help confirm their orientation. The problem is that paying such close attention to the sexual process takes attention away from the experience itself, resulting in reduced arousal and poor performance as a self-fulfilling prophecy.

Obsessions Surrounding Sexual Deviance

Many people with sexually themed OCD worry about having inappropriate sexual desires, such as an attraction to children, family members, religious figures, or even animals. People with such worries often try very hard not to think about sexual matters as this triggers OCD-related worries. For example, one of my patients asked, "If I have sexual feelings about my husband, but my baby is in the bed with us, could that mean I am actually attracted to my son?" She avoided anything that might cause sexual arousal, as she worried that the feelings would somehow transfer to her baby and make her a pedophile. As you can imagine, there was not much sexual happiness in the home.

Contamination Fears

Over a quarter of those with OCD have contamination fears, and many of these people worry about germs that can cause a dreaded illness or disease. Perhaps the most feared disease is HIV, with other sexually transmitted diseases (i.e., herpes, HPV) also possible causes of concern. People with these worries will avoid places and situations that evoke disease-related obsessions, such as public restrooms, medical facilities, and, above all, sexual contact. These fears are not rational, and OCD patients may have concerns about partners who are faithful and certified disease-free. OCD sufferers may have themselves tested repeatedly for STDs and demand their partners do the same.

Others with contamination fears in OCD may not worry about infection per se; rather, they find sexual fluids unbearably disgusting. As a result, long postintercourse decontamination rituals become necessary to regain peace of mind. This may involve hours of compulsive washing and scrubbing in scalding water, as well as laundering all bed linens, clothes, and towels that may have been witness to sexual activity. In the face of such onerous rituals, it becomes easier to avoid sexual activity altogether.

Anxiety and Depression Reduces Sex Drive

Although laboratory studies suggest that some types of anxiety may facilitate sexual feelings (i.e., watching a scary movie, crossing a rickety bridge), anxiety associated with mental disorders generally leads to sexual dysfunction. One reason for this is that high levels of anxiety may be associated with mental distractions (such as worry, obsessions, and hypervigilance) that can interfere with sexual responding (Bradford & Meston, 2006). People with OCD are generally anxious about any number of things, sexual and nonsexual, and this can reduce sex drive or interfere with being mentally engaged during the sexual experience.

Additionally, the reality of having chronic, unwanted thoughts—no matter what the content—is just distressing. Therefore, it is not surprising that over half of those with OCD also struggle with a diagnosable depressive disorder. Depression alone can result in a loss of sexual interest.

Medication Side Effects

Selective-serotonin reuptake inhibitor (SSRI) medications, used widely as antidepressants, are a first-line treatment for OCD. SSRIs and other similar medications usually reduce anxious feelings but will also cause sexual dysfunction in at least a third of patients (Bystritsky, 2004). Furthermore, people with OCD typically require higher doses than people using SSRIs for depression, making sexual dysfunction more likely. For many, relief from OCD symptoms is enough to overcome the resulting sexual problems, but for others the medication itself makes intercourse impossible.

Talking to Partners

Sexual problems caused by OCD can increase the stress level in a relationship that is already bearing the weight of the disorder in other areas. Partners may be frustrated by the apparent lack of sexual interest shown by their loved one. It is important to emphasize to partners that sexual dysfunction is a symptom of the illness and does not reflect a lack of love or caring. The person with OCD may simply be too overwhelmed with worries to feel sexual.

Getting professional help for OCD is an important step in the right direction, but be aware that treatment can also contribute to the problem, at least at first. Exposure-based therapy for OCD may be stressful, temporarily contributing to decreased interest in sex, and medication can result in difficulties that may be temporary or long-term. It is important to discuss these issues with clients in advance, and couples sessions may be a necessary part of the process. Understanding and patience is critical, but if both partners are motivated, OCD can be beaten and love life restored.

Relationship OCD

Although not without controversy, emerging studies in OCD research have begun to examine a dimension of OCD sometimes called relationship OCD (R-OCD). Individuals with R-OCD experience distressing thoughts, images, or urges that are directly related to interpersonal relationships. The obsessions can be categorized into two unique symptom presentations: *relationship-focused* and *partner-focused*. While worries about relationships may be present in other dimensions of OCD, the content of obsessions in individuals with R-OCD are significantly more focused on their relationships and partners as compared with individuals who are primarily experiencing symptoms associated with other OCD dimensions. Similarly to other dimensions of OCD, individuals with R-OCD experience intense feelings of guilt, impairment with interpersonal functioning, and sexual dysfunction (Doron, Derby, Szepsenwol, Nahaloni, & Moulding, 2016; Doron, Mizrahi, Szepsenwol, & Derby, 2014).

Relationship-focused obsessions generally question the quality of the relationship. For example, an individual may constantly question whether or not the relationship "feels right." Individuals with relationship-focused

R-OCD may also question whether or not they are sufficiently in love with a partner or whether or not they are sufficiently sexually attracted to a partner. Partner-focused obsessions hone in on potential flaws with the partner. Thoughts may focus on physical aspects of a partner such as, "Are they attractive enough?" or about physical features of the body or face. Partner-focused obsessions can also go beyond the physical appearance and attach to worries about a partner's intelligence, social ability, motivation, or stability (e.g. "Are they smart enough?" "Are they motivated enough to be successful?"). The person with OCD may also wonder obsessively about their partner's attraction to others or even their fidelity.

Much like other obsessive-compulsive symptom dimensions, these thoughts are the opposite of what is valued. Those who question the "rightness" of their relationship, or their love for their partner are likely to acknowledge being very much in love with their partner and value their relationship. When worrying about the physical attractiveness or competence of a partner, the person may hold a value that looks do not matter in relationships or may readily acknowledge the partner's intelligence, social grace, or motivation. The discord between the content of obsessions and a person's values or beliefs is what causes the distress, and like other symptoms of OCD, compulsions are performed to temporarily lower the anxiety. The compulsions can span a variety of behaviors, but some common compulsions associated with R-OCD may include reassurance-seeking, comparing and analyzing features and behaviors of a partner, or constantly evaluating how attracted one feels toward a partner.

The distress associated with R-OCD can cause significant impairment in emotional and sexual functioning, as well as relationship satisfaction. The constant worries that consume an individual with R-OCD can naturally weaken the sense of closeness one feels with a partner and can put tremendous strain on the relationship as a whole. The constant questioning of physical and personal qualities of a partner may result in tremendous guilt and negative views toward oneself. Questioning the partner's attraction to others can put a tremendous strain on the relationship, as it makes the partner feel untrusted and disrespected. One of our clients had been demanding that her husband show her the text messages he sent to a female coworker each day.

While sex is usually a way in which a couple becomes closer, R-OCD can turn sexual encounters into experiences that create doubt, and the obsessions of R-OCD can interfere with experiencing pleasure from sex.

Sexual activity presents an opportunity to evaluate the encounter for satisfaction, intensity, and attraction. For example, "Was I aroused enough by my partner?" or "Did I enjoy sex with my partner as much as I should have?" Unfortunately, the combination of guilt, constant doubt, and experiencing sex that is more distressing than pleasurable frequently results in a reduction in sexual activity and dissatisfaction with the relationship in general.

There is limited research with regards to specific treatment for R-OCD, but given the similarities to other symptoms of OCD in how R-OCD is maintained (anxiety, compulsion, temporary relief) and the similar cognitive processes to OCD in general (e.g., overvaluing thoughts, worry that thoughts will result in action), R-OCD is likely to respond to traditional OCD treatment. For example, to address a common worry regarding the level of attraction or arousal toward or from the partner, an exposure may be to engage in sexual activity but not perform the corresponding compulsion, such as mentally reviewing the experience, asking the partner if they were satisfied or adequately aroused during sex, or comparing the pleasure of the recent encounter to the past. Clients may tell themselves statements such as, "Maybe I (or my partner) did enjoy sex, maybe not. I don't know." They may even agree with the OCD obsessions and say something like, "I was not attracted to my partner at all, and I hated having sex," or "My partner was not aroused at all because they are not attracted to me."

For worries that may be less easily addressed with in vivo exposures, such as the level of acceptable attractiveness, intelligence, or motivation, imaginal exposures may be helpful. The therapist and client may write a story that incorporates all of the client's greatest fears surrounding the partner's potential physical and personality flaws. The client may write about how they are in a committed relationship with a person who is incredibly unattractive, while assigning their partner with physical qualities that are repulsive. The partner might be portrayed in the story as extremely dull, unmotivated, or unintelligent; with close attention to add as many details to depict the character flaws as possible.

Consequences of having an unattractive partner should also be detailed in the imaginal exposure. For example, if the client is worried about losing sexual desire, the story should include the inability to become aroused during sex; if the worries are surrounding being stuck with the wrong person, the imaginal exposure should include details of all of the other wonderful, potential partners and experiences that are lost by being in the current relationship; or if worries include ridicule from others, the exposure could include details of what others might say and how the client feels hearing such mockery. Similarly to in vivo exposures, clients should not engage in any compulsions, such as mental review, reassurance, or engaging in positive thoughts about the partner in an effort to balance negative thoughts.

Summary

Through research and clinical practice, we know that OCD can put tremendous strain on individuals, and recent studies have begun to focus on the distress OCD causes on the family system as well. The symptoms cause impairment to an afflicted individual's desire and ability to connect with others, which, in turn, can leave a person feeling isolated and loved ones feeling neglected. Consequences of OCD on the family system negatively impact communication, intimacy, and relationship satisfaction.

When obsessions are sexual in nature, symptoms may be compounded by guilt, which may further isolate an individual and delay the seeking of treatment. The content of sexual obsessions can span a wide range of worries and can be easily triggered everyday activities. The distress causes not only compulsions but also an array of avoidance behavior, including physical and emotional intimacy with partners. Partners may find themselves noticing distress but not fully understand the cause of the anxiety, since loved ones are likely to be very reluctant to share the upsetting thoughts and images that invade their minds on a regular basis.

Loved ones frequently find themselves in a position to try to alleviate the distress of a partner or loved one through accommodating behavior. Partners may offer repeated assurance of sexual orientation or sexual performance or even reassure their partner that they would never act out in a violent or aggressive manner. Behaviors and schedules may also be modified, so as to shield the afflicted individual from scary situations or to allow for the completion of rituals. Such accommodations can be taxing for the partner and family members and, ultimately, maintain the obsessive-compulsive cycle.

When living with a partner or loved one with OCD, it is important to know that treatment is available and that the family can be very helpful in the therapeutic process. Support from loved ones can take many forms in the therapeutic process, from attending therapy sessions on a regular basis, to attending a few sessions, to helping with exposures and encouragement to work through distressing moments without performing rituals. Therapy may even include helping loved ones work through their own frustrations and sadness before getting involved in the treatment of the afflicted partner. Whatever involvement the family has, sessions should provide a strong foundation of psychoeducation, as well as an emphasis on supportive intervention that is free from shaming, criticism, and judgment.

The treatment should augment individual therapy with family sessions that provide psychoeducation for the partner and family, so that there is a clear understanding as to how the OCD cycle is maintained and perpetuated. It is also important to understand OCD so that the treatment rationale is clear, as many of the treatment methods can seem counterintuitive. Partners and families should have a clear understanding of accommodation behaviors that are practiced within the family system, and through individual and family work, they can strive to eliminate accommodation behaviors and learn to develop a supportive environment to recover from OCD. Family therapy should also consider the cultural components of the individual and family and help the family structure support with sensitivity to values and beliefs that exist within the system, which may be different from Western or non-Hispanic White cultures.

8
Troubleshooting Common Problems, Issues, and Resources

Monnica T. Williams, Erin C. Nghe, John Hart, and Chad T. Wetterneck

There are a number of issues, foreseen and unforeseen, that may arise in the treatment process. The very nature of the content makes sexually themed obsessive-compulsive disorder (S-OCD) tricky to treat. Even among those with healthy attitudes toward sex, it is often a difficult topic to discuss. However, more complicating is that the sexual issues in S-OCD are alien to the client, provoking greater anxiety, embarrassment, guilt, and shame. Negative stigma is a problem that encompasses all psychiatric disorders including obsessive-compulsive disorder (OCD), with sexually intrusive thoughts more stigmatizing than other types of intrusive thoughts (Cathey & Wetterneck, 2013).

Many of the barriers to treatment are similar to problems clients have when they are experiencing OCD with other themes. Building motivation, increasing treatment adherence, creating effective and safe exposures, family and caregiver issues and working with comorbid depression are among the many problems that emerge in treating this disorder. Here we address some of the most common questions asked by therapists, clients, and family members about treatment issues in S-OCD.

Therapist Discomfort Discussing Sexual Topics

Sex and sexuality often comes up in clinical work, and as clinicians we need to be willing to address it. Hopefully, most of us already feel competent that we can address clinical issues involving sexual functioning with our clients. However, in S-OCD, the content of clients' obsessions are often disturbing and morbid, as they may involve incest, bestiality, and rape. Obviously, if we are disturbed, then that must be but a fraction of how disturbed our clients feel. An important thing to keep in mind is that we are treating OCD and not sexual disorders. To confuse the two would be a breakdown in the understanding and relationship between the therapist and the client. In fact, it is not uncommon for S-OCD clients to seek out sex therapists. However, after a thorough assessment, it should be apparent that the client's obsession is ego alien and not an actual part of their sexuality.

New clinicians may continue to be uneasy with the nature of client obsessions and may want to seek consultation from a more experienced OCD clinician. The best way therapists can address their discomfort is through practice. We usually have our trainees practice giving assessments to each other before assessing clients. Therapists can role-play any number of deviant sexual obsessions with each other and stumble through finding the right wording to adequately explicate the hypothetical problem. It is important that when therapists do discuss these issues with clients, they do not seem embarrassed or hesitant, as the S-OCD client may interpret this as evidence of the unacceptability of their thoughts. Similar to the client's experience in therapy, many of us as treatment professionals will have to habituate to uncomfortable therapy material. In addition to role-plays, reading de-identified imaginal exposures of previous clients is helpful in training (see Chapters 5 and 6 for examples). We find the best approach is typically when the therapist can approach the material in a warm and caring but matter-of-fact matter.

Troubleshooting for Busy Professionals

OCD does not discriminate whom it affects, as we have seen people from all walks of life our practice. We have treated construction workers, fast-food workers, surgeons, nurses, elementary school teachers, and university professors for the debilitating effects of S-OCD. Finding time to complete homework with the stress of a professional life and family life is often a challenge for our clients. Sometimes clients need support from the therapist on how to prioritize self-monitoring and exposure homework while trying to juggle the rest of life's demands. Therapists should first assess whether difficulty with homework stems from avoidance, as this is often the case. Clients should also be prepped during the initial consultation sessions about the demands of homework, as sometimes it is not only tedious but also emotionally draining to detail the compulsive events of each day. We also stress that as clients decrease in their compulsions, they are able to find more time to complete homework.

We have had clients who work long, 12-hour days where exposure homework and self-monitoring seems almost impossible due to their schedules. Recording rituals immediately after they occur allows for better accuracy, but some occupations make carrying a form and recording rituals on the spot difficult. We encourage our clients to get creative by briefly writing them down in their smart-phones or recording them on a voice memo. Though we do not endorse any specific technology, we may encourage a client to explore whether anxiety-tracking applications on their phone would allow for more ease in this area. We also work with our clients to find ways to incorporate exposures throughout their workday, if spending 45 to 60 minutes on exposures after work isn't always possible. For example, if a client fears pedophilia obsessions, we encourage them to keep a child's small toy, a picture of children, etc. in their pockets and touch it while walking about their offices or look at it during a free moment at their desk.

Occasionally, there are times when we have to assess clients in their work environment. We do this by obtaining consent from the client to collaborate with the employer so that the employer is able to make reasonable accommodations for the client's OCD in accordance with the Americans with Disabilities Act. This generally allows us to assess the client for avoidance in the workplace and find additional exposures that are relevant to that setting. For example, a man with gay obsessions could have a calendar featuring male actors or athletes or the kind male firefighters/police officers sell for raising funds. A person with pedophilia obsessions could keep pictures of all of their children, nieces, nephews, etc. on their desk. Those with bestiality could have calendars, a screen saver, or pictures of pets that a typical pet lover would have. On occasion, a client's severity level is so extreme that they may need to take a leave of absence from work. Of course, we try to evaluate whether there is impaired functioning in the work setting versus more avoidance.

Insurance Coverage for 90-Minute Session

One unique aspect of OCD treatment is the session format. We generally utilize 90 minutes in each session to make sure there is enough time for the exposure therapy we do. Insurance companies will typically allow the first hour of the 90 minutes without an issue, but sometimes they will not automatically cover the additional 30 minutes. A few insurance companies will even balk at the 60-minute session in favor of a 45-minute one.

We advise all of our clients to contact their insurance company before scheduling with us and ask if they will cover the code for an extended session (the additional CPT° code is 99355). If so, they should ask if preauthorization is required. If the answer is yes, we get the contact information from the client of their insurance company's behavioral health department. Then we explain that the 90-minute session is needed to conform with best practices for OCD treatment to get this authorized for the client.

If 90 minutes cannot be covered, the treatment can be done in shorter sessions but generally will require more weeks to complete.

Client Has Comorbid Depression

It's normal for clients with OCD to also be depressed. It is not unreasonable to imagine that it can be depressing when your brain won't stop going places that are scary! As noted previously, over half of those with OCD have a comorbid unipolar depressive disorder, and almost a quarter have a comorbid bipolar disorder. Research shows that for clients with mild to moderate depression, exposure and response prevention (Ex/RP) is just as effective, but for client with severe depression, outpatient treatment does not work as well (Abramowitz, Franklin, Street, Kozak, & Foa, 2000). Since treatment is very energy intensive, people who are depressed may not have the energy or motivation to stick to the treatment plan. Exposures are hard, and consistency is important. When people are severely depressed, it can be hard to even brush your teeth, much less do some anxiety-provoking homework.

There are a number of good strategies for helping with depression in OCD. If the client has enough motivation, we usually engage the person in behavioral activation (Dimidjian, Barrera, Martell, Muñoz, & Lewinsohn, 2011), which works very well. If clients are able to be consistent with their daily behavioral activation homework (which, unlike OCD homework, tends to be enjoyable and not aversive), we usually start to see some mood improvements in a week or two. If the client is too depressed to engage in behavioral activation homework, we recommend a psychiatric consult for medication management. If medications and therapy are not enough, higher levels of care, including residential services, have shown good success in treating both OCD and depression (Wetterneck, Adams, et al., 2017).

As mentioned in Chapter 1, exercise also seems to be a good adjunct to OCD treatment, either as part of a behavioral activation plan or as an additional separate treatment. There is good research showing that exercise is good for depression and also a small amount of research showing that exercise is helpful for OCD, whether or not the person has a mood disorder. So we encourage all clients, if they are sedentary, to do something active at least every other day, even if just going for a walk.

Client Won't Adhere to CBT Treatment Elements (Sessions, Homework, Etc.)

Sometimes clients have expectations about how treatment should be done that is not in line with the actual treatment protocol or effective cognitive-behavioral therapy (CBT) principles. This could be because the client had another form of therapy in the past where the only expectation was that the client would talk about what was on their mind, or it could be that the person doesn't believe the techniques are effective or appropriate. We often tell clients that we are dealing with a part of the brain that doesn't listen to reason so talking to it doesn't help. If you could just reason with the OCD part of the brain or just talk to it, then you would be better already. This part of the brain needs to be "shown" through the experience of Ex/RP.

There is often a considerable amount of shame around needing help or embarrassment about the nature of their obsessions. Whatever the reasons, not sticking to the plan is a major roadblock to treatment. The client has shown up, has an OCD diagnosis, and paid their fee, but now they don't want to do it your way. This type of resistance usually shows up early in treatment when exposures are introduced but could also be surrounding other treatment issues, like number of sessions per week, length of sessions, homework requirements, etc.

One way to handle such patients is to fall back on the concept of the "treatment contract." We outline the requirements of treatment at the onset and will not proceed unless the client has agreed. This is most often useful when dealing with clients who have borderline personality disorder but can be helpful in other cases as well. The following are the key points to consider:

- We do offer a sympathetic ear, but ultimately it is the exposure piece that works. A sympathetic ear may help ease distress after arguing with a spouse or a disappointing outcome at work, but it is not an effective treatment for OCD.
- We know that our treatments work. The client doesn't design the treatment, any more than we would tell our dentist how to treat an infected tooth. Rather, the client describes the problem, and the therapist determines the treatment that will be effective. It is our responsibility as competent therapists to provide the client with the treatment we believe will work and to review the pros and cons of their options.
- The clients make a choice to engage in treatment. That choice cannot be taken from them, and they cannot give it away.
- If they want to do something other than a treatment that we believe will work, they are rejecting the treatment contract with us, and we will discontinue services. It would be unethical for us to take their money and provide a treatment that will not help. That would also contribute to disillusionment with therapy in general and make them less likely to try treatment again since they will later think, "It didn't work." We make it clear that clients are free to come back if and when they are ready to engage in the treatment we have prescribed. Within this process, we are not abandoning the client. The client is making an informed decision not to use our services, as is their right. Therapists should not feel pressured into doing something ineffective, and sometimes no therapy is the right thing.
- However, working with resistant clients requires patience. Ex/RP is difficult and counterintuitive to many people with OCD, and getting them settled into treatment can take some time. Utilizing techniques from motivational interviewing for OCD (Zuckoff, Balán, &, Simpson, 2015) can help that client enter into the difficult first stage of treatment. In motivational interviewing, treatment resistance or lack of adherence is considered "ambivalence." Clients are caught between wanting to reduce the impact of OCD on their lives, the perceived cost and benefits of not changing, and/or the avoidance of the aversive nature of the Ex/RP. Motivational interviewing strategies can help clients work through this ambivalence (see Rosengren, 2009, for a review).
- Should the client ask who else might want to do the treatment they seem to prefer, it's justifiable to say, "I don't know of anyone." However, we always provide a list of referrals to others in the area who perform

effective treatments for OCD but note that the treatment will not be substantially different than what we offer.

Client Does Some Exposures but Refuses to Do Exposures That Don't Feel "Safe Enough"

Sometimes clients will express a willingness to do exposures that are "what normal people would do" but refuse to do exposures that seem "extreme" or "unsafe." They may rationalize this by saying, "I'll never need to wear a rainbow bracelet in real life, so why do I need to 'practice' doing it in therapy." The issue is that the success of the treatment rests on being willing to take some risk, even if those behaviors are outside of what the client would normally do. The purpose of such exposure is not to be extreme per se, but to promote full recovery. We often ask such client's the follow questions:

- Would a good cancer doctor only take out half the tumor?
- What happens if you have an infection and only take half your bottle of antibiotics?
- Would I be a good therapist if I only give you half of the treatment you need to get well?

Usually clients understand these analogies right away and recognize that treatment needs to be complete to be effective. You should underscore that failure or relapse will be the result of not moving all the way through the hierarchy. If there are exposures that are outside the norm of everyday activity, then these exposures can be linked to something useful or valuable in their lives. These "outside the norm" exposures such as wearing a rainbow bracelet may ultimately lead to more flexible social and occupational experiences.

Furthermore, clients must to be willing to face the uncertainty that a painful fear has already come true (e.g., "I am really a pedophile and have been one all along,") and therefore take the risk that they are living in denial. After all, there are no certainties in life, and no one can 100% guarantee that any person will or will not become a pedophile.

We have also seen people willing to tolerate a level of suffering they have decided is suitable and stay that way for a very long time. The question is whether the person thinks they are losing something of value to their OCD or not. Why does the client avoid all television but sports? Sports have plenty of pedophile OCD triggers, but the client just isn't willing to give up sports. You might consider making the discussion exclusively about what the client is willing to give up versus what they are not, and the cost/benefit of simply "improving" versus really "getting better."

Client Says, "I Cannot Stop Mental Compulsions"

It can seem impossible to clients to think that they can simply stop their mental compulsions, especially when they have been performing them for a long period of time and they feel "automatic." However, we know from decades of experience that if clients apply themselves to this goal, it can be done. It will not happen overnight, but we do expect clients to try. Like anything, with practice they will get better at it.

Therapists may mistakenly teach clients to identify mental compulsions using self-statements like "That's my OCD"; however, this can become a compulsion. For example, a client might say "It's only OCD" whenever she has an obsessional thought to reassure herself that there is no danger associated with her fear. Instead, clients should be taught to respond to mental compulsions by resisting them or better yet, using exposure statements that target their core fear. For example, a client who reassures himself that he will not go crazy each time he takes his young daughter to the bathroom should be instructed to replace self-reassurance with statements like, "I might go crazy from seeing my daughter naked." As with overt rituals, clients are instructed to "spoil" mental compulsions that occur (sometimes automatically) by using exposure statements.

Client Worried about Getting Sexually Aroused during Exposure

Most clients are very afraid of getting sexually aroused in the presence of anything other than their preferred sexual target because of what they imagine this might mean about themselves. Often frightening experiences like this were the catalyst for the client's S-OCD, so they definitely don't want it to happen again! This is why psychoeducation about sexual issues is vitally important at the beginning of treatment, so that clients understand that sexual arousal is only a part of what constitutes their sexual orientation. Sexual orientation is more than just about what images causes momentary sexual excitement but also about the client's values and what sort of person they want to be intimate with, physically and emotionally. It's quite common for people to feel sexually aroused by unexpected people and situations. For example, we explain to clients with sexual orientation S-OCD that "it's common for straight people to have an occasional gay thought and gay people to have an occasional straight thought," so such sensations are not to be feared or avoided. It is quite possible that clients may have a sexual feeling during exposures because the exposures remind them of sex, but we don't ascribe any additional meaning to the feelings. Clients should be warned that they may have momentary feelings of sexual arousal when they don't want to and that is important for the treatment process because it demonstrates that they can have incongruent sexual feelings without acting on them or experiencing a change in sexual orientation.

Is Sending Clients to a Gay Club Too Extreme?

When sending clients to social venues for exposures, it has been argued that perhaps it's wrong to send them out in the community under false identities and then have them do things that could possibly affect the lives of others negatively. For example, when going to a gay bar as an exposure, what might be the effect of trying to pick up another person, with no intention of having a real relationship? Could this amount to using people and manipulating them to our own ends? Are we teaching patients that other people are just out there to be used? Is it okay to play with the feelings of others in this way? Could it lead to unintended negative consequences for that other person?

In our opinion, this particular homework assignment goes too far. We have frequently assigned clients to go to gay bars and to simply spend time there or have friendly conversations with others but not to give out a phone number or go on a date. We may go to a club and watch a performance, such as a drag show or best bootie contest. Clients can even just sit there and tell themselves that this is where they belong because they "are really gay." This is generally all the exposure someone with such symptoms needs. We should always try to do the utmost for our clients, but we also need to consider the repercussions of how we have them interact with others and show sensitivity and consideration.

Is Treating Clients with Sexual Orientation OCD Any Different than Reparative Therapy?

OCD is a disabling mental disorder and is not at all the same as sexual identity confusion or internalized homophobia/heterosexism. Individuals with sexual orientation-themed OCD are having severe, unrelenting doubts that tell them they may have a different sexual identity than the one they actually have. These clients are highly anxious about anything to do with sex, dating, and relationships. They do not go out of their way to have same-sex relationships on purpose or otherwise. Their situations generally don't get out of control, and, if anything, they are highly overcontrolled. They generally do not do things spontaneously, such as unexpected or random sexual encounters. It is very important to understand that those with thoughts that they may be gay are generally not gay. They don't need to go to LGBTQ-affirming therapy groups to figure out their identities. A genetically based brain disorder is making them doubtful and uncertain about an important topic with meaning to the client. Trying to figure out if they are gay or not is the source of their compulsive behaviors—something we are trying to get them to stop doing. Trying to evaluate their identities is precisely what they need to resist. Ex/RP is staying with what the person fears and then resisting any type of escape or avoidance to build up a tolerance to the anxiety caused by the thoughts.

Furthermore, there is no scientific evidence that reparative therapy is effective for LGBTQ individuals, much less people with sexual orientation-themed OCD. In fact, there is a great deal of concern among the mental health community that reparative therapy can cause psychological maladjustment and even suicidal thoughts. Sadly, we have encountered people with sexual orientation-themed OCD who did try reparative therapy and were consequently traumatized as a result. As of this writing, several states have made reparative therapy illegal.

Imaginal Exposure Not Causing Anxiety

Imaginal exposure is useful to confront patients with their anticipated catastrophes related to their obsessions but should not be used when an effective in vivo exposure is possible. So the first thing to do to troubleshoot a nonworking imaginal is to determine if an in vivo would be better. Imaginal exposures are best for situations that cannot be disproven through in vivo exposure, such as those in which the patient fears they may change in a fundamental way (e.g., sexual orientation), cause a distal catastrophe (e.g., starting a chain of events that results in an airplane crash), or when the result of failing to do a ritual is far in the future (e.g., dying from HIV; Gillihan, Williams, Malcoun, Yadin, & Foa, 2012). Assuming this is the type of fear you are attacking, then an imaginal exposure is the right approach.

The next likely problem is that the core fear has not been identified. It is important to identify early in therapy the underlying core fear that feeds the abundance of compulsions. Some common examples of the obsessional fear that can feed the sufferer's fears are being responsible for harm, losing control, being an immoral person, going to jail, suffering, being an outcast, or going to hell. It is crucial to identify the precise core fear(s), as it may not be apparent at first. For example, one client with obsessions related to the possibility of being gay was not very distressed by an imagined scenario of having a torrid gay love affair; rather, his core fear was that he would realize he was gay, come out to his family, and as a result would lose the people in his life that he loved the most (Gillihan et al., 2012).

We find that for people with S-OCD the use of imaginal exposure to the worst-case scenario (in combination with appropriate in vivo exposures and ritual prevention) yields the best results. After repeated use of these imaginal exposure techniques, patients are better able to tolerate the distress associated with the imagined disaster. As a result, they are able to give up behaviors that they believe are needed to neutralize their distress or prevent their feared outcome from happening. Additionally, as previously discussed, imaginal exposure provides a major opportunity for disconfirmation of a client's belief that thinking about terrible outcomes can make them happen.

"Exposures Are Not Working"

This could be a multifaceted problem that requires a thorough assessment of the amount, type, and manner in which exposure work is completed. While this concern may be a product of the doubt most with OCD have (i.e., "I will be one of the rare few in which this does not work"), there are typically identifiable reasons for why the client is not seeing any benefit.

The first assessment should be on what a client believes is "working." Some may want no more obsessions or emotional experiences (e.g., fear, disgust, or shame) at all. This is not possible—we cannot remove all emotions or a previous thought or image. It could also be the client focusing on the remaining or worst parts of the OCD experience that are still present while ignoring that they have made gains.

As mentioned earlier, a client needs to work on relevant exposures and doing in vivo exposures when possible are preferred. If a client is starting a hierarchy and is more distressed or their life has greater interference by areas or items higher in the hierarchy, we may need to shift the focus to those areas if repeated homework on lower level exposures or areas are not recognized as effective. While we recommend starting at a challenging but manageable level, as most people won't tolerate a flooding approach, the client and therapist can agree to start on higher level exposures or more difficult areas if needed.

As detailed in the chapter on Ex/RP, it is incredibly important for clients to refrain from rituals while doing exposure work. When the amount and level of exposures are being performed correctly but habituation is not occurring, a client likely has hidden rituals they may or may not be aware of. The therapist may have to do more in vivo work during the session and ask for the client to detail all internal and external experiences noting when the client reassure themselves, shifts attention away from the exposure, focuses on doubt at what is actually occurring, stopping the exposure once there is a slight drop in the unwanted emotion, and not allowing more robust habituation or anything else that detracts from the procedure.

Another possible explanation is that the client is not doing enough exposure work in terms of time or trials. Although a good therapist can typically tell when not enough exposure time or trials are being spent to be effective, it helps to have a record of this to make that as apparent to the client as possible. In our more intensive settings where clients do exposure work for three or more hours per day, we set a guideline of at least five exposure trials of five separate exposures. We may assign a checklist that the client and therapist keep track of on a daily basis of Ex/RP trials (and any other work such as behavioral activation or valued living activities) and graph the number of trials and time spent per day on the work. These visual depictions, along with the daily recording (and checking in on it at intensive programs or via a message left with the therapist's voicemail or email) typically give the more parsimonious answer that not enough time or trials are being completed. We have had many conversations with clients where we review this and state, "Of course, it is possible that exposure may not be working for you, but given that over the past two weeks you have only completed on average 9 out of 25 trials a day and/or only spent 27 minutes instead of the 2.5 to 3 hours per day we recommended, we can't conclude that exposure isn't working because we are at a lower dose than what we have found useful."

How Explicit Should Exposures Be?

Whatever thoughts, images, and fears that the client experiences need to be included in *imaginal exposures*. Although the idea is to exaggerate the feared outcomes, there is no need to dwell on or elaborate on gratuitous sexual details that the client doesn't experience. That being said, if it's in the client's head, it needs to be addressed. For example, one client had obsessional intrusive images of engaging in incestuous same-sex anal intercourse, and so all of that needed to be included in the exposure.

Like with imaginal exposures, we want the *in vivo exposures* to include material the client is already using (i.e., pornographic material used for reassurance can be repurposed for exposures) or unreasonably avoiding (i.e., bathing their children). However, there is no need for clients to engage in more extreme behavior, such as exploring alternative sexual experiences, unless that is one of the client's treatment goals.

Issues with Adolescents and Their Parents/Caregivers

When adolescents enter OCD treatment, often it's because their parents have first developed concerns about their child's well-being. Beginning and maintaining treatment with adolescents can pose challenges within the therapeutic relationship because of some of the following:

- Teens often have busy extracurricular, school, and travel schedules.
- Treatment is the parents' idea, and the young client is not motivated.
- The client has "helicopter" parents who observe and help too much.

Taking some extra time for rapport-building and use of motivational interviewing can be helpful in addressing all of these issues (Zuckoff et al., 2015). Spending time during the initial sessions to work on the relationship between the therapist and child can set the tone for future sessions, where a foundation of trust can be built. This can be done by playing games, watching videos/movies, having sessions outdoors or at arcade venues, and even encouraging the teen to ask the therapist questions that may initially seem unrelated to OCD. Validating the young person while also delineating their caregiver's concerns can be a balancing act. Therapists can ask questions like:

- Are there any parts of your parents' concerns that you think are valid? Why or why not?
- How do your parents' concerns about OCD affect you?
- What might be some concerns outside of your parents' that you could use help with?
- How has OCD ever hurt and even ever helped you with anything?
- Even if you feel safe or comfortable enough with your current ability to manage your OCD (e.g., through avoidance and other compulsions), if you do not challenge your OCD how might it affect your ability to be similar to same-age peers—for example, having pets, dating, going to college, having a roommate, being able to be in or change in a locker room or dressing room, starting a family, etc.?

Once trust has been established and the client is open to continuing with treatment, it is useful to remind both the young person and parent how demanding OCD treatment can be due to exposure homework and ritual monitoring. Stressing the importance of prioritizing treatment with other activities is a necessary discussion as parents may be concerned that the child's schoolwork may suffer. Therapists can ease these concerns by working with families to plan realistic schedules that allow for OCD homework, school work, and their child's social needs to be met. However, families should be aware that some adjustments to the child's schedule will be necessary to effectively complete treatment. Therapists can discuss how temporary adjustments to their child's social life or extracurricular activities may be warranted to accomplish long-term health/OCD goals.

Sometimes challenges within the parent–child relationship can also impact treatment. Teens may feel that their parents are overbearing or overly concerned with their behaviors. This can even play out in therapy sessions if parents attempt to dictate the kinds of exposures their child is given because they feel that the exposures are too harsh or inappropriate. You might also discover parents completing OCD homework for the child even though the child needs to do the homework to get well! Though these behaviors may seem surprising, sometimes it is a reflection of the dynamic that the parent and child have in other settings outside of treatment, for example, at school or at home.

In these instances, we generally work with the parents on establishing practical boundaries by discussing how their child cannot benefit from treatment if they are overly involved in their OCD homework. We do discuss how and when involvement is needed if the child is having difficulty understanding an assignment or needs the occasional reminder when not doing homework consistently. Therapists should inform parents that the clinician will notify them when and if the child has challenges with assignments that require parental intervention. Parents also need reminding that it is okay to encourage their child, but that nagging or forcing a child to do homework/exposure, or doing it for them, may ultimately cause a struggle for power that results in the child inevitably becoming resistant.

Working to establish trust with the parents is also vital as it will allow them to feel more confident that the assignments given are based on a client's clinical need and not simply assigned to be inappropriate or to scare their son or daughter. Therapists can discuss how overinvolvement in treatment sessions can decrease the amount of time that the therapist and child have to complete exposures. Therapists and parents should also have discussions on how accommodating can prevent the progress that their child can make in treatment and promote avoidance. However, it is important not to shame family members because nearly all families engage in some level of accommodations for a family member with OCD.

When unwanted behaviors are a result of the parent's own mental health concerns or marital problems, clinicians can schedule sessions without the teen to discuss these issues. Parents should be made aware of how their mental health issues can impede the success of their child's treatment plan and should be encouraged to seek a therapist of their own. Ideally, the child's therapist would provide referrals to support the parent in finding someone that would adequately meet their needs. Preferably this referral should be to a clinician familiar with OCD. If such a referral is not available, it is essential that there needs to be collaboration between clinicians because the parent's therapy and the child's therapy can easily be in cross purposes. If the parents are unwilling to get their own treatment when needed, therapists might consider adding "parent sessions" in addition to individual/family sessions with the young person.

When a child is unable or unwilling to participate in treatment, then a viable alternative is parent training. This is essentially teaching the parent how to be the therapist in the home. Recently a programs such as the Supportive Parenting for Anxious Childhood Emotions (SPACE; Lebowitz, Omer, Hermes, & Scahill, 2014) have been developed to circumvent the problems of treatment resistant children and adolescents. Programs such as SPACE are exclusively parent-based and are delivered without direct involvement with young person from the clinician.

Issues with Clients with Developmental and Cognitive Delays

Clients with intellectual and developmental delays may vary in their presentation of obsessions and compulsions. Unfortunately, this may mean that their OCD symptoms have gone undiagnosed for quite a while. Like other clients, individuals with delays can benefit from medication; however, it is important to ensure that the medication doesn't negatively impact any other neurological deficits (Gautame & Bhatia, 2015). When our clients have developmental or intellectual delays, we find it important and useful to conduct intellectual and achievement testing. If the client has already been evaluated, it is important to review those records. This allows us to be aware of client strengths and weakness and then structure psychoeducation in a way that will best suit clients' learning styles. Therapists may find that more psychoeducational sessions are needed in the beginning, compared to other clients. Clients with delays may also benefit from more visual and interactive learning. If the client is an adult, with consent, involving a family member during the sessions can be useful as they can reinforce what is learned in session, if the client lives in the home with their family.

Clients with delays may be thought to have behavioral issues or strange mannerisms, when, in reality, these behaviors are a result of their OCD (Gautam & Bhatia, 2015). For example, a young adult we treated would spend hours at a time either running the shower or sitting in the bathtub. Her family was frustrated because they thought she was being defiant by not listening to their requests to conserve the water. She also hit herself on the head with her pinkie finger extended, which her family thought to be odd. Both examples were actually compulsions that helped to relieve her anxiety. The sound of the water calmed her and slowly helped her bad thoughts to leave, and hitting her head also helped to eliminate those thoughts. Research has shown that clients with delays may better benefit from focusing on their behaviors, compared to identifying and processing internal feelings of anxiety (Gautam & Bhatia, 2015), and that is exactly how we were able to effectively work with this client. Along with Ex/RP, we utilized behavioral charts at home and in session, where the client was able to win rewards by earning a determined number of points each week at home and each session in our office. This was highly motivating for our client and improved the family dynamic because the parents and grandparents were able to participate in rewarding the client even though she was an adult. It also helped the family to be more aware of the client's progress over time.

Shame, Guilt, and Embarrassment in Adolescents

It is not uncommon to see expressions of guilt, shame, or embarrassment in clients with OCD. This is especially true for clients with taboo or unacceptable thoughts, which are sexual or violent in nature or related to religious obsessions (Glazier, Wetterneck, Singh, & Williams, 2015). Shame is something that should be addressed rather than making the assumption that it will diminish once a client has successfully completed OCD treatment, as it is not uncommon for feelings of shame to still be present once treatment is over (Singh, Wetterneck, Williams, & Knott, 2016). Embarrassment or shame can be especially strong in adolescents, due to being in a stage of life that is heavily focused on fitting in.

An example of this was seen in one of our teenage clients who had put great effort into trying to hide his compulsions, due to fear of being labeled strange at school and his family's overdramatized response whenever they witnessed his compulsions. He spent so much time hiding his compulsions that once he entered into treatment, he spent several sessions denying that he had any concerns. Even while carrying out compulsions in front of the therapist, he pretended that they were simply silly, erratic behaviors that he engaged in because he was a child. In this instance, rapport-building, being in tune with the client, and providing psychoeducation on OCD were essential strategies, as well as specifically working with the client to address his shame. Specifically, addressing shame is important because of its correlation with suicide (Weingarden, Renshaw, Wilhelm, Tangney, & DiMauro, 2016), effect on a client's mood (Woien, Ernst, Patock-Peckham, & Nagoshi, 2003), and impact on quality of life (Singh et al., 2016). Destigmatizing OCD through psychoeducation and doing work around shame can improve the client's self-perception and better support their OCD treatment goals overall.

When OCD Clients Mention Suicide

As clients can have various dimensions of OCD, we thought it important to consider how to approach those who have obsessions about suicide or harming themselves. As discussed earlier, having comorbid depression along with OCD is a common occurrence. Moreover, clients with OCD have increased risk of suicide attempts and dying from suicide at rates that are comparable to other disorders such schizophrenia and bipolar disorder and greater than posttraumatic stress disorder and alcohol use disorders (de la Cruz et al., 2016). Working with clients that fear harming themselves as part of their OCD can be scary and tricky, as the therapist must determine whether the thoughts are real suicidal thoughts versus OCD obsessions—especially when clients are already depressed. As with other forms of OCD, like S-OCD, clients don't want to have these thoughts. Despite having persistent, distressing thoughts of hurting themselves or killing themselves, individuals with suicide obsessions don't want to die and work hard to avoid these thoughts, unlike individuals that are actually suicidal (Wetterneck, Williams, Tellawi, & Bruce, 2016).

It is important for therapists to be aware of these differences as it can be harmful to the client's ability to obtain the appropriate treatment for OCD, as well as harmful to the therapeutic relationship if OCD thoughts are confused with suicidal ideation. Being in tune as to whether the clients' thoughts are intrusive in nature and whether the client avoids these thoughts is a good starting point when first meeting a client that presents with these concerns. Incorporating OCD measures early, when a client's thoughts seem intrusive, can support therapists in preventing harm that could come from overly assessing for suicide risk (Al-Zaben, 2011).

OCD and Substance Use

Because substance use and addictions can often be associated with feelings of shame, our approach is to give clients an opportunity to disclose chemical dependence upfront, by using structured measures like the Mini International Neuropsychiatric Interview (MINI) that include questions about alcohol, street drugs, and prescription drug usage. If we suspect addiction, even when not endorsed, our goal is to create an environment that allows clients to disclose this information, even if it takes several sessions. To facilitate discussion, we've found it helpful to discuss hypothetical scenarios that allow us to address whether or not the client would ever feel comfortable sharing this information with us if an addiction developed later. If discussed during rapport-building sessions, we've found that clients do eventually disclose due to the trust built within the therapeutic relationship. If clients endorse abusing alcohol or drugs in the past, we encourage them to refrain from usage as it can interfere with treatment.

Therapists shouldn't be afraid of working with individuals that have co-morbid addictions along with OCD. When clients have disclosed substance use problems after several sessions into treatment, we start by thanking them for trusting us with such sensitive information and then empathize with them on how difficult it must have been to not be able to previously tell us. Clients should not be referred out immediately as this may seem punitive. Instead, therapists and clients should work to develop more trust by agreeing to honesty when discussing addiction in future sessions. Therapists can work with clients on exploring what things make them feel like they need to abuse drugs and may discover that clients abuse substances as a coping mechanism for their OCD (Mancebo, Grant, Pinto, Eisen, & Rasmussen, 2009). The client and therapist can develop a plan that can support the client when they feel like using again. The client should also be encouraged to participate in an addiction program like 12-step, SMART Recovery, or something comparable in conjunction with OCD treatment. We may also ask them to see a separate alcohol and other drug abuse (AODA) counselor and keep in contact with that professional to highlight how important both aspects of treatment are. When clients receive treatment for both OCD and substance abuse, they are found to have better-improved OCD symptoms (Fals-Stewart & Schafer, 1992).

However, if clients are not willing or able to work on their substance use problem, we will usually suspend OCD treatment and refer them out for specialized treatment for the substance use problem. We make sure there is an understanding that they will return for OCD treatment once the substance problem is under control.

Support Groups for S-OCD

Support groups can be extremely useful as an adjunct to individual therapy, especially for those who are struggling with motivation and trepidation about doing exposures. The sense of common humanity can be both supportive and motivating for clients. If a client is willing to reveal their obsession, this can break the sense of shame since there is likely to be another member having the same experience. Even if there aren't other members struggling with S-OCD, people with other forms of OCD can often be empathic and understanding toward S-OCD. Often clients believe that they are the only one with this problem and/or have never spoken to another person with OCD. Additionally, support groups frequently have members who have gone through Ex/RP and can be effectively encouraging. If there isn't a support group in your area, then you can start one. The International Obsessive-Compulsive Foundation can provide information about how to get one started. These support groups can be in-person, but many of our clients have found them equally effective if done through video-teleconferencing such as Skype, Vsee, GoToMeeting, etc.

Issues with Exposures in Public Locations

It is ideal and most effective to utilize Ex/RP to treat OCD in those natural environments that typically create anxiety for clients whenever possible. For a client that has contamination fears that are specific to airplanes, realistically the therapist or client usually cannot purchase plane tickets every day to complete an exposure. However, there are many OCD fears that can benefit from stepping outside of the office setting. It is typical for OCD therapists to take the clients with contamination OCD to complete exposures in public restrooms, port-a-potties, pet stores, and even nearby sewers to help clients habituate to the fear of being near something that might be dirty. For S-OCD, exposures out of the office may include trips to LGBTQ centers, strip clubs, animal parks, or playgrounds.

When therapists need to conduct therapy outside of the treatment clinic, consideration should be made to address how to maintain a client's confidentiality in the event that the therapist or client crosses paths with an acquaintance, as well as how to support a client if they have a panic attack in a public setting. This requires advanced planning on the therapist's part prior to each session. Therapists can strategize with the client on preparing a "pseudo relationship" so that a client does not feel obligated to introduce the therapist to a family member or friend if they are spotted out and about together. Or, they could decide to simply be open about the therapist–client relationship, which gets people to go away quicker and then there is no need to keep stories straight.

When one of our clients with religious S-OCD had fears of entering a church, our initial exposures were spent in the church parking lot while sitting in the car and then sitting on the benches in front of the church. Prior to being able to enter the church sanctuary, we spent time in the church's cafeteria and bookstore. This particular client did have a panic attack, but because we spent time discussing how to approach the anxiety and slowly built up to this exposure based on her hierarchy, the therapist was able to help de-escalate the client's anxiety by utilizing exposure statements and breathing retraining with the client. The client was able to handle this experience so successfully that she was eager to quickly jump back into the exposure in the bookstore, because she was determined to overcome her anxiety once she saw first-hand how treatment really worked to address her fears. By the time the client was ready to do exposures in the sanctuary (the area that was high on her hierarchy), she was able to do so without having an anxiety attack and was able to remain within the exposure for long periods of time to habituate. Though public panic attacks can be challenging for the client and therapist, as they can draw unwanted attention, they can be effectively managed.

Reducing Accommodations

Accommodations come in many varieties and are problematic to the treatment. The most frequent is the asking for reassurance by the client. Other accommodations include caregivers altering their behavior in response to the client's fears, performing rituals for the client, etc.

Working with accommodations has been covered in previous chapters, yet accommodations are often one of the biggest barriers to progress. Caregivers often feel guilty about giving accommodations. Often clinicians will inadvertently add to this guilt when they are encouraging caregivers to eliminate reassurances. It is helpful to note that reassurance, although associated with the maintenance of OCD, has also been shown to be associated with relationship strength between caregivers and clients (Lee et al., 2015).

Troubleshooting for Unsupportive Home Life and Family

Having the support of family members when entering OCD treatment can be invaluable. When this exists, clients are able to depend on their family for emotional support when challenges arise. Family members can also shed light on the details of the OCD from a different perspective. For example, family members often have additional insight into a client's compulsions, how the OCD has impacted the client inside and outside of the home, and how the OCD has impacted the family unit. Healthy dynamics within the family makes allowance for members to point out behaviors that a client may be unaware of, including avoidance and reassurance-seeking. Relatives can even serve as homework partners when clients need support with exposures.

Unfortunately, we don't live in a world where families always have the healthiest dynamics. If we did, some of us might lose job security as clinicians! Unhealthy dynamics within the family unit can impede a client's progress while in treatment. If clients feel like they are on the same team with their family members, motivation is heightened, and there are fewer distractions compared to clients with ongoing family conflict. In other words, family members can play a large role in the failure or success of the treatment. Although clients may not intend for their treatment to include family therapy, if they are unable to navigate these difficulties on their own, one or more family sessions may be needed. This can be vitally important to help family members understand the difficulties their loved one is experiencing and how they can be part of the solution.

Helping Family Members Motivate Individuals with OCD into Treatment

Often clinicians will be contacted by family members about getting their loved one into treatment. Many individuals with OCD are treatment resistant before they have even gone to a single appointment! Or they've been a client of another therapist whose expertise was not OCD, or they pressed too hard initially to get the client into Ex/RP. Whatever the reason, families and other caregivers often find themselves in "survival mode" just trying to get through each day. Frequently in these situations the OCD is holding the household or family hostage with reassurance-seeking, accommodating rituals, and changes in typical family functioning.

If the person is refusing to come into treatment, clinicians will often see the parents, spouse, or other caregiver to help map out a strategy. The person with OCD should be made aware that this is happening and that some sort of change is coming. Since change in family functioning is coming, it would be better if the OCD sufferer would collaborate on the plan. Helping caregivers understand the nature and treatment of OCD is the first step. Understanding the powerful neurobiological nature of OCD can provide increased empathy and patience with the client but also increased patience and understanding for themselves.

Working with caregivers in the absence of the OCD sufferer proceeds in a similar way to Ex/RP. A hierarchy is developed as to what OCD symptoms are interfering with the family functioning. The caregiver's hierarchy is built on their responses to the OCD symptoms. Changing the caregiver's response moves up the hierarchy just as Ex/RP does. For instance, a person with S-OCD or pedophilia-themed S-OCD (P-OCD) may try to dictate what is watched on the television as a way of avoiding obsession triggers. The caregiver(s) would announce that at a certain date this would no longer be accommodated. A person with P-OCD may prevent the family from having children at the house, which can isolate caregivers from family and friends. The P-OCD sufferer is given sufficient warning before the appearance of a child so they have time to decide their response. The goal of these caregiver responses is not to treat the person's OCD; rather, it serves the dual purpose of restoring healthy caregiver(s) functioning and to motivate the OCD sufferer to engage in treatment. It needs to be kept in mind that reducing reassurance and OCD accommodations is a type emotional exposure for the caregiver(s). Caregivers often give in to accommodations to avoid or reduce feeling painful emotions such as guilt, anxiety, and anger.

What Are Some Good Books for Clients and Family Members about S-OCD?

There is nothing written specifically for clients about S-OCD, but the following books include some information about the topic that could be helpful for clients and their loved ones.

Abramowitz, J. (2009). *Getting over OCD: A 10-step workbook for taking back your life* (1st ed.). New York, NY: Guilford.

This is one of the leading self-help books for OCD. It does a good comprehensive overview of the different types of OCD obsessions. It addresses sexual obsessions directly albeit briefly during the book. Sexual obsessions are explained in the first chapter of the book and then again in a brief paragraph in Chapter 2. Sexual obsessions are brought up directly in the chapter on "defeating obsessional thoughts" as well. This section includes a one-page description of different exposures individuals with sexual obsessions could use.

Baer, L. (2002). *The imp of the mind: Exploring the silent epidemic of obsessive bad thoughts*. New York, NY: Plume.

This book includes a number of references to sexual obsessions in OCD, including multiple cases studies. The author does a fairly thorough job defining and explaining the possible underlying causes of sexual obsessions. In a total of nine chapters, sexual obsessions are mentioned in all of them. Chapter 6 includes a detailed case study of almost 10 pages on cognitive therapy specifically for sexual obsessions. The book wraps up with details on treatment options, including serotonin reuptake inhibitor drugs and their benefits for those with sexual obsessions.

Foa, E., & Wilson, R. (2001). *S.T.O.P. obsessing! How to overcome your obsessions and compulsions*. New York, NY: Banta.

Stop Obsessing! Is a self-help book meant to be used by individuals suffering from OCD. It covers the common subtypes of OCD including contamination, ordering, hoarding, worry, and obsessional thinkers. The authors note that one common type of obsession for obsessional thinkers is the fear of committing a sexually immoral act. Sexual obsessions are only addressed on this one page.

Grayson, J. (2014). *Freedom from obsessive-compulsive disorder: A personalized recovery program for living with uncertainty.* New York, NY: Berkley.

This self-help book includes general information about OCD as well as self-assessment tests, therapy scripts, and therapy techniques. Throughout the first few chapters, sexual obsessions are mentioned very generally, if at all. In Chapter 6, "Exposure and Response Prevention," sexual obsessions are included on multiple checklists. The topic is not mentioned again, however, until Chapter 12, which has a 10-page section dedicated to sexual obsessions including steps for imaginal exposure and multiple sample hierarchies.

Hershfield, J., & Corboy, T. (2013). *The mindfulness workbook for OCD: A guide to overcoming obsessions and compulsions using mindfulness and cognitive behavioral therapy.* Oakland, CA: New Harbinger.

This is a popular self-help workbook aimed at helping individuals suffering from various types of OCD to use mindfulness in conjunction with CBT to overcome their obsessions. This book examines at several forms of OCD including relationship OCD, pedophile OCD, and sexual orientation OCD. The book has a 12-page chapter on addressing sexual orientation OCD with CBT. The chapter includes tools on how to identify sexual orientation OCD as well as tools on confronting sexual OCD.

Hyman, B., & Pedrick, C. (2010). *The OCD workbook: Your guide to breaking free from obsessive-compulsive disorder* (3rd ed.). Oakland, CA: New Harbinger.

This is a popular self-help book that guides individuals through the treatment process for OCD. There is a chapter devoted to helping individuals identify which types of obsessions they have. One of the subtypes mentioned is obsessional thinking, including sexual obsessions. The book also contains a 15-page chapter on overcoming obsessional thinking. This chapter does not focus purely on sexual obsessions, but it does mention them.

Purdon, C., & Clark, D. (2005). *Overcoming obsessive thoughts: How to gain control of your OCD.* Oakland, CA: New Harbinger.

Overcoming Obsessive Thoughts is written as a self-help book for individuals suffering with OCD. This book particularly focuses on overcoming disturbing obsessional thoughts. This book does not have a section dedicated to sexual obsessions, but it does mention them on three separate pages of the beginning of book in relation to helping individuals categorize their symptoms. None of the treatment strategies presented in the book are specific to sexual obsessions.

Schwartz, J. (1996). *Brain lock: Free yourself from obsessive compulsive behavior*. New York, NY: Harper-Collins.

Brain Lock is a self-help book that gives readers four clear steps to addressing their OCD: relabeling, reattributing, refocusing, and revaluating. This book does not address sexual obsessions at all or even the subtypes of OCD. The book is primarily focused on empowering the reader and comparing their four-step treatment method to traditional treatments for OCD.

Landsman, K. J., Rupertus, K. M., & Pedrick, C., & (2005). *Loving someone with OCD: Help for you and your family*. New York, NY: New Harbinger.

Loving Someone with OCD is book that focuses on someone who has a partner with OCD. It emphasizes how to work together to understand and work on treatment based on behavioral principles and appropriate compassion for both individuals. Much of the advice can apply to various relationships including other family members who could have OCD (e.g., children or other relatives).

Where Can Therapists Learn More about Treating This Kind of OCD?

As we discussed in the introduction, there are very few accessible sources of information about S-OCD. However, for clinicians who want to learn more, we recommend the following resources.

Case Studies

Bruce, S. L., Ching, T., & Williams, M. T. (2018). Pedophilic obsessions in obsessive compulsive disorder: Assessment and treatment with exposure and response prevention. *Archives of Sexual Behavior, 47*(2), 389–402. doi:10.1007/s10508-017-1031-4.

Reid, A. M., Flores, C., Olsen, B., Barthle, M. A., Rahmani, M., Rakhshani, A. C., . . . McNamara, J. H. (2016). Treatment of sexual obsessive-compulsive symptoms during exposure and response prevention. In E. A. Storch & A. B. Lewin (Eds.), *Clinical handbook of obsessive-compulsive and related disorders: A case-based approach to treating pediatric and adult populations* (pp. 23–38). Cham, Switzerland: Springer International. doi:10.1007/978-3-319-17139-5_3

O'Neil, S. E., Cather, C., Fishel, A. K., & Kafka, M. (2005). "Not knowing if I was a pedophile . . ." Diagnostic questions and treatment strategies in a case of OCD. *Harvard Review of Psychiatry, 13*(3), 186–196.

Ung, D., Ale, C. M., & Whiteside, S. H. (2016). Treatment of sexual obsessions in childhood obsessive-compulsive disorder. In E. A. Storch & A. B. Lewin (Eds.), *Clinical handbook of obsessive-compulsive and related disorders: A case-based approach to treating pediatric and adult populations* (pp. 117–130). Cham, Switzerland: Springer International. doi:10.1007/978-3-319-17139-5_9

Williams, M. T., Slimowicz, J., Tellawi, G., & Wetterneck, C. (2014). Sexual orientation symptoms in obsessive compulsive disorder: Assessment and treatment with cognitive behavioral therapy. *Directions in Psychiatry, 34*(1), 37–50.

Williams, M. T., Davis, D. M., Tellawi, G., & Slimowicz, J. (2015). Assessment and treatment of sexual orientation obsessions in obsessive-compulsive disorder. *Australian Clinical Psychologist, 1*(1), 12–18.

Williams, M. T., Crozier, M., & Powers, M. B. (2011). Treatment of sexual orientation obsessions in obsessive-compulsive disorder using exposure and response prevention. *Clinical Case Studies, 10*, 53–66.

Organizational Resources

- International OCD Foundation (IOCDF) P.O. Box 961029, Boston, MA 02196, (617) 973-5801, http://www.iocdf.org Resources: This organization has a Q&A email service, a Behavior Therapy Training Institute, and an annual conference for clinicians, researchers, and consumers.
- Association of Behavioral and Cognitive Therapies (ABCT) 305 7th Avenue, 16th Fl., New York, NY 10001, (212) 647-1890, http:///www.abct.org Resources: This organization has an active clinician listserv an annual conference for clinicians and researchers.
- Anxiety and Depression Association of America (ADAA) 8701 Georgia Ave. #412, Silver Spring, MD 20910, (240) 485-1001, http://www.adaa.org Resources: This organization has online expert guidelines, regular webinars for therapists, and an annual conference for clinicians and researchers.

Expert Supervisors

Therapists who want to learn more about treating OCD can contact the authors to receive help and training. Contact us directly to inquire about group peer supervision, individual supervision, and costs.

Summary

This chapter covered many of the barriers and pitfalls in treating S-OCD. What is covered here is not exhaustive, as the disorder comes with many permutations and idiosyncrasies. Even an experienced clinician will find something new in a client or get stumped on how to motivate or how to construct an exposure. It cannot be emphasized enough that it is important to seek supervision from a knowledgeable OCD therapist when there are questions and concerns about treating a client.

APPENDICES

APPENDIX A

Materials for Clients

Handout 1

+

Obsessive Compulsive Disorder Symptom Dimensions

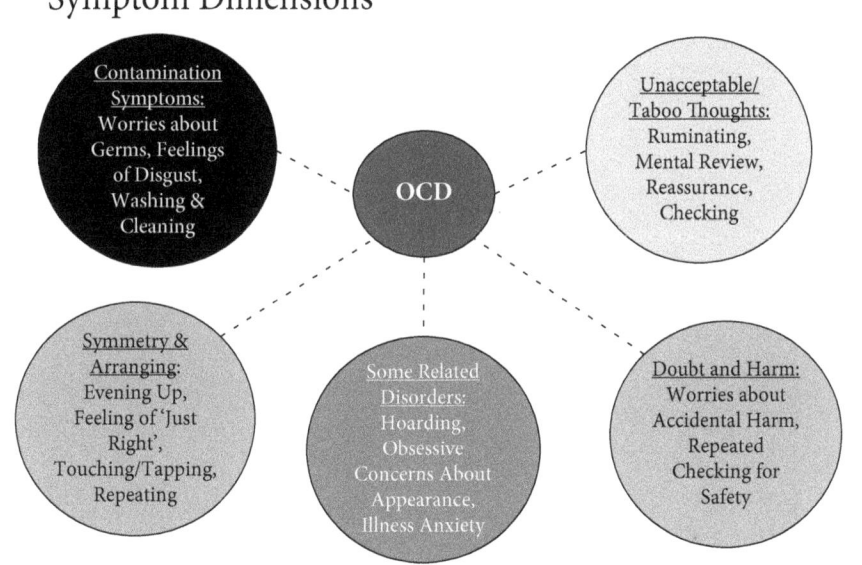

- **Contamination Symptoms:** Worries about Germs, Feelings of Disgust, Washing & Cleaning
- **Unacceptable/Taboo Thoughts:** Ruminating, Mental Review, Reassurance, Checking
- **OCD**
- **Symmetry & Arranging:** Evening Up, Feeling of 'Just Right', Touching/Tapping, Repeating
- **Some Related Disorders:** Hoarding, Obsessive Concerns About Appearance, Illness Anxiety
- **Doubt and Harm:** Worries about Accidental Harm, Repeated Checking for Safety

What causes OCD?
Which kind of OCD do you have?
Do you notice symptoms in more than one area?
How have you coped with the symptoms?
Many experience feelings of shame about symptoms. Your experience?

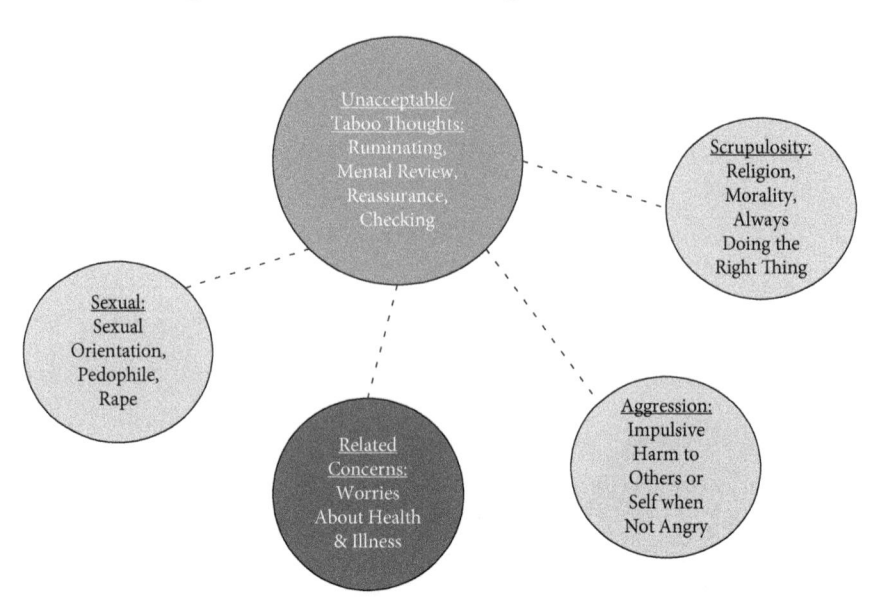

Unacceptable Taboo Thoughts

Unacceptable/Taboo Thoughts: Ruminating, Mental Review, Reassurance, Checking

Sexual: Sexual Orientation, Pedophile, Rape

Related Concerns: Worries About Health & Illness

Aggression: Impulsive Harm to Others or Self when Not Angry

Scrupulosity: Religion, Morality, Always Doing the Right Thing

Handout 2

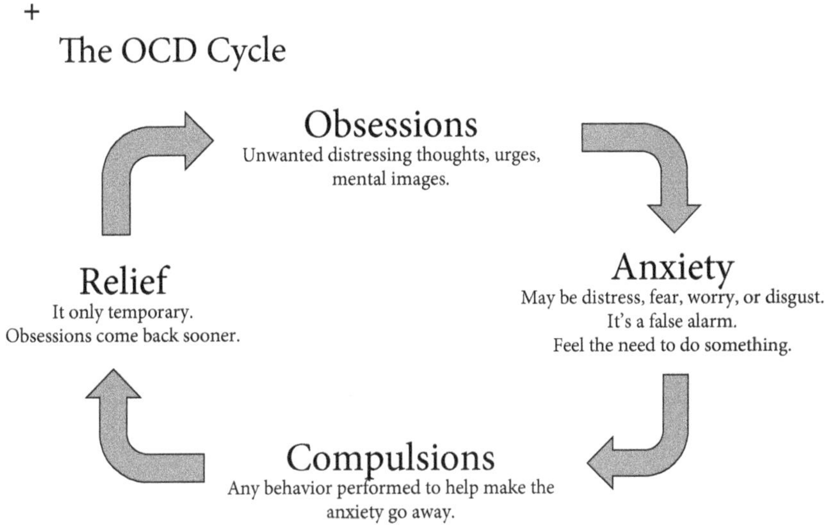

The OCD Cycle

Obsessions
Unwanted distressing thoughts, urges, mental images.

Anxiety
May be distress, fear, worry, or disgust.
It's a false alarm.
Feel the need to do something.

Compulsions
Any behavior performed to help make the anxiety go away.

Relief
It only temporary.
Obsessions come back sooner.

Handout 3A

Compulsion & Avoidance Monitoring Log

Use the "Compulsion & Avoidance Monitoring Log" form to record the following information:

- The first column lists the time in 30-minute increments.
- In the second column, note a brief description of the thought or situation that prompted you to engage in your compulsion/ritual(s) or to avoid.
- In the third column, record your level of discomfort using the SUDS ratings of zero to 100 (0 = completely calm; 100 = extremely upset/distressed), just prior to doing the compulsion (or if you had resisted the compulsion).
- In the fourth column, describe the compulsion you engaged in (for example, "mental replaying," "reassurance seeking," "washing," or "repeating prayers") or your avoidance behavior.
- In the last column, note the actual number of minutes you spent engaging in that ritual or avoiding.

For mental compulsions: Record how many minutes or seconds you spent engaging in mental repetition of special words, mental reviewing, mental undoing, etc. Record the elapsed time from the start of the activity until you finished it.

For reassurance seeking rituals: Record how many minutes or seconds you spent seeking reassurance. Record the time elapsed from when you started seeking reassurance until you stopped seeking reassurance.

For somatic checking rituals: Record how many minutes or seconds you spent evaluating your body signs. Record the elapsed time from when you started checking until you stopped checking.

For washing or cleaning compulsions: Record how many minutes or seconds you spent washing, bathing, or cleaning. Record the amount of time from the start of cleaning until you finished.

For any other excessive checking: Record how many minutes you spent checking. Record the elapsed time from the time you started checking a particular item until you finish checking that item and leave the situation. Alternately, you can list the number of times you checked, if that is easier.

For avoidance: Record the approximate amount of time you spent avoiding situations/activities/thoughts relevant to your obsessions.

Complete the form for the whole day. Complete one form per day. Contact your therapist if you need more forms before your next session.

Example Self-Monitoring Form:

Time of Day	Situation that Triggered the Compulsion or Avoidance	SUDS (0–100)	Description of Compulsion/ Avoidance	Number of Minutes Spent on Compulsion
6–6:30 AM	Working out at the gym around other men	60	Working at stations far from other men	30 minutes
6:30–7 AM	Working out at the gym around other men	60	Checking for arousal around other men	10 minutes
7–7:30 AM				
7:30–8 AM	Kissing daughter goodbye before leaving for work	80	Mentally reviewing that the kiss was not inappropriate	10 minutes
8–8:30 AM				
8:30–9 AM	Ended brief meeting with female secretary in the office	70	Calling wife after to seek reassurance that the meeting was "normal" and not "predatory"	5 minutes 30 seconds

Handout 3B

Compulsion & Avoidance Monitoring Log

Name		Date	

Time of Day	Situation that Triggered the Compulsion or Avoidance	SUDS (0–100)	Description of Compulsion/ Avoidance	Number of Minutes Spent on Compulsion
6:00–6:30 AM				
6:30–7:00				
7:00–7:30				
7:30–8:00				
8:00–8:30				
8:30–9:00				
9:00–9:30				
9:30–10:00				
10:00–10:30				
10:30–11:00				
11:00–11:30				
11:30–12:00 PM				
12:00–12:30				
12:30–1:00				
1:00–1:30				
1:30–2:00				
2:00–2:30				
2:30–3:00				
3:00–3:30				
3:30–4:00				
4:00–4:30				
4:30–5:00				
5:00–5:30				

Time of Day	Situation that Triggered the Compulsion or Avoidance	SUDS (0–100)	Description of Compulsion/ Avoidance	Number of Minutes Spent on Compulsion
5:30–6:00				
6:00 – 6:30				
6:30–7:00				
7:00–7:30				
7:30–8:00				
8:00–8:30				
8:30–9:00				
9:00–9:30				
9:30–10:00				
10:00–10:30				
10:30–11:00				
11:00–11:30				
11:30–12:00 AM				
12:00–6:00				

Notes:

Handout 4A

About Sexual Obsessive-Compulsive Disorder (S-OCD)

Symptoms of S-OCD

It is estimated that worldwide over 112 million people have obsessive-compulsive disorder (OCD), many of whom suffer from unwanted sexual thoughts as part of their OCD (S-OCD). S-OCD can afflict anyone and is found in males and females of all age groups, from school-aged children to older adults. S-OCD typically develops in adolescence but may also develop in childhood or early adulthood. S-OCD seems to be more common in males but more distressing in females. S-OCD typically has a gradual onset, but it usually gets worse over time if not treated. Symptom severity can fluctuate, usually in relation to stressful events. Affected individuals may remember when their symptoms began disrupting their lives but may not remember exactly when S-OCD started for them. People can sometimes remember a specific incident that triggered it.

As the name implies, the symptoms of OCD include *obsessions* and *compulsions*:

Common Obsessions

- Unwanted or upsetting doubts
- Upsetting thoughts about harm, contamination, sex, religious themes, or health
- Mental images of disturbing acts or events

Common Compulsions

- Too much washing, checking, praying, repeating routine activities
- Special thoughts designed to counteract negative thoughts

You also may notice that certain situations, places, or objects trigger the worrisome thoughts and lead to urges to do *rituals* (also called compulsions). Rituals are actions you do to try to feel better after you have an obsession. You may also find yourself avoiding situations, places, and objects that bother you.

The symptoms of S-OCD may include the following:

- Sexual *obsessions*, including:
  - Unwanted thoughts about engaging in undesirable sexual acts
  - Unwanted sexual mental images
  - Fears about a change in one's sexual orientation (sometimes called SO-OCD or H-OCD)
  - Unwanted thoughts about having sexual contact with a child
  - Unwanted sexual thoughts about religious figures
  - Unwanted thoughts about sexual aggression
  - Fears about becoming pregnant or impregnating others through unlikely means

- Related *compulsions*
  - Mental compulsions (e.g., mental repetition of special words, mental reviewing, mental undoing, etc.)
  - Reassurance-seeking
  - Somatic checking (monitoring of body signs)
- *Avoidance* of situations/activities/thoughts that trigger sexual obsessions and urge to ritualize

What Causes S-OCD?

It is not entirely known why some people develop symptoms of S-OCD while others don't. However, different theories have been considered. For example, some experts believe that thinking errors occur in S-OCD:

- If I'm thinking about something bad, that's the same as doing it, or wanting to do it.
- I should be able to control all of my thoughts at all times.
- If I don't try to prevent harm, it's the same as causing harm.
- I am always responsible for harm, regardless of the circumstances.
- Having bad thoughts means I am a bad person.

Of course, this is all absolute rubbish. People actually have much less control over their thoughts than they think they do. Everyone is constantly bombarded by a stream of "garbage thoughts" that we simply dismiss most of the time. People without S-OCD have all the same repugnant thoughts as those with S-OCD, but the difference is that people with S-OCD grab on to those thoughts, examine them, and try to figure out what they mean. They don't just dismiss the thoughts, and in the process of dwelling on the thoughts, the thoughts start to take on life of their own and don't just go away.

Other researchers have pointed to possible brain chemistry abnormalities involving serotonin (a brain chemical important for brain functioning) as a cause for OCD. For example, unusual serotonin levels have been observed in people with all types of OCD, and medications that treat S-OCD symptoms also have an effect on serotonin levels. However, it is not known whether serotonin chemistry is truly a reason for the development of S-OCD or just a related finding. Research is ongoing at this point.

There is also evidence that OCD runs in families. It is difficult to know how much of this is a result of what children learn from their family while growing up (nurture) and how much is genetic (nature). However, people with S-OCD often have other family members with OCD or related disorders like anxiety, depression, and hoarding. It does appear that OCD has a very strong genetic component.

Why Do You Have S-OCD?

Many affected individuals would like to know why or how they developed S-OCD. Most likely it is a combination of genetic and environmental factors that contribute to the development of S-OCD. Stress, recreational or street drugs, and trauma can trigger OCD in people who are susceptible to the disorder. But usually it is not possible to know exactly what caused OCD for any particular person. Many people spend a lot of time trying to figure out how they got it, but this is not really useful. Fortunately, there are effective treatments for the disorder that do not require an explanation for why or how a person developed S-OCD.

Additionally, we do know a great deal about the symptoms of S-OCD, which is important for treating the disorder. By learning more about your S-OCD symptoms, you will get more improvement from treatment. S-OCD is essentially a set of habits that first involves obsessions (intrusive and unwanted thoughts, ideas, images, or impulses) that cause feelings of extreme discomfort or anxiety, as well as strong urges to do something to reduce the distress. Subsequently, because of these feelings and urges, affected individuals develop the habit of compulsive rituals (performing various unique thoughts or actions) to try to eliminate the distress. These habits of thinking, feeling, and acting are unpleasant, unproductive, and difficult to get rid of on your own.

Two Important Associations in S-OCD

Two types of associations or connections are an important part of OCD and understanding both of them will help with your therapy (Yadin, Lichner, & Foa, 2012). Therapy is designed to break both types of associations.

- *Association 1*: First is the association (connection) between certain objects, thoughts, or situations and anxiety/discomfort. For example, think about something that you try to avoid or that you endure with suffering because it makes you upset. It is likely that you have an association between this situation and the distress it causes you.
- *Association 2:* The second type of association is a connection between doing a ritual/compulsions and decreasing the distress. In other words, after you do your S-OCD rituals, you temporarily feel a little better. Therefore, you continue to do the behavior more often to get more relief.

Try to identify what situations increase your discomfort (Association 1) and then the behaviors or thoughts that you do to reduce the discomfort (Association 2). Doing this will help you in your treatment.

In treating S-OCD, the aforementioned associations have to be weakened or broken. Your therapy is designed for this, and your therapist work with you on exercises that will help you accomplish this goal. These exercises are called exposure and response prevention (Ex/RP), and you will learn more about them from your therapist.

Reference

Yadin, E., Lichner, T. K., & Foa, E. B. (2012). *Treating your OCD with exposure and response (ritual) prevention: Workbook*. Philadelphia, PA: Oxford University Press.

Handout 4B

About Sexual Obsessive-Compulsive Disorder (S-OCD) Quiz

NAME: _____   DATE: _____

1. Which of the following are common types of sexual obsessions characteristic of S-OCD?
   Circle all that apply.
   A. Unwanted sexual mental images
   B. Reassurance seeking regarding sexual orientation
   C. Unwanted thoughts about having sexual contact with a child
   D. Fears about becoming pregnant through unlikely means

2. OCD
   A. Is extremely rare.
   B. Sometimes involves special thoughts designed to counteract negative thoughts.
   C. Includes compulsions, which are good for long-term anxiety relief.
   D. Treatment will need to target association areas in the brain, including Wernicke's.

3. What is "somatic checking"?
   A. A S-OCD type of therapy
   B. Monitoring of body signs
   C. Checking whether or not you remember ever liking someone of the same sex
   D. A type of obsession

4. What is another word for "compulsion" in OCD?
   _____

5. Chris persistently worries that he is gay. He has been in a relationship with a girl for a year now, but he convinces himself that he is faking sexual arousal and has been gay his whole life. He has been attracted to females since kindergarten, yet he can't seem to shake his fear that he might be attracted to males. He joins an OCD forum online, realizing that he experiences many of the same symptoms as other people on the forum. He repeatedly asks other members whether or not they really think he has "H-OCD" or if he is truly gay. What is he engaging in by doing this?
   Circle all that apply.
   A. A ritual
   B. Ex/RP
   C. Reassurance-seeking
   D. An appropriate treatment strategy

6. Explain the two key associations that are important to address for S-OCD in therapy?

_____
_____
_____
_____

7. Some experts believe that thinking errors contribute to the development of S-OCD and OCD in general. Which is *not* a common thinking error?
   A. If I'm thinking about something bad, that's the same as doing it, or wanting to do it.
   B. I should be able to control all of my thoughts at all times.
   C. Thoughts are random and come and go. I am not my thoughts.
   D. If I don't try to prevent harm, it's the same as causing harm.

8. S-OCD treatment *needs* to include
   A. Finding the root of why you have OCD.
   B. Avoidance of situations which create distress and often induce compulsions.
   C. Weakening or breaking the link between the two associations.
   D. Medication.

9. OCD is "caused" by
   A. genetics.
   B. a stressful life event.
   C. certain parenting patterns.
   D. trick question: OCD is not attributed to one cause, but rather a variety of factors.

10. Often people with S-OCD may _____ certain situations or people that trigger their sexual obsessions or urge to ritualize.

Handout 5A

OCD and Unacceptable Thoughts

Pure Obsessionals & Covert Compulsions

OCD is well known for its curious obsessions and repetitive, often bizarre, compulsions. In fact, compulsions are usually the most noticeable part of the disorder. However, many people with OCD find they have no visible compulsions, only the repetitive mental agony of upsetting thoughts that won't go away. These thoughts usually are about aggression, religion, and sex (also called *taboo thoughts*). Interestingly, you almost never hear about people with this kind of OCD. Why? Because most of the action is taking place inside the person's head. Unlike people who wash their hands repeatedly or who keep checking locks, you don't really see the OCD action. These people are sometimes called pure-obsessionals, or *pure-o* for short.

The OCD Cycle

Although we don't know the exact cause of OCD, we do know quite a bit about what keeps the disorder going. You can think of OCD as a set of habits that involve intrusive thoughts that something very bad might happen (obsessions), followed by an urge to do something to prevent the bad thing from happening (a compulsion). The compulsion reduces the distress momentarily, and so the person gets into the habit of using these various special behaviors to get rid of the anxiety. When someone does this over and over again, we call it a compulsive ritual. Of course, rituals are only a temporary fix, as the obsession always comes back. In fact, the more compulsions you do, the stronger the OCD becomes.

This understanding of the OCD cycle is what gives us therapists our strongest tool for taking down the OCD demon, using a treatment called exposure and response prevention (Ex/RP). Interestingly, the fewer compulsions the person does, the weaker the OCD gets, so clients are taught how to stop doing rituals and embrace the anxiety. You can think of OCD as a fire, and every time you do a compulsion, you're throwing it a log. Once the fuel stops coming, the fire dies out.

So, based on what we know about how OCD is maintained, it is actually impossible for someone with OCD to only have obsessions, because OCD will eventually disappear with no compulsions to feed it. In short, pure-o can't exist.

The Pure Obsessional

So, where did we even get the idea that the pure-obsessionals may be out there at all? The first study to really take a scientific look at OCD symptom clusters was published by Dr. Lee Baer in 1994. He studied 107 OCD patients who had completed a long checklist of OCD symptoms called the Yale–Brown Obsessive-Compulsive checklist. He found three types of OCD that he called Symmetry/Hoarding, Contamination/Checking, and Pure Obsessions. This last subtype included people with aggressive, sexual, and religious obsessions, but no compulsions. Thus it was believed that the "Pure Obsessions" group had no rituals, just their own troubled thoughts.

However, at that time no one was really taking a good hard look at other types of compulsions that aren't so flashy. For example, consider a woman with OCD who gets unwanted thoughts to stab her husband with a steak knife. She might do any number of compulsions to make the thought go away. She might mentally retrace her steps to be sure she didn't touch a knife. She might do repetitive silent prayers that no harm comes to her husband. She might take a mental inventory of all the good things she's done to convince herself that she's a morally upright person. She might ask for reassurance from her husband that she's a good person and would never do such a terrible thing. These types of behaviors are sometimes called *covert rituals* because you don't actually see the compulsions in the same way you do when someone can't stop washing their hands.

Another example would be a young man who worries that he might become gay or fears that perhaps he has been gay all along. Mental rituals can include many different compulsions that take place in the mind. An example of a mental ritual would be if he mentally reviews experiences with the opposite sex to convince himself that he enjoyed being with females, thus confirming he is not gay. He might try to visualize two men kissing, and if he felt a negative gut reaction, he may be temporarily satisfied that he is not turning gay. If he doesn't feel the desired reaction, he repeats the mental imagery until he experiences the desired result. He may also avoid being around other men in a locker room or at the pool, as seeing other men triggers his worries.

Covert rituals can include a variety of behaviors, such as mental compulsions and reassurance-seeking. Mental compulsions may include mental repetition of special words, mental reviewing, and mental undoing. Reassurance-seeking may include asking others for reassurance, self-assurance, or confessing to others. Even Internet searching can be a covert compulsion as the person with OCD seeks reassurance online in forums, chat rooms, or information websites—much in the same way a hypochondriac seeks reassurance from doctors.

Pure-O and Covert Compulsions: The Link

Current research shows that if Baer had included these types of rituals in his study, he might have had some very different findings. When mental rituals and reassurance-seeking are added into the picture, they fall neatly into the category that Baer had termed "Pure Obsessional." So, it seems quite possible that the pure obsessional just doesn't exist.

The bottom line: people who think they are pure-o are likely doing covert compulsions. Ex/RP for OCD is extremely effective, but it requires a thorough examination of both a person's obsessions and compulsions. If someone with OCD gets Ex/RP, but the covert rituals are not addressed, then treatment will be incomplete. This can lead to a speedy relapse. Therapists treating OCD need to always address covert rituals. People with OCD need to understand that these acts are part of the clinical picture.

Handout 5B

Unacceptable Thoughts Quiz

1. The "Pure Obsessional" type of OCD [*choose all that apply*]
   A. Does not exist. Even when people are without obvious symptoms, they still most likely have repetitive and upsetting mental compulsions.
   B. Does exist. Many people with OCD simply do not have any kind of compulsions.
   C. Is how people with OCD have been categorized when they have no obvious symptoms.
   D. Is a misnomer; the compulsions take place inside the person's head.

2. What kinds of obsessions are common in people experiencing repetitive mental thoughts?
   A. Aggression, religion, and sex
   B. Politics, the media, cultures
   C. Animals, other people, sports
   D. All of the above

3. Explain the cycle of OCD and how it persists.
   _____
   _____
   _____

4. What term is used to describe "special behaviors" used to get rid of anxiety brought on by obsessions?
   A. Persistent thoughts
   B. Scatter brained
   C. Compulsive rituals
   D. Mental rituals

5. What therapy has been shown to be very effective in the treatment of OCD?
   _____

6. What assessment instrument is most commonly used to assess OCD and considered the "gold standard"?
   A. BDI: Beck Depression Inventory
   B. Y-BOCS: Yale–Brown Obsessive-Compulsive Scale
   C. OCI-R: Obsessive Compulsive Inventory-Revised
   D. No assessments are used. Only clinical interviews.

7. What three types of OCD did Baer find in his 1994 study?
   1. _____
   2. _____
   3. _____

8. Which type(s) of OCD mentioned in the previous question likely does not exist considering what we know about the nature of OCD?
   A. Symmetry/Hoarding
   B. Contamination/Checking
   C. Contamination and Pure Obsessions
   D. Pure Obsessions

9. Helen has OCD. She gets bombarded with thoughts that she will push her mother in front of a train. To make these thoughts go away, she asks her mother for reassurance that she is a nonviolent person with strong morals. She repeats the same prayer over and over that nothing bad will happen to her mother. Asking for reassurance and repeating prayers for her mother would be referred to as what?

   _____

10. OCD can be effectively treated even if covert rituals are not addressed by the therapist.
    A. No, if covert rituals are not discovered, the patient will likely relapse.
    B. Yes, as long as the obsessions are controlled, covert rituals will take care of themselves.
    C. Yes, covert rituals are not as disruptive as visible ones like washing and checking.
    D. Both B and C

Handout 6A

Understanding Cognitive-Behavioral Therapy for OCD

What to Expect in Therapy

Starting therapy for OCD can be anxiety-provoking or even frightening. Knowing ahead of time what to expect can help put your mind at ease and make the treatment feel less daunting. The following describes the major components of cognitive-behavior therapy (CBT) specifically for OCD. CBT is a form of psychotherapy that treats problems and improves quality of life by modifying emotions, behaviors, and thoughts. CBT focuses on solutions, encouraging individuals to challenge distorted thoughts ("cognitive therapy") and change dysfunctional patterns of behavior ("behavioral therapy").

Psychotherapy for OCD

Exposure and ritual prevention (Ex/RP) is an effective type of CBT treatment for OCD. The word *response* in Ex/RP is often replaced by *ritual* as the word *response* is too broad—not all responses are compulsions. Though behaviorally based, Ex/RP includes both behavioral and cognitive techniques. A more cognitive approach, called simply "cognitive therapy" (CT), is advocated by some and may be useful for clients who are not responding well to behavioral strategies. However, Ex/RP and CT both typically include both behavioral and cognitive elements. Ex/RP has been used in a variety of formats, including individual and group treatment, family-based treatment, computer-based treatment, self-help techniques, and intensive programs. This article will describe the important components of Ex/RP and CT for OCD.

In Vivo Exposure

Exposure is the cornerstone of EX/RP treatment. In vivo exposure has been shown to reduce obsessions and related distress. This technique involves repeated and prolonged confrontation with situations that cause anxiety. Exposure sessions may last anywhere from 30 minutes to two hours. The immediate goal is for the client to remain in the situation long enough to experience some reduction in anxiety and to realize that the feared "disastrous" consequences do not occur. With repeated exposures, the peak of the distress as well as the overall distress decreases over sessions. Thus, the client habituates to upsetting stimuli in two ways, within the session and between sessions.

Typically, exposure is gradual, and the client begins by facing objects and situations that result in only moderate levels of anxiety. Constructed in collaboration with the client, the therapist will put together a list of distress-evoking stimuli in a hierarchical manner, beginning with the least distressing and gradually proceeding to more distressing ones. A rating scale of zero to 100 (often called SUDS for Subjective Units of Distress/Discomfort Scale) is used to rate the expected amount of distress associated with each item. After an item from the hierarchy is confronted in session with a therapist, the client then practices self-exposure to the same item as daily homework. Once mastered, the client faces the next progressively more distressing object or situation. The client learns (a) that the feared consequence will not occur, (b) to better tolerate anxiety, and (c) that anxiety diminishes over time even without performing the rituals. As the client progresses up the hierarchy, each next items become a bit easier.

Imaginal Exposure

In some cases, it is not possible to construct an in vivo exposure to a client's fear, and in these instances an exposure can be done in the imagination. Situations especially appropriate for an imaginal exposure are those in which the client fears they may change in a fundamental way (i.e., shifting in sexual orientation or becoming a serial killer), cause a distal catastrophe (i.e., starting a chain of events that results in harm coming to unknown people), or that the outcome of failing to do a ritual is far in the future (i.e., going to hell or dying from cancer).

To conduct an imaginal exposure, the therapist and client develop a detailed scene together based on the client's worst fear. The story will describe a catastrophe befalling the client and/or loved ones as a direct result of the client's failure to perform rituals. The therapist might first recount the story aloud and then have the client do the same, ideally in the present tense to make the events seem more real. SUDS levels are taken at various points throughout the narrative (i.e., every 5 minutes) to assure that the story is evoking enough anxiety to be productive. The exposure is typically recorded to facilitate repeated listening as homework.

Imaginal exposure is effective when it evokes the same distress in a person as the actual obsession. A person with OCD typically fights the obsession because they believe that if they entertain the ideas, the feared outcome will be more likely to occur. However, fighting the obsession only strengthens it. By repeating the distressing ideas in the form of a narrative, the person with OCD habituates to the fears and also learns that dwelling on the thoughts does not make them happen. The person gains a new perspective on the fear and is able to attend to it more objectively.

Response/Ritual Prevention

The ritual or response prevention component involves instructions for the client not to engage in compulsions or rituals of any sort. This is important because people with OCD often think that the compulsions prevent the occurrence of a feared outcome. Only by stopping the compulsions do clients learn that rituals do not protect them from their obsessional concerns. In the vast majority of cases, rituals have a functional relationship with the obsessional thought (i.e., "Washing will prevent me from becoming ill," or "If I don't wash, I will be distressed forever and will fall apart"); many times this functional relationship is logical (e.g., "Checking will prevent me from making mistakes"), but sometimes it has a magical flavor (i.e., "If I smell perfume, I will sexually assault a woman, so I will exhale whenever I think of a woman"). Sometimes clients cannot articulate any negative outcome that is prevented by performing the rituals. Rather, the performance of the ritual "just feels right"; in this case, the function of the ritual is to reduce anxiety or discomfort, and the disastrous consequence is psychological, such as falling apart.

Putting ritual prevention into practice involves a detailed analysis of all compulsions or rituals performed by the client. Typically, clients are asked to keep daily logs of all rituals performed. The therapist uses these logs initially to identify the rituals that need to be stopped, and, as treatment progresses, it is used to identify areas of difficulty that need more therapeutic attention.

Cognitive Therapy

OCD clients feel anxious or distress when engaging with their obsessional thoughts or images, because they interpret them as warnings of events that are dangerous and likely to occur. CT is designed to help clients identify these automatic unrealistic thoughts and change the interpretations of the thoughts, resulting in decreased obsessions and distressing compulsions.

In the first stage of CT, clients are taught to identify their worries as obsessions and their rituals as compulsions. The client keeps a daily diary of obsessions, called a thought record. In the thought record, clients write down their obsessions and the interpretations associated with the obsessions. Important details to record may include what the client was doing when the obsession began, the content of the obsession, the meaning attributed to the obsession, and what the client did in response to the obsession (usually a compulsion).

The therapist reviews the thought records with the client with an emphasis on how the obsession was interpreted. Using reasoning and gentle questioning, the therapist helps the client challenge their unrealistic beliefs. This helps the client to identify the cognitive distortion, typically a faulty assessment of danger, an exaggerated sense of responsibility, or fears that thinking something negative will make it come true (called "thought–action fusion").

Once clients are able to identify their obsessions and compulsions as symptoms of OCD, the therapist may do a few behavioral experiments to disprove errors in thinking about cause and effect. For example, if a client believes that praying three times will prevent her family from being harmed in a house fire, the therapist may instruct the client to pray only two times and then wait to see if family members are actually harmed that day in a house fire. The therapist may then use the results of this experiment as material for discussion about other types of magical thinking. Over time, clients learn to identify and re-evaluate beliefs about the potential consequences of engaging in or refraining from compulsive behaviors and subsequently begin to eliminate compulsions.

Summary

Ex/RP for OCD is challenging and even counter-intuitive at times. However, clients who learn to master these skills soon have mastery over their OCD. There is no cure for OCD, but with steady practice, it can be controlled and life restored.

Handout 6B

Understanding CBT for S-OCD

NAME: _____   DATE: _____

1. Ex/RP stands for _____

2. What is *in vivo* exposure?
   A. Thought-action fusion
   B. Imagining that you are confronting your fears
   C. A real-life confrontation with something that causes you anxiety
   D. Magical thinking

3. What is the immediate goal of in vivo exposure?
   A. To remain long enough in the situation to experience some reduction in anxiety and realize that something disastrous isn't going to happen
   B. To feel completely at ease
   C. To eliminate all compulsions
   D. To imagine the obsession and conquer the associated fear

4. What is the overall, more long-term goal? *[Circle all that apply.]*
   A. To understand that the feared consequence will not occur
   B. To better tolerate anxiety
   C. Thought-action fusion
   D. That anxiety will actually diminish over time by not performing rituals

5. Typically, exposure is *[Circle all that apply.]*
   A. Gradual.
   B. Performed in a hierarchical manner, starting with smaller fears and building up to larger ones.
   C. One session.
   D. Efficient because it involves overcoming the most anxiety-producing obsession from the start.

6. Explain ritual prevention. Why is it important?
   _____
   _____
   _____

7. When is imaginal exposure effective?
   A. When you meditate by repeating a group of words
   B. When you act on a compulsion
   C. When the therapist says it is
   D. When it produces distress similar to the actual obsession

8. Only by _____ the rituals do patients learn that rituals do not protect them from their obsessional concerns.

9. Explain how cognitive therapy works with OCD:

   _____
   _____
   _____

10. During the initial stage of cognitive therapy for OCD, a patient might use a thought record so that
    A. The therapist can begin to understand how the patient interprets their obsessions.
    B. The patient can write down what he or she was doing when the compulsion started.
    C. The therapist can gently challenge the patient's interpretations about obsessions.
    D. All of the above

Handout 7

Unwanted Sexual Thoughts

Having unwanted thoughts related to harming others or being impulsive is more common than most realize, with a few studies noting that 80% to 90% of the general population admit to these kind of thoughts. Few studies have looked at thoughts related to sexual themes, but those that do note similarly high rates, regardless of gender. The following table is a partial list of unwanted sexual thoughts by 292 undergraduate students (148 woman and 144 men) between 17 and 45 years old. The thoughts are from the Sexual Cognitions Checklist, which consists of 56 questions and are answered based on a scale ranging from zero (*I have never had this thought*) to 6 (*I have this thought frequently during the day*). Participants answered these questions depending on the frequency of having these thoughts when it was positive and again when it was considered negative. The following is a portion of the results of those who had negative thoughts toward common sexual thoughts that map onto common themes in sexually themed OCD (S-OCD; e.g., orientation, acting impulsively, pedophilia, sexual aggression, etc.). For reference, of the 144 men who participated, 50% of those men felt negatively about sexual thoughts about engaging in sexual activity contrary to their sexual orientation.

Percentage Who Felt Negatively About Thought

Sexual Thoughts	Men (%)	Women (%)
Engaging in sexual activity contrary to my sexual orientation	50.0	43.2
Having sex with someone much younger than me	54.2	25.0
Lifting my skirt or dropping my pants, thereby indecently exposing myself in public	42.4	25.0
Having incestuous sexual relations	38.2	20.9
Engaging in a sexual act which violates my religious principles	27.8	30.4
Having sex with an animal or non-human object	34.0	17.6
Being aroused by watching someone urinate	19.4	11.5
Masturbating in a public place	35.4	12.8
Being sexually victimized	43.8	62.2
Engaging in a sexual act with someone who is "taboo"	41.0	30.4
Exposing myself provocatively	36.8	37.8
Forcing someone to do something sexually	52.1	26.4

From C. A. Renaud & E. S. Byers, 1999, Exploring the frequency, diversity and content of university students' positive and negative sexual cognitions, *Canadian Journal of Human Sexuality*, 8(1), 17–30.

Handout 8A

Instructions for Therapists: Creating the SUDS Scale

Give the client the Subjective Units of Discomfort/Distress Scale handout (p. 338–341) and explain it as follows:

> As you know, the treatment program consists of exposing you gradually to situations that make you anxious or uncomfortable. To put together your treatment program, I am putting together a list of the specific situations that make you uncomfortable. We need to determine just how much discomfort each situation generates in you. So that I know we're both on the same page in terms of your anxiety, let's put the degree of discomfort into numbers. Look at this scale, which we call the Subjective Units of Discomfort/Distress Scale or SUDS (see handout), that ranges from zero to 100, where zero means that you feel no discomfort at all (perfectly at peace) and 100 indicates that you are very upset from anxiety, in fact, it is the most anxiety you've ever felt. Most people when experiencing this level of distress would be shaking, crying, or screaming.
>
> We need to create some anchoring points on this scale. We'll start with zero. Can you think of a time when you've felt no anxiety at all and experienced perfect peace? That would be zero on our scale. For many people it could be being on vacation at the beach, watching the ocean. But some people don't like vacations, in which case that wouldn't be a good zero for them. What about you?

Don't use examples from the patient's OCD. The distress caused by OCD is expected to change over the course of treatment, and we want to pick anchors that will stay the same.

Assist the client in establishing anchor points for zero, 25, 50, 75, and 100 SUDs. It's ideal to choose real situations that the client has experienced, but sometimes the client will not have had any experiences that rise to the 90 to 100 level, and in such cases a hypothetical example will have to do. For example, a 100 might be, "You get a call from the hospital that your whole family has been in a tragic accident, and the doctors don't know if they will live or die."

The following table can be used as an example for how the SUDS scale will be used, once complete.

Example of how SUDS is used for José's fear of dogs

Situation	SUDS
Looking at pictures of dogs	25
Holding a puppy	55
Touching a very small adult dog	65
Watching someone walk a large dog on a leash at the park	75
Seeing a barking medium sized dog from behind a chain-link fence	80
Being in the same room with a large dog	95
Petting a large dog	100

NAME _____   DATE_____

The Subjective Units of Discomfort/Distress Scale (SUDS) for OCD

Guidelines:

- Establish anchor points for zero, 25, 50, 75, 100 SUDs
- Try to choose real situations that you have experienced.
- Don't use examples from your OCD!

Can do activities with relative ease. They cause little to no distress.

Challenging but manageable. Might to prefer to avoid these activities if possible.

Would avoid thinking about or engaging in behaviors that result in this level of distress.

0	10	20	30	40	50	60	70	80	90	100
No Distress				**Moderate Distress**				**Extreme Distress**		

APPENDIX A. MATERIALS FOR CLIENTS 339

Handout 8B

NAME José P.   DATE_____

The Subjective Units of Discomfort/Distress Scale (SUDS) for OCD

Guidelines:
- Establish anchor points for 0, 25, 50, 75, 100 SUDs
- Try to choose real situations that you have experienced
- Don't use examples from your OCD!

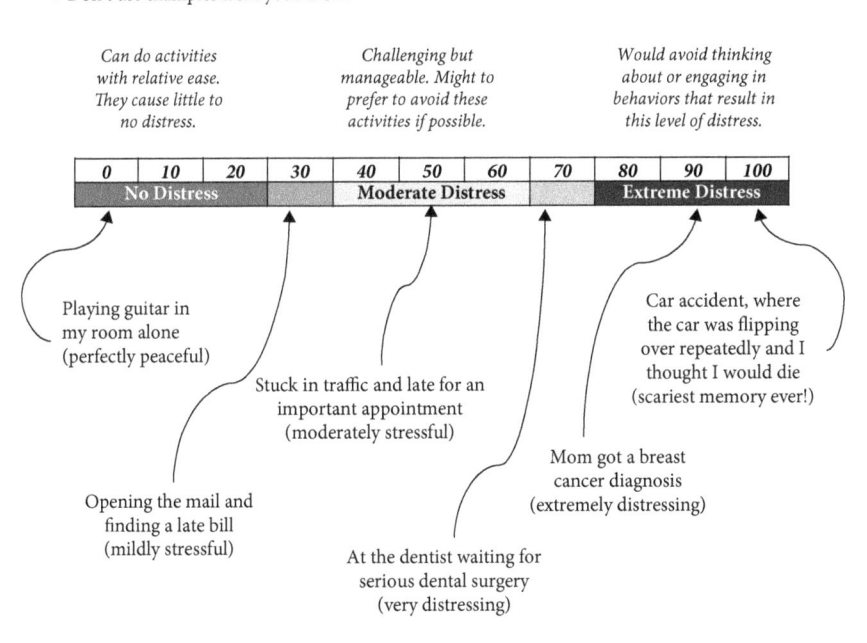

Can do activities with relative ease. They cause little to no distress.

Challenging but manageable. Might to prefer to avoid these activities if possible.

Would avoid thinking about or engaging in behaviors that result in this level of distress.

0	10	20	30	40	50	60	70	80	90	100
No Distress				**Moderate Distress**				**Extreme Distress**		

Playing guitar in my room alone (perfectly peaceful)

Car accident, where the car was flipping over repeatedly and I thought I would die (scariest memory ever!)

Stuck in traffic and late for an important appointment (moderately stressful)

Mom got a breast cancer diagnosis (extremely distressing)

Opening the mail and finding a late bill (mildly stressful)

At the dentist waiting for serious dental surgery (very distressing)

APPENDIX A. MATERIALS FOR CLIENTS

NAME Monnica W.   DATE _____

The Subjective Units of Discomfort/Distress Scale (SUDS) for OCD

Guidelines:
- Establish anchor points for 0, 25, 50, 75, 100 SUDs
- Try to choose real situations that you have experienced
- Don't use examples from your OCD!

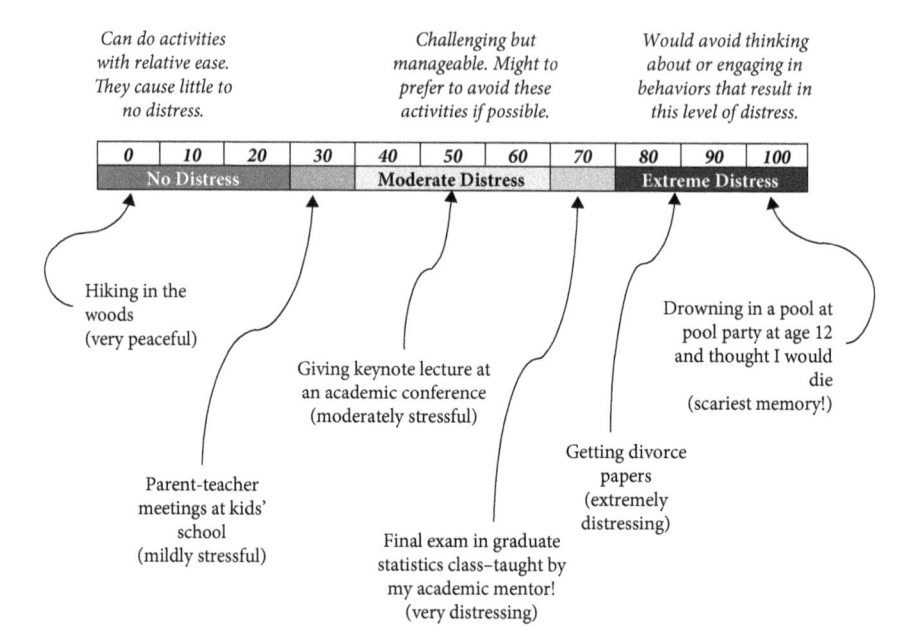

Can do activities with relative ease. They cause little to no distress.

Challenging but manageable. Might to prefer to avoid these activities if possible.

Would avoid thinking about or engaging in behaviors that result in this level of distress.

0	10	20	30	40	50	60	70	80	90	100
No Distress				**Moderate Distress**				**Extreme Distress**		

- Hiking in the woods (very peaceful)
- Parent-teacher meetings at kids' school (mildly stressful)
- Giving keynote lecture at an academic conference (moderately stressful)
- Final exam in graduate statistics class—taught by my academic mentor! (very distressing)
- Getting divorce papers (extremely distressing)
- Drowning in a pool at pool party at age 12 and thought I would die (scariest memory!)

NAME Chad W.   DATE

The Subjective Units of Discomfort/Distress Scale (SUDS) for OCD

Guidelines:
- Establish anchor points for 0, 25, 50, 75, 100 SUDs
- Try to choose real situations that you have experienced
- Don't use examples from your OCD!

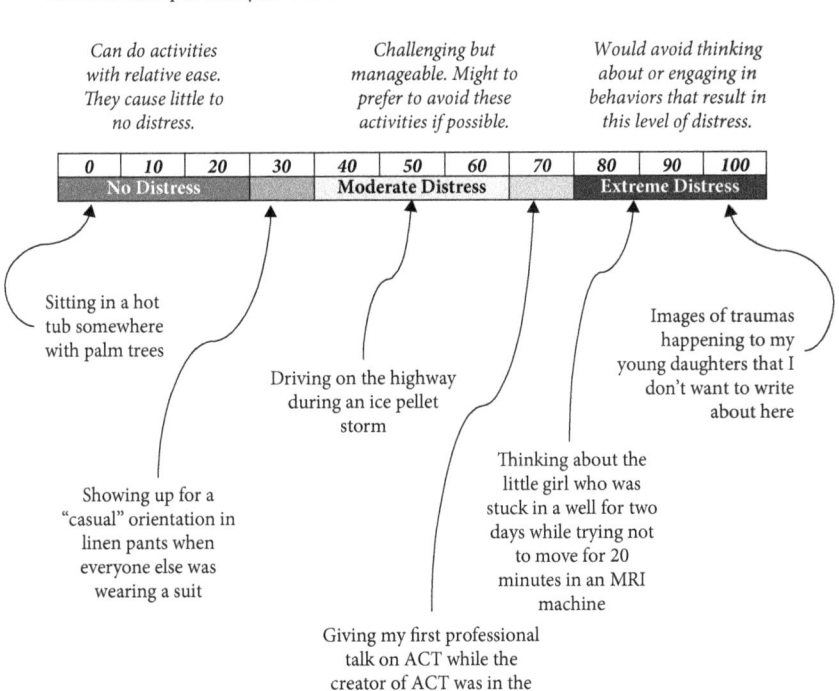

Can do activities with relative ease. They cause little to no distress.

Challenging but manageable. Might to prefer to avoid these activities if possible.

Would avoid thinking about or engaging in behaviors that result in this level of distress.

0	10	20	30	40	50	60	70	80	90	100
No Distress				**Moderate Distress**				**Extreme Distress**		

- Sitting in a hot tub somewhere with palm trees
- Showing up for a "casual" orientation in linen pants when everyone else was wearing a suit
- Driving on the highway during an ice pellet storm
- Giving my first professional talk on ACT while the creator of ACT was in the audience
- Thinking about the little girl who was stuck in a well for two days while trying not to move for 20 minutes in an MRI machine
- Images of traumas happening to my young daughters that I don't want to write about here

Handout 9A

Daily Homework & Task Sheet

Exposure: _____

Amount of Time to Spend: _____

Date Conducted: _____ Start Time: _____ Finish Time: _____

SUDS (0–100): Start _____ Peak _____ End _____

Exposure: _____

Amount of Time to Spend: _____

Date Conducted: _____ Start Time: _____ Finish Time: _____

SUDS (0–100): Start _____ Peak _____ End _____

Exposure: _____

Amount of Time to Spend: _____

Date Conducted: _____ Start Time: _____ Finish Time: _____

SUDS (0–100): Start _____ Peak _____ End _____

Tasks to Complete Before Next Session:

1. _____
2. _____
3. _____

Areas of Difficulty:

1. _____
2. _____

Daily Homework Sheet

Exposure: _____

Amount of Time to Spend: _____

Date Conducted: _____ Start Time: _____ Finish Time: _____

SUDS (0–100): Start _____ Peak _____ End _____

Exposure: _____

Amount of Time to Spend: _____

Date Conducted: _____ Start Time: _____ Finish Time: _____

SUDS (0–100): Start _____ Peak _____ End _____

Exposure: _____

Amount of Time to Spend: _____

Date Conducted: _____ Start Time: _____ Finish Time: _____

SUDS (0–100): Start _____ Peak _____ End _____

Exposure: _____

Amount of Time to Spend: _____

Date Conducted: _____ Start Time: _____ Finish Time: _____

SUDS (0–100): Start _____ Peak _____ End _____

Exposure: _____

Amount of Time to Spend: _____

Date Conducted: _____ Start Time: _____ Finish Time: _____

SUDS (0–100): Start _____ Peak _____ End _____

Weekly Homework Sheet

Exposure: _____

Amount of Time to Spend: _____

Date Conducted: _____ Start Time: _____ Finish Time: _____

SUDS (0–100): Start _____ Peak _____ End _____

Date Conducted: _____ Start Time: _____ Finish Time: _____

SUDS (0–100): Start _____ Peak _____ End _____

Date Conducted: _____ Start Time: _____ Finish Time: _____

SUDS (0–100): Start _____ Peak _____ End _____

Date Conducted: _____ Start Time: _____ Finish Time: _____

SUDS (0–100): Start _____ Peak _____ End _____

Exposure: _____

Amount of Time to Spend: _____

Date Conducted: _____ Start Time: _____ Finish Time: _____

SUDS (0–100): Start _____ Peak _____ End _____

Date Conducted: _____ Start Time: _____ Finish Time: _____

SUDS (0–100): Start _____ Peak _____ End _____

Date Conducted: _____ Start Time: _____ Finish Time: _____

SUDS (0–100): Start _____ Peak _____ End _____

Date Conducted: _____ Start Time: _____ Finish Time: _____

SUDS (0–100): Start _____ Peak _____ End _____

Areas of Difficulty:

1. _____

2. _____

Handout 9B

Exposure Homework Plan Sheet

Complete a new page for each day and bring to session or email to your therapist.

Name	
Time to Practice	

1.	

DATE:	SUDs		SUDs
Beginning		30 minutes	
5 minutes		40 minutes	
10 minutes		50 minutes	
20 minutes		60 minutes	

2.	

DATE:	SUDs		SUDs
Beginning		30 minutes	
5 minutes		40 minutes	
10 minutes		50 minutes	
20 minutes		60 minutes	

3.	

DATE:	SUDs		SUDs
Beginning		30 minutes	
5 minutes		40 minutes	
10 minutes		50 minutes	
20 minutes		60 minutes	

Comments or difficulties:

Handout 10

Guidelines for "Normal Behavior"

General Guidelines:

- Continue to expose yourself weekly to objects, people, places, or situations that used to disturb you.
- If anything is still somewhat disturbing, expose yourself to it twice weekly.
- Do not avoid situations that cause some discomfort.
- If you notice a tendency to avoid a situation, make a point to confront it deliberately twice per week.

Checking:

- Do not check more than once any objects or situations that used to trigger an urge to check.
- Do not check even once in situations that your therapist has said do not require checking.
- Do not avoid situations that trigger an urge to check.
- Do not ask friends or family members to check things for you.

Mental Compulsions:

- Do not exceed two acts of mental repetition of special words per week.
- Do not exceed two acts of mental reviewing per week.
- Do not engage in mental undoing.

Reassurance Seeking:

- Do not exceed two acts of reassurance seeking per week.

Somatic Checking:

- Do not check even once for arousal in situations that your therapist has advised you do not require checking.

Washing:

- Do not take more than one 15-minute shower daily.
- Do not wash your hands more than 5 times per day, no more than 20 seconds each.
- Limit handwashing to: before meals, after using the bathroom, after handling greasy or visibly dirty things.

Other Guidelines:

_____

_____

_____

_____

_____

_____

_____

Handout 11

OCD Relapse Prevention: Quick Tips

Intrusive Thoughts are Expected and May Hang Around

- Remember that even people without obsessive-compulsive disorder (OCD) experience some intrusive thoughts, so it is OK if you still get them, even after treatment.
- You may notice that the frequency of your intrusive thoughts fluctuates during therapy. That's OK!
- Times of stress may cause OCD symptoms to increase—remember to use the tools you learned in therapy to manage, even if it seems hard.
- New situations can cause symptoms to flare up, such as new romantic relationship, having a child, or change of job.
- If you are on medication for OCD and stop taking it, your obsessions may get stronger.

Remember That Resisting Compulsions Keeps OCD Away

- When you notice intrusive thoughts, pay close attention to your response to the thoughts.
  - Am I avoiding?
  - Am I performing rituals?
- If you answered "yes," remember to do the opposite of what OCD is telling you to do: Confront fears and resist rituals!

Be Your Own Therapist

- If some OCD anxiety returns, doing the things you learned in therapy will eventually get you feeling better again.
- Even if you are not experiencing high anxiety, remember to regularly challenge yourself to practice nonavoidance and conduct "real-life" exposures.
- Keep a list of helpful strategies learned in therapy so that you can review them after treatment.
- Before treatment ends, make sure to work with your therapist to come up with a plan to help you deal with any remaining challenges on your own.

Lapse versus Relapse

- Know the difference between a "lapse" and "relapse."
  - Lapse—a partial return of prior symptoms
  - Relapse—a return to symptoms and level of functioning prior to treatment
- Intervene early: A lapse does not have to lead to relapse!

End Therapy with Helpful Resources

- Do not hesitate to call your therapist for help, even if you are only experiencing a lapse.
- Find local or online support groups.
- If family was involved in treatment, they may be a source of support during challenging times.
- Follow-up: Check in with your therapist every 3–6 months to make sure the OCD isn't slipping back in.

Handout 12

Association Splitting: Tips and Reminders

Seek Out an Appropriate Setting for Practice

- You should practice the technique in your own time in a quiet setting with a relaxing atmosphere. This setting should not contain any triggers for your obsessive-compulsive disorder (OCD) concerns.

Practice Only When You Are Not Experiencing Obsessions or Compulsive Urges

- Make sure that you are not experiencing obsessions or compulsive urges at the time of practice! The practice of association splitting itself should not become a compulsive ritual to neutralize the anxiety that comes with obsessions.

Avoid Associations That Deny or Run Directly Counter to Your Obsessions

- Do not generate associations such as "infant" → "I would never touch an infant inappropriately!" These types of counterassociations have no alternative meanings and tend to backfire. Instead, focus on building up alternative meanings when generating new associations.

Check the Direction of Your New Associations

- Your new associations should lead out of your OCD-relevant semantic network (i.e., "gay" → "day," "gay" → "gaze," "gay" → "happy," etc.), instead of the other way round (i.e., "day" → "gay," "gaze" → "gay," "happy" → "gay," etc.).

Be as Creative as Possible!

- For example, you can introduce humor into your new associations. The positive emotions that accompany such associations will help in combating the negative emotions associated with your obsessive thoughts.

Use Visual Images Whenever Possible

- Attaching vivid visual images to your new associations is also helpful, since visual images help to form stronger associations. Constructing an association-splitting diagram with your therapist will also help with your practice as an easy reference.

Practice Regularly, and Don't Give Up!

- You should practice association splitting daily. Each practice session should last no more than 10 minutes. Practice sessions may be difficult at first but will likely become easier as your new associations are strengthened over time. Don't give up!

APPENDIX B

Measures

Family Accommodation Scale for Obsessive-Compulsive Disorder Interviewer-Rated (FAS-IR)

Developed by
Lisa Calvocoressi, Ph.D., Carolyn M. Mazure, Ph.D.,
Barbara Van Noppen, Ph.D., and Lawrence H. Price, M.D.

Copyright and Permissions

The Family Accommodation Scale for Obsessive Compulsive Disorder Copyright © 1999 by Lisa Calvocoressi, Ph.D., Carolyn M. Mazure, Ph.D., Barbara Van Noppen, Ph.D., and Lawrence H. Price, M.D.

The Family Accommodation Scale for Obsessive Compulsive Disorder includes a modified version of the Yale Brown Obsessive Compulsive Scale (YBOCS) Checklist and items based on the YBOCS scale, copyright © 1986, 1989, with permission.

References

Calvocoressi, L., Mazure, C. M., Kasl, S. V., Skolnick, J., Fisk, D., Vegso, S. J., . . . Price, L. H. (1999). Family accommodation of obsessive-compulsive symptoms: Instrument development and assessment of family behavior. *Journal of Nervous and Mental Disease*, 187, 636–642.

Calvocoressi, L., Mazure, C. M., Van Noppen, B., & Price, L. H. (1999). The family accommodation scale for obsessive-compulsive disorder. In Steketee G. (Ed.), *Overcoming obsessive-compulsive disorder: A behavioral and cognitive protocol for the treatment of OCD* (pp. 185–200). Oakland, CA: New Harbinger.

Correspondence

Lisa Calvocoressi, Ph.D., Yale University School of Public Health, Yale University School of Medicine: lisa.calvocoressi@yale.edu.

Family Accommodation Scale for Obsessive-Compulsive Disorder Interviewer-Rated (FAS-IR)

Developed by
Lisa Calvocoressi, Ph.D., Carolyn M. Mazure, Ph.D.,
Barbara Van Noppen, Ph.D., and Lawrence H. Price, M.D.

GENERAL INFORMATION AND INSTRUCTIONS FOR ADMINISTERING THE FAMILY ACCOMMODATION SCALE FOR OBSESSIVE-COMPULSIVE DISORDER

The Family Accommodation Scale for Obsessive-Compulsive Disorder assesses the extent to which relatives of patients with OCD engage in 12 types of accommodating behaviors. The FAS-IR is a semistructured interview administered by a clinician or trained lay interviewer. Questions and statements read aloud to the family member by the interviewer are enclosed in quotation marks. Instructions for the interviewer are written in italics.

The FAS includes two areas of inquiry. First, the interviewer obtains information from the family member regarding the patient's current symptoms. Second, the interviewer assesses the extent to which the family member is involved in accommodating the patient's symptoms. Each item includes common examples of accommodating behaviors, but the interviewer may wish to develop additional examples based on information gleaned from the family member's report of patient symptoms.

Each item is scored on a scale ranging from zero (none/not at all) to 4 (everyday/extreme). Total FAS scores range from zero to 48 and are obtained by summing the item scores. A scoring sheet is included.

Family Accommodation Scale for Obsessive-Compulsive Disorder Interviewer-Rated (FAS-IR)

Relative of Client:_____   Date: _____

Interviewer: _____

Introduction and General Instructions for the Family Member

"The purpose of this interview is to learn about the ways in which you may be modifying your behavior or routines to accommodate (*name of patient*)'s symptoms. During this interview, I will first ask you about the obsessive-compulsive symptoms that (*name of patient*) has been experiencing, and then I will ask you about the ways in which you have responded to these symptoms. This interview will last about 30 minutes. If, at any time, you are uncertain about what I am asking, please let me know and I will try to clarify the question for you."

Family Member's Report of Patient's Symptoms

INSTRUCTIONS FOR THE FAMILY MEMBER: "I will define obsessions, compulsions, and other symptoms related to OCD and ask you if (*name of patient*) has experienced any of these symptoms <u>during the past week</u>."

*(Read the description of each symptom, check all that apply, and then ask the family member to describe the patient's specific symptoms. Record specific symptoms on the sheet entitled **Patient Symptom List**.)*

Obsessions

"Obsessions are distressing ideas, thoughts, images or impulses that repeatedly enter a person's mind and may seem to occur against his or her will. The thoughts may be repugnant or frightening, or may seem senseless to the person who is experiencing them."

"I will now review a list of different types of obsessions common in OCD. Please tell me if (*name of patient*) has experienced any of these obsessions <u>during the past week</u>."

_____ HARMING OBSESSIONS

"During the past week, has (*name of patient*) experienced obsessions involving fears of harming self or others, stealing things, blurting out obscenities or insults, acting on unwanted impulses, or doing something else embarrassing? Has (*name of patient*) had fears associated with being responsible for something terrible happening, such as a fire or burglary, or has s/he complained of experiencing violent or horrific images?"

_____ CONTAMINATION OBSESSIONS

"During the past week, has (*name of patient*) experienced excessive concerns about or disgust with bodily waste or secretions, dirt, or germs? Has s/he had excessive concerns about contamination due to environmental toxins, for example, asbestos, radiation, or toxic waste? Has (*name of patient*) feared contamination due to household cleansers or solvents, or to animals, such as insects? Has s/he experienced discomfort with sticky substances or residues, feared illness because of a contaminant, or been concerned about contaminating others?"

_____ SEXUAL OBSESSIONS

"During the past week, has (*name of patient*) experienced obsessions concerning forbidden or improper sexual thoughts, images, or impulses, or has s/he had repeated thoughts of incest, sexual involvement with children, or aggressive sexual behavior toward others?"

_____ SAVING/LOSING OBSESSIONS

"During the past week, has (*name of patient*) experienced obsessions related to saving things or an unfounded fear of losing something valuable?"

_____ RELIGIOUS OBSESSIONS

"During the past week, has (*name of patient*) experienced obsessions involving irreverent, sacrilegious, or blasphemous thoughts? Has s/he had excessive concerns about right and wrong?"

_____ OBSESSION WITH NEED FOR SYMMETRY OR EXACTNESS

"During the past week, has (*name of patient*) experienced obsessions related to a need for things to be symmetrical or in exactly the right place? Does s/he insist that certain items not be moved or touched (e.g., must have canned goods lined up or clothes organized alphabetically)?"

_____ SOMATIC OBSESSIONS

"During the past week, has (*name of patient*) experienced excessive concerns about illness or disease (such as AIDS or cancer)?"

_____ MISCELLANEOUS OBSESSIONS

"During the past week, has (*name of patient*) evidenced an excessive need to know or remember, a fear of losing things, obsessions regarding saying certain things or not saying just the right thing, a discomfort with certain sounds or noises, or has s/he had repeated thoughts of lucky or unlucky numbers?"

Compulsions

"Compulsions are defined as behaviors or acts that a person feels driven to perform, although s/he may recognize them as senseless or excessive. It may be difficult or anxiety provoking for a person to resist performing these behaviors."

"I will now review a list of different types of compulsions common in OCD. Please tell me if (*name of patient*) has experienced any of these compulsions during the past week."

_____ CLEANING/WASHING COMPULSIONS

"During the past week, has (*name of patient*) engaged in excessive or ritualized hand washing, showering, bathing, tooth brushing, grooming, or toilet routine? Has s/he engaged in excessive cleaning of household items or other inanimate objects, or pursued other measures to remove or prevent contact with contaminants?"

_____ CHECKING COMPULSIONS

"During the past week, has (*name of patient*) excessively checked locks, stove, appliances or other items? Has s/he engaged in checking to ensure that s/he did not or will not harm self or others, that nothing terrible did or will happen, or that s/he did not make a mistake? Has (*name of patient*) engaged in checking tied to fears of illness or contamination?"

_____ REPEATING RITUALS

"During the past week, has (*name of patient*) had to re-read or re-write things, or has s/he repeated routine activities, for example, getting up and down from a chair?"

_____ COUNTING COMPULSIONS

"During the past week, has (*name of patient*) engaged in compulsions involving counting things (e.g., counting floor tiles, books on a shelf, or words in a sentence)?"

_____ ORDERING/ARRANGING COMPULSIONS

"During the past week, has (*name of patient*) engaged in compulsions involving ordering or arranging things? This includes excessive straightening of papers on a desk, adjusting furniture or picture frames."

_____ SAVING/COLLECTING COMPULSIONS

"During the past week, has (*name of patient*) engaged in compulsions involving saving (such as old newspapers or junk mail) or collecting things?"

_____ MISCELLANEOUS COMPULSIONS

"During the past week, has (*name of patient*) engaged in mental rituals, excessive list making, measures to prevent harm to self or others, or to prevent terrible consequences, or has s/he evidenced a need to tell, ask, or confess?"

Other OCD-Related Problems

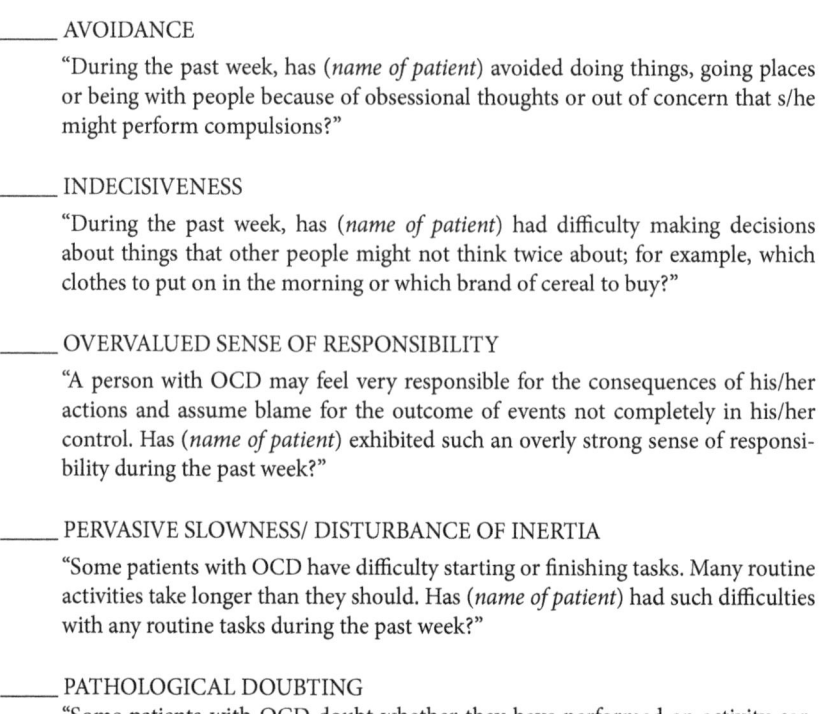

_____ AVOIDANCE

"During the past week, has (*name of patient*) avoided doing things, going places or being with people because of obsessional thoughts or out of concern that s/he might perform compulsions?"

_____ INDECISIVENESS

"During the past week, has (*name of patient*) had difficulty making decisions about things that other people might not think twice about; for example, which clothes to put on in the morning or which brand of cereal to buy?"

_____ OVERVALUED SENSE OF RESPONSIBILITY

"A person with OCD may feel very responsible for the consequences of his/her actions and assume blame for the outcome of events not completely in his/her control. Has (*name of patient*) exhibited such an overly strong sense of responsibility during the past week?"

_____ PERVASIVE SLOWNESS/ DISTURBANCE OF INERTIA

"Some patients with OCD have difficulty starting or finishing tasks. Many routine activities take longer than they should. Has (*name of patient*) had such difficulties with any routine tasks during the past week?"

_____ PATHOLOGICAL DOUBTING

"Some patients with OCD doubt whether they have performed an activity correctly, or whether they did it at all. When carrying out routine activities they may find that they don't trust their senses; that is, what they see, hear, or touch. Has (*name of patient*) exhibited such doubting during the past week?"

Patient Symptom List

(Describe main symptoms reported by the family member and refer to this list when posing the remaining questions.)

Obsessions

1. _____
2. _____
3. _____
4. _____
5. _____
6. _____

Compulsions

1. _____
2. _____
3. _____
4. _____
5. _____
6. _____

Other OCD-Related Problems

1. _____
2. _____
3. _____
4. _____
5. _____
6. _____

Family Member's Report of Accommodating Behaviors

INSTRUCTIONS FOR THE FAMILY MEMBER: "You have told me that *(name of patient)* has the following symptoms *(review patient symptom list)*. I am now going to ask you about ways in which you may have responded to *(name of patient)* and his/her symptoms during the past week." *(Formulate examples of accommodation for each question using the specific symptoms on the Patient Symptom List.)*

1. Providing Reassurance

"During the past week, when *(name of patient)* has expressed worries, fears, or doubts related to obsessions or compulsions, have you reassured him/her that s/he doesn't have to worry, that there are no grounds for his/her concerns, or that the rituals s/he already performed have taken care of his/her concerns? Examples might include telling your relative that s/he is not contaminated, or that s/he has done enough cleaning or checking."

"During the past week, on how many occasions did you provide reassurance to *(name of patient)* that was directly related to an obsession or compulsion? [Do not include instances in which you provided more general reassurance that s/he will overcome symptoms or feel better soon, or reassurance about matters unrelated to OCD.]"

N/A = Not applicable. Patient did not experience OCD symptoms this week.
0 = None
1 = 1/week
2 = 2-3/week
3 = 4-6/week
4 = Everyday

2. Watching the Patient Complete Rituals

"During the past week, did you deliberately watch *(name of patient)* complete rituals at his/her request or because you thought s/he would want you to do so?"

"During the past week, how many times did you watch *(name of patient)* complete rituals? [Do not include those instances in which you just happened to see him/her performing rituals.]"

N/A = Not applicable. Patient did not experience OCD symptoms this week.
0 = None
1 = 1/week
2 = 2-3/week
3 = 4-6/week
4 = Everyday

3. Waiting for the Patient

"During the past week, did you wait for (*name of patient*) to complete compulsive behaviors, resulting in interference with plans you had made?"

"During the past week, how many times did you wait for (*name of patient*) because of his/her OCD?"

N/A = Not applicable. Patient did not experience OCD symptoms this week.
0 = None
1 = 1/week
2 = 2-3/week
3 = 4-6/week
4 = Everyday

4. Refraining from Saying/Doing Things

"During the past week, were there things that you did not do or say because of (*name of patient*)'s OCD? For example, family members may stop themselves from entering some areas of the house, refrain from physical contact with the relative with OCD, or avoid conversation topics related to the relative's obsessions."

"During the past week, how often did you stop yourself from saying or doing things because of (*name of patient*)'s OCD?"

N/A = Not applicable. Patient did not experience OCD symptoms this week.
0 = None
1 = 1/week
2 = 2-3/week
3 = 4-6/week
4 = Everyday

5. Participating in Compulsions

"During the past week, did you engage in (*name of patient*)'s compulsions or in behaviors which you consider odd or senseless at his/her request, or because you thought (*name of patient*) would want you to do these things? For example, family members might wash their hands more times than they feel is necessary (or in a ritualized way) or they may check the burners on the stove repeatedly even though they believe the burners are not lit."

"During the past week, how many times did you directly participate in (*name of patient*)'s rituals or in behaviors that you consider odd or senseless?"

N/A = Not applicable. Patient did not experience OCD symptoms this week.
0 = None
1 = 1/week
2 = 2-3/week
3 = 4-6/week
4 = Everyday

6. Facilitating Compulsions

"Were there times in this past week in which your actions made it possible for (*name of patient*) to complete his/her rituals (without you being directly involved in performing the rituals)? For example, a family member may provide a relative with OCD with things s/he needs to perform rituals or compulsions, such as buying excessive quantities of soap or cleaning products. Other examples include driving the car back to the house so the relative can check that doors are locked, or creating extra space in the house for the relative's saved items."

"During the past week, how many times did you do something that helped (*name of patient*) complete rituals? [Do not include those instances in which you directly participated in rituals as noted in the last question (item 5).]"

N/A = Not applicable. Patient did not experience OCD symptoms this week.
0   = None
1   = 1/week
2   = 2-3/week
3   = 4-6/week
4   = Everyday

7. Facilitating Avoidance

"In the past week, did you get involved in (**name of patient**)'s efforts to avoid people, places, or things? Or did you do anything that allowed him/her avoid? For example, family members may make excuses for a relative who says s/he cannot attend a social function because of OCD-related concerns, take a roundabout driving route because the relative wants to avoid a 'contaminated' area, or open a door so the relative does not have to touch a "contaminated" door handle."

"During the past week, on how many occasions did you do something that helped (*name of patient*) avoid people, places, or things? [Do not include instances in which you participated in compulsions or did something that helped your relative to complete compulsions, as noted in the last two questions (items 5 and 6).]"

N/A = Not applicable. Patient did not experience OCD symptoms this week.
0   = None
1   = 1/week
2   = 2-3/week
3   = 4-6/week
4   = Everyday

8. Tolerating Odd Behaviors/Household Disruption

"During the past week, did you put up with odd behaviors on (*name of patient*)'s part (e.g., repetitive actions such as going in and out of a doorway), or did you put up with unusual conditions in your home because of (*name of patient*)'s OCD; for example leaving the home cluttered with old newspapers or ignoring repeated closing and opening of doors?"

"During the past week, to what extent did you tolerate odd behaviors or unusual conditions in your home because of (*name of patient*)'s OCD? [This question is specific to behaviors or conditions that you allow to occur. Do not include instances in which you took action to participate in or facilitate compulsions or avoidance noted under the last three questions (items 5-7).]" *(RATER SCORED)*

N/A = Not applicable. Patient did not experience OCD symptoms this week.
0 = Not at all.
1 = Mild; tolerated slightly unusual behavior/conditions.
2 = Moderate; tolerated behavior/conditions that are somewhat unusual.
3 = Severe; tolerated very unusual behavior/conditions.
4 = Extreme; tolerated extremely aberrant behavior/conditions.

9. Helping the Patient with Tasks of Daily Living or Simple Decisions

"During the past week, did you help (*name of patient*) complete simple tasks of daily living or make simple decisions when his/her ability to function was impaired by OCD; for example, helping him/her to get dressed, to bathe, or to decide what to eat?"

"During the past week, on how many occasions did you help (*name of patient*) with simple tasks or decisions because s/he was impaired by OCD? [Do not include instances or in which doing a task for your relative included doing something that helped him/her avoid an OCD-related fear (item 7) or in which making a decision for your relative consisted of providing reassurance about an OCD-related concern (item 1).]"

N/A = Not applicable. Patient did not experience OCD symptoms this week.
0 = None
1 = 1/week
2 = 2-3/week
3 = 4-6/week
4 = Everyday

10. Taking on Patient's Responsibilities

"Do you take on tasks that are (*name of patient*)'s responsibility but which he/she cannot adequately perform because of his/her OCD? Examples include paying his/her bills, or taking care of his/her children."

"During the past week, to what extent did you take on (*name of patient*)'s responsibilities due to OCD? [Do not include doing simple tasks of daily living for your relative, as noted under the last question (item 9).]" *(RATER SCORED)*

N/A = Not applicable. Patient did not experience OCD symptoms this week.
0 = Not at all.
1 = Mild; occasionally handles one of patient's responsibilities, but there has been no substantial change in his/her role.
2 = Moderate; has assumed patient's responsibilities in one area.
3 = Severe; has assumed patient's responsibilities in more than one area.
4 = Extreme; has assumed most or all of patient's responsibilities.

11. Modifying Your Personal Routine

"Are you currently modifying your leisure time activities, or your work or family responsibilities, because of (*name of patient*)'s OCD? Examples of modifying one's personal routine might include spending less time socializing or exercising, or changing one's work schedule to spend more time attending to the person with OCD."

"During the past week, to what extent did you modify your personal routine because of (*name of patient*)'s OCD?" *(RATER SCORED)*

N/A = Not applicable. Patient did not experience OCD symptoms this week.
0 = Not at all.
1 = Mild; slightly modified routine, but was able to fulfill family and/or work responsibilities and to engage in leisure time activities.
2 = Moderate; definitely modified routine in one area (family, work, or leisure time).
3 = Severe; definitely modified routine in more than one area.
4 = Extreme; unable to attend to work or family responsibilities or to have any leisure time because of relative's OCD.

12. Modifying the Family Routine

"Are you currently modifying what you consider an ordinary family routine because of (*name of patient*)'s OCD? Examples might include modifying the family's cooking or cleaning practices."

"During the past week, to what extent did you modify the family routine because of (*name of patient*)'s OCD? To what degree has your relative's OCD necessitated changes in family activities or practices?" *(RATER SCORED)*

N/A = Not applicable. Patient did not experience OCD symptoms this week.
0 = Not at all.
1 = Mild. The family routine was slightly modified, but remained substantially unchanged.
2 = Moderate. The family routine was definitely modified in one area.
3 = Severe. The family routine was definitely modified in more than one area.
4 = Extreme. The family routine was disrupted in most or all areas.

Scoring Sheet

Family Accommodation Scale for Obsessive-Compulsive Disorder

Interviewer-Rated (FAS-IR)

Name:_____   Interviewer:_____

Total Score:_____   Date:_____

	N/A	None	Mild	Moderate	Severe	Extreme
1: Providing Reassurance	0	0	1	2	3	4
2: Watching the Patient Complete Rituals	0	0	1	2	3	4
3: Waiting for the Patient	0	0	1	2	3	4
4: Refraining From Saying/ Doing Things	0	0	1	2	3	4
5: Participating in Compulsions	0	0	1	2	3	4
6: Facilitating Compulsions	0	0	1	2	3	4
7: Facilitating Avoidance	0	0	1	2	3	4
8: Tolerating Odd Behavior/ Household Disruption	0	0	1	2	3	4
9: Helping with Simple Tasks	0	0	1	2	3	4
10: Taking on Patient's Responsibilities	0	0	1	2	3	4
11: Modifying Personal Routine	0	0	1	2	3	4
12: Modifying Family Routine	0	0	1	2	3	4

(Sum item scores to obtain total score.)

COPYRIGHT © 1999 by Lisa Calvocoressi, Ph.D., Carolyn M. Mazure, Ph.D., Barbara Van Noppen, Ph.D., and Lawrence H. Price, M.D.

Family Accommodation Scale for Obsessive-Compulsive Disorder Self-Rated Version (FAS-SR)

Developed by:
Anthony Pinto, Ph.D., Barbara Van Noppen, Ph.D., & Lisa Calvocoressi, Ph.D.

Copyright and Permissions

The Family Accommodation Scale for Obsessive Compulsive Disorder - Self-Rated Version (FAS-SR) Copyright © 2012 by Anthony Pinto, Ph.D., Barbara Van Noppen, Ph.D., & Lisa Calvocoressi, Ph.D.

The Family Accommodation Scale for Obsessive Compulsive Disorder–Self-Rated Version (FAS-SR) includes a modified version of the Yale–Brown Obsessive Compulsive Scale (YBOCS) Checklist. Copyright © 1986, 1989, with permission.

Reference

Pinto, A., Van Noppen, B., & Calvocoressi, L. (2013). Development and preliminary psychometric evaluation of a self-rated version of the Family Accommodation Scale for Obsessive-Compulsive Disorder. *Journal of Obsessive- Compulsive and Related Disorders*, 2, 457–465.

Correspondence

For permission to use or adapt this instrument for clinical or research purposes, please contact Lisa Calvocoressi, Ph.D., Yale University School of Public Health, Yale University School of Medicine: lisa.calvocoressi@yale.edu.

Family Accommodation Scale for OCD
Self-Rated Version (FAS-SR)

Name: _____   Today's Date: _____

I am the patient's _____
[What is your relation to the patient?] *(circle one)*
1 = parent   2 = spouse   3 = partner   4 = adult child   5 = sibling   6 = other

Introduction for the Family Member

You have been asked to complete this questionnaire because you have a relative or significant other who has been diagnosed with obsessive-compulsive disorder (OCD) and who has identified you as the family member who is most involved with him/her and the OCD. Throughout this questionnaire, your relative/significant other with OCD is referred to as "your relative" and you are referred to as the "family member."

Part I of this questionnaire describes obsessions and compulsions and asks you to identify your relative's current OCD symptoms to the best of your knowledge. Part II of this questionnaire asks you to identify possible ways in which you may be modifying your behavior or routines in response to your relative's OCD.

Part I: Report of Relative's OCD Symptoms

Obsessions

Obsessions are distressing ideas, thoughts, images or impulses that repeatedly enter a person's mind and may seem to occur against his or her will. The thoughts may be repugnant or frightening, or may seem senseless to the person who is experiencing them.

Below is a list of different types of obsessions common in OCD. Please place a check mark by each type of obsession that your relative experienced (to the best of your knowledge) **during the past week**.

_____HARMING OBSESSIONS

Examples: fears of harming oneself or others, stealing things, blurting out obscenities or insults, acting on unwanted or embarrassing impulses; being responsible for something terrible happening (e.g., a fire or burglary); experiencing violent or horrific images.

_____CONTAMINATION OBSESSIONS

Examples: excessive concerns about or disgust with bodily waste, secretions, blood, germs; excessive concerns about being contaminated by environmental toxins (e.g., asbestos, radiation, or toxic waste), household cleansers/solvents, or animals (e.g., insects); discomfort with sticky substances or residues; fears of contaminating others.

_____ SEXUAL OBSESSIONS

Examples: unwanted, repeated thoughts with forbidden or perverse sexual themes (e.g., sexual involvement with children).

_____ HOARDING/SAVING OBSESSIONS

Examples: worries about throwing out seemingly unimportant things, resulting in accumulation of possessions that fill up or clutter active living areas or the workplace.

_____ RELIGIOUS OBSESSIONS

Examples: intrusive blasphemous thoughts; excessive concerns about right and wrong/morality.

_____ OBSESSION WITH NEED FOR SYMMETRY OR EXACTNESS

Examples: worries about whether items have been moved; worries that possessions are not properly aligned; worries about calculations or handwriting being perfect.

_____ SOMATIC OBSESSIONS

Examples: excessive concerns about having an illness like AIDS or cancer, despite reassurance to the contrary; excessive concerns about a part of the body or aspect of appearance.

_____ MISCELLANEOUS OBSESSIONS

Examples: an excessive need to know or remember unimportant details; a fear of losing things; a fear of saying certain words; a fear of not saying just the right thing; a discomfort with certain sounds or noises; or repeated thoughts of lucky or unlucky numbers.

Compulsions

Compulsions (also called rituals) are defined as behaviors or mental acts that a person feels driven to perform, although s/he may recognize them as senseless or excessive. It may be difficult or anxiety provoking for a person to resist performing these behaviors.

Below is a list of different types of compulsions common in OCD. Please place a check mark by each type of compulsion that your relative experienced (to the best of your knowledge) **during the past week.**

_____ CLEANING/WASHING COMPULSIONS

Examples: excessive or ritualized handwashing, showering, bathing, toothbrushing, grooming, or toilet routine; excessive cleaning of household items; efforts to prevent contact with contaminants.

_____CHECKING COMPULSIONS

Examples: excessively checking locks, stove, appliances; checking to ensure that nothing terrible did or will happen, or that s/he did not make a mistake; checking tied to fears of illness.

_____REPEATING RITUALS

Examples: rereading and/or rewriting things; repeating routine activities (e.g., going in/out of door, getting up/down from chair).

_____COUNTING COMPULSIONS

Examples: counting floor tiles, books on a shelf, or words in a sentence.

_____ORDERING/ARRANGING COMPULSIONS

Examples: excessive straightening of papers on a desk, adjusting furniture or picture frames.

_____HOARDING/SAVING/COLLECTING COMPULSIONS

Examples: saving old newspapers, junk mail, wrappers, broken tools since they may be needed one day; picking up useless objects from the street or garbage cans.

_____MISCELLANEOUS COMPULSIONS

Examples: seeking reassurance (e.g., by repeatedly asking the same question); excessive list-making; taking measures to prevent harm to self or others, or to prevent terrible consequences; mental rituals other than checking or counting (e.g., reviewing, ritualized praying); need to touch or tap things; ritualized eating behaviors.

Part II: Report of Family Member's Responses to OCD

INSTRUCTIONS: Keeping in mind your relative's OCD symptoms that you identified in Part I, the next set of items describe possible ways that you may have responded to those symptoms during the past week. For each item, please indicate the **number of days during the past week** that you responded to your relative in the way specified. For each item, fill in a circle in the NUMBER OF DAYS column. If an item refers to something you did not do at all in the last week, fill in the circle for "none/never happened."

	NUMBER OF DAYS THIS PAST WEEK				
	None/ Never	1 day	2-3 days	4-6 days	Every day
1. I reassured my relative that there were no grounds for his/her OCD-related worries. *Examples: reassuring my relative that s/he is not contaminated or that s/he is not terminally ill.*	0	1	2	3	4
2. I reassured my relative that the rituals he/she already performed took care of the OCD-related concern. *Examples: reassuring my relative that s/he did enough ritualized cleaning or checking.*	0	1	2	3	4
3. I waited for my relative while s/he completed compulsive behaviors.	0	1	2	3	4
4. I directly participated in my relative's compulsions. *Examples: doing repeated washing or checking at my relative's request.*	0	1	2	3	4
5. I did things that made it possible for my relative to complete compulsions. *Examples: driving back home so my relative can check if the doors are locked; creating extra space in the house for my relative's saved items.*	0	1	2	3	4
6. I provided my relative with OCD with items s/he needs to perform rituals or compulsions. *Examples: shopping for excessive quantities of soap or cleaning products for my relative.*	0	1	2	3	4

APPENDIX B. MEASURES 371

	NUMBER OF DAYS THIS PAST WEEK				
	None/ Never	1 day	2-3 days	4-6 days	Every day
7. I did things that allowed my relative to avoid situations that might trigger obsessions or compulsions. *Examples: touching public door knobs for my relative so s/he wouldn't have to.*	0	1	2	3	4
8. I helped my relative make simple decisions when s/he couldn't do so because of OCD. *Examples: deciding which clothes my relative should put on in the morning or what brand of cereal s/he should buy.*	0	1	2	3	4
9. I helped my relative with personal tasks, such as washing, grooming, toileting, or dressing, when his/her ability to function was impaired by OCD.	0	1	2	3	4
10. I helped my relative prepare food when s/he couldn't do so because of OCD.	0	1	2	3	4
11. I took on family or household responsibilities that my relative couldn't adequately perform due to OCD. *Examples: doing bills, shopping, and/or taking care of children for my relative (when, except for OCD, I wouldn't have done so).*	0	1	2	3	4
12. I avoided talking about things that might trigger my relative's obsessions or compulsions.	0	1	2	3	4
13. I stopped myself from doing things that could have led my relative to have obsessions or compulsions. *Examples: not moving items that my relative has carefully lined up.*	0	1	2	3	4
14. I made excuses or lied for my relative when s/he missed work or a social activity because of his/her OCD.	0	1	2	3	4
15. I didn't do anything to stop unusual OCD-related behaviors by my relative. *Examples: tolerating my relative's repetitive actions such as going in and out of a doorway or touching/tapping objects a certain number of times.*	0	1	2	3	4

	\multicolumn{5}{c}{NUMBER OF DAYS THIS PAST WEEK}
	None/ Never	1 day	2-3 days	4-6 days	Every day
16. I put up with unusual conditions in my home because of my relative's OCD. *Examples: leaving the home cluttered with papers that my relative won't throw away.*	0	1	2	3	4
17. I cut back on leisure activities because of my relative's OCD. *Examples: spending less time socializing, doing hobbies, exercising.*	0	1	2	3	4
18. I changed my work or school schedule because of my relative's OCD.	0	1	2	3	4
19. I put off some of my family responsibilities because of my relative's OCD. *Examples: I spent less time than I would have liked with other relatives; I neglected my household chores.*	0	1	2	3	4
TOTAL SCORE *(sum of responses to items 1–19)*					

Family Accommodation Scale for Obsessive-Compulsive Disorder Patient Version (FAS-PV)

Developed by:
Anthony Pinto, Ph.D., Barbara Van Noppen, Ph.D., Monica S. Wu, M.A.,
& Lisa Calvocoressi, Ph.D.

Copyright and Permissions

The Family Accommodation Scale for Obsessive Compulsive Disorder–Patient Version (FAS-PV) Copyright © 2015 by Anthony Pinto, Ph.D., Barbara Van Noppen, Ph.D., Monica S. Wu, M.A., & Lisa Calvocoressi, Ph.D.

The Family Accommodation Scale for Obsessive Compulsive Disorder–Patient Version (FAS-PV) includes a modified version of the Yale–Brown Obsessive Compulsive Scale (YBOCS) Checklist. Copyright © 1986, 1989, with permission. *Reprinted with the permission of the authors.*

Correspondence

For permission to use or adapt this instrument for clinical or research purposes, please contact Lisa Calvocoressi, Ph.D., Yale University School of Public Health, Yale University School of Medicine: lisa.calvocoressi@yale.edu.

Family Accommodation Scale for OCD Patient Version (FAS-PV)

Name: _____   Today's Date: ____/____/____

Identify the relative who is most involved with you and your obsessive-compulsive symptoms. *(circle one)*
1 = parent   2 = spouse   3 = partner   4 = adult child   5 = sibling   6 = other

Overview

You have been asked to complete this questionnaire because you have been identified as having significant obsessive-compulsive symptoms and have identified a family member who is most involved with you and these symptoms. Throughout this questionnaire, your relative/significant other is referred to as "your relative."

Part I of this questionnaire describes obsessions and compulsions and asks you to identify your current obsessive-compulsive symptoms. Part II of this questionnaire asks you to identify possible ways in which your relative may be modifying his/her behavior or routines in response to your obsessive-compulsive symptoms.

Part I: Report of Your Obsessive-Compulsive Symptoms
Obsessions

Obsessions are distressing ideas, thoughts, images or impulses that repeatedly enter a person's mind and may seem to occur against his or her will. The thoughts may be repugnant or frightening, or may seem senseless to the person who is experiencing them. Below is a list of different types of obsessions common in people who have obsessive-compulsive disorder (OCD). Please place a check mark by each type of obsession that you experienced **during the past week**.

____ HARMING OBSESSIONS
Examples: fears of harming oneself or others, stealing things, blurting out obscenities or insults, acting on unwanted or embarrassing impulses; being responsible for something terrible happening (e.g., a fire or burglary); experiencing violent or horrific images.

____ CONTAMINATION OBSESSIONS
Examples: excessive concerns about or disgust with bodily waste, secretions, blood, germs; excessive concerns about being contaminated by environmental toxins (e.g.,

asbestos, radiation, or toxic waste), household cleansers/solvents, or animals (e.g., insects); discomfort with sticky substances or residues; fears of contaminating others.

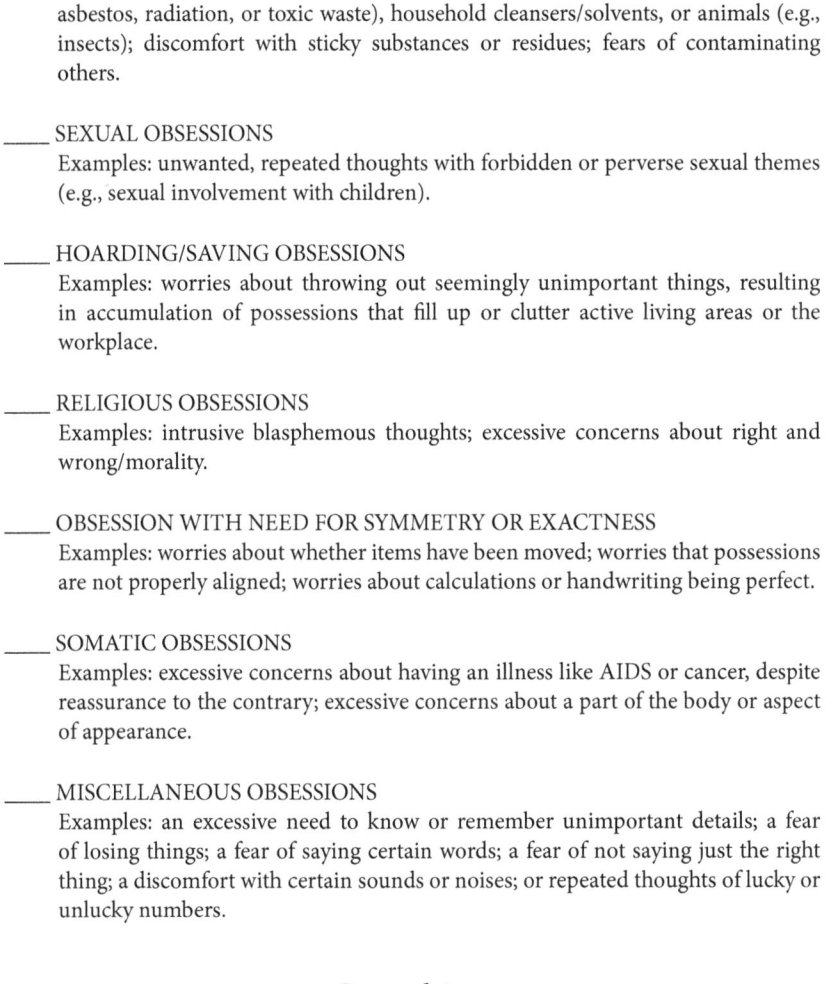

____ SEXUAL OBSESSIONS
Examples: unwanted, repeated thoughts with forbidden or perverse sexual themes (e.g., sexual involvement with children).

____ HOARDING/SAVING OBSESSIONS
Examples: worries about throwing out seemingly unimportant things, resulting in accumulation of possessions that fill up or clutter active living areas or the workplace.

____ RELIGIOUS OBSESSIONS
Examples: intrusive blasphemous thoughts; excessive concerns about right and wrong/morality.

____ OBSESSION WITH NEED FOR SYMMETRY OR EXACTNESS
Examples: worries about whether items have been moved; worries that possessions are not properly aligned; worries about calculations or handwriting being perfect.

____ SOMATIC OBSESSIONS
Examples: excessive concerns about having an illness like AIDS or cancer, despite reassurance to the contrary; excessive concerns about a part of the body or aspect of appearance.

____ MISCELLANEOUS OBSESSIONS
Examples: an excessive need to know or remember unimportant details; a fear of losing things; a fear of saying certain words; a fear of not saying just the right thing; a discomfort with certain sounds or noises; or repeated thoughts of lucky or unlucky numbers.

Compulsions

Compulsions (also called rituals) are defined as behaviors or mental acts that a person feels driven to perform, although s/he may recognize them as senseless or excessive. It may be difficult or anxiety provoking for a person to resist performing these behaviors. Below is a list of different types of compulsions common in people who have OCD. Please place a check mark by each type of compulsion that you experienced **during the past week**.

____ CLEANING/WASHING COMPULSIONS
Examples: excessive or ritualized hand washing, showering, bathing, toothbrushing, grooming, or toilet routine; excessive cleaning of household items; efforts to prevent contact with contaminants.

____ CHECKING COMPULSIONS
Examples: excessively checking locks, stove, appliances; checking to ensure that nothing terrible did or will happen, or that s/he did not make a mistake; checking tied to fears of illness.

____ REPEATING RITUALS
Examples: re-reading and/or re-writing things; repeating routine activities (e.g., going in/out of door, getting up/down from chair).

____ COUNTING COMPULSIONS
Examples: counting floor tiles, books on a shelf, or words in a sentence.

____ ORDERING/ARRANGING COMPULSIONS
Examples: excessive straightening of papers on a desk, adjusting furniture or picture frames.

____ HOARDING/SAVING/COLLECTING COMPULSIONS
Examples: saving old newspapers, junk mail, wrappers, broken tools since they may be needed one day; picking up useless objects from the street or garbage cans.

____ MISCELLANEOUS COMPULSIONS
Examples: seeking reassurance (e.g., by repeatedly asking the same question); excessive list making; taking measures to prevent harm to self or others, or to prevent terrible consequences; mental rituals other than checking or counting (e.g., reviewing, ritualized praying); need to touch or tap things; ritualized eating behaviors.

Part II: Report of Family Member's Responses to Obsessive-Compulsive Symptoms

INSTRUCTIONS: Keeping in mind your current obsessive-compulsive symptoms (identified in Part I), the next set of items describe possible ways that your relative may have responded to those symptoms during the past week. For each item, please indicate the number of days during the past week that your relative responded to you in the way specified. For each item, fill in a circle in the NUMBER OF DAYS column. If an item refers to something your relative did not do at all in the last week, fill in the circle for "none/never happened."

	NUMBER OF DAYS THIS PAST WEEK				
	None/ Never	1 Day	2–3 Days	4–6 Days	Every Day
1. My relative reassured me that there were no grounds for my OCD-related worries. *Examples: reassuring me that I am not contaminated or that I am not terminally ill.*	0	1	2	3	4
2. My relative reassured me that the rituals I already performed took care of the OCD-related concern. *Examples: reassuring me that I did enough ritualized cleaning or checking.*	0	1	2	3	4
3. My relative waited for me while I completed compulsive behaviors.	0	1	2	3	4
4. My relative directly participated in my compulsions. *Examples: doing repeated washing or checking at my request.*	0	1	2	3	4
5. My relative did things that made it possible for me to complete compulsions. *Examples: driving back home so I can check if the doors are locked; creating extra space in the house for my saved items.*	0	1	2	3	4
6. My relative provided me with items I need to perform rituals or compulsions. *Examples: shopping for excessive quantities of soap or cleaning products for me.*	0	1	2	3	4

| | NUMBER OF DAYS THIS PAST WEEK |||||
	None/ Never	1 Day	2–3 Days	4–6 Days	Every Day
7. My relative did things that allowed me to avoid situations that might trigger obsessions or compulsions. *Examples: touching public door knobs for me so I wouldn't have to.*	0	1	2	3	4
8. My relative helped me make simple decisions when I couldn't do so because of my obsessive-compulsive symptoms. *Examples: deciding which clothes I should put on in the morning or what brand of cereal I should buy.*	0	1	2	3	4
9. My relative helped me with personal tasks, such as washing, grooming, toileting, or dressing, when my ability to function was impaired by my obsessive-compulsive symptoms.	0	1	2	3	4
10. My relative helped me prepare food when I couldn't do so because of my obsessive-compulsive symptoms.	0	1	2	3	4
11. My relative took on family or household responsibilities that I couldn't adequately perform due to my obsessive-compulsive symptoms. *Examples: doing bills, shopping, and/or taking care of children for me (when, except for my obsessive-compulsive symptoms, my relative wouldn't have done so).*	0	1	2	3	4
12. My relative avoided talking about things that might trigger my obsessions or compulsions.	0	1	2	3	4
13. My relative stopped himself/herself from doing things that could have led me to have obsessions or compulsions. *Examples: not moving items that I have carefully lined up.*	0	1	2	3	4

	NUMBER OF DAYS THIS PAST WEEK					
	None/ Never	1 Day	2–3 Days	4–6 Days	Every Day
14. My relative made excuses or lied for me when I missed work or a social activity because of my obsessive-compulsive symptoms.	0	1	2	3	4
15. My relative didn't do anything to stop my unusual obsessive-compulsive behaviors. *Examples: tolerating my repetitive actions such as going in and out of a doorway or touching/tapping objects a certain number of times.*	0	1	2	3	4
16. My relative put up with unusual conditions in his/her home because of my obsessive-compulsive symptoms. *Examples: leaving the home cluttered with papers that I won't throw away.*	0	1	2	3	4
17. My relative cut back on leisure activities because of my obsessive-compulsive symptoms. *Examples: spending less time socializing, doing hobbies, exercising.*	0	1	2	3	4
18. My relative changed his/her work or school schedule because of my obsessive-compulsive symptoms.	0	1	2	3	4
19. My relative put off some of his/her family responsibilities because of my obsessive-compulsive symptoms. *Examples: My relative spent less time than he/she would have liked with other family members; my relative neglected his/her household chores.*	0	1	2	3	4
TOTAL SCORE (*sum of responses to items 1–19*)					

Sexual Orientation Obsessions and Reactions Test (SORT)

NAME: _____   DATE: _____

Circle the answer that best corresponds with how you have been feeling over the last week. LGBTQ refers to people who identify as lesbian, gay, bisexual, transgender, and/or queer.

		Never	Rarely	Sometimes	Often	Always
1.	I worry about the thoughts I am having about people of the same sex.	[0]	[1]	[2]	[3]	[4]
2.	My sexual fantasies scare me.	[0]	[1]	[2]	[3]	[4]
3.	I try to reassure myself that I am not LGBTQ.	[0]	[1]	[2]	[3]	[4]
4.	I check myself to see if I am aroused by sexual images.	[0]	[1]	[2]	[3]	[4]
5.	I worry that other people will think I am LGBTQ.	[0]	[1]	[2]	[3]	[4]
6.	I just need to know for sure if I am straight.	[0]	[1]	[2]	[3]	[4]
7.	I worry that my sexual orientation may change.	[0]	[1]	[2]	[3]	[4]
8.	I check myself to see if I am sexually aroused around other people.	[0]	[1]	[2]	[3]	[4]
9.	An unwanted sexual thought or image means I really want to do it.	[0]	[1]	[2]	[3]	[4]
10.	I worry a lot if I don't get sexually aroused when I want to.	[0]	[1]	[2]	[3]	[4]
11.	I just want to be like everyone else.	[0]	[1]	[2]	[3]	[4]
12.	I worry that I will lose control and become LGBTQ.	[0]	[1]	[2]	[3]	[4]

Scoring: Score test by summing all items, with each item scored from zero to 4. Both heterosexual and LGBTQ individuals scoring over 10 should be assessed for OCD.

Means: heterosexual undergraduates 5.9 (SD = 5.8), LGBTQ undergraduates 8.8 (SD = 7.5), LGBTQ community 6.4 (SD = 4.9) heterosexual SO-OCD patients 21.6 (SD = 11.7), heterosexual patients with other forms of OCD 12.4 (SD = 12.6).

Citation: Williams, M. T., Ching, T. H. W., Tellawi, G., Siev, J., Dowell, J., Schlaudt, V., Slimowicz, J., & Wetterneck, C. T. (2018). Assessing sexual orientation symptoms in obsessive-compulsive disorder: Development and validation of the Sexual Orientation Obsessions and Reactions Test (SORT). *Behavior Therapy, 49,* 715–729. doi: 10.1016/j.beth.2017.12.005

Adult OCD Impact Scale (AOIS)

OCD-Related Problems in Functioning

Please indicate whether you have difficulties in these situations or avoid these situations due to your OCD concerns.

	Work/School Problems	*No Problem*	*Slight Problem*	*Moderate Problem*	*Significant Problem*	*Extreme Problem*
1.	Getting to work/school on time	[0]	[1]	[2]	[3]	[4]
2.	Absent from work	[0]	[1]	[2]	[3]	[4]
3.	Getting to appointments/class on time	[0]	[1]	[2]	[3]	[4]
4.	Oral presentations/reports	[0]	[1]	[2]	[3]	[4]
5.	Being prepared for meetings/class	[0]	[1]	[2]	[3]	[4]
6.	Writing out tasks, reports, emails, etc.	[0]	[1]	[2]	[3]	[4]
7.	Completing projects	[0]	[1]	[2]	[3]	[4]
8.	Getting good evaluations/grades	[0]	[1]	[2]	[3]	[4]
9.	Attending work functions outside of office hours	[0]	[1]	[2]	[3]	[4]
10.	Concentrating on work	[0]	[1]	[2]	[3]	[4]
11.	Going to bathroom at work	[0]	[1]	[2]	[3]	[4]
12.	Going on work-related outings	[0]	[1]	[2]	[3]	[4]

	Home/Family Problems	*No Problem*	*Slight Problem*	*Moderate Problem*	*Significant Problem*	*Extreme Problem*
13.	Getting dressed in the morning	[0]	[1]	[2]	[3]	[4]
14.	Bathing/grooming in the morning	[0]	[1]	[2]	[3]	[4]
15.	Bathing/grooming other times	[0]	[1]	[2]	[3]	[4]
16.	Doing indoor household chores (e.g., washing dishes, cleaning bathroom, vacuuming, etc.)	[0]	[1]	[2]	[3]	[4]
17.	Doing outdoor household chores (e.g., mowing lawn, washing car, etc.)	[0]	[1]	[2]	[3]	[4]
18.	Eating meals at home	[0]	[1]	[2]	[3]	[4]
19.	Watching TV/listening to music	[0]	[1]	[2]	[3]	[4]
20.	Reading for fun	[0]	[1]	[2]	[3]	[4]
21.	Shopping for food	[0]	[1]	[2]	[3]	[4]
22.	Preparing food	[0]	[1]	[2]	[3]	[4]
23.	Eating food	[0]	[1]	[2]	[3]	[4]
24.	Getting ready for bed at night	[0]	[1]	[2]	[3]	[4]
25.	Sleeping at night	[0]	[1]	[2]	[3]	[4]
26.	Going to bathroom	[0]	[1]	[2]	[3]	[4]
27.	Getting along with children	[0]	[1]	[2]	[3]	[4]
28.	Going on vacation	[0]	[1]	[2]	[3]	[4]
29.	Going to temple or church	[0]	[1]	[2]	[3]	[4]
30.	Pumping gas	[0]	[1]	[2]	[3]	[4]

	Intimacy/Significant Relationship Problems	No Problem	Slight Problem	Moderate Problem	Significant Problem	Extreme Problem
31.	Touching a significant other (e.g., hugging, holding hands, massage)	[0]	[1]	[2]	[3]	[4]
32.	Kissing a significant other	[0]	[1]	[2]	[3]	[4]
33.	Sexual intercourse	[0]	[1]	[2]	[3]	[4]
34.	Oral sex	[0]	[1]	[2]	[3]	[4]
35.	Getting along with spouse/ significant other	[0]	[1]	[2]	[3]	[4]
36.	Having boyfriend/ girlfriend	[0]	[1]	[2]	[3]	[4]
37.	Kissing a child or other close family member	[0]	[1]	[2]	[3]	[4]
38.	Touching with a child (e.g., hugging, giving a bath, etc.)	[0]	[1]	[2]	[3]	[4]
39.	Touching/playing with a family pet	[0]	[1]	[2]	[3]	[4]

	Social Problems	No Problem	Slight Problem	Moderate Problem	Significant Problem	Extreme Problem
40.	Making new friends	[0]	[1]	[2]	[3]	[4]
41.	Keeping friends	[0]	[1]	[2]	[3]	[4]
42.	Leaving the house	[0]	[1]	[2]	[3]	[4]
43.	Being with familiar people	[0]	[1]	[2]	[3]	[4]
44.	Being with a group of strangers	[0]	[1]	[2]	[3]	[4]
45.	Going to friend's house during day	[0]	[1]	[2]	[3]	[4]
46.	Having a friend at house during day	[0]	[1]	[2]	[3]	[4]
47.	Being an overnight guest at friend's house	[0]	[1]	[2]	[3]	[4]
48.	Having house guests spend the night	[0]	[1]	[2]	[3]	[4]
49.	Someone touching/ using things	[0]	[1]	[2]	[3]	[4]

	Social Problems	*No Problem*	*Slight Problem*	*Moderate Problem*	*Significant Problem*	*Extreme Problem*
50.	Being touched (e.g., shaking hands, getting haircut)	[0]	[1]	[2]	[3]	[4]
51.	Going to movies	[0]	[1]	[2]	[3]	[4]
52.	Going shopping/ trying on clothes	[0]	[1]	[2]	[3]	[4]
53.	Eating in restaurant/ fast food	[0]	[1]	[2]	[3]	[4]
54.	Eating in other public places	[0]	[1]	[2]	[3]	[4]
55.	Eating lunch with colleagues, clients, Etc.	[0]	[1]	[2]	[3]	[4]
56.	Engaging in professional relationships at work/ school	[0]	[1]	[2]	[3]	[4]
57.	Engaging in friendly relationships at work/ school	[0]	[1]	[2]	[3]	[4]
58.	Visiting relatives	[0]	[1]	[2]	[3]	[4]

For clinical purposes the items are grouped together in areas of impairment. If you are interested in using this measure for research please contact the authors to obtain a copy of the original ordering and numbering of the measure. Sum all items for a total score. Items with asterisks are provided for further research are unscored.

Wetterneck, C. T., Knott, L., Kinnear, K., & Storch, E. (2019). *Development of the Adult OCD Impact Scale (AOIS): A measure of psychosocial functioning for adults with OCD.* Manuscript submitted for publication.

Dimensional Obsessive-Compulsive Scale (DOCS)

This questionnaire asks you about several different types of concerns that you might or might not experience. For each type there is a description of the kinds of thoughts (sometimes called *obsessions*) and behaviors (sometimes called *rituals* or *compulsions*) that are typical of that particular concern, followed by 5 questions about your experiences with these thoughts and behaviors. Please read each description carefully and answer the questions for each category based on your experiences in the last month.

Category 1: Concerns about Germs and Contamination

Examples

- Thoughts or feelings that you are contaminated because you came into contact with (or were nearby) a certain object or person.
- The feeling of being contaminated because you were in a certain place (such as a bathroom).
- Thoughts about germs, sickness, or the possibility of spreading contamination.
- Washing your hands, using hand sanitizer gels, showering, changing your clothes, or cleaning objects because of concerns about contamination.
- Following a certain routine (e.g., in the bathroom, getting dressed) because of contamination.
- Avoiding certain people, objects, or places because of contamination.

The next questions ask about your experiences with thoughts and behaviors related to contamination <u>over the last month</u>. Keep in mind that your experiences might be different than the examples listed above. Please circle the number next to your answer:

1. About how much time have you spent each day thinking about contamination and engaging in washing or cleaning behaviors because of contamination?
   0 None at all
   1 Less than 1 hour each day
   2 Between 1 and 3 hours each day
   3 Between 3 and 8 hours each day
   4 8 hours or more each day

2. To what extent have you avoided situations in order to prevent concerns with contamination or having to spend time washing, cleaning, or showering?
   0 None at all
   1 A little avoidance
   2 A moderate amount of avoidance
   3 A great deal of avoidance
   4 Extreme avoidance of nearly all things

3. If you had thoughts about contamination but could not wash, clean, or shower (or otherwise remove the contamination), how distressed or anxious did you become?
   0 Not at all distressed/anxious
   1 Mildly distressed/anxious
   2 Moderately distressed/anxious
   3 Severely distressed/anxious
   4 Extremely distressed/anxious

4. To what extent has your daily routine (work, school, self-care, social life) been disrupted by contamination concerns and excessive washing, showering, cleaning, or avoidance behaviors?
   0 No disruption at all.
   1 A little disruption, but I mostly function well.
   2 Many things are disrupted, but I can still manage.
   3 My life is disrupted in many ways and I have trouble managing.
   4 My life is completely disrupted and I cannot function at all.

5. How difficult is it for you to disregard thoughts about contamination and refrain from behaviors such as washing, showering, cleaning, and other decontamination routines when you try to do so?
   0 Not at all difficult
   1 A little difficult
   2 Moderately difficult
   3 Very difficult
   4 Extremely difficult

Category 2: Concerns about being Responsible for Harm, Injury, or Bad Luck

Examples

- A doubt that you might have made a mistake that could cause something awful or harmful to happen.
- The thought that a terrible accident, disaster, injury, or other bad luck might have occurred and you weren't careful enough to prevent it.
- The thought that you could prevent harm or bad luck by doing things in a certain way, counting to certain numbers, or by avoiding certain "bad" numbers or words.
- Thought of losing something important that you are unlikely to lose (e.g., wallet, identify theft, papers).
- Checking things such as locks, switches, your wallet, etc. more often than is necessary.
- Repeatedly asking or checking for reassurance that something bad did not (or will not) happen.
- Mentally reviewing past events to make sure you didn't do anything wrong.
- The need to follow a special routine because it will prevent harm or disasters from occurring.
- The need to count to certain numbers, or avoid certain bad numbers, due to the fear of harm.

The next questions ask about your experiences with thoughts and behaviors related to harm and disasters <u>over the last month</u>. Keep in mind that your experiences might be slightly different than the examples listed above. Please circle the number next to your answer:

1. About how much time have you spent each day thinking about the possibility of harm or disasters and engaging in checking or efforts to get reassurance that such things do not (or did not) occur?
    0 None at all
    1 Less than 1 hour each day
    2 Between 1 and 3 hours each day
    3 Between 3 and 8 hours each day
    4 8 hours or more each day

2. To what extent have you avoided situations so that you did not have to check for danger or worry about possible harm or disasters?
    0 None at all
    1 A little avoidance
    2 A moderate amount of avoidance
    3 A great deal of avoidance
    4 Extreme avoidance of nearly all things

3. When you think about the possibility of harm or disasters, or if you cannot check or get reassurance about these things, how distressed or anxious did you become?
   0 Not at all distressed/anxious
   1 Mildly distressed/anxious
   2 Moderately distressed/anxious
   3 Severely distressed/anxious
   4 Extremely distressed/anxious

4. To what extent has your daily routine (work, school, self-care, social life) been disrupted by thoughts about harm or disasters and excessive checking or asking for reassurance?
   0 No disruption at all.
   1 A little disruption, but I mostly function well.
   2 Many things are disrupted, but I can still manage.
   3 My life is disrupted in many ways and I have trouble managing.
   4 My life is completely disrupted and I cannot function at all.

5. How difficult is it for you to disregard thoughts about possible harm or disasters and refrain from checking or reassurance-seeking behaviors when you try to do so?
   0 Not at all difficult
   1 A little difficult
   2 Moderately difficult
   3 Very difficult
   4 Extremely difficult

> ## Category 3: Unacceptable Thoughts
>
> *Examples*
>
> - Unpleasant thoughts about sex, immorality, or violence that come to mind against your will.
> - Thoughts about doing awful, improper, or embarrassing things that you don't really want to do.
> - Repeating an action or following a special routine because of a bad thought.
> - Mentally performing an action or saying prayers to get rid of an unwanted or unpleasant thought.
> - Avoidance of certain people, places, situations or other triggers of unwanted or unpleasant thoughts.

The next questions ask about your experiences with unwanted thoughts that come to mind against your will and behaviors designed to deal with these kinds of thoughts <u>over the last month</u>. Keep in mind that your experiences might be slightly different than the examples listed above. Please circle the number next to your answer:

1. About how much time have you spent each day with unwanted unpleasant thoughts and with behavioral or mental actions to deal with them?
   0 None at all
   1 Less than 1 hour each day
   2 Between 1 and 3 hours each day
   3 Between 3 and 8 hours each day
   4 8 hours or more each day

2. To what extent have you been avoiding situations, places, objects and other reminders (e.g., numbers, people) that trigger unwanted or unpleasant thoughts?
   0 None at all
   1 A little avoidance
   2 A moderate amount of avoidance
   3 A great deal of avoidance
   4 Extreme avoidance of nearly all things

3. When unwanted or unpleasant thoughts come to mind against your will how distressed or anxious did you become?
   0 Not at all distressed/anxious
   1 Mildly distressed/anxious
   2 Moderately distressed/anxious
   3 Severely distressed/anxious
   4 Extremely distressed/anxious

4. To what extent has your daily routine (work, school, self-care, social life) been disrupted by unwanted and unpleasant thoughts and efforts to avoid or deal with such thoughts?
   0 No disruption at all.
   1 A little disruption, but I mostly function well.
   2 Many things are disrupted, but I can still manage.
   3 My life is disrupted in many ways and I have trouble managing.
   4 My life is completely disrupted and I cannot function at all.

5. How difficult is it for you to disregard unwanted or unpleasant thoughts and refrain from using behavioral or mental acts to deal with them when you try to do so?
   0 Not at all difficult
   1 A little difficult
   2 Moderately difficult
   3 Very difficult
   4 Extremely difficult

Category 4: Concerns about Symmetry, Completeness, and the Need for Things to be "Just Right"

Examples

- The need for symmetry, evenness, balance, or exactness.
- Feelings that something isn't "just right."
- Repeating a routine action until it feels "just right" or "balanced."
- Counting senseless things (e.g., ceiling tiles, words in a sentence).
- Unnecessarily arranging things in "order."
- Having to say something over and over in the same way until it feels "just right."

The next questions ask about your experiences with feelings that something is not "just right" and behaviors designed to achieve order, symmetry, or balance over the last month. Keep in mind that your experiences might be slightly different than the examples listed above. Please circle the number next to your answer:

1. About how much time have you spent each day with unwanted thoughts about symmetry, order, or balance and with behaviors intended to achieve symmetry, order or balance?
    0   None at all
    1   Less than 1 hour each day
    2   Between 1 and 3 hours each day
    3   Between 3 and 8 hours each day
    4   8 hours or more each day

2. To what extent have you been avoiding situations, places or objects associated with feelings that something is not symmetrical or "just right?"
    0   None at all
    1   A little avoidance
    2   A moderate amount of avoidance
    3   A great deal of avoidance
    4   Extreme avoidance of nearly all things

3. When you have the feeling of something being "not just right," how distressed or anxious did you become?
    0   Not at all distressed/anxious
    1   Mildly distressed/anxious
    2   Moderately distressed/anxious
    3   Severely distressed/anxious
    4   Extremely distressed/anxious

4. To what extent has your daily routine (work, school, self-care, social life) been disrupted by the feeling of things being "not just right," and efforts to put things in order or make them feel right?
   0 No disruption at all.
   1 A little disruption, but I mostly function well.
   2 Many things are disrupted, but I can still manage.
   3 My life is disrupted in many ways and I have trouble managing.
   4 My life is completely disrupted and I cannot function at all.

5. How difficult is it for you to disregard thoughts about the lack of symmetry and order, and refrain from urges to arrange things in order or repeat certain behaviors when you try to do so?
   0 Not at all difficult
   1 A little difficult
   2 Moderately difficult
   3 Very difficult
   4 Extremely difficult

> ## Category 5: Sexually Intrusive Thoughts
>
> *Examples*
>
> - Unpleasant thoughts about someone of the same sex if you are heterosexual
> - Thoughts about doing awful, improper, or embarrassing things of a sexual nature that you don't really want to do (including sexual acts with children or authority figures)
> - Thoughts about forcing someone to do something sexually or of being forced to do a sexual act
> - Repeating an action or following a special routine because of sexually intrusive thoughts
> - Mentally performing an action or saying prayers to get rid of an unwanted or unpleasant sexual thought
> - Avoidance of people, place, situations, or other triggers of sexually intrusive thoughts

The next questions ask about your experiences with sexual thoughts that come to mind against your will and behaviors designed to deal with these thoughts <u>over the last month</u>. Keep in mind that your experiences might be slightly different than the examples listed above. Please circle the number next to your answer:

1. About how much time have you spent each day with sexually intrusive thoughts and with behavioral or mental actions to deal with them?
   - 0 None at all
   - 1 Less than 1 hour each day
   - 2 Between 1 and 3 hours each day
   - 3 Between 3 and 8 hours each day
   - 4 8 hours or more each day

2. To what extent have you been avoiding situations, places, objects and other reminders (e.g., numbers, people) that trigger sexually intrusive thoughts?
   - 0 None at all
   - 1 A little avoidance
   - 2 A moderate amount of avoidance
   - 3 A great deal of avoidance
   - 4 Extreme avoidance of nearly all things

3. When sexually intrusive thoughts come to mind against your will how distressed or anxious did you become?
   - 0 Not at all distressed/anxious
   - 1 Mildly distressed/anxious
   - 2 Moderately distressed/anxious
   - 3 Severely distressed/anxious
   - 4 Extremely distressed/anxious

4. To what extent has your daily routine (work, school, self-care, social life) been disrupted by sexually intrusive thoughts and efforts to avoid or deal with such thoughts?
   0 No disruption at all.
   1 A little disruption, but I mostly function well.
   2 Many things are disrupted, but I can still manage.
   3 My life is disrupted in many ways and I have trouble managing.
   4 My life is completely disrupted and I cannot function at all.

5. How difficult is it for you to disregard sexually intrusive thoughts and refrain from using behavioral or mental acts to deal with them when you try to do so?
   0 Not at all difficult
   1 A little difficult
   2 Moderately difficult
   3 Very difficult
   4 Extremely difficult

Citations:

Abramowitz, J. S., Deacon, B. J., Olatunji, B. O., Wheaton, M. G., Berman, N. C., Losardo, D., . . . Hale, L. (2010). Assessment of obsessive-compulsive symptom dimensions: Development and evaluation of the dimensional obsessive-compulsive scale. *Psychological Assessment, 22*, 180-198.

Wetterneck, C. T., Siev, J., Smith, A. H., Adams, T.G., & Slimowicz, J.C. (2015). Assessing Sexually Intrusive Thoughts: Parsing Unacceptable Thoughts on the Dimensional Obsessive-Compulsive Scale. *Behavior Therapy, 46*(4). doi: 10.1016/j.beth.2015.05.006

Self-Assessment of Sexual Orientation

I. Sexual Attractions

The following six questions are asked to assess how frequently and intensely you are sexually attracted to men and women. Consider times you had sexual fantasies, daydreams, or dreams about a man or woman, or have been sexually aroused by a man or woman.

1. **During the past year, how many different men were you sexually attracted to?** (circle one answer)
   a. None
   b. 1
   c. 2
   d. 3–5
   e. 6–10
   f. 11–49
   g. 50–99
   h. 100 or more

2. **During the past year, on average, how often were you sexually attracted to a man?** (circle one answer)
   a. Never
   b. Less than one time per month
   c. 1–3 times per month
   d. 1 time per week
   e. 2–3 times per week
   f. 4–6 times per week
   g. Daily

3. **During the past year, the most I was sexually attracted to a man was . . .** (circle one answer)
   a. Not at all sexually attracted
   b. Slightly sexually attracted
   c. Mildly sexually attracted
   d. Moderately sexually attracted
   e. Significantly sexually attracted
   f. Very sexually attracted
   g. Extremely sexually attracted

4. **During the past year, how many different women were you sexually attracted to?** (circle one answer)
   a. None
   b. 1
   c. 2
   d. 3–5
   e. 6–10
   f. 11–49
   g. 50–99
   h. 100 or more

5. **During the past year, on average, how often were you sexually attracted to a woman?** (circle one answer)
   a. Never
   b. Less than one time per month
   c. 1–3 times per month
   d. 1 time per week
   e. 2–3 times per week
   f. 4–6 times per week
   g. Daily

6. **During the past year, the most I was sexually attracted to a woman was . . .** (circle one answer)
   a. Not at all sexually attracted
   b. Slightly sexually attracted
   c. Mildly sexually attracted
   d. Moderately sexually attracted
   e. Significantly sexually attracted
   f. Very sexually attracted
   g. Extremely sexually attracted

II. Sexual Contact

The following four questions are asked to assess your sexual contacts. Consider times when you had contact between your body and another man or woman's body for the purpose of sexual arousal or gratification.

1. **During the past year, how many different men did you have sexual contact with?** (circle one answer)
   a. None
   b. 1
   c. 2
   d. 3–5
   e. 6–10
   f. 11–49
   g. 50–99
   h. 100 or more

2. **During the past year, on average, how often did you have sexual contact with a man?** (circle one answer)
   a. Never
   b. Less than one time per month
   c. 1–3 times per month
   d. 1 time per week
   e. 2–3 times per week
   f. 4–6 times per week
   g. Daily

3. **During the past year, how many different women did you have sexual contact with?** (circle one answer)
   a. None
   b. 1
   c. 2
   d. 3–5
   e. 6–10
   f. 11–49
   g. 50–99
   h. 100 or more

4. **During the past year, on average, how often did you have sexual contact with a woman?** (circle one answer)
   a. Never
   b. Less than one time per month
   c. 1–3 times per month
   d. 1 time per week
   e. 2–3 times per week
   f. 4–6 times per week
   g. Daily

III. Sexual Identity

The following two questions are asked to assess your sexual identity.

1a. **I consider myself . . .** (circle one answer)
   a. Not at all LGBTQ
   b. Slightly LGBTQ
   c. Mildly LGBTQ
   d. Moderately LGBTQ
   e. Significantly LGBTQ
   f. Very LGBTQ
   g. Extremely LGBTQ

1b. **I consider myself . . .** (circle one answer)
   a. Not at all attracted to someone of the same sex
   b. Slightly attracted to someone of the same sex
   c. Mildly attracted to someone of the same sex
   d. Moderately attracted to someone of the same sex
   e. Significantly attracted to someone of the same sex
   f. Very attracted to someone of the same sex
   g. Extremely attracted to someone of the same sex

2a. **I consider myself . . .** (circle one answer)
   a. Not at all heterosexual
   b. Slightly heterosexual
   c. Mildly heterosexual
   d. Moderately heterosexual
   e. Significantly heterosexual
   f. Very heterosexual
   g. Extremely heterosexual

2b. **I consider myself . . .** (circle one answer)
   a. Not at all attracted to someone of the other sex
   b. Slightly attracted to someone of the other sex
   c. Mildly attracted to someone of the other sex
   d. Moderately attracted to someone of the other sex
   e. Significantly attracted to someone of the other sex
   f. Very attracted to someone of the other sex
   g. Extremely attracted to someone of the other sex

Citation: Sell, R. L. (1996). The Sell Assessment of Sexual Orientation: Background and scoring. *Journal of Gay, Lesbian, & Bisexual Identity, 1*(4), 295–310.

Behavioral Activation for Depression Scale–Short Form (BADS-SF)

NAME: _____ DATE: _____

Please read each statement carefully and then circle the number which best describes how much the statement was true for you DURING THE PAST WEEK, INCLUDING TODAY.

	Not at All	A Little		A Lot		Completely	AC	AV	T
1. There were certain things I needed to do that I didn't do.	[0]	[1]	[2]	[3]	[4]	[5]	[6]	–		R
2. I am content with the amount and types of things I did.	[0]	[1]	[2]	[3]	[4]	[5]	[6]	–		–
3. I engaged in many different activities.	[0]	[1]	[2]	[3]	[4]	[5]	[6]	–		–
4. I made good decisions about what type of activities and/or situations I put myself in.	[0]	[1]	[2]	[3]	[4]	[5]	[6]	–		–
5. I was an active person and accomplished the goals I set out to do.	[0]	[1]	[2]	[3]	[4]	[5]	[6]	–		–
6. Most of what I did was to escape from or avoid something unpleasant.	[0]	[1]	[2]	[3]	[4]	[5]	[6]		–	R
7. I spent a long time thinking over and over about my problems.	[0]	[1]	[2]	[3]	[4]	[5]	[6]		–	R
8. I engaged in activities that would distract me from feeling bad.	[0]	[1]	[2]	[3]	[4]	[5]	[6]		–	R
9. I did things that were enjoyable.	[0]	[1]	[2]	[3]	[4]	[5]	[6]	–		–

Citation: Kanter, J. W., Mulick, P. S., Busch, A. M., Berlin, K. S., & Martell, C. R. (2012). Behavioral Activation for Depression Scale (BADS) (Long and Short Form). Measurement Instrument Database for the Social Science. Retrieved from http://www.midss.ie

APPENDIX C

Session Notes

C0: Consultation

Patient Name:	Date & Time:
Therapist:	Type of Session & Fee:

1. Brief description of presenting problem (i.e., OCD, possible comorbid depression):

_____
_____
_____
_____
_____

2. Administer self-report scales (e.g., DOCS, SORT, etc.)

Instrument	Date	Score

3. Review and describe:
   - ❑ Handouts on *OC Symptom Dimensions, Unacceptable/Taboo Thoughts*, and the *OCD Cycle*
   - ❑ *Compulsion & Avoidance Monitoring Log*
   - ❑ Rationale for treatment and treatment format (Ex/RP)

4. Initial impression(s) according to relevant DSM-5 diagnostic criteria:

_____
_____
_____
_____
_____

5. Plan/recommendation:

_____
_____
_____
_____

6. Assign homework:
    - ❏ Provide the *Family Accommodations Scale* to client to give to any family members involved in rituals (if applicable)
    - ❏ Provide handouts on *OCD Symptom Dimensions* and *the OCD Cycle*

Therapist's signature: _____

C1: Assessment & Diagnosis

Patient Name:	Date & Time:
Therapist:	Type of Session & Fee:

1. Measurements Summary (reference self-report measures)

Instrument	Date	Score	Instrument	Score	Date	Instrument	Date	Score

2. Background Information:

DOB:	Age:
Sex: M / F / Other	Race/Ethnicity:
Marital status:	Children (ages):

Presenting problem (description; new or recurrent; onset; triggers/causes):
_____
_____
_____
_____
_____
_____
_____
_____

Current vocational and/or academic functioning:

Education:	Employment:

_____
_____
_____
_____
_____
_____
_____

Other current problems (i.e., in the past month; e.g., depression, anxiety, compulsion, drug/alcohol use; description; new or recurrent; onset; triggers/causes):

Current treatment status (past month: purpose/for what symptoms; treatment setting, nature, duration, and outcome etc.; current medications):

Treatment history (date/age; purpose/for what symptoms; treatment setting, nature, duration, and outcome etc.):

Family psychiatric history:

3. Social Functioning

Previous and current relationship with parents:
_____
_____
_____
_____
_____

Previous and current relationship with siblings (if applicable):
_____
_____
_____
_____
_____

Previous and current relationships with friends, co-workers, etc.:
_____
_____
_____
_____
_____

Dating/sexual history/current sexual functioning:
_____
_____
_____
_____
_____

Previous and current relationship with spouse/partner (if applicable):
_____
_____
_____
_____
_____

4. Most Likely DSM-5 Diagnoses with diagnostic code(s) and reasons (reference structured interview, e.g. MINI):

_____
_____
_____
_____
_____
_____

DSM-5 diagnoses to be ruled out (and reasons):

_____
_____
_____
_____
_____
_____

5. Plan/Recommendation:

_____
_____
_____
_____
_____
_____
_____

6. Review (if relevant):

- ❏ Rationale for treatment
- ❏ Treatment plan and format (i.e., Ex/RP, Prolonged Exposure, Behavioral Activation, etc.)
- ❏ Other: _____
- ❏ Other: _____

7. Homework (if client has OCD):

- ❏ Self-monitoring of rituals (give *Compulsion & Avoidance Monitoring Log* and *Instructions*)
- ❏ Provide *Understanding S-OCD* handout
- ❏ Other: _____
- ❏ Other: _____

Therapist's signature: _____

C2: Case Formulation Part 1

Client Name:	Date & Time:
Therapist:	Type of Session & Fee:

Primary DSM-5 Diagnosis and Code:

Instrument	Date	Score	Instrument	Date	Score	Instrument	Date	Score

1. Review:
   - ❐ Handouts on *OCD Symptom Dimensions*, the *OCD Cycle*, if needed
   - ❐ Review *Family Accommodations Scale*
   - ❐ Review *Compulsion & Avoidances Log*

2. Administer YBOCS-II and record of client responses based on the Y-BOCS-II.

Significant reported obsessions [for each, record: (a) time occupied; (b) distress; (c) functional interference; (d) degree of control; (e) length of average obsession-free interval; and (f) insight]:

_____
_____
_____
_____
_____
_____

Significant reported compulsions [record: (a) resistance against compulsion; (b) degree of control; (c) distress if compulsion is not performed; (d) time occupied; (e) functional interference; and (f) insight]:

_____
_____
_____
_____
_____
_____

Significant reported avoidant behaviors [for each, record: (a) distress if unavoidable; (b) time occupied; (c) functional interference; and (d) insight]:

_____
_____
_____
_____
_____
_____
_____

Note judgment of severity and include YBOCS-II severity scale score:

_____
_____
_____
_____
_____
_____
_____

3. Provide psychoeducation about OCD, sexual issues, and other areas as needed:

_____
_____
_____
_____

4. Review rationale for treatment and format:

_____
_____
_____
_____

5. **Homework:**
   ❑ *Compulsion & Avoidances Log* form
   ❑ Read *OCD and Unacceptable Thoughts* handout

Therapist's signature: _____

C3: Case Formulation Part 2

Patient Name:	Date & Time:
Therapist:	Type of Session & Fee:

Primary DSM-5 Diagnosis and Code:

1. **Review:**
   - ❒ Describe plan for session
   - ❒ Review homework: handout on *Understanding S-OCD*
   - ❒ Review the *Compulsion & Avoidance Monitoring Log*

2. **Prepare for treatment:**
   - ❒ Provide psychoeducation about OCD
   - ❒ Describe treatment plan

3. **Case formulation:** Identify relationship between triggers, obsessions, feared outcomes, compulsions, and avoidances (use attached forms as necessary)

   _____
   _____
   _____
   _____
   _____
   _____

4. **Plan/recommendation:**

   _____
   _____
   _____
   _____
   _____
   _____

5. **Homework:**
   - ❒ Self-monitoring of compulsions (provide *Compulsion & Avoidance Monitoring Logs*)
   - ❒ Read handout *OCD and Unacceptable Thoughts*

Therapist's signature: _____

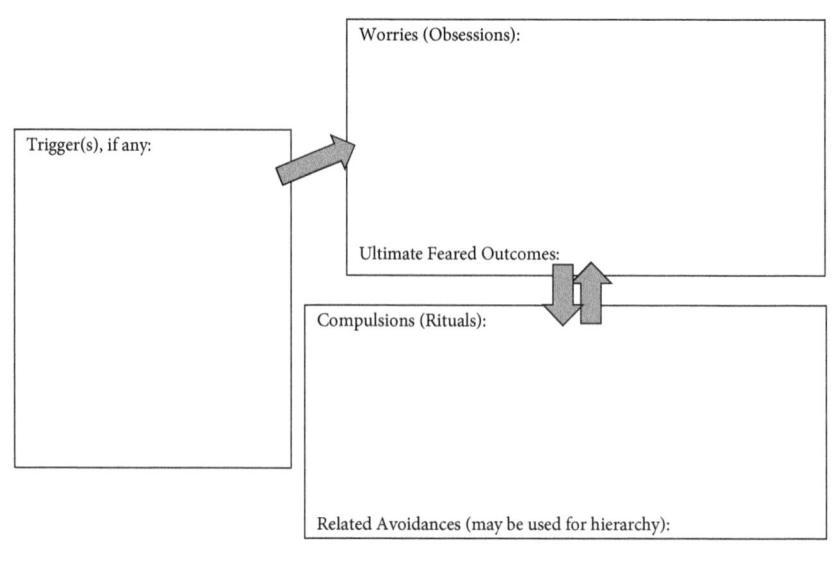

408 APPENDIX C. SESSION NOTES

Trigger(s), if any:

Worries (Obsessions):

Ultimate Feared Outcomes:

Compulsions (Rituals):

Related Avoidances (may be used for hierarchy):

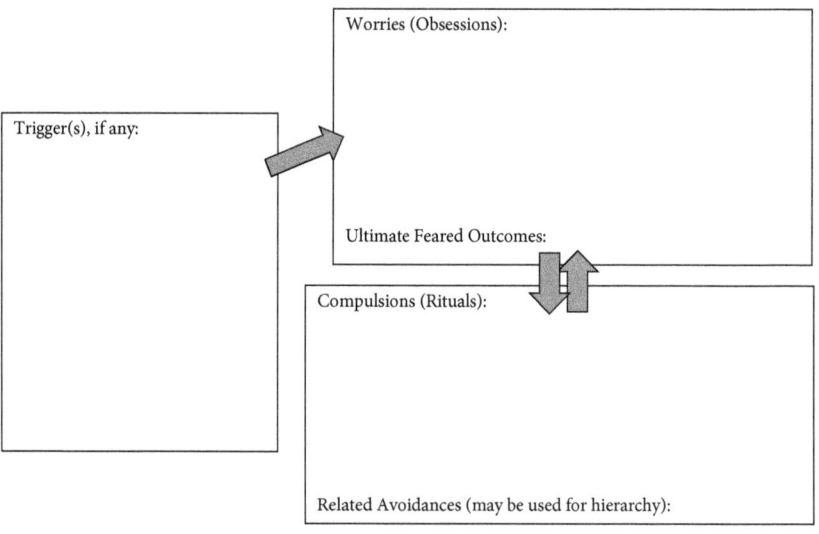

Trigger(s), if any:

Worries (Obsessions):

Ultimate Feared Outcomes:

Compulsions (Rituals):

Related Avoidances (may be used for hierarchy):

C4: Treatment Planning

Patient Name:	Date & Time:
Therapist:	Type of Session & Fee:

Primary DSM-5 Diagnosis and Code:

Instrument	Date	Score	Date	Score	Date	Score	Date	Score

1. Review:
    - ☐ *Compulsion & Avoidances Monitoring Log*
    - ☐ Handout on *OCD and Unacceptable Thoughts*
    - ☐ Rationale for treatment and treatment format (Ex/RP)

2. Comments about client's self-monitoring:
   _____
   _____
   _____
   _____

3. Prepare for treatment:
    - ☐ Introduce the Subjective Units of Discomfort Scale (SUDS) and related handout
    - ☐ Create a SUDS scale with the client (list anchors below)

0:	
25:	
50:	
100:	

4. Generate rank-ordered hierarchy of situations with client (next page).

5. **Plan:**

_____
_____
_____
_____

6. **Homework:**
   - ❒ Provide *Compulsion & Avoidances Monitoring Logs*
   - ❒ Read *Understanding CBT for OCD* handout

Therapist's signature: _____

| Patient Name: | Date & Time: |

Exposure Hierarchy

Rank	Situation	SUDs

C5: Psychological Progress Note with Exposure

Client Name:	Date & Time:
Therapist(s):	Sessions Type & Fee:

Primary DSM-5 Diagnosis and Code:

Review of Homework:
___
___

Assessment & Progress:
___
___

Intervention(s):
___
___
___
___

In-session exposures can be skipped once client has successfully completed all items on hierarchy. (*Note: Therapists should model all exposures before client attempts them.*)

Exposure:	Start	5 min	10 min	15 min	20 min	25 min	30 min	35 min	40 min	50 min	60 min
Time											
SUDS (0-100)											

Recommendations/Plan:
___
___

Homework Assigned: (include *Exposure Homework Forms* and *Compulsion & Avoidance Log*, as needed)
___
___
___

Therapist's signature: ___

APPENDIX C. SESSION NOTES 413

C6: Final Session Form for OCD

Client Name:	Date & Time:
Therapist(s):	Sessions Type & Fee:

Primary DSM-5 Diagnosis and Code:

1. **Measurements Summary** (reference clinical interviews and self-report measures)

Instrument	Date (pre-treatment)	Score	Date (post-treatment)	Score
YBOCS-II Severity Scale				
DOCS (four scales)				
DOCS Sexually Intrusive Thoughts Scale				
Family Accommodations Scale				

2. **Review of Homework** (progress with self-directed exposures and adherence to Guidelines for Normal Behavior):

_____
_____
_____
_____

3. **Assessment & Progress:**

_____
_____
_____
_____

4. Relapse Prevention Plan:

_____
_____
_____
_____
_____

5. Follow-Up Plan (if no further regular meetings, schedule a three- to six-month check-in):

_____
_____
_____
_____

6. Review and provide:
   ❐ *Guidelines for Relapse Prevention* handout

Therapist's signature: _____

References

Abramowitz, J. S. (1996). Variants of exposure and response prevention in the treatment of obsessive-compulsive disorder: A meta-analysis. *Behavior Therapy, 27*(4), 583–600.

Abramowitz, J. S., Deacon, B. J., Olatunji, B. O., Wheaton, M. G., Berman, N. C., Losardo, D., . . . Hale, L. (2010). Assessment of obsessive-compulsive symptom dimensions: Development and evaluation of the dimensional obsessive-compulsive scale. *Psychological Assessment, 22*, 180–198.

Abramowitz, J. S., Franklin, M. E., Street, G. P., Kozak, M. J., & Foa, E. B. (2000). Effects of comorbid depression on response to treatment for obsessive-compulsive disorder. *Behavior Therapy, 31*(3), 517–528. doi:10.1016/S0005-7894(00)80028-3

Abramowitz, J. S., & Jacoby, R. J. (2014). Obsessive-compulsive disorder in the DSM-5, *Clinical Psychology: Science and Practice, 21*(3), 221–235.

Ahmed, M., Westra, H. A., & Stewart, S. H. (2008). A self-help handout for benzodiazepine discontinuation using cognitive behavioral therapy. *Cognitive and Behavioral Practice, 15*(3), 317–324. doi:10.1016/j.cbpra.2007.05.003

Aksaray, G., Yelken, B., Kaptanoglu, C., Oflu, S., & Özaltin, M. (2001). Sexuality in women with obsessive compulsive disorder. *Journal of Sex & Marital Therapy, 27*, 273–277.

Al-Zaben, F. N. (2011). suicidal obsessions in a patient with obsessive compulsive disorder: A case report. *Journal of King Abdulaziz University Medical Science, 19*(4), 121–127.

Albert, U., Maina, G., Forner, F., & Bogetto, F. (2004). DSM-IV obsessive-compulsive personality disorder: Prevalence in patients with anxiety disorders and in healthy comparison subjects. *Comprehensive Psychiatry, 45*(5), 325–332.

Alegría, M., Canino, G., Ríos, R., Vera, M., Calderón, J., Rusch, D., & Ortega, A. N. (2002). Inequalities in use of specialty mental health services among Latinos, African Americans, and non-Latino whites. *Psychiatric Services, 53*, 1547–1555.

Alonso, P., Menchón, J. M., Pifarré, J., Mataix-Cols, D., Torrres, L., Salgado, P., & Vallejo, J. (2001). Long-term follow-up and predictors of clinical outcome in obsessive-compulsive patients treated with serotonin reuptake inhibitors and behavioral therapy. *Journal of Clinical Psychiatry, 62*, 535–540.

Alonso, P., Segalàs, C., Real, E., Pertusa, A., Labad, J., Jiménez-Murcia, S., . . . Menchón, J. M. (2010). Suicide in patients treated for obsessive–compulsive disorder: A prospective follow-up study. *Journal of Affective Disorders, 124*(3), 300–308.

Alvidrez, J., Snowden, L. R., & Kaiser, D. M. (2008). The experience of stigma among Black mental health consumers. *Journal of Health Care for the Poor and Underserved, 19*, 874–893.

American Psychiatric Association. (2013). *Diagnostic and statistical manual of mental disorders* (5th ed.). Arlington, VA: American Psychiatric Association.

Amir, N., Freshman, M., & Foa, E. B. (2000). Family distress and involvement in relatives of obsessive-compulsive disorder patients. *Journal of Anxiety Disorders, 14*(3), 209–217.

Anderson, J. R. (1974). Retrieval of prepositional information from long-term memory. *Cognitive Psychology, 6*, 451–474.

Anderson, J. R. (1983). A spreading activation theory of memory. *Journal of Verbal Learning and Verbal Behavior, 22*, 261–295.

Anderson, J., & Bower, G. H. (1973). *Human associative memory*. Washington, DC: Winston.

Anderson, J. R., & Pirolli, P. L. (1984). Spread of activation. *Journal of Experimental Psychology: Learning, Memory, and Cognition, 10*, 791–798.

Arch, J. J., & Abramowitz, J. S. (2015). Exposure therapy for obsessive–compulsive disorder: An optimizing inhibitory learning approach. *Journal of Obsessive-Compulsive and Related Disorders, 6*, 174–182.

Arciniega, G. M., Anderson, T. C., Tovar-Blank, Z. G., & Tracey, T. J. G. (2008). Toward a fuller conception of machismo: Development of a traditional machismo and caballerismo scale. *Journal of Counseling Psychology, 55*, 19–33.

Armstrong, A. B., Morrison, K. L., & Twohig, M. P. (2013). A preliminary investigation of acceptance and commitment therapy for adolescent obsessive-compulsive disorder. *Journal of Cognitive Psychotherapy, 27*(2), 175–190.

Ayuso-Mateos, J. L. (2006, August 21). *Global burden of obsessive-compulsive disorder in the year 2000*. Global Program on Evidence for Health Policy (GPE) Global Burden of Disease 2000. Geneva, Switzerland: World Health Organization.

Bach, N., & Williams, M. T. (2013, March). Help! I'm married to OCD [Web log post]. *Psychology Today*. Retrieved from https://www.psychologytoday.com/blog/culturally-speaking/201303/help-i-m-married-ocd

Baer, L. (1994). Factor analysis of symptom subtypes of obsessive-compulsive disorder and their relation to personality and tic disorders. *Journal of Clinical Psychiatry, 55*, 18–23.

Ball, S. G., Baer, L., & Otto, M. W. (1996). Symptom subtypes of obsessive-compulsive disorder in behavioral treatment studies: A quantitative review. *Behaviour Research and Therapy, 34*(1), 47–51. doi:10.1016/0005-7967(95)00047-2

Barlow, D. H., Levitt, J. T., & Bufka, L. F. (1999). The dissemination of empirically supported treatments: A view to the future. *Behaviour Research and Therapy, 37*, 147–162.

Barney, J. Y., Field, C. E., Morrison, K. L., & Twohig, M. P. (2017). Treatment of pediatric obsessive compulsive disorder utilizing parent-facilitated acceptance and commitment therapy. *Psychology in the Schools, 54*(1), 88–100.

Beck, A. T. (1990). *Beck Anxiety Inventory*. San Antonio, TX: Psychological Corporation.

Beck, A. T., Steer, R. A., & Brown, G. K. (1996). *Beck depression inventory* (2nd ed.). San Antonio, TX: Psychological Corporation.

Beck, A. T., Ward, C. H., Mendelson, M., Mock, J., & Erbaugh, J. (1961). An inventory for measuring depression. *Archives of General Psychiatry, 4*, 561–571.

Belus, J. M., Baucom, D. H., & Abramowitz, J. S. (2014). The effect of a couple-based treatment for OCD on intimate partners. *Journal of Behavior Therapy and Experimental Psychiatry, 45*(4), 484–488.

Besiroglu, L., Cilli, A. S., & Askin, R. (2004). The predictors of healthcare seeking behavior in obsessive-compulsive disorder. *Comprehensive Psychiatry, 45*, 99–108.

Bhattacharyya, S., Fusar-Poli, P., Borgwardt, S., Martin-Santos, R., Nosarti, C., O'Carroll, C., . . . McGuire, P. (2009). Modulation of mediotemporal and ventrostriatal function in humans by Δ9-tetrahydrocannabinol: A neural basis for the effects of cannabis sativa on learning and psychosis. *Archives of General Psychiatry, 66*(4), 442–451. doi:10.1001/archgenpsychiatry.2009.17

Blanco, C., Olfson, M., Stein, D., Simpson, H. Gameroff, M., & Narrow, W. (2006). Treatment of obsessive compulsive disorder by US psychiatrists. *Journal of Clinical Psychiatry, 67*(6), 946–951.

Bluett, E. J., Homan, K. J., Morrison, K. L., Levin, M. E., & Twohig, M. P. (2014). Acceptance and commitment therapy for anxiety and OCD spectrum disorders: An empirical review. *Journal of Anxiety Disorders, 28*(6), 612–624.

Boeding, S. E., Paprocki, C. M., Baucom, D. H., Abramowitz, J. S., Wheaton, M. G., Frabricant, L. E., et al. (2013). Let me check that for you: symptom accommodation in romantic partners of adults with obsessive-compulsive disorder. *Behaviour Research and Therapy, 51*, 316–322.

Boschen, M. J., & Vuksanovic, D. (2007). Deteriorating memory confidence, responsibility perceptions and repeated checking: Comparisons in OCD and control samples. *Behaviour Research and Therapy, 45*(9), 2098–2109.

Bradford, A., & Meston, C. M. (2006). The impact of anxiety on sexual arousal in women. *Behaviour Research and Therapy, 44* (8), 1067–1077.

Bruce, S. L., Ching, T., & Williams, M. T. (2018). Pedophilia-themed obsessive compulsive disorder: Assessment, differential diagnosis, and treatment with exposure and response prevention. *Archives of Sexual Behavior, 47*(2), 389–402. doi:10.1007/s10508-017-1031-4

Bystritsky, A. (2004). Pharmacological treatments for obsessive-compulsive disorder. *Essential Psychopharmacology, 5*(4), 251–272.

Calamari, J. E., Cohen, R. J., Rector, N. A., Szacun-Shimizu, K., Riemann, B. C., & Norberg, M. M. (2006). Dysfunctional belief-based obsessive-compulsive disorder subgroups. *Behaviour Research and Therapy, 44*(9), 1347–1360.

Calvocoressi, L., Lewis, B., Harris, M., Trufan, S. J., Goodman, W. K., McDougle, C. J., & Price, L. H. (1995). Family accommodation in obsessive-compulsive disorder. *The American Journal of Psychiatry, 152*(3), 441–443.

Cathey, A., & Wetterneck, C. T. (2013). Stigma and disclosure of intrusive thoughts about sexual themes. *Journal of Obsessive Compulsive & Related Disorders, 2*, 439–444.

Chadwick, B., Miller, M. L., & Hurd, Y. L. (2013). Cannabis use during adolescent development: Susceptibility to psychiatric illness. *Frontiers in Psychiatry, 4*, art. 129. doi:10.3389/fpsyt.2013.00129

Chase, T. E., Wetterneck, C. T., Bartsch, R., Leonard, R. C., & Riemann, B. C. (2015). Investigating treatment outcomes across obsessive compulsive symptoms in a clinical sample. *Cognitive Behaviour Therapy*, 26, 1–12.

Cheon, B. K., & Chiao, J. Y. (2012). Cultural variation in implicit mental illness stigma. *Journal of Cross-Cultural Psychology*, 43, 1058–1062.

Ching, T. H. W., Goh, W. D., & Tan, G. (2015). Exploring dimensionality in the contamination-relevant semantic network with simulated obsessions and association splitting. *Journal of Obsessive-Compulsive and Related Disorders*, 6, 39–48.

Ching, T. H. W., & Williams, M. T. (2018). Association splitting of the sexual orientation-OCD-relevant semantic network. *Cognitive Behaviour Therapy*, 47 (3), 229–245. doi:10.1080/16506073.2017.1343380

Chowdhury, A. N., Mukherjee, H., Ghosh, K., & Chowdhury, S. (2003). Puppy pregnancy in humans: A culture-bound disorder in rural West Bengal, India. *International Journal of Social Psychiatry*, 49(1), 35–42.

Clark, D. A. (2004). *Cognitive-Behavioral Therapy for OCD*. New York: Guilford Press.

Coles, M. E., & Coleman, S. L. (2010). Barriers to treatment seeking for anxiety disorders: Initial data on the role of mental health literacy. *Depression and Anxiety*, 27, 63–71. doi:10.1002/da.20620

Collins, A. M., & Loftus, E. F. (1975). A spreading-activation theory of semantic processing. *Psychological Review*, 82, 407–428.

Craske, M. G., Treanor, M., Conway, C. C., Zbozinek, T., & Vervliet, B. (2014). Maximizing exposure therapy: An inhibitory learning approach. *Behaviour Research and Therapy*, 58, 10–23.

Cromer, K. R., Schmidt, N. B., & Murphy, D. L. (2007). An investigation of traumatic life events and obsessive-compulsive disorder. *Behaviour Research and Therapy*, 45, 1683–1691.

David Mataix-Cols, Scott L. Rauch, Peter A. Manzo, Michael A. Jenike & Lee Baer (1999). Use of Factor-Analyzed Symptom Dimensions to Predict Outcome With Serotonin Reuptake Inhibitors and Placebo in the Treatment of Obsessive- Compulsive Disorder. *American Journal of Psychiatry*, 156(9), 1409–1416.

Davis, D. M., Steever, A. M., Terwilliger, J. M., & Williams, M. T. (2012). The relationship between the culture-bound syndrome koro and obsessive-compulsive disorder. In G. R. Hayes & M. H. Bryant (Eds.), *Psychology of culture* (pp. 213–221). Hauppauge, NY: Nova Science.

de la Cruz, L. F., Barrow, F., Bolhuis, K., Krebs, G., Volz, C., Nakatani, E., . . . Mataix-Cols, D. (2013). Sexual obsessions in pediatric obsessive-compulsive disorder: Clinical characteristics and treatment outcomes. *Depression and Anxiety*, 30(8), 732–740. doi:10.1002/da.22097

de la Cruz L. F., Rydell M., Runeson B., Onofrio, M. D., Brander, G., Ruck, C., . . . Mataix-Cols, D. (2016). Suicide in obsessive–compulsive disorder: A population-based study of 36,788 Swedish patients. *Molecular Psychiatry*, 22, 1626–1632. doi:10.1038/mp.2016.115

Dell'Osso, L., Casu, G., Carlini, M., Conversano, C., Gremigni, P., & Carmassi, C. (2012). Sexual obsessions and suicidal behaviors in patients with mood disorders, panic disorders and schizophrenia. *Annals of General Psychiatry*, 11(1), 27.

Dimidjian, S., Barrera, M., Jr., Martell, C., Muñoz, R. F., & Lewinsohn, P. M. (2011). The origins and current status of behavioral activation treatments for depression. *Annual Review of Clinical Psychology, 7*, 1–38.

Doron, G., Derby, D., Szepsenwol, O., Nahaloni, E., & Moulding, R. (2016). Relationship obsessive-compulsive disorder: Interference, symptoms, and maladaptive Beliefs. *Frontiers in Psychiatry, 7*, art. 58.

Doron, G., Mizrahi, M., Szepsenwol, O., & Derby, D. (2014). Right or flawed: Relationship obsessions and sexual satisfaction. *Journal of Sexual Medicine, 11*(9), 2218–2224.

Eisen, J. L., Coles, M. E., Shea, M. T., Pagano, M. E., Stout, R. L., Yen, S., . . . Rasmussen, S. A. (2006). Clarifying the convergence between obsessive-compulsive personality disorder criteria and obsessive-compulsive disorder. *Journal of Personality Disorders, 20*, 294–305.

Fals-Stewart, W., & Schafer, J. (1992). The treatment of substance abusers diagnosed with obsessive-compulsive disorder: An outcome study. *Journal of Substance Abuse Treatment, 9*(4), 365–370.

First, M. B., Spitzer, R. L., Gibbon, M., & Williams, J. B. W. (2002). *Structured Clinical Interview for DSM-IV-TR Axis I Disorders - Research Edition*. New York State Psychiatric Institute, Biometrics department, New York.

Foa, E. B., Huppert, J. D., Leiberg, S., Langner, R., Kichic, R., Hajcak, G., & Salkovskis, P. M. (2002). The obsessive-compulsive inventory: Development and validation of a short version. *Psychological Assessment, 14*, 485–496.

Foa, E. B., Kozak, M. J., Goodman, W. K., Hollander, E., Jenike, M. A., & Rasmussen, S. A. (1995). DSM-IV Field Trial: Obsessive compulsive disorder. *American Journal of Psychiatry, 152*, 90–96.

Foa, E. B., Liebowitz, M. R., Kozak, M. J., Davies, S., Campeas, R., Franklin, M. E., . . . Tu, X. (2005). Randomized, placebo-controlled trial of exposure and ritual prevention, clomipramine, and their combination in the treatment of obsessive-compulsive disorder. *The American Journal Of Psychiatry, 162*(1), 151–161. doi:10.1176/appi.ajp.162.1.151

Foa, E. B., Yadin, E., & Lichner, T. K. (2012). *Exposure and response (ritual) prevention for obsessive-compulsive disorder: Therapist guide* (2nd ed.). New York, NY: Oxford University Press.

Fogel, J. (2003). An epidemiological perspective of obsessive-compulsive disorder in children and adolescents. *Canadian Child and Adolescent Psychiatry Review, 12*(2), 33–36.

Fontenelle, L. F., Cocchi, L., Harrison, B. J., Shavitt, R. G., do Rosário, M. C., Ferrão, Y. A., . . . Torres, A. R. (2012). Towards a post-traumatic subtype of obsessive-compulsive disorder. *Journal of Anxiety Disorders, 26*(2), 377–383. doi:10.1016/j.janxdis.2011.12.001

Franklin, M. E., & Foa, E. B. (2011). Treatment of obsessive compulsive disorder. *Annual Review of Clinical Psychology, 7*, 229–243.

Franklin, M. E., & Foa, E. B. (2014). Obsessive-compulsive disorder. In D. H. Barlow's *Clinical handbook of psychological disorders* (pp. 155–205). New York, NY: Guilford.

Fullana, M. A., Mataix-Cols, D., Caspi, A., Harrington, H., Grisham, J. R., Moffitt, T. E., & Poulton, R. (2009). Obsessions and compulsions in the community: Prevalence, interference, help-seeking, developmental stability, and co-occurring psychiatric conditions. *American Journal of Psychiatry, 166*, 329–336.

Garyfallos, G., Katsigiannopoulos, K., Adamopoulou, A., Papazisis, G., Karastergiou, A., & Bozikas, V. P. (2010). Comorbidity of obsessive-compulsive disorder with obsessive-compulsive personality disorder: Does it imply a specific subtype of obsessive-compulsive disorder? *Psychiatry Research, 177*(1-2), 156–160.

Gautame, P., & Bhatia, M. S. (2015). Obsessive-compulsive disorder with intellectual disability: A diagnostic and therapeutic challenge. *Journal of Clinical and Diagnostic Research, 9* (9), VD01–VD02.

Gillihan, S. J., Williams, M. T., Malcoun, E., Yadin, E., & Foa, E. B. (2012). Common pitfalls in exposure and ritual prevention (Ex/RP) for obsessive-compulsive disorder. *Journal of Obsessive-Compulsive & Related Disorders, 1*(4), 251–257.

Glazier, K., Calixte, R., Rothschild, R., & Pinto, A. (2013). High rates of OCD symptom misidentification by mental health professionals. *Annals of Clinical Psychiatry, 25,* 201–209.

Glazier, K., Swing, M., & McGinn, L. (2015). Half of obsessive-compulsive disorder cases misdiagnosed: Vignette-based survey of primary care physicians. *Journal of Clinical Psychiatry, 76,* e761–e767.

Glazier, K., Wetterneck, C. T., Singh, S., & Williams, M. T. (2015). Stigma and shame as barriers to treatment in obsessive-compulsive and related disorders. *Journal of Depression and Anxiety, 4*(3), 191. doi:10.4191/2167-1044.1000191

Gomes, J. B., Van Noppen, B., Pato, M., Braga, D. T., Meyer, E., Bortoncello, C. F., & Cordioli, A. V. (2014). Patient and family factors associated with family accommodation in obsessive–compulsive disorder. *Psychiatry and Clinical Neurosciences, 68*(8), 621–630.

Goodman, W. K., Price, L. H., Rasmussen, S. A., Mazure, C., Delgado, P., Heninger, G. R., & Charney, D. S. (1989). The Yale–Brown Obsessive Compulsive Scale. II. Validity. *Archives of General Psychiatry, 46,* 1012–1016.

Goodwin, R., Koenen, K. C., Hellman, F., Guardino, M., & Struening, E. (2002). Helpseeking and access to mental health treatment for obsessive-compulsive disorder. *Acta Psychiatrica Scandinavica, 106*(2), 143–149.

Gordon, W. M. (2002). Sexual obsessions and OCD. *Sexual and Relationship Therapy, 17*(4), 343–354.

Grabe, H. J., Goldschmidt, F., Lehmkuhl, L., Gänsicke, M., Spitzer, C., & Freyberger, H. J. (1999). Dissociative symptoms in patients with obsessive-compulsive disorder. *Psychopathology, 32,* 319–324.

Graham, C. A., Bancroft, J., Doll, H. A., Greco, T., & Tanner, A. (2007). Does oral contraceptive-induced reduction in free testosterone adversely affect the sexuality or mood of women? *Psychoneuroendocrinology, 32,* 246–255.

Grant, J. E., Pinto, A., Gunnip, B., Mancebo, M. C., Eisen, J. L., & Rasmussen, S. A. (2006). Sexual obsessions and clinical correlates in adults with obsessive-compulsive disorder. *Comprehensive Psychiatry, 47,* 325–329.

Greenberg, W., Blenenfield, D., Memon, M., & Talavera, F. (2014, April). Obsessive compulsive disorder medication. *Medscape.* Retrieved from http://emedicine.medscape.com/article/1934139-medication

Grisham, J. R., Anderson, T. M., & Sachdev, P. S. (2008). Genetic and environmental influences on obsessive-compulsive disorder. *European Archives of Psychiatry and Clinical Neuroscience, 258,* 107–116.

Hampton, N., & Sharp, S. E. (2014). Shame-focused attitudes toward mental health problems: The role of gender and culture. *Rehabilitation Counseling Bulletin, 57,* 170–181.

Hand, I. (1991). Aggression and social deficits in psychological disorders. In W. Pöldinger (Ed.), *Aggression and autoaggression* (pp. 27–45). Berlin, Germany: Springer.

Hart, J., & Fountain, K. (2008, March). *Using chromatic drawings in imaginal exposure therapy for harm obsessions.* Presentation to the Anxiety Rounds at the 28th Annual Anxiety Disorders Association of America, Savannah, GA.

Hasler, G., LaSalle-Ricci, V. H., Ronquillo, J. G., Crawley, S. A., Cochran, L. W., Kazuba, D., . . . Murphy, D. L. (2005). Obsessive–compulsive disorder symptom dimensions show specific relationships to psychiatric comorbidity. *Psychiatry Research, 135,* 121–132.

Hayes, S. C. (2004). Acceptance and commitment therapy, relational frame theory, and the third wave of behavioral and cognitive therapies. *Behavior Therapy, 35,* 639–665.

Hayes, S. C., Levin, M. E., Plumb-Vilardaga, J., Villatte, J. L., & Pistorello, J. (2013). Acceptance and commitment therapy and contextual behavioral science: Examining the progress of a distinctive model of behavioral and cognitive therapy. *Behavior Therapy, 44,* 180–198.

Hayes, S. C., Luoma, J. B., Bond, F. W., Masuda, A., & Lillis, J. (2006). Acceptance and commitment therapy: Model, processes and outcomes. *Behaviour Research and Therapy, 44,* 1–25.

Hayes, S. C., Pistorello, J., & Levin, M. E. (2012). Acceptance and commitment therapy as a unified model of behavior change. *The Counseling Psychologist, 40*(7), 976–1002. doi:10.1177/0011000012460836

Heyman, I., Mataix-Cols, D., & Fineberg, N. A. (2006). Obsessive-compulsive disorder. *BMJ, 333,* 424–429.

Himle, J. A., Muroff, J. R., Taylor, R. J., Baser, R. E., Abelson, J. M., Hanna, G. L., . . . Jackson, J. S. (2008). Obsessive-compulsive disorder among African Americans and Blacks of Caribbean descent: Results from the national survey of American life. *Depression and Anxiety, 25,* 993–1005.

Himle, J. A., Taylor, R. J., & Chatters, L. M. (2012). Religious involvement and obsessive compulsive disorder among African Americans and Black Caribbeans. *Journal of Anxiety Disorders, 26*(4), 502–510. doi:10.1016/j.janxdis.2012.02.003

Hiss, H., Foa, E. B., & Kozak, M. J. (1994). Relapse prevention program for treatment of obsessive-compulsive disorder. *Journal of Consulting and Clinical Psychology, 62*(4), 801–808. doi:10.1037/0022-006X.62.4.801

Hodgson, R. J., & Rachman, S. (1977). Obsessional-compulsive complaints. *Behaviour Research and Therapy, 15,* 389–395.

Hottenrott, B., Jelinek, L., Kellner, M., & Moritz, S. (2011). Association splitting as an additional intervention for patients with obsessive-compulsive disorder: A case description. *Verhaltenstherapie, 21*, 109–115.

Huppert, J. D., Siev, J., & Kushner, E. S. (2007). When religion and obsessive-compulsive disorder collide: Treating scrupulosity in ultra-Orthodox Jews. *Journal of Clinical Psychology, 63*(10), 925–941. doi:10.1002/jclp.20404

Jacoby, R. J., & Abramowitz, J. S. (2016). Inhibitory learning approaches to exposure therapy: A critical review and translation to obsessive-compulsive disorder. *Clinical Psychology Review, 49*, 28–40.

Jacoby, R. J., Leonard, R. C., Riemann, B. C., & Abramowitz, J. S. (2016). Self-punishment as a maladaptive thought control strategy mediates the relationship between beliefs about thoughts and repugnant obsessions. *Cognitive Therapy and Research, 40*(2), 179–187.

Jelinek, L., Hauschildt, M., Hottenrott, B., Kellner, M., & Moritz, S. (2014). Further evidence for biased semantic networks in obsessive-compulsive disorder (OCD): When knives are no longer associated with buttering bread but only with stabbing people. *Journal of Behavior Therapy and Experimental Psychiatry, 45*, 427–434.

Jelinek, L., Hottenrott, B., & Moritz, S. (2009). When cancer is associated with illness but no longer with animal or zodiac sign: Investigation of biased semantic networks in obsessive-compulsive disorder (OCD). *Journal of Anxiety Disorders, 23*, 1031–1036.

Kanter, J. W., Mulick, P. S., Busch, A. M., Berlin, K. S., & Martell, C. R. (2012). *Behavioral Activation for Depression Scale (BADS)* (Long and short form). Measurement Instrument Database for the Social Science. Retrieved from www.midss.ie

Kashdan, T. B., & Rottenberg, J. (2010). Psychological flexibility as a fundamental aspect of health. *Clinical Psychology Review, 30*(7), 865–878. doi:10.1016/j.cpr.2010.03.001

Kassam, A., Glozier, N., Leese, M., Henderson, C., & Thornicroft, G. (2010). Development and responsiveness of a scale to measure clinician's attitudes to people with mental illness (medical student version). *Acta Psychiatrica Scandinavica, 122*, 153–161.

Kellner, M. (2010). Drug treatment of obsessive-compulsive disorder. *Dialogues Clin Neuroscience, 12*(2), 187–197. PMID: 20623923.

Knauft, B. (2010). Spirits, sex, and celebration. In M. Ryan (Ed.), *The Gebusi: Lives transformed in a rainforest world* (pp. 66–77). New York, NY: McGraw Hill.

Koran, L. M., Hanna, G. L., Hollander, E., Nestadt, G., & Simpson H. B. (2007). Practice guideline for the treatment of patients with obsessive-compulsive disorder. *American Journal of Psychiatry, 164* (7 Suppl), 5–53.

Koran, L., & Simpson, H. B. (2013). *Guideline watch (2013): Practice guidelines for the treatment of obsessive-compulsive disorder.* Retrieved from http://psychiatryonline.org

Koran, L. M., Thienemann, M. L., & Davenport, R. (1996). Quality of life for patients with obsessive-compulsive disorder. *American Journal of Psychiatry, 153*(6), 783–788.

Kouyoumdjian, H., Zamboanga, B. L., & Hansen, D. J. (2003). Barriers to community mental health services for Latinos: Treatment considerations. *Clinical Psychology: Science and Practice, 10*, 394–422.

Kulz, A. K., Hassenpflug, K., Riemann, D., Linster, H. W., Dornberg, M., & Voderholzer, U. (2009). Psychotherapeutic care in OCD outpatients: Results from an anonymous therapist survey. *Psychotherapy and Psychosomatics, 59*, 1–8.

Lang, R. A., & Frenzel, R. R. (1988). How sex offenders lure children. *Annals of Sex Research, 1*(2), 303–317. doi:10.1007/BF00852802

Larsen, K. E., Schwartz, S. A., Whiteside, S. P., Khandker, M., Moore, K. M., & Abramowitz, J. S. (2006). Thought control strategies used by parents reporting postpartum obsessions. *Journal of Cognitive Psychotherapy: An International Quarterly, 20*, 435–445.

Lauber, C., Nordt, C., Braunschweig, C., & Rossler, W. (2006). Do mental health professionals stigmatize their clients? *Acta Psychiatrica Scandinavica, 113*(429), 51–59.

Lebowitz, E. R., Omer, H., Hermes, H., & Scahill, L. (2014). Parent training for childhood anxiety disorders: The SPACE program. *Cognitive and Behavioral Practice, 21*(4), 456–469.

Leckman, J. F., Grice, D. E., Barr, L. C., de Vries, A., Martin, C., Cohen, D. J., . . . Rasmussen, S. A. (1995). Tic-related vs. non-tic related obsessive compulsive disorder. *Anxiety, 1*, 208–221.

Lee, E., Steinberg, D., Phillips, L., Hart, J., Smith, A., & Wetterneck, C. (2015). Examining the effects of accommodation and caregiver burden on relationship satisfaction in caregivers of individuals with OCD. *Bulletin of the Menninger Clinic, 79*(1), 1–13.

Leonard, R., & Riemann, B. (2012). The co-occurrence of obsessions and compulsions in OCD. *Journal of Obsessive- Compulsive and Related Disorders, 1*(3), 211–215.

Leong, F. T., Kim, H. H., & Gupta, A. (2011). Attitudes toward professional counseling among Asian-American college students: Acculturation, conceptions of mental illness, and loss of face. *Asian American Journal of Psychology, 2*, 140–153.

Levin, M. E., Hildebrandt, M. J., Lillis, J., & Hayes, S. C. (2012). The Impact of treatment components suggested by the psychological flexibility model: A meta-analysis of laboratory-based component studies. *Behavior Therapy, 43*(4), 741–756.

Maina, G., Saracco, P., & Albert, U. (2006). Family-focused treatments for obsessive-compulsive disorder. *Clinical Neuropsychiatry, 3*(6), 382–390.

Mancebo, M. C., Grant, J. E., Pinto, A., Eisen, J. L., & Rasmussen, S. A. (2009). Substance use disorders in an obsessive compulsive disorder clinical sample. *Journal of Anxiety Disorders, 23*(4), 429–435.

Marques, L., LeBlanc, N. J., Weingarden, H. M., Timpano, K. R., Jenike, M., & Wilhelm, S. (2010). Barriers to treatment and service utilization in an internet sample of individuals with obsessive-compulsive symptoms. *Depression and Anxiety, 27*, 470–475.

Martinez-Alvarez, R. (2015). Ablative surgery for obsessive-compulsive disorders. In B. Sun & A. De Salles (Eds.), *Neurosurgical treatments for psychiatric disorders* (pp. 105–112). New York, NY: Springer Science. doi:10.1007/978-94-017-9576-0_10

Masuda, A., Hayes, S. C., Sackett, C. F., & Twohig, M. P. (2004). Cognitive defusion and self-relevant negative thoughts: Examining the impact of a ninety year old technique. *Behaviour Research and Therapy, 42*, 477–485.

Mataix-Cols, D., & Marks, I. M. (2006). Self-help with minimal therapist contact for obsessive-compulsive disorder: A review. *European Psychiatry, 21*, 75–80.

McDermott, K. B., & Watson, J. M. (2001). The rise and fall of false recall: The impact of presentation duration. *Journal of Memory and Language, 45*, 160–176.

McKay, D. (1997). A maintenance program for obsessive-compulsive disorder using exposure with response prevention: 2-year follow-up. *Behaviour Research and Therapy, 35*(4), 367–369. doi:10.1016/S0005-7967(96)00105-2

McKay, D., Sookman, D., Neziroglu, F., Wilhelm, S., Stein, D. J., Kyrios, M., . . . Veale, D. (2015). Efficacy of cognitive-behavioral therapy for obsessive–compulsive disorder. *Psychiatry Research, 225*(3), 236–246.

McNamara, T., & Altarriba, J. (1988). Depth of spreading activation revisited: Semantic mediated priming occurs in lexical decisions. *Journal of Memory and Language, 27*, 545–559.

Mehta, M. (1990). A comparative study of family-based and patient-based behavioural management in obsessive-compulsive disorder. *British Journal of Psychiatry, 157*, 133–135.

Meyer, V. (1966). Modifications of expectations in cases with obsessional rituals. *Behaviour Research and Therapy, 4*, 273–280. doi:10.1016/0005- 7967(66)90083-0

Meyer, T. J., Miller, M. L., Metzger, R. L., & Borkovec, T. D. (1990). Development and validation of the Penn State Worry Questionnaire. *Behaviour Research and Therapy, 28*, 487–495.

Moodley, R., & Sutherland, P. (2010). Psychic retreats in other places: Clients who seek healing with traditional healers and psychotherapists. *Counselling Psychology Quarterly, 23*(3), 267–282. doi:10.1080/09515070.2010.505748

Moore, T. M., Zammit, S., Lingford-Hughes, A., Barnes, T. E., Jones, P. B., Burke, M., & Lewis, G. (2007). Cannabis use and risk of psychotic or affective mental health outcomes: A systematic review. *The Lancet, 370*(9584), 319–328. doi:10.1016/S0140-6736(07)61162-3

Moritz, S., & Jelinek, L. (2007). *Association splitting: Self-help guide for reducing obsessive thoughts*. Hamburg, Germany: VanHam Campus.

Moritz, S., & Jelinek, L. (2011). Further evidence for the efficacy of association splitting as a self-help technique for reducing obsessive thoughts. *Depression and Anxiety, 28*, 574–581.

Moritz, S., Jelinek, L., Klinge, R., & Naber, D. (2007). Fight fire with fireflies! Association splitting: A novel cognitive technique to reduce obsessive thoughts. *Behavioral and Cognitive Psychotherapy, 35*, 631–635.

Moritz, S., & Russu, R. (2013). Further evidence for the efficacy of association splitting in obsessive-compulsive disorder: An Internet study in a Russian-speaking sample. *Journal of Obsessive-Compulsive and Related Disorders, 2*, 91–98.

Moritz, S., Timpano, K. R., Wittekind, C. E., & Knaevelsrud, C. (2013). Harnessing the web: Internet and self-help therapy for people with obsessive-compulsive disorder and posttraumatic stress disorder. In E. Storch & D. McKay (Eds.), *Handbook of treating variants and complications in anxiety disorders* (pp. 375–397). New York, NY: Springer.

Moritz, S., Wittekind, C. E., Hauschildt, M., & Timpano, K. R. (2011). Do it yourself? Self-help and online therapy for people with obsessive-compulsive disorder. *Current Opinion in Psychiatry, 24*, 541–548.

Mowrer, O. H. (1939). A stimulus-response analysis of anxiety and its role as a reinforcing agent. *Psychological Review, 46*, 553–65.

Mowrer, O. H. (1960). *Learning theory and behavior.* New York, NY: Wiley.

Murphy, T. K., Storch, E. A., Lewin, A. B., Edge, P. J., & Goodman, W. K. (2012). Clinical Factors associated with pediatric autoimmune neuropsychiatric disorders associated with streptococcal (PANDAS) infections. *Journal of Pediatrics, 160*(2). 314–319.

National Institute for Health and Clinical Excellence. (2006). *Obsessive-compulsive disorder: Core interventions in the treatment of obsessive-compulsive disorder and body dysmorphic disorder.* The British Psychological Society & The Royal College of Psychiatrists. Retrieved from http://www.nice.org.uk

Newth, S., & Rachman, S. (2001), The concealment of obsessions. *Behaviour Research and Therapy, 39*(4), 457–464.

Nicolini, H., Orozco, B., Giuffra, L., Páez, F., Mejía, J., de Carmona, M. S., . . . de la Fuente, J. R. (1997). Age of onset, gender and severity in obsessive-compulsive disorder: A study on a Mexican population. *Salud Mental, 20*, 1–4.

O'Neil, S. E., Cather, C., Fishel, A. K., & Kafka, M. (2005). "Not knowing if i was a pedophile . . ." Diagnostic questions and treatment strategies in a case of OCD. *Harvard Review of Psychiatry, 13*(3), 186–196.

Obsessive Compulsive Cognitions Working Group. (2003). Psychometric validation of the Obsessive Beliefs Questionnaire and the Interpretation of Intrusions Inventory: Part 1. *Behaviour Research and Therapy, 41*, 1245–1264.

Olatunji, B. O., Davis, M. L., Powers, M. B., & Smits, J. A. (2013). Cognitive-behavioral therapy for obsessive-compulsive disorder: A meta-analysis of treatment outcome and moderators. *Journal of Psychiatric Research, 47* (1), 33–41.

Osegueda, A., Wetterneck, C. T., Williams, M. T., Hart, J., & Bjorgvinsson, T. (2013, April). *Sexual obsessions in OCD: Effects on depression and suicidal ideation.* Poster presented at the Anxiety and Depression Association of America Annual Conference, San Diego, CA.

Öst, L. G., Havnen, A., Hansen, B., & Kvale, G. (2015). Cognitive behavioral treatments of obsessive–compulsive disorder. A systematic review and meta-analysis of studies published 1993-2014. *Clinical Psychology Review, 40*, 156–169.

Panzer, C., Wise, S., Fantini, G., Kang, D., Munarriz, R., Guay, A., & Goldstein, I. (2006). Impact of oral contraceptives on sex hormone-binding globulin and androgen levels: A retrospective study in women with sexual dysfunction. *Journal of Sexual Medicine, 3*, 104–113.

Pinto, A., Greenberg, B. D., Grados, M., Bienvenu, O., III, Samuels, J., Murphy, D., . . . Nestadt, G. (2008). Further development of Y-BOCS dimensions in the OCD Collaborative Genetics Study: Symptoms vs. categories. *Psychiatry Research, 160*, 83–93.

Pinto, A., Van Noppen, B., & Calvocoressi, L. (2013). Development and preliminary psychometric evaluation of a self-rated version of the Family Accommodation Scale for Obsessive-Compulsive Disorder. *Journal of Obsessive-Compulsive and Related Disorders*, 2(4), 457–465.

Pouchly, C. A. (2012). A narrative review: arguments for a collaborative approach in mental health between traditional healers and clinicians regarding spiritual beliefs. *Mental Health, Religion & Culture*, 15(1), 65–85.

Rachman, S. (1997). A cognitive theory of obsessions. *Behavior Research and Therapy*, 35 (9), 793–802.

Rachman, S. (2004). Fear of contamination. *Behaviour Research and Therapy*, 42, 1227–1255.

Rady, A., Salama, H., Wagdy, M., & Ketat, A. (2013). Obsessive compulsive phenomenology in a sample of Egyptian adolescent population. *The European Journal of Psychiatry*, 27(2), 89–96.

Rassin, E., Diepstraten, P., Merckelbach, H., & Muris, P. (2001). Thought-action fusion and thought suppression in obsessive-compulsive disorder. *Behaviour Research and Therapy*, 39(7), 757–764.

Real, E., Labad, J., Alonso, P., Segalàs, C., Jiménez-Murcia, S., Bueno, B., . . . Menchón, J. M. (2011). Stressful life events at onset of obsessive-compulsive disorder are associated with a distinct clinical pattern. *Depression and Anxiety*, 28, 367–376.

Rector, N. A., Richter, M. A., Lerman, B., & Regev, R. (2015). A pilot test of the additive benefits of physical exercise to CBT for OCD. *Cognitive Behaviour Therapy*, 44(4), 328–340.

Reid, A. M., Flores, C., Olsen, B. Barthle, M. A., Rahmani, M., Rakhshani, A. C., . . . McNamara, J. P. H. (2016). Treatment of sexual obsessive-compulsive symptoms during exposure and response prevention. In E. A. Storch & A. B. Lewin (eds.), *Clinical handbook of obsessive-compulsive and related disorders: A case-based approach to treating pediatric and adult populations* (pp. 23–38). Cham, Switzerland: Springer.

Reisberg, D. (2001). Associative theories of long-term memory. In D. Reisberg (Ed.), *Cognition: Exploring the science of the mind* (pp. 235–270). New York, NY: Norton.

Renaud, C. A., & Byers, E. S. (1999). Exploring the frequency, diversity, and content of university students' positive and negative sexual cognitions. *Canadian Journal of Human Sexuality*, 8, 17–30.

Riggs, D. S., Hiss, H., & Foa, E. B. (1992). Marital distress and the treatment of obsessive compulsive disorder. *Behavior Therapy*, 23(4), 585–597.

Rodríguez-Martín, B. C., Moritz, S., Molerio-Pérez, O., & Gil-Pérez, P. (2013). Effectiveness of association splitting in reducing unwanted intrusive thoughts in a nonclinical sample. *Behavioural and Cognitive Psychotherapy*, 41, 433–440.

Roediger, H. L., III, Balota, D. A., & Watson, J. M. (2001). Spreading activation and arousal of false memories. In H. L. Roediger III, J. S. Nairne, I. Neath, & A. M. Surprenant (Eds.), *The nature of remembering: Essays in honor of Robert G. Crowder* (pp. 95–115). Washington, DC: American Psychological Association.

Roediger, H. L., III, & McDermott, K. B. (2000). Tricks of memory. *Current Directions in Psychological Science*, 9, 123–127.

Röper, G., Rachman, S., & Marks, I. (1975). Passive and participant modelling in exposure treatment of obsessive-compulsive neurotics. *Behaviour Research and Therapy*, *13*(4), 271–279. doi:10.1016/0005-7967(75)90032-7

Rosengren, D. B. (2009). *Building motivational interviewing skills: A practitioner workbook*. New York, NY: Guilford.

Roy, D., Hazarika, S., Bhattacharya, A., Das, S., Nath, K., & Saddichha, S. (2011). Koro: Culture bound or mass hysteria? *Australian & New Zealand Journal of Psychiatry*, *45*(8), 683.

Ruscio, A. M., Stein, D. J., Chiu, W. T., & Kessler, R. C. (2010). The epidemiology of obsessive- compulsive disorders in the National Comorbidity Survey Replication. *Molecular Psychiatry*, *15*(1), 53–63.

Saez, P. A., Casado, A., & Wade, J. C. (2009). Factors influencing masculinity ideology among Latino men. *Journal of Men's Studies*, *17*, 116–128.

Safer, D. L., Bullock, K. D., & Safer, J. D. (2016). Obsessive compulsive disorder presenting as gender dysphoria/gender incongruence: A case report and literature review. *AACE Clinical Case Reports*, *2*, e268–e271. doi:10.4158/EP161223.CR

Samuels, J., Eaton, W. W., Bienvenu, O. J., III, Brown, C. H., Costa, P. T., Jr., & Nestadt, G. (2002). Prevalence and correlates of personality disorders in a community sample. *British Journal of Psychiatry*, *180*, 536–542.

Sarris, J., Camfield, D., & Berk, M. (2012). Complementary medicine, self-help, and lifestyle interventions for obsessive compulsive disorder (OCD) and the OCD spectrum: A systematic review. *Journal of Affective Disorders*, *138*(3), 213–221. Doi:10.1016/j.jad.2011.04.051

Schneider, B. C., Wittekind, C. E., Talhof, A., Korrelboom, K., & Moritz, S. (2015). Competitive memory training (COMET) for OCD: A self-treatment approach to obsessions. *Cognitive Behaviour Therapy*, *44*, 142–152.

Schweitzer, I., Maguire, K., & Ng, C. (2009). Sexual side-effects of contemporary antidepressants: Review. *Australian and New Zealand Journal of Psychiatry*, *43*, 795–808.

Segraves, R. T. (2007). Sexual dysfunction associated with antidepressant therapy. *Urologic Clinics of North America*, *34*, 575–579.

Sell, R. L. (1996). The sell assessment of sexual orientation: Background and scoring. *Journal of Gay, Lesbian, & Bisexual Identity*, *1*(4), 295–310.

Shafran, R., Thordarson, D. S., & Rachman, S. (1996). Thought-action fusion in obsessive compulsive disorder. *Journal of Anxiety Disorders*, *10*(5), 379–391.

Sharma, M., Saleh, E., Deogaonkar, M., & Rezai, A. (2015). DBS for obsessive-compulsive disorder. In B. Sun & A. De Salles (Eds.), *Neurosurgical treatments for psychiatric disorders* (pp. 113–123). New York, NY: Springer Science. Doi:10.1007/978-94-017-9576-0_11

Sheehan, D. V., Lecrubier, Y., Sheehan, K. H., Amorim, P., Janavs, J., Weiller, E., Hergueta, T., Baker, R., & Dunbar, G. C. (1998). The Mini-International Neuropsychiatric Interview (M.I.N.I.): the development and validation of a structured diagnostic psychiatric interview for DSM-IV and ICD-10. *Journal of Clinical Psychiatry*, *59*(Suppl 20), 22–33.

Silverman, W. K., & Albano, A. M. (1996). *Anxiety disorders interview schedule for DSM-IV*. Graywind Publications Inc., Boulder.

Simmons, A., Williams, M., Matusko, N., Abelson, J. L., Bach, N., & Himle, J. A. (2012, November). Help-seeking behaviors of African Americans with anxiety disorders. Paper presented at the 2012 Association for Behavioral and Cognitive Therapies Convention, National Harbor, MD.

Simpson, H. B., Foa, E. B., Liebowitz, M. R., Huppert, J. D., Cahill, S., Maher, M. J., McLean, . . . Campeas, R. (2013). A randomized controlled trial of cognitive-behavioral therapy vs risperidone for augmenting serotonin reuptake inhibitors in obsessive-compulsive disorder. *Journal of the American Medical Association Psychiatry, 70*(11), 1190–1199. Doi:10.1001/jamapsychiatry.2013.1932.

Simpson, H. B., Foa, E. B., Liebowitz, M. R., Ledley, D. R., Huppert, J. D., Cahill, S., . . . Petkova, E. (2008). A randomized, controlled trial of cognitive-behavioral therapy for augmenting pharmacotherapy in obsessive-compulsive disorder. *American Journal of Psychiatry, 165*(5), 621–630. Doi:10.1176/appi.ajp.2007.07091440

Simpson, H. B., & Zuckoff, A. (2011). Using motivational interviewing to enhance treatment outcome in people with obsessive-compulsive disorder, *Cognitive and Behavioral Practice, 18*, 28–37.

Singh, R., Wetterneck, C. T., Williams, M. T., & Knott, L. E. (2016). The role of shame and symptom severity on quality of life in obsessive-compulsive and related disorders. *Journal of Obsessive Compulsive and Related Disorders, 11*, 49–55.

Smith, A. H., Wetterneck, C. T., & Harpster, R. (2011). Sexually intrusive thoughts in a non-clinical sample: The effects of content and direct experience on distress level and thought appraisal. *Canadian Journal of Human Sexuality, 20*, 151–156.

Smith, A. H., Wetterneck, C. T., Hart, J. M., Short, M. B., & Björgvinsson, T. (2012). Differences in obsessional beliefs and emotion appraisal in obsessive compulsive symptom presentation *Journal of Obsessive-Compulsive and Related Disorders, 1*(1), 54–61.

Son, D., & Shelton, J. (2011). Stigma consciousness among Asian Americans: Impact of positive stereotypes in interracial roommate relationships. *Asian American Journal of Psychology, 2*, 51–60.

Steinberg, D., & Wetterneck, C. T. (2017). OCD taboo thoughts and stigmatizing attitudes in clinicians. *Community Mental Health Journal, 53*(3), 275–280. Doi:10.1007/s10597-016-0055-x.

Steketee, G., Frost, R., & Bogart, K. (1996). The Yale–Brown Obsessive Compulsive Scale: Interview versus self-report. *Behaviour Research and Therapy, 34*, 675–684.

Steketee, G., & Van Noppen, B. (2003). Family approaches to treatment for obsessive compulsive disorder. *Revista Brasileira de Psiquiatria, 25*(1), 43–50.

Storch, E. A., Rasmussen, S. A., Price, L. H., Larson, M. J., Murphy, T. K., & Goodman, W. K. (2010). Development and psychometric evaluation of the Yale–Brown Obsessive-Compulsive Scale—Second Edition. *Psychological Assessment, 22*(2), 223–232. Doi:10.1037/a0018492

Summerfeldt, L. (2004). Understanding and treating incompleteness in obsessive-compulsive disorder. *Journal of Clinical Psychology, 60*(11), 1155–1168.

Sussman, N. (2003). Obsessive-compulsive disorder: A commonly missed diagnosis in primary care. *Primary Psychiatry, 10*(12), 14.

Swain, J., Hancock, K., Hainsworth, C., & Bowman, J. (2013). Acceptance and commitment therapy in the treatment of anxiety: A systematic review. *Clinical Psychology Review, 33*, 965–978.

Swedo, S. E., Leckman, J. F., & Rose, N. R. (2012). From research subgroup to clinical syndrome: Modifying the PANDAS criteria to describe PANS (pediatric acute-onset neuropsychiatric syndrome). *Pediatrics and Therapeutics, 2*(2), art. 113.

Szymanski, D. M., Kashubeck-West, S., & Meyer, J. (2018). Internalized Heterosexism: A Historical and Theoretical Overview. *The Counseling Psychologist, 36*(4), 510–524. https://doi.org/10.1177/0011000007309488

Taylor, S., Abramowitz, J. S., McKay, D., Calamari, J. E., Sookman, D., Kyrios, M., . . . Carmin, C. (2006). Do dysfunctional beliefs play a role in all types of obsessive-compulsive disorder? *Journal of Anxiety Disorders, 20*(1), 85–97.

Taylor, S., Thordarson, D. S., Spring, T., Yeh, A. H., Corcoran, K. M., Eugster, K., & Tisshaw, C. (2003). Telephone-administered cognitive behavior therapy for obsessive-compulsive disorder. *Cognitive Behaviour Therapy, 32*(1), 13–25.

Tellawi, G., Dimitrova, V., Bach, N., Steinberg, D., Williams, M. T., & Wetterneck, C. (2014, March). *Experiential avoidance and romantic relationships in OCD*. Poster presented at the Anxiety and Depression Association of America Annual Conference, Chicago, IL.

Tellawi, G., Viscusi, J., Miller, A., Williams, M., & Chasson, G. S. (2015, August). *OCD and marital satisfaction: A comparison of individuals with OCD and their spouses*. Poster presented at the International OCD Foundation Conference, Boston, MA.

Tellawi, G., Williams, M. T., & Chasson, G. (2016). Interpersonal hostility and suspiciousness in obsessive-compulsive disorder. *Psychiatry Research, 243*, 295–302.

Terwilliger, J. M., Bach, N., Bryan, C., & Williams, M. T. (2013). Multicultural versus colorblind ideology: Implications for mental health and counseling (pp. 111–122). In A. Di Fabio (Ed.), *Psychology of counseling*. Hauppauge, NY: Nova Science.

Thompson, V. L. S., Bazile, A., & Akbar, M. (2004). African Americans' perceptions of psychotherapy and psychotherapists. *Professional Psychology: Research and Practice, 35*, 19–26.

Thompson-Hollands, J., Abramovitch, A., Tompson, M. C., & Barlow, D. H. (2015). A randomized clinical trial of a brief family intervention to reduce accommodation in obsessive-compulsive disorder: A preliminary study. *Behavior Therapy, 46*(2), 218–229.

Thompson-Hollands, J., Edson, A., Tompson, M. C., & Comer, J. S. (2014). Family involvement in the psychological treatment of obsessive–compulsive disorder: A meta-analysis. *Journal of Family Psychology, 28*(3), 287.

Tükel, R., Polat, A., Genç, A., Bozkurt, O., & Atli, H. (2004). Gender-related differences among Turkish patients with obsessive-compulsive disorder. *Comprehensive Psychiatry, 45*(5), 362–366.

Tumkaya, S., Karadag, F., Jellema, T., Oguzhanoglu, N. K., Ozdel, O., Atesci, F. C., & Varma, G. (2014). Involuntary social cue integration in patients with obsessive compulsive disorder. *Comprehensive Psychiatry, 55*(1), 137–144.

Tumkaya, S., Karadag, F., Mueller, S. T., Ugurlu, T. T., Oguzhanoglu, N. K., Ozdel, O., . . . Bayraktutan, M. (2013). Situation awareness in obsessive-compulsive disorder. *Psychiatry Research, 209*(3), 579–588.

Twohig, M. P. (2009). The application of acceptance and commitment therapy to obsessive compulsive disorder. *Cognitive and Behavioral Practice, 16*, 18–28.

Twohig, M. P. (2012). Introduction: The basics of acceptance and commitment therapy. *Cognitive and Behavioral Practice, 19*, 499–507.

Twohig, M. P., Hayes, S. C., & Masuda, A. (2006). Increasing willingness to experience obsessions: Acceptance and commitment therapy as a treatment for obsessive-compulsive disorder. *Behavior Therapy, 37*(1), 3–13.

Twohig, M. P., Hayes, S. C., Plumb, J. C., Pruitt, L. D., Collins, A. B., Hazlett-Stevens, H., & Woidneck, M. R. (2010). A randomized clinical trial of acceptance and commitment therapy versus progressive relaxation training for obsessive-compulsive disorder. *Journal of Consulting and Clinical Psychology, 78*(5), 705.

Twohig, M. P., Plumb-Vilardaga, J. C., Levin, M. E., & Hayes, S. C. (2015). Changes in psychological flexibility during acceptance and commitment therapy for obsessive compulsive disorder. *Journal of Contextual Behavioral Science, 4*, 196–202.

Twohig, M. P., Abramowitz, J. S., Smith, B. M., Fabricant, L. E., Jacoby, R. J., Morrison, K. L., . . . Ledermann, T. (2018). Adding acceptance and commitment therapy to exposure and response prevention for obsessive-compulsive disorder: A randomized controlled trial. *Behaviour Research and Therapy, 108*, 1–9.

Van Ameringen, M., Simpson, W., Patterson, B., Dell'Osso, B., Fineberg, N., Hollander, E., . . . Zohar, J. (2014). Pharmacological treatment strategies in obsessive compulsive disorder: A cross-sectional view in nine international OCD centers. *Journal of Psychopharmacology, 28*(6), 596–602. https://doi.org/10.1177/0269881113517955

Van Noppen, B., & Steketee, G. (2009). Testing a conceptual model of patient and family predictors of obsessive compulsive disorder (OCD) symptoms. *Behaviour Research and Therapy, 47*(1), 18e25. doi: j.brat.2008.10.005.

Wegner, D. M., Schneider, D. J., Carter, S. R., & White, T. L. (1987). Paradoxical effects of thought suppression. *Journal of Personality and Social Psychology, 53*(1), 5–13. doi:10.1037/0022-3514.53.1.5

Wegner, D. M., & Zanakos, S. (1994). Chronic thought suppression. *Journal of Personality, 62*, 615–640.

Weingarden, H., Renshaw K. D., Wilhelm, S., Tangney, J. P., & DiMauro, J. (2016). Anxiety and shame as risk factors for depression, suicidality, and functional impairment in body dysmorphic disorder and obsessive compulsive disorder. *Journal of Nervous and Mental Disease, 204*(11), 832–839. doi:10.1097/NMD.0000000000000498

Wetterneck, C. T., Adams, T. G., Leonard, R. C., Riemann, B. C., & Franklin, M. E. (2017). *The effects of level of depression on OCD treatment: Results from an intensive residential program.* Manuscript submitted for publication.

Wetterneck, C. T., Knott, L., Kinnear, K., & Storch, E. (2017). *Development of the Adult OCD Impact Scale (AOIS): A measure of psychosocial functioning for adults with OCD.* Manuscript submitted for publication.

Wetterneck, C. T., Lee, E. B., Hart, J. M., & Smith, A. H. (2013). Courage, self-compassion and values in obsessive compulsive disorder. *Journal of Contextual Behavioral Science*, 2, 68–73.

Wetterneck, C. T., Little, T. E., Rinehart, K. L., Cervantes, M. E., & Burgess, A. J. (2010, November). *Differences in psychotherapy expectations between Caucasians and Hispanics.* Poster presented at the 2010 Association for Behavioral and Cognitive Therapies Convention, San Francisco, CA.

Wetterneck, C. T., Siev, J., Smith, A. H., Adams, T. G., & Slimowicz, J. C. (2015). Assessing sexually intrusive thoughts: parsing unacceptable thoughts on the dimensional obsessive-compulsive scale. *Behavior Therapy*, 46(4). doi:10.1016/j.beth.2015.05.006

Wetterneck, C. T., Smith, A. H., Hart, J. M., & Burgess, A. J. (2011). Distress from sexual thoughts: Do religiosity, emotions, and thought appraisal matter? *Journal of Cognitive Psychotherapy*, 25, 189–202.

Wetterneck, C. T., Williams, M. T., Tellawi, G., & Bruce, S. (2016). Treatment of suicide obsessions in obsessive-compulsive disorder with comorbid major depressive disorder. In E. Storch & A. Lewin (Eds.), *Clinical handbook of obsessive-compulsive and related disorders: A case-based approach to treating pediatric and adult populations* (pp. 431–445). Cham, Switzerland: Springer.

Whiteside, S. P., & Abramowitz, J. S. (2005). The expression of anger and its relationship to symptoms and cognitions in obsessive-compulsive disorder. *Depression and Anxiety*, 21(3), 106–111.

Williams, M. T. (2008). Homosexuality anxiety: A misunderstood form of OCD. In L. V. Sebeki (Ed.), *Leading-edge health education issues* (pp. 195–205). Hauppauge, NY: Nova.

Williams, M. T. (2016, June 12). When clients confess to crimes they did not commit [Web log post]. *Psychology Today.* Retrieved from https://www.psychologytoday.com/blog/culturally-speaking/201606/when-clients-confess-crimes-they-did-not-commit

Williams, M. T., Domanico, J., Marques, L., Leblanc, N., & Turkheimer, E. (2012). Barriers to Treatment Among African Americans with Obsessive-Compulsive Disorder. *Journal of Anxiety Disorders*, 26(1), 555–563. doi:10.1016/j.janxdis.2012.02.009

Williams, M. T., Chapman, L. K., Simms, J. V., & Tellawi, G. (2017). Cross-cultural phenomenology of obsessive-compulsive disorder. In J. Abramowitz, D. McKay, & E. Storch (Eds.), *The Wiley handbook of obsessive-compulsive related disorders* (pp. 56–74). New York: Wiley.

Williams, M. T., & Ching, T. H. W. (2016). Transgender anxiety, cultural issues, and cannabis in obsessive compulsive disorder. *Endocrine Practice*, 2(3), e276–e277. doi:10.4158/ep161356.co

Williams, M. T., Ching, T. H. W., Tellawi, G., Siev, J., Dowell, J., Schlaudt, V., . . . Wetterneck, C. T. (2018). Assessing sexual orientation symptoms in obsessive-compulsive disorder: Development and validation of the Sexual Orientation Obsessions and Reactions Test (SORT). *Behavior Therapy*, 49, 715–729.

Williams, M. T., Crozier, M., & Powers, M. B. (2011). Treatment of sexual orientation obsessions in obsessive-compulsive disorder using exposure and ritual prevention. *Clinical Case Studies*, 10, 53–66.

Williams, M. T., Davis, D. M., Powers, M., & Weissflog, L. O. (2014). Current trends in prescribing medications for obsessive-compulsive disorder: Best practices and new research. *Directions in Psychiatry, 34* (4), 247–261.

Williams, M. T., Davis, D. M., Tellawi, G., & Slimowicz, J. (2015). Assessment and treatment of sexual orientation obsessions in obsessive-compulsive disorder. *Australian Clinical Psychologist, 1*(1), 12–18.

Williams, M. T., Domanico, J., Marques, L., Leblanc, N., & Turkheimer, E. (2012). Barriers to treatment of African Americans with obsessive-compulsive disorder. *Journal of Anxiety Disorders, 26,* 555–563.

Williams, M. T., Elstein, J., Buckner, E., Abelson, J., & Himle, J. (2012). Symptom dimensions in two samples of African Americans with obsessive-compulsive disorder. *Journal of Obsessive-Compulsive & Related Disorders, 1*(3), 145–152.

Williams, M. T., & Farris, S. G. (2011). Sexual orientation obsessions in obsessive-compulsive disorder: Prevalence and correlates. *Psychiatry Research, 187,* 156–159.

Williams, M. T., Farris, S. G., Turkheimer, E., Franklin, M. E., Simpson, H. B., Liebowitz, M., & Foa, E. B. (2014). The impact of symptom dimensions on outcomes for exposure and ritual prevention therapy for obsessive-compulsive disorder. *Journal of Anxiety Disorders, 28*(6), 553–558. doi:10.1016/j.janxdis.2014.06.001

Williams, M. T., Gooden, A. M., & Davis, D. (2012). African Americans, European Americans, and pathological stereotypes: An African-centered perspective. In G. R. Hayes & M. H. Bryant (Ed.), *Psychology of culture* (pp. 25–46). Hauppauge, NY: Nova Science.

Williams, M. T., Mugno, B., Franklin, M. E., & Faber, S. (2013). Symptom dimensions in obsessive-compulsive disorder: Phenomenology and treatment with exposure and ritual prevention. *Psychopathology, 46,* 365–376. doi:10.1159/000348582

Williams, M., Powers, M., & Foa, E. (2012). Obsessive-compulsive disorder. In P. Sturmey & M. Hersen (Eds.), *Handbook of evidence-based practice in clinical psychology* (Vol. 2, pp. 313–335). Hoboken, NJ: Wiley.

Williams, M. T., Sawyer, B., Ellsworth, M., Singh, R., & Tellawi, G. (2017). Obsessive-compulsive and related disorders in ethnoracial minorities: attitudes, stigma, & barriers to treatment. In J. Abramowitz, D. McKay, & E. Storch (Eds.), *The Wiley handbook of obsessive-compulsive disorder across the lifespan.* Hoboken, NJ: Wiley.

Williams, M. T., Sawyer, B., Leonard, R. C., Ellsworth, M., Simms, J. V., & Riemann, B. C. (2015). Minority participation in a major residential and intensive outpatient program for obsessive-compulsive disorder. *Journal of Obsessive-Compulsive and Related Disorders, 5,* 67–75. doi:10.1016/j.jocrd.2015.02.004

Williams, M. T., Slimowicz, J., Tellawi, G., & Wetterneck, C. (2014). Sexual orientation symptoms in obsessive compulsive disorder: Assessment and treatment with cognitive behavioral therapy. *Directions in Psychiatry, 34*(1), 37–50.

Williams, M. T., & Steever, A. (2015). Cultural manifestations of obsessive-compulsive disorder. In C. W. Lack (Ed.), *Obsessive-compulsive disorder: Etiology, phenomenology, and treatment* (pp. 63–84). Hoboken, NJ: Wiley.

Williams, M. T., Tellawi, G., Davis, D. M., & Slimowicz, J. (2015). Assessment and treatment of sexual orientation obsessions in obsessive-compulsive disorder. *Australian Clinical Psychologist, 1,* 12–18.

Williams, M. T., Wetterneck, C. T., Tellawi, G., & Duque, G. (2015). Domains of distress among people with sexual orientation obsessions. *Archives of Sexual Behavior, 44,* 783–789. doi:10.1007/s10508-014-0421-0

Williams, M. T., Wetterneck, C. T., Thibodeau, M., & Duque, G. (2013). Validation of the Yale–Brown Obsessive Compulsive Severity Scale in African Americans with obsessive-compulsive disorder. *Psychiatry Research, 209*(2), 214–221.

Wilson, K. G., Sandoz, E. K., Kitchens, J., & Roberts, M. (2010). The Valued Living Questionnaire: Defining and measuring valued action within a behavioral framework. *Psychological Record, 60,* 249–272.

Woien, S. L., Ernst, H. A. H., Patock-Peckham, J. A., & Nagoshi, C. T. (2003). Validation of the TOSCA to measure shame and guilt. *Personality and Individual Differences, 35,* 313–326.

Wolpe, J. (1969). *The practice of behavior therapy.* Oxford, England: Pergamon.

Woods, C. M., Vevea, J. L., Chambless, D. L., & Bayen, U. J. (2002). Are compulsive checkers impaired in memory? A meta-analytic review. *Clinical Psychology: Science & Practice, 9,* 353–366.

Yadin, E., Lichner, T. K., & Foa, E. B. (2012). *Treating your OCD with exposure and response (ritual) prevention: Workbook.* Philadelphia, PA: Oxford University Press.

Zohar, J., Fostick, L., Black, D., & Lopez-Ibor, J. (2007). Special populations. *CNS Spectrums, 12*(2 Suppl 3), 36–42.

Zuckoff, A., Balán, I. C., & Simpson, H. B. (2015). Enhancing the effectiveness of exposure and response prevention in the treatment of obsessive–compulsive disorder: Exploring a role for motivational interviewing. In H. Arkowitz, W. Miller, & S. Rollnick (Eds.), *Motivational Interviewing in the treatment of psychological problems* (2nd ed., pp. 56–82). New York, NY: Guildford.

Index

Note: Tables, figures, and boxes are indicated by *t*, *f*, and *b* following the page number.

acceptance and commitment therapy (ACT), 120–25
   and association splitting, 144–46
access to care, 181
accommodation in OCD
   Family Accommodation Scale for Obsessive-Compulsive Disorder, 339–45
   reducing, 305–6
adolescents
   and caregivers or parents, issues with, 297–300
   and medications for OCD, 75
   shame, guilt, and embarrassment among, 301–2
Adult OCD Impact Scale (AOIS), 57–58
African Americans, hesitancy to disclose obsessions, 18–19, 152
alternative treatments, for obsessive-compulsive disorder, 34–35
   traditional healers, communication with, 83, 85–86
antipsychotics, issues encountered with, 78
anxiety
   assessment in OCD patients, 59
   sexual problems encountered with, 277–80, 279
Asian Americans, barriers to treatment among, 153
assessment, 48–59
   and comorbidity in OCD, 51
   assessment instruments, 51–59
   in pedophilic obsession, case example, 214–16
   in sexual-orientation obsession, case example, 167–68

intake questionnaire, 48–51
interviews, general psychopathology, 51–55
interviews, obsessive-compulsive disorder, 55–56
recommended measures for clients with sexually themed OCD, 53*t*
relationship scales, 59
role in treatment, 93–94
self-report instruments, 56–59
Assessment for Anxiety Disorders Clinical Interview Schedule (ADIS), 52
assessment instruments, 51–59
   interviews, general psychopathology, 51–55
   interviews, obsessive-compulsive disorder, 55–56
   pedophilic obsessions, 214–15
   recommended measures for clients with sexually themed OCD, 53*t*
   relationship scales, 59
   self-report instruments, 56–59
   sexual-orientation obsession, 167–68
assessment of progress
   in treatment of pedophilic obsession, 217–38
   in treatment of sexual-orientation obsession, 170–72, 173*t*, 174–80
association splitting
   case description, 142–43
   client handout on, 336–37
   cognitive technique of, 140–42
   diagram, 160*f*
   rationale for use, 151–54
   research evidence for efficacy of, 146–51
   semantic network, associations in, 137–40

association splitting (cont.)
  step-by-step guide, 154–56, 157t, 158–61, 158t
  vs. other approaches to treating OCD, 143–46

barriers to care, 181
Barriers to Treatment Questionnaire (BTQ), 58
Beck Anxiety Inventory, 59, 168
Beck Depression Inventory, 58, 168, 214
Behavioral Activation Depression Scale-Short Form, 214
behavioral experiments, in cognitive therapy, 117–18
benzodiazepines, issues encountered with, 77–78
bestiality, S-OCD and fears regarding, 71–72
brain surgery for OCD, 37, 38

care, access and barriers to, 181
caregivers, and adolescent clients, 297–300
case conceptualization
  in pedophilic obsession, case example, 216
  in sexual-orientation obsession, case example, 168–70
case studies, for therapists treating S-OCD, 310–11
checking rituals, as symptom presentation of OCD, 11–12
child protective services (CPS), communication with, 82–83, 84b
children
  and medications for OCD, 73, 75
  S-OCD in, 17–18
cleaning rituals, as symptom presentation of OCD, 10–11
client assessment, 48–59
  and comorbidity in OCD, 51
  assessment instruments, 51–59
  intake questionnaire, 48–51
  interviews, general psychopathology, 51–55
  interviews, obsessive-compulsive disorder, 55–56
  recommended measures for clients with sexually themed OCD, 53t
  relationship scales, 59
  self-report instruments, 56–59
client consultation, 39–48
  diagnosis, client doubts regarding, 45–46
  disarming shame in, 39–42
  OCD cycle, explaining, 42–43
  symptoms, discussing origin of, 43–44
  talk therapy, ineffectiveness of for OCD, 44–45
  treatment, preparation for, 46–48
clients, materials and handouts for, 315–37
  About Sexual Obsessive-Compulsive Disorder (S-OCD), 318–20
  Association Splitting: Tips and Reminders, 336–37
  Guidelines for "Normal Behavior," 332–33
  OCD and Unacceptable Thoughts, 321–22
  OCD Cycle, 317
  OCD Relapse Prevention: Quick Tips, 334–35
  OCD Symptom Dimensions, 315
  Unacceptable Taboo Thoughts, 316
  Understanding Cognitive-Behavioral Therapy for OCD, 323–25
  Unwanted Sexual Thoughts, 326
clinical treatment of S-OCD
  among ethnoracial minority populations, 19–20
  instructional materials, availability of, 3–4
  questions commonly asked, 4
  treatment options for OCD, 33–38
  treatment-refractory OCD, options for treatment, 36–38
cognitive delays, clients with, 300–301
cognitive-behavioral therapy (CBT), 325
  and association splitting, 145–46
  and facing fears, 90–92
  behavioral experiments, 117–18
  building mental fitness in, 92–93
  clients noncompliant with, 289–91
  concealment, experimenting with dropping, 118–20
  effectiveness of, 87–88
  understanding CBT for OCD, 323–25
  usefulness for OCD, 116–17

INDEX 437

communication, with other mental
   healthcare providers, 79–83, 85–86
 physicians, 79–81
 social workers, 82–83, 84b
 therapists, 81–82
community domain, values-based
   exposures in, 221–23, 223t
comorbidity in OCD, 51
 depression, 288–89
 substance use, 303–4
complicating factors
 in pedophilic obsessions, case
   example, 238
 in sexual-orientation obsession, case
   example, 180–81
compulsions
 common compulsions in S-OCD, 318–19
 examples of, 31
 resisting compulsions
  monitoring
  spoiling
concealment, experimenting with
   dropping, 118–20
consultation, client, 39–48
 diagnosis, client doubts regarding, 45–46
 disarming shame in, 39–42
 OCD cycle, explaining, 42–43
 symptoms, discussing origin of, 43–44
 talk therapy, ineffectiveness of for
   OCD, 44–45
 treatment, preparation for, 46–48
contamination fears
 as symptom presentation of OCD, 10–11
 overlapping S-OCD, 89
 sexual problems encountered
   with, 278–79
coping strategies, for intrusive
   thoughts, 89
covert compulsions, and pure
   obsessionals, 321–22
cross-cultural presentation of
   S-OCD, 20–21
cultural perspectives, on family counseling
   and interventions, 276–77
culture-bound disorders, examples of, 20–21

danger, and people with sexual
   obsessions, 31–32

deep brain stimulation (DBS), and
   treatment for OCD, 38
depression
 assessment in OCD patients, 58
 clients with comorbid, 288–89
 rates of in S-OCD, 17
 sexual problems encountered with, 279
developmental delays, clients with,
   300–301
diagnosis
 client doubts regarding, 45–46
 pedophilic OCD, issues in
   diagnosing, 63–65
*Diagnostic and Statistical Manual of
   Mental Disorders (DSM-5),* 7–9
differential diagnosis, and assessing clients
   with sexual obsessions, 59–72
 bestiality, fears 71–72
 pedophilic disorder *vs.* OCD,
   59–63, 69–71
 pedophilic OCD, issues in
   diagnosing, 59–63
 sexual identity confusion *vs.* OCD, 65–67
 transgender identity, 67–69
Dimensional Obsessive Compulsive Scale
   (DOCS), 56, 168, 214, 346–55
distress, differentiating among types of, 110b
domains and values, descriptions of,
   220–23, 221t
doubting rituals, as symptom presentation
   of OCD, 11–12
DSM-IV Field Trial, 2, 3

ethnic minorities, S-OCD and, 18–20
expectancy violation, in Ex/RP
   therapy, 115
experiential avoidance, 124
exposure and response prevention
   (Ex/RP) therapy
 assessment for, 93–94
 availability as treatment for OCD, 35
 basics of, 101–2
 client fears regarding arousal, 292–93
 clients noncompliant with, 291–92
 combined with medication, 72–74
 distress-evoking situations, building a
   hierarchy of, 97–104, 98t, 173t
 effectiveness of, 88

exposure and response prevention
(Ex/RP) therapy (*cont.*)
  exposures in public locations, issues with, 304–5
  exposures, addressing ineffectiveness of, 295–97
  exposures, determining explicitness of, 297
  habituation, necessity for, 114–16
  homework, role in treatment, 112–14
  imaginal exposure, 109–11, 324
  imaginal exposure, judging appropriateness of, 294–95
  imaginal exposure, pedophilic obsessions, 249–61
  imaginal exposure, sexual-orientation obsessions, 187–206
  in acceptance and commitment approach, 121
  in sexual-orientation obsession, case example, 175–80
  in vivo exposure, 106–7, 323–24
  in vivo exposure, judging appropriateness of, 293–94
  in vivo exposures, pediatric obsessions, 241–49
  in vivo exposures, sexual-orientation obsessions, 183–87
  inhibitory learning, 114–16
  out-of-office exposures, 107–8
  response/ritual prevention, 324–25
  rituals, discrediting, 104
  rituals, monitoring, 105–6
  rituals, prevention of, 102–4
  role in treatment, 93–97
  session-by-session outline for, 130–36
  Subjective Units of Distress/Discomfort Scale (SUDS), 95–97
  values-based exposures in parenting domain, 220–23, 222*t*
  values-based exposures in spiritual/community domain, 221–23, 223*t*
  values-based exposures in well-being domain, 222–23, 224*t*

families
  and adolescent clients, 297–300
  and motivating clients to seek treatment, 307–8

family accommodations, S-OCD and, 267–68, 283–84
family counseling and interventions, 269–77, 283–84
family counseling and interventions, cultural perspectives on, 276–77
measuring accommodation by, 59
perspectives on mental illness, 274–76
unsupportive families, 306
useful books for, 308–0
Family Accommodation Scale for Obsessive-Compulsive Disorder, 59, 339–45
family history
  in pedophilic obsession, case example, 213
  in sexual-orientation obsession, case example, 166
family mental health history
  in pedophilic obsession, case example, 212–13
  in sexual-orientation obsession, case example, 166
fantasies, *vs.* obsessions, 29, 266
fear
  client experience in Ex/RP, 291–92
  using CBT to face, 90–92
follow-up to treatment
  pedophilic obsession, case example, 238
  sexual-orientation obsession, case example, 181–82
fusion, concept of in acceptance and commitment therapy, 124–25, 124*n*1

guardians, and adolescent clients, 297–300

habituation, necessity for, 114–16
handouts for clients, 315–37
  About Sexual Obsessive-Compulsive Disorder (S-OCD), 318–20
  Association Splitting: Tips and Reminders, 336–37
  Guidelines for "Normal Behavior," 332–33
  OCD and Unacceptable Thoughts, 321–22
  OCD Cycle, 317
  OCD Relapse Prevention: Quick Tips, 334–35
  OCD Symptom Dimensions, 315

Unacceptable Taboo Thoughts, 316
Understanding Cognitive-Behavioral
    Therapy for OCD, 323–25
Unwanted Sexual Thoughts, 326
hierarchy, of distress-evoking situations,
    97–104, 98t, 173t
Hispanic Americans, hesitancy to disclose
    obsessions, 153
history, patient
    in pedophilic obsession, case
        example, 207–14
    in sexual-orientation obsession, case
        example, 165–66
home visits, 108
homework, role in treatment, 112–14
hormonal contraceptives, issues, 79

imaginal exposure, 109–11, 324
    judging appropriateness of, 294–95
    pedophilic obsessions, 249–61
    sexual-orientation obsessions, 177,
        187–206
impregnating obsessions in
    obsessive-compulsive
    disorder, 29–31, 277–78
in vivo exposure, 106–7, 323–24
    judging appropriateness of, 293–94
    pedophilic obsessions, 241–49
    sexual-orientation obsessions, 183–87
inhibitory learning, 114–16
instructional materials, and treatment of
    S-OCD, 3–4
insurance coverage, 90-minute sessions
    and, 287–88
intake questionnaire, client assessment
    and, 48–51
interviews
    general psychopathology, 51–55
    obsessive-compulsive disorder, 55–56
intrusive thoughts
    in context of OCD, 89
    universality of, 87, 88–90

koro, culture-bound disorder, 21

Latino Americans, hesitancy to disclose
    obsessions, 153
learning, inhibitory, 114–16

marijuana, and treatment for OCD, 35
marriages
    challenges of S-OCD for, 5
    discussing sexual problems, 280
    family accommodations, S-OCD and,
        267–68, 283–84
    family counseling and interventions,
        269–77, 283–84
    family counseling and interventions,
        cultural perspectives on, 276–77
    impact of OCD on, 269
    impact of sexual obsessions on,
        263–67, 283–84
    psychoeducation of spouses, 269–74
medications, for OCD, 35–36, 72–79
    antipsychotics, issues, 78
    benzodiazepines, issues, 77–78
    combining with therapy, 72–74
    dealing with ineffectiveness of, 74
    hormonal contraceptives, issues, 79
    mood stabilizers, issues, 78
    serotonin reuptake inhibitors (SSRIs),
        74–76, 279
    sexual side effects of, 76–77, 279
mental compulsions, client fears
    regarding, 292
mental fitness, building in
    cognitive-behavioral
    treatment, 92–93
mental illness, family perspectives
    on, 274–76
mental rituals, as symptom presentation of
    OCD, 14–15
mindfulness techniques, 120, 124–25
MINI International Neuropsychiatric
    Interview, 52, 168, 215
minority populations, S-OCD and, 18–20
misidentification, of common S-OCD
    presentations, 1–2
mood stabilizers, issues encountered
    with, 78
motivational interviewing, and treatment
    for OCD, 34

neuroanatomy, of obsessive-compulsive
    disorder, 37
neuromodulation, and treatment for
    OCD, 38

obsessions
 examples of, 31
 semantic network conceptualization of, 137–40
 vs. fantasies, 29, 266
 vs. ruminations, 110b
 vs. worries, 110b
obsessive-compulsive disorder (OCD), 7–10, 38
 and family perspectives on mental illness, 274–76
 and substance use, 303–4
 associated emotions, 90
 case studies for therapists, 310–11
 coexisting conditions, 7
 cycle of, 42–43
 definition of, 7–9
 family accommodations and, 267–68, 283–84
 family counseling and interventions for, 269–77, 283–84
 family counseling and interventions, cultural perspectives on, 276–77
 interviews for assessing, 55–56
 medications, sexual side effects of, 76–77, 279
 neuroanatomy of, 37
 OCD cycle, 317, 321
 organizational resources, 311
 origin of symptoms, discussing with client, 43–44
 psychoeducation of partners and spouses, 269–74
 psychotherapy for, 323
 pure obsessionals, and covert compulsions, 321–22
 rituals in, 102–6
 self-reports for assessing, 56–59
 symptom dimensions, 315
 treatment options, 33–38
 understanding CBT for, 323–25
 useful books for clients and family members, 308–10
 variety of presentations, 10–15
Obsessive-Compulsive Inventory, The, 57
onset
 age of
 of pedophilic obsessions, 207–10

 of sexual-orientation obsessions, 165
ordering rituals, as symptom presentation of OCD, 12–14
organizational resources, for treating OCD, 311
out-of-office exposures, 107–8

parenting domain, values-based exposures in, 220–23, 222t
parents, and adolescent clients, 297–300
patient history
 in pedophilic obsession, 207–14
 in sexual-orientation obsession, case example, 165–66
pedophilic disorder, vs. pedophilic obsessions in obsessive-compulsive disorder, 59–63
pedophilic obsessions
 in obsessive-compulsive disorder (P-OCD), 22–23
 issues in diagnosing, 63–65, 69–71
 vs. pedophilic disorder, 59–63
pedophilic obsessions, treatment
 assessment of progress, case example, 217–38
 assessment, case example, 214–16
 case conceptualization, case example, 216
 clinicians, recommendations to, 240–41
 complicating factors, case example, 238
 course of treatment, case example, 217–38
 domains and values, descriptions of, 220–23, 221t
 follow-up to treatment, case example, 238
 imaginal exposures, examples of, 249–61
 in vivo exposures, suggestions for, 241–49
 onset of obsessions, case example, 207–10
 parenting domain, values-based exposures in, 221t, 222t
 patient history, case example, 207–14
 presenting complaints, case example, 207
 resources, 261
 spiritual/community domain, values-based exposures in, 223t
 treatment implications, case example, 239–40
 well-being domain, values-based exposures in, 224t

physicians, communication with, 79–81
presentations of sexual obsession in OCD
   in pedophilic obsessions, 207
   in sexual-orientation
      obsessions, 163–65
   misidentification of, 1–2
prevalence of S-OCD, 2–3
prognosis, for S-OCD, 32–33
progress, assessment of
   in treatment of pedophilic
      obsession, 217–38
   in treatment of sexual-orientation
      obsession, 170–72, 173t, 174–80
psychoeducation, 88–93
   and family perspectives on mental
      illness, 274–76
   commitment to treatment, 92–93
   fears, confronting in CBT, 90–92
   of partners and spouses, 269–74, 284
   universality of intrusive thoughts, 88–90
psychosurgery, for treatment-refractory
   OCD, 36–38
psychotherapies, for obsessive-compulsive
   disorder, 33–34, 323
puppy pregnancy, culture-bound disorder
   of, 20–21
pure obsessionals, and covert
   compulsions, 321–22

racial minorities, S-OCD and, 18–20
relapse prevention, 126–29, 128b
   client handout on, 334–35
relational frame theory (RFT), 144
relationship obsessions in
   obsessive-compulsive disorder
   (R-OCD), 280–83
relationship scales, and client
   assessment, 59
relationships
   family accommodations, S-OCD
      and, 267–68
   family counseling and
      interventions, 269–77
   impact of sexual obsessions on,
      263–67, 283–84
   perspectives on mental illness, 274–76
religious sexual obsession in obsessive-
   compulsive disorder, 26–27

reparative therapy vs. treatment of
   S-OCD, 294
resources
   books for clients and family
      members, 308–10
   pedophilic obsessions, treatment of, 261
   sexual-orientation obsessions,
      treatment of, 206
rituals
   discrediting, 104
   monitoring, 105–6
   prevention of, 102–4
   spoiling
romantic partners
   challenges of S-OCD for, 5
   discussing sexual problems, 280
   family accommodations, S-OCD
      and, 267–68
   family counseling and
      interventions, 269–77
   impact of OCD on, 269
   impact of sexual obsessions on, 263–67
   psychoeducation of, 269–74, 284
ruminations, vs. obsessions and
   worries, 110b

safety, client fears regarding, 291–92
scrupulosity, 26–27, 89
selective serotonin reuptake inhibitors
   (SSRIs), 279
   in treating OCD, 74–76
   use in children, 73, 75
self-report instruments, and client
   assessment, 56–59
semantic network conceptualization of
   obsessions, 137–40
sexual deviance obsessions, sexual
   problems encountered with, 278
sexual history
   in pedophilic obsession, case
      example, 213–14
   in sexual-orientation obsession, case
      example, 166
sexual identity confusion, vs. sexually
   themed OCD, 65–67
sexual obsessions
   family counseling and interventions
      for, 269–77

sexual obsessions in obsessive-compulsive disorder (S-OCD), 15–18
and children, 17–18
and family perspectives on mental illness, 274–76
and racial and ethnic minorities, 18–20
bestiality, fears regarding, 71–72
cross-cultural presentation of, 20–21
depression, rates of, 17
difficulty of treating, 87
family accommodations and, 267–68, 283–84
family counseling and interventions for, 269–77, 283–84
family counseling and interventions, cultural perspectives on, 276–77
impregnating obsessions, 29–31
issues diagnosing, 69–71
medications for OCD, 35–36, 72–79
benzodiazapines
dealing with ineffectiveness of, 74
issues encountered with, 77–79
serotonin reuptake inhibitors, 74–76
sexual side effects of, 76–77, 279
misidentification of common presentations, 1–2
origins of, 319–20
pedophile obsessions (P-OCD), 22–23
pedophile obsessions (P-OCD), issues in diagnosing, 69–71
pedophilic OCD, issues in diagnosing, 63–65
prevalence of, 2–3
prognosis for individuals who experience, 32–33
psychoeducation of partners and spouses, 269–74
relationships, impact on, 263–67
religious sexual obsession, 26–27
rituals in, 102–6
romantic partners, challenges for, 5
scrupulosity, 26–27
sexual-assault obsessions, 27–29
sexual-orientation obsessions (SO-OCD), 23–26, 160f
support groups, 304
symptoms and common compulsions, 318–19
therapy, combining with medication, 72–74

threat posed by individuals who experience, 31–32
transgender identity, differential diagnosis and, 67–69
treatment options, 33–38
types of sexual obsessions, 22–31
vs. pedophilic disorder, 59–63
vs. sexual identity confusion, 65–67
sexual obsessions, assessing clients with, 86
and medications for OCD, 72–79
assessment, 48–59
bestiality, fears regarding, 71–72
client consultation, 39–48
communication with other care providers, 79–83, 85–86
differential diagnosis, 59–72
OCD vs. pedophilic disorder, 59–63
pedophilic OCD, issues in diagnosing, 63–65, 69–71
recommended measures for, 53t
therapy, combining with medication, 72–74
transgender identity, differential diagnosis and, 67–69
Sexual Orientation Obsessions and Reactions Test (SORT), 56–57
sexual problems
discussing with spouses and partners, 280
encountered in relationship-focused OCD (R-OCD), 281–83
encountered with anxiety, 277–80
sexual side effects, of medication for OCD, 76–77, 279
sexual topics, therapist discomfort with, 285–86
sexual-assault obsessions in obsessive-compulsive disorder, 27–29
sexual-orientation obsessions
cross-cultural presentation of, 21
diagram of, 160f
in obsessive-compulsive disorder (SO-OCD), 23–26, 160f
sexual problems encountered with, 278
sexual-orientation obsessions, treatment of
access and barriers to care, case example, 181
assessment of progress, case example, 170–72, 173t, 174–80

assessment, case example, 167–68
case conceptualization, case
  example, 168–70
complicating factors, case
  example, 180–81
course of treatment, case
  example, 170–72, 173t, 174–80
follow-up to treatment, case
  example, 181–82
imaginal exposure, case example, 177
imaginal exposure, examples of,
  187–206
in vivo exposure suggestions, 183–87
onset of obsessions, case example, 165
patient history, case example, 165–66
presenting complaints, case
  example, 163–65
recommendations to clinicians, 182–83
resources, 206
shame, disarming in client
  consultation, 39–42
side effects, of medication for OCD,
  76–77, 279
social history of clients
  in pedophilic obsession, case
    example, 213
  in sexual-orientation obsession, case
    example, 166
social workers, communication with,
  82–83, 84b
spiritual domain, values-based exposures
  in, 221–23, 223t
Structured Clinical Interview for DSM-IV
  Disorders (SCID), 52, 54–55
Subjective Units of Distress/Discomfort
  Scale (SUDS), 95–97
  instructions for therapists on
    creating, 327–31
substance use, among clients with
  OCD, 303–4
suicide, client discussion of, 302
support groups, and treatment of
  S-OCD, 304
suppression, of intrusive thoughts
  in context of OCD, 89
  ineffectiveness of, 87
symmetry obsessions, as symptom
  presentation of OCD, 12–14
symptoms, discussing origin
  of, 43–44

taboo thoughts, and symptom
  presentations of OCD, 14–15
talk therapy, ineffectiveness of for
  OCD, 44–45
therapists
  case studies for, 310–11
  communication with, 81–82
  supervision available for, 312
therapists, handouts and materials for
  Dimensional Obsessive Compulsive
    Scale (DOCS), 346–55
  Family Accommodation Scale
    for Obsessive-Compulsive
    Disorder, 339–45
  Instructions for Therapists: Creating the
    SUDS Scale, 327–31
therapy, combining with
  medication, 72–74
thought action fusion (TAF), 40, 94, 109,
  124, 333
thoughts, and symptom presentations of
  OCD, 14–15
traditional healers, communication
  with, 83, 85–86
transcranial magnetic stimulation (TMS),
  and treatment for OCD, 38
transgender identity, and differential
  diagnosis of S-OCD, 67–69
trauma history
  in pedophilic obsession, case
    example, 213
  in sexual-orientation obsession, case
    example, 166
treatment of S-OCD
  among ethnoracial minority
    populations, 19–20
  case studies for therapists, 310–11
  effectiveness of CBT, 87–88
  effectiveness of Ex/RP, 88
  ethnoracial minority clients and,
    18–19, 152–53
  family counseling and
    interventions, 269–77
  instructional materials, availability of, 3–4
  medications and, 72–79, 279
  organizational resources, 311
  patient commitment to, 92–93
  questions commonly asked, 4
  termination and relapse prevention,
    126–29, 128b

treatment of S-OCD (*cont.*)
    traditional difficulty of, 87
    treatment options for OCD, 33–38
    treatment-refractory OCD, options for treatment, 36–38
treatment of S-OCD, step-by-step
    acceptance and commitment therapy, 120–25
    cognitive therapy, use of, 116–20
    distress-evoking situations, building a hierarchy of, 97–104, 98*t*, 173*t*
    exposure and response prevention (Ex/RP), 93–97, 101–11
    exposure and response prevention (Ex/RP), session-by-session outline for, 130–36
    guide to association splitting, 154–56, 157*t*, 158–61, 158*t*
    habituation, necessity for, 114–16
    homework, role of, 112–14
    inhibitory learning, 114–16
    mindfulness techniques, 120, 124–25
    psychoeducation, 88–93
    relapse prevention, 126–29, 128*b*
    session-by-session schedule, 99*t*
treatment of S-OCD, troubleshooting problems, 312
    accommodating patient schedules, 286–87
    adolescent clients, and issues with caregivers or parents, 297–300
    adolescent clients, shame, guilt, and embarrassment among, 301–2
    and clients with developmental and cognitive delays, 300–301
    client discussion of suicide, 302
    clients noncompliant with CBT treatment, 289–91
    clients noncompliant with Ex/RP treatments, 291–92
    depression, clients with comorbid, 288–89
    expert supervisors available, 312
    exposures in public locations, issues with, 304–5
    exposures, addressing ineffectiveness of, 295–97
    exposures, determining explicitness of, 297
    families, and motivating clients to seek treatment, 307–8
    imaginal exposure, judging appropriateness of, 294–95
    in vivo exposures, judging appropriateness of, 293–94
    insurance coverage for 90-minute sessions, 287–88
    mental compulsions, client fears regarding, 292
    OCD and substance use, 303–4
    reducing accommodation, 305–6
    reparative therapy *vs.* treatment of S-OCD, 294
    sexual arousal during exposure, client fears regarding, 292–93
    support groups for S-OCD, 304
    therapist discomfort with sexual topics, 285–86
    unsupportive families, 306
    useful books for clients and family members, 308–10
treatment, course of
    in pedophilic obsession, 217–38
    in sexual-orientation obsession, 170–72, 173*t*, 174–80
treatment-refractory obsessive-compulsive disorder
    options for treatment, 36–38

Unacceptable Taboo Thoughts, handout for clients, 316
universality, of intrusive thoughts, 87, 88–90

Valued Living Questionnaire, 215, 215*t*, 238*t*
values-based exposures
    in parenting domain, 220–23, 222*t*
    in spiritual/community domain, 221–23, 223*t*
    in well-being domain, 222–23, 224*t*

well-being domain, values-based exposures in, 222–23, 224*t*
worries, *vs.* obsessions and ruminations, 110*b*

Yale-Brown Obsessive-Compulsive Scale, 53, 55–56, 60, 84, 146, 147, 167–68, 214, 217, 228, 230, 234, 236, 237, 239

Milton Keynes UK
Ingram Content Group UK Ltd.
UKHW020638020624
443206UK00013B/143